Contents

Maps   ix

Prologue   3

PART ONE
THE RISE

1. The Lessons of Logan Way   15
2. Stick-up Man   37
3. The University of Alcatraz   49
4. Becoming Untouchable   72
5. Just Don't Clip Anyone   98
6. Southie Is His Hometown   115

PART TWO
THE REIGN

7. A Beautiful Friendship   141
8. Lancaster Street   170
9. Circles Within Circles   181

10. Overreach   210

11. The Wrong Man   241

12. Deep in The Haunty   270

PART THREE
THE RUN

13. A Head Start   307

14. Where's Whitey?   335

15. St. Monica's West   361

16. Uncontrolled Wickedness   383

17. Captured: The Man Without a Country   400

Afterword   423

Notes   453

Acknowledgments   487

Index   493

More praise for

Whitey Bulger

A *New York Times* Bestseller

A #1 *Boston Globe* Bestseller

"Whitey committed every crime outside. He lived years in prison and was certain that prison was preferable to the risks and disgrace in his life of South Boston." —Jimmy Breslin, Pulitzer Prize–winning columnist, and author of *The Gang That Couldn't Shoot Straight* and *The Good Rat*

"This is *the* Whitey Bulger book by the two expert journalists who know the turf best. An unflinching look at the culture of silence and death fostered by Bulger—and by his friends in high and low places— and an important affirmation for young people growing up in *today's* neighborhoods of good people besieged by thuggery, corruption, and codes of silence." —Michael Patrick MacDonald, best-selling author of *All Souls: A Family Story from Southie*

"[Cullen and Murphy] reveal the complicated man amid the swirls and crosscurrents of Boston's peculiar past. *Whitey Bulger*, in that sense, is as much a social history as a biography or manhunt thriller. . . . Cullen and Murphy are stellar journalists . . . and both have covered Whitey for decades; their institutional knowledge and reportorial skills are evident throughout, and they weave decades of material and dozens of characters into a gripping narrative."

—Sean Flynn, *Boston Globe*

"Comprehensive, deeply reported, invested with an understanding of place and character, and the subtle, at times pernicious, ways they interact. . . . The authors, Polk Award–winning *Boston Globe* reporters (Cullen also has a Pulitzer), have been on the Bulger trail for nearly 30 years. Their expertise infuses *Whitey Bulger* with authority, a depth and an engagement that makes it less a work of true crime than a social history."

—David Ulin, *Los Angeles Times*

"What is it about this story that's so compelling? This book, by two *Boston Globe* reporters who have spent decades covering the Bulger story, provides the answer. . . . In fact, it reads so much like a movie that it's probably best to look at it as what they call in the film business 'a treatment.' "

—Jeff Greenfield, *Washington Post*

"I have a very strong recommendation if you like real crime stories, or very well-told biographies—or if you like both, which I happen to. If you have not read *Whitey Bulger: America's Most Wanted Gangster and the Manhunt That Brought Him to Justice,* by *Boston Globe* columnist Kevin Cullen and reporter Shelley Murphy, get it now. You'll thank me. It's riveting, graphic and a great tale of real life in South Boston, one of the most compelling neighborhoods in American history."

—Peter King, SportsIllustrated.com

"Riveting."

—*The Economist*

"Compelling." —Maureen Dowd, *New York Times*

"[Cullen and Murphy] seem to know Mr. Bulger better than he knows himself." —Dan Barry, *New York Times*

"Explosive." —*Irish Central*

"*Whitey Bulger* is nothing short of a masterpiece of true crime writing, relentlessly researched and cross-checked, historically fascinating and more than a little frightening." —Tod Goldberg, *Las Vegas City Life*

U. S. PENITENTIARY
ALCATRAZ
1428
11 16 59

Whitey Bulger

AMERICA'S MOST WANTED GANGSTER AND
THE MANHUNT THAT BROUGHT HIM TO JUSTICE

KEVIN CULLEN
and
SHELLEY MURPHY

W. W. NORTON & COMPANY   New York • London

For our spouses, Martha and Regis, and for our children,
Patrick, Brendan, Liam, Ryan, Jessica, and Kerry

Copyright © 2013 by Globe Newspaper Company, Inc.

For information about permission to reproduce selections from this book,
write to Permissions, W. W. Norton & Company, Inc.,
500 Fifth Avenue, New York, NY 10110

For information about special discounts for bulk purchases, please contact
W. W. Norton Special Sales at specialsales@wwnorton.com or 800-233-4830

Manufacturing by Courier Westford
Book design by Helene Berinsky
Production manager: Julia Druskin

Library of Congress Cataloging-in-Publication Data

Cullen, Kevin, Journalist.
Whitey Bulger : America's most wanted gangster and the manhunt that brought him to
justice / Kevin Cullen and Shelley Murphy. — First edition.
pages cm
Includes bibliographical references and index.
ISBN 978-0-393-08772-7 (hardcover)
1. Bulger, Whitey, 1929- 2. Gangsters—Massachusetts—Boston—Biography. 3. Fugitives from
justice—United States—Biography. 4. Organized crime—MassachusettsBoston—Case studies.
I. Murphy, Shelley. II. Title.
HV6452.M4C85 2013
364.1092—dc23
[B]
2012050752

ISBN 978-0-393-34725-8 pbk.

W. W. Norton & Company, Inc.
500 Fifth Avenue, New York, N.Y. 10110
www.wwnorton.com

W. W. Norton & Company Ltd.
Castle House, 75/76 Wells Street, London W1T 3QT

2 3 4 5 6 7 8 9 0

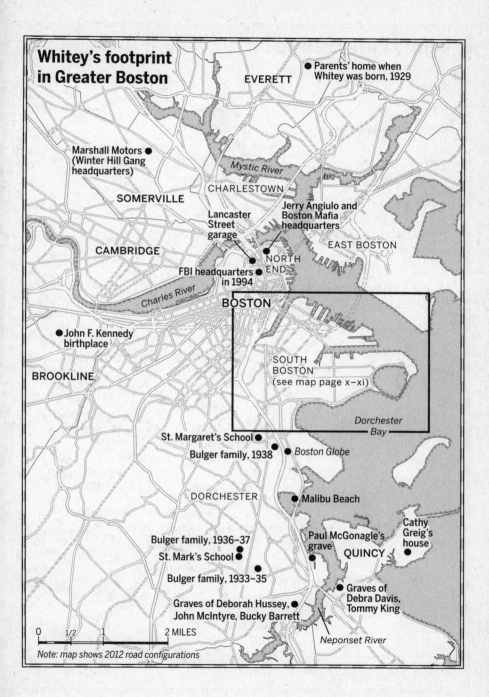

Whitey's footprint
in Greater Boston

EVERETT

● Parents' home when
   Whitey was born, 1929

● Marshall Motors
  (Winter Hill Gang
  headquarters)

Mystic River

CHARLESTOWN

SOMERVILLE

Lancaster
Street
garage

Jerry Angiulo and
Boston Mafia
headquarters

CAMBRIDGE

EAST BOSTON

NORTH
END

FBI headquarters ●
in 1994

BOSTON

Charles River

● John F. Kennedy
  birthplace

SOUTH
BOSTON
(see map page x–xi)

BROOKLINE

*Dorchester
Bay*

St. Margaret's School ●

Bulger family, 1938 ● *Boston Globe*

DORCHESTER

● Malibu Beach

Bulger family, 1936–37
St. Mark's School ●

● Paul McGonagle's
  grave

Cathy
Greig's
house

QUINCY

Bulger family, 1933–35 ●

Graves of Deborah Hussey, ●
John McIntyre, Bucky Barrett

● Graves of
  Debra Davis,
  Tommy King

Neponset River

0   1/2   1   2 MILES

Note: map shows 2012 road configurations

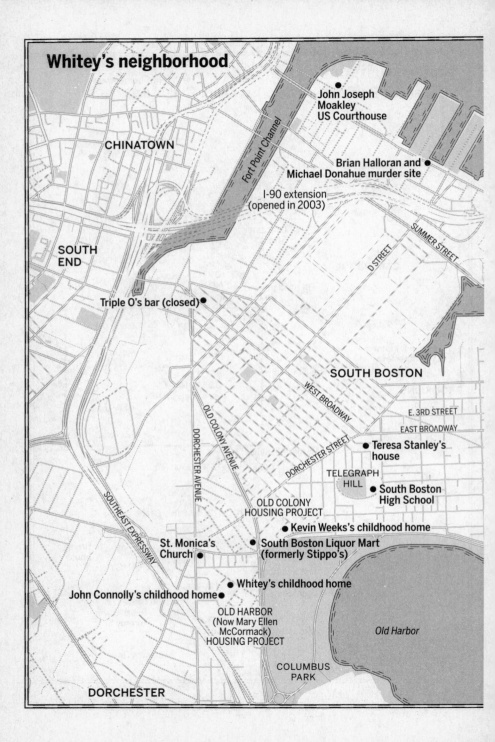

Whitey's neighborhood

John Joseph Moakley US Courthouse

CHINATOWN

Fort Point Channel

Brian Halloran and Michael Donahue murder site

I-90 extension (opened in 2003)

SOUTH END

SUMMER STREET

D STREET

Triple O's bar (closed)

SOUTH BOSTON

WEST BROADWAY

E. 3RD STREET

EAST BROADWAY

OLD COLONY AVENUE

DORCHESTER AVENUE

DORCHESTER STREET

Teresa Stanley's house

SOUTHEAST EXPRESSWAY

TELEGRAPH HILL

South Boston High School

OLD COLONY HOUSING PROJECT

Kevin Weeks's childhood home

St. Monica's Church

South Boston Liquor Mart (formerly Stippo's)

Whitey's childhood home

John Connolly's childhood home

OLD HARBOR (Now Mary Ellen McCormack) HOUSING PROJECT

Old Harbor

COLUMBUS PARK

DORCHESTER

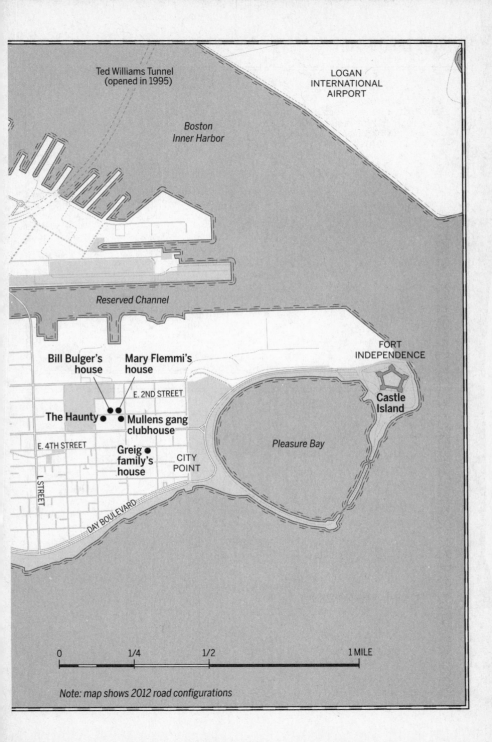

Ted Williams Tunnel
(opened in 1995)

LOGAN
INTERNATIONAL
AIRPORT

*Boston
Inner Harbor*

Reserved Channel

FORT
INDEPENDENCE

Bill Bulger's
house

Mary Flemmi's
house

E. 2ND STREET

**Castle
Island**

The Haunty

Mullens gang
clubhouse

E. 4TH STREET

Greig
family's
house

CITY
POINT

Pleasure Bay

L STREET

DAY BOULEVARD

0   1/4   1/2   1 MILE

Note: map shows 2012 road configurations

Whitey on the run

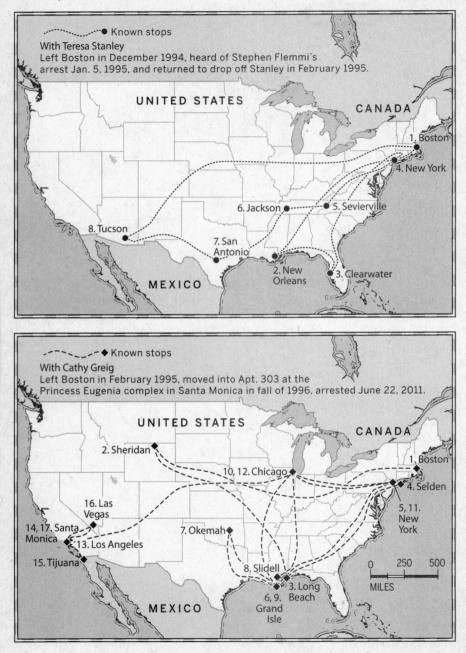

Known stops

With Teresa Stanley
Left Boston in December 1994, heard of Stephen Flemmi's
arrest Jan. 5, 1995, and returned to drop off Stanley in February 1995.

UNITED STATES

CANADA

1. Boston
4. New York
6. Jackson
5. Sevierville
8. Tucson
7. San Antonio
2. New Orleans
3. Clearwater
MEXICO

Known stops

With Cathy Greig
Left Boston in February 1995, moved into Apt. 303 at the
Princess Eugenia complex in Santa Monica in fall of 1996, arrested June 22, 2011.

UNITED STATES

CANADA

2. Sheridan
10, 12. Chicago
1. Boston
4. Selden
16. Las Vegas
5, 11. New York
14, 17. Santa Monica
7. Okemah
13. Los Angeles
15. Tijuana
8. Slidell
3. Long Beach
6, 9. Grand Isle
MEXICO

0   250   500
MILES

Whitey
Bulger

Prologue

He sat in the back of a black SUV wearing blue jeans, handcuffs, and a scowl. After sixteen years on the run, Whitey Bulger had returned to the South Boston waterfront, to a town that had changed so much that he stared uncomprehendingly out the window. He no longer really belonged in this place, where once he had wielded such power, and nothing about it now belonged to him. The city's history had outrun him, even as his own had caught up with him.

The case against Whitey had originated in the old downtown courthouse named for John McCormack, the US Speaker of the House who was instrumental in building the South Boston housing project where Whitey grew up. Now he was on his way to the new federal courthouse on the Southie waterfront named for one of his neighbors from that housing project, Joseph Moakley, the longtime congressman. When he was a young bank robber, driving an Oldsmobile convertible at a time when hardly anyone in the neighborhood could afford a car, Whitey would pull over if he saw Moakley's mother walking home with groceries and give her a lift.

It was a small world, Whitey's world.

The courthouse was just up the street from the spot where, in 1982, Whitey used a rifle to kill a hoodlum named Brian Halloran who had tried to turn him in to the Federal Bureau of Investigation (FBI). Halloran had stumbled into the crosshairs because he didn't know that the FBI was willing to let him die to protect their secret, that Whitey was their informant. An innocent man, a truck driver named Michael Donahue, had also fallen that day, killed by the same spray of bullets—and now his family was waiting inside the courthouse, waiting to lay eyes on the man who had ripped hope from their lives twenty-nine years before.

The faded, peeling waterfront where Whitey Bulger gunned down those two men was long gone, replaced while he was on the lam by sprawling restaurants, gleaming bars, and high-rise hotels that cater to the young and the moneyed, the new Bostonians for whom the name Bulger means little or nothing. As he eyed this shiny new section of town, Whitey said a few words to his guards about the stunning transformation, about the new Boston he didn't know.

As the SUV pulled into the courthouse's underground garage, a Coast Guard boat idled in Boston Harbor, behind the courthouse, an officer manning a machine gun mounted on deck, an almost ludicrous show of force. The idea that anyone would mount a daring or suicidal operation to kill or spring Whitey was preposterous. Sixty-five when he fled, Whitey was eighty-one years old now, and everybody had turned on him—everybody except his girlfriend, Cathy Greig; his immediate family; and John Connolly, the FBI agent who grew up with the Bulgers in the projects and then used his badge to protect the Bulger name. Greig, who had been captured along with Whitey in Santa Monica, was in custody in the courthouse, too. Connolly was also locked up, doing forty years in Florida for helping Whitey kill a potential witness, someone who could have exposed Whitey's Faustian partnership with the FBI decades earlier. Whitey's younger brother Bill was a few miles away, getting ready to leave his South Boston home for the short drive to the courthouse.

Whitey rode the elevator to the fifth floor, surrounded by deputy US Marshals who kept their sunglasses on indoors. As he waited in an anteroom for his case to be called, Michael Donahue's widow, Patricia, sat in Courtroom 10 with her three sons, Michael Jr., Shawn, and Tommy, who had grown up without a father. The special agent in charge of the FBI in Boston walked in and took an empty seat on the right side of the gallery, directly in front of the Donahues, but said nothing to them. He didn't know them, or any of the families of Whitey's victims, who sat clustered together.

When Whitey shuffled into the courtroom, he quickly spotted his brother Bill out in the spectators' gallery and mouthed a cheerful hello even before he made it to the defendant's table. For many years one of the most powerful politicians in Massachusetts, Bill smiled and nodded back.

Whitey's $822,198 in cash, hidden in the wall of his apartment in Santa Monica, was of no use to him now. The thirty guns hidden in those same walls proved useless, relics of a time when he'd always had a gun within easy reach. There had been no defiant, bloody standoff with the law before his arrest, a drama that would have better served his legend. His years of gunplay behind him, the old man had surrendered quietly and almost with a smile. The Whitey Bulger standing there in the courtroom, in his ill-fitting blue jeans, white smock, and sneakers, looked like any other casually dressed octogenarian or a Southern California retiree, which is what he had been just a few days before.

Over the next few weeks, there would be more court appearances as the feds tried to figure out what to do with him. Each time, the black SUV drove him up the Southeast Expressway, the main road into Boston, taking him past some of the spots where he had buried his secrets. To the right, next to a railway bridge over the Neponset River, were the soggy graves of Debra Davis and Tommy King. A little farther up, under the sand at Tenean Beach, there was Paulie McGonagle's. Off to the left of the highway, beneath some mounds of dirt across from the firefighters' hall, there was the oversize makeshift grave that held Deborah Hussey and Bucky Barrett and John McIntyre. They were just six of the nineteen people Whitey was charged with killing.

Whitey hid the bodies to lessen the risk of prosecution. It's never good business to leave a corpse behind: no body, no case. But he also did it to preserve his image in the Town, as South Boston natives call their neighborhood. It was especially important to Whitey that his role in the demise of the two women remain hidden. He was a criminal, he would readily admit, but he was an honorable criminal. Gangsters with scruples don't kill women, and Whitey insists to this day that he did not kill Debra Davis or Deborah Hussey. He says the last years of his life will be spent clearing his name, not just in the killing of the women but in this whole matter of his being an FBI informant. "I never put one person in prison in my life," he claimed in a letter to a friend.[1]

This is the illusion Whitey lived by and where his legend as the good bad guy began. He will most likely die in prison, now that the trial has ended. Nothing seems more certain to die there with him than that legend.

There have been other books written about Whitey Bulger, many of them told through the eyes of people who worked for him or pretended to. Other, more serious accounts were written when knowledge of Whitey was limited or, in some cases, incomplete or incorrect. This book aims to provide the first complete and authoritative accounting of this man, of his rise, reign, and final reckoning. We aim, in short, to present Whitey in full. Many descriptions of him, and much of the lore about him, have traded in caricature, making him a two-dimensional figure more monstrous than human, if you hate him, more human than monster, if you don't. Whitey was more complicated, more compelling, more frightening than that.

In the sixteen years that he was on the run, Whitey's place in the public consciousness seemed to grow less, not more, nuanced. Popular culture cluttered public perception, as it evolved in his absence.

Myth overgrew reality. Frank Costello, the venal, scheming Southie mob boss played by Jack Nicholson in Martin Scorsese's film *The Departed*, was loosely based on Whitey. Costello was a sociopath, devoid of conscience or redeeming values, with blood literally dripping from his hands. Nicholson's captivating and brilliant portrayal didn't really capture the man it was modeled on. Others painted with an even broader brush. One former criminal associate wrote a book describing Whitey as a closet homosexual who once had a liaison with the actor Sal Mineo. The FBI, which used and protected him for decades, suddenly described the fugitive Whitey as a pervert who had sex with girls as young as twelve. After he disappeared, Whitey's portrayal evolved from that of a cunning criminal to a sleaze.

A closer inspection of Whitey's life reveals a more intriguing character, a strange and complex amalgam of the depraved and the blandly conventional. If Whitey spent his youth running away from the warmth and stability of his family home, he spent much of his adult life trying to re-create something he saw as a traditional, nurturing domestic environment. That he did so while maintaining two separate households with two separate women is just one of the many incongruities that define him. Whitey saw no contradiction in slaughtering someone with a machine gun and then, an hour later, sitting down to dinner with one of his mistresses and her children. At those nightly family dinners, he insisted that no one answer the phone should it ring during the meal and lectured the kids on staying away from bad influences.

He considered himself more paternal than pathological, nothing like the other bad guys. Yes, he was a criminal, but to hear him tell it he only hurt those who threatened his business. Whitey, though, was expert at blurring that line. Two accomplished men assisted in this preening self-portrait: Bill Bulger, who could never fully face what a menace his brother was, and one of Bill's protégés, FBI agent John Connolly. Connolly cast Whitey as an indispensable ally in the FBI's war against the Mafia. The truth was otherwise; almost everything Whitey knew about the Mafia he gleaned from his partner, Steve Flemmi, who enjoyed similar protection from Connolly and the FBI. Connolly reaped the rewards of being one of the FBI's top Mafia fighters, but his ulterior motive was to ensure that the Bulgers, the family he'd grown up with and which had helped him in his formative years, would not suffer the ignominy of seeing Whitey publicly accused of sordid crimes. To understand why Connolly would risk his career and ultimately his freedom to protect the good name of the Bulger family is to understand South Boston, whose residents valued loyalty to family, neighbors and neighborhood over all else. Like the waterfront Whitey came home to, that South Boston is largely gone today, a victim of demographics and time. It is the town Whitey looked for out the window of that black SUV but didn't see.

If this book is the first comprehensive biography of Whitey Bulger, it is also a social history of a time in Boston when a life like Whitey's was possible. It begins during Roosevelt's New Deal, which brought the Bulgers to South Boston in the first place, and encompasses the years when the city's working-class enclaves were still places where political loyalty ensured jobs and social mobility, the years when the Irish took full control of Boston's politics and sought control of its criminal rackets, too. Whitey's rise also embraced the divisive era of court-ordered integration of the city's schools, when those working-class enclaves felt besieged as never before. Whitey joined that struggle, waging a symbolic, sometimes violent battle on behalf of Southie—a story this book tells for the first time. *Whitey Bulger* also encompasses the years during which ethnic divisions pitted Irish and Italian gangsters against each other, a fight the FBI joined on the side of the Irish, enabling Whitey's rise and ultimate hegemony. Whitey, in fact, faced criminal charges only because a confederation of Massachusetts State Police, Boston police, and federal drug agents dared to challenge the FBI's role as the nation's, and the region's, premier law enforcement agency.

And so, in his own bloody way, Whitey Bulger's life was fused with the modern history of the city. During his career he became one of its most recognizable icons. Boston is the city of John Adams, John Kennedy, and Ted Williams, but there are few names better known or more deeply associated with the city than Bulger's. Certainly he is Boston's most infamous criminal. After his capture, he suggested to a friend that he might have now replaced Al Capone and Machine Gun Kelly as the most intriguing of Alcatraz's former denizens.[2] He might be right. And yet so much of what is known about him is crudely embellished or simply wrong.

We grounded our understanding of Whitey Bulger in our decades of covering his career as reporters for the *Boston Globe* and other Boston media, but not with any direct input from our subject or his family. Whitey Bulger refused to be interviewed by the authors. He ignored letters written by us to him in jail. Indeed, Whitey was more than uncooperative; he was outright hostile to this project, as he spelled out in letters to a friend from his Alcatraz years. Whitey will never forgive the *Globe* for the way it covered the court-ordered busing that desegregated Boston's public schools and championed it on its editorial pages. Busing, he maintains, ruined South Boston.[3] He has said he hates Shelley Murphy for writing stories about him and his brother Bill that were, in his view, hurtful to his family. He also considers her a traitor: Murphy grew up in Dorchester, attended South Boston High School, and was herself caught up in the busing crisis. She has also broken many of the most important stories about Whitey over the years. Kevin Cullen, part of the *Globe* team that outed Whitey as an FBI informant in 1988, was, Whitey said, "another lowlife . . . who has lied about my family and me." Cullen lived in South Boston through much of Whitey's reign, and many of his relatives still live there.

We believe Whitey saw a request for an interview for this book not as an attempt to get his side of the story but as a threat. "I hate the *Globe*," he wrote to a friend. "Shelley, Cullen . . . they will twist my words and sensationalize it."[4] Despite his cynicism about our motives, we have sought to be fair to Whitey in this book, though of course there is no diminishing his crimes. We have tried, above all, to describe him in all his complexity.

The public record about Whitey changed considerably, and deepened greatly, in the decade between the appearance of the first books about Whitey Bulger and his trial. The passage of time has made it easier to parse what is true and what isn't. Many who once lived in fear of speaking publicly now open up about him. We grounded much of this book in the accounts of some of the principals in Whitey's life, including some of his key criminal comrades. Their still vivid recollections help to flesh out long-ago scenes and dialogue. Also, some of those principals—Whitey's criminal associates Steve Flemmi, John Martorano, Kevin Weeks—have testified repeatedly in court, making it possible to corroborate their claims in interviews with their sworn testimony. We have made every effort to verify their words and deeds, but there are times when they are the only source for what was said or done. Their recollections are detailed—almost photographic, in many cases—and they ring true, or we wouldn't have used them. But the reader, like the authors, should bear in mind that these are what they are—recollections, from men, in some cases, with mixed motives. Weeks; Patrick Nee, one of Whitey's rivals turned associate; and Teresa Stanley, Whitey's girlfriend of thirty years, gave multiple interviews to the authors. Richard Sunday, Whitey's prison friend, gave the authors many interviews and access to a series of letters Whitey sent him after his June 2011 arrest, which serve as a window into Whitey's own version of his story and his thinking.

But the bulk of the book is based on the authors' long and detailed knowledge of Whitey Bulger, the fruit of more than twenty-five years of reporting on his exploits, interviewing the FBI agents who protected him, the criminals who worked with him, the lawmen who hunted him down, and the families he destroyed. We have covered dozens of hearings and trials, from Boston to Miami to Los Angeles, and followed his story from Massachusetts to Florida to Ireland to Louisiana to California to Iceland. It is an account made richer by interviews with some of those who spent time in prison with Whitey and by the examination of thousands of pages from his prison file. It is a story bolstered by interviews with those whom Whitey and Catherine Greig met and befriended during their sixteen years on the run, from the bayous of Louisiana to a modest apartment complex a few blocks from the beach in Santa Monica. And it is a story underwritten by the institutional authority of the *Boston Globe*, which first exposed Whitey's deal with the FBI and has driven understanding of the narrative of his life ever since.

More than anything, this book tries to capture the contradictions that fill in the silhouette that is Whitey Bulger—a man who considered himself a patriot even as he used murder and the threat of it to amass a fortune, a man who could fall asleep moments after killing someone but couldn't watch a sick dog be put down, a man who held loyalty to be the highest moral value even as he traded damning information about friends to the FBI. There is great sweep and nuance to his story, but it is striking, in the end, how small Whitey's world was, just a couple of miles, as the crow flies, from the soggy graves of Neponset to City Point, where Whitey regularly had dinner at the home of his politician brother. It is an epic tale with many characters, but one ultimately sketched on a very small canvas.

Shortly after his arrest in June 2011, Whitey was flown by Coast Guard helicopter from his jail cell in Plymouth, south of Boston, to the waterfront courthouse, giving him an aerial view of the shoreline. Those old graves had been dug up, the bodies exhumed, while Whitey hid in open view on the other side of the country. Now he was back in South Boston, his hometown, in chains, made to answer for those bodies and thirteen others. As he looked down from the helicopter, it may have dawned on him that he might still be in charge in his corner of this world if he had never stepped beyond those few square miles where all the shakedowns and killings were plotted and carried out, where Whitey first met his FBI handler, where, for all his misdeeds, he was embraced and not shunned by his brothers and sisters, his nieces and nephews, and his women.

Inside that narrow space, he was untouchable, protected by a tradition of neighborhood loyalty fostered on the stoops of that housing project in Southie, protected by the arrogance and corruption of an FBI and a Justice Department that tolerated murder as an acceptable price of doing effective law enforcement. His capture after a worldwide manhunt that was, by turns, intense and incurious, epic and inept, put the spotlight back on the life, the legends, the lies and the myths, on families protected and families ruined, on the neighborhood where loyalty was everything and where now, for him, it was nothing.

PART ONE
THE RISE

1

The Lessons of Logan Way

On the map of coastal Boston, South Boston doesn't look like anything special, just a stubby peninsula jutting out into the harbor, but in this case geography deceives. It is in fact a place apart, an island more than a peninsula, imbued almost since it was first settled with a proud separatism, an overweening sense of self. It might be a function of its having been so unwanted for so long. It might also be that for those who landed here, it was all they had, the first taste of security and possession and home.

Out of this place would come James "Whitey" Bulger. And from the shadows, he would one day rule it.

Before bridges connected it to the rest of the city in the nineteenth century, South Boston actually was an island at high tide, a place that was home to more cows than people. In 1673, James Foster, one of the Puritans who settled in the area, built the first house on Leek Hill, near the present-day intersection of E and Silver streets. By the start of the Revolutionary War, there were a dozen families living in what was called Dorchester Neck, but they fled as British forces flooded Boston. It was a bitter but timely retreat. The redcoats swept the Neck in February 1776 and burned down all the buildings. Within a month, this first incursion of unwelcome outsiders into Southie would be avenged when colonial forces used Dorchester Heights, overlooking the bay, to aim cannon at the enemy fleet.

Southie's hilly topography afforded the rebels' cannon, dragged to Boston from Fort Ticonderoga on Lake Champlain, an unobstructed shot at the warships below. The hasty, humiliating exit of the British fleet, the first victory for colonial forces under the command of General George Washington, helped give birth to the notion of Southie Pride, the sense that this place and the people who live there were special. The city still celebrates the memory of the British retreat on what is known locally as Evacuation Day, a secular holiday that happily coincides with St. Patrick's Day, a holy day and occasion for garrulous celebration for the Irish, especially in Southie.

After the Revolution, succeeding generations built bridges to the peninsula, but paradoxically the connection to the mainland contributed to an even more insular attitude. Over the bridges came waves of new immigrants, changing the neighborhood's demographics and its politics. In 1850, before those waves of newcomers arrived, a Democrat didn't stand a chance in Southie, which was, like Boston generally and like much of the Northeast, a Republican stronghold. The antislavery party, the Republicans, were also in Boston the party of the old colonial families, the old money, and the Protestant power structure it supported. They were about to be overwhelmed. By 1900, after a huge influx of Irish, the situation reversed. The term South Boston Republican became an oxymoron, as Democrats took charge of the city; only one Republican was elected mayor after 1910, none after 1930. Though the neighborhood was in fact a blend of many immigrant groups, the Irish would dominate, in numbers and in moxie, and produce a string of leaders and notable souls.

James Connolly was Southie's first well-known Irish son. Having studied his way to Harvard, he asked for a leave of absence to participate in the first modern Olympic Games in Athens in 1896. When Harvard denied his request, he simply dropped out and won the gold medal in the triple jump. When Babe Ruth was courting his future wife, Helen Woodford, a Southie girl, he was known to haunt the bars of Broadway, Southie's main thoroughfare, but this was five years before he was sold by the Red Sox to the Yankees and became baseball's biggest star. Helen lived on Silver Street, the same narrow, one-way side street Whitey Bulger would later live on with one of his girlfriends and her children.[1]

Southie was perhaps best known for producing priests and politicians. Cardinal Richard Cushing, who grew up in City Point—a relatively prosperous section near the tip of the peninsula—ran the Catholic Church in Boston for a quarter-century and presided over John F. Kennedy's wedding, inauguration, and funeral. Cushing was born in a three-decker almost directly across from the East Third Street home where Whitey and his confederates killed and secretly buried three people. John McCormack, one of eight children born to immigrant parents near Southie's gritty Andrew Square, was elected to the House of Representatives in 1928 and became its speaker in 1962.

But if politics, both in church and state, was the Irish strong suit, they weren't bad at the rackets, either. Frank Wallace and his brothers led the Gustin Gang, named for a Southie street, for about a decade. Wallace's demise in 1931 offered a cautionary tale about the threat from outsiders: He and an associate were shot to death in an ambush when they went over the bridge and into the North End, Boston's Italian neighborhood, to discuss a bootlegging dispute with the ruthless characters who would later be known as the Mafia. The demise of the Gustin Gang established an Italian criminal supremacy in Boston that would go unchallenged for a half century, until another Southie gangster emerged to take them on. That gangster, Whitey Bulger, would become Southie's most infamous product even though he was the sort that in Southie they call a blow-in.

James Joseph Bulger Jr. wasn't born in the neighborhood, or in
Boston at all, but rather in Everett, the first city to the north. He
only found his way to Southie, with his family, as a young child. His
father, for whom he was named, was born in Newfoundland and,
as an eleven-year-old, arrived in Boston on the Fourth of July.[2] He
settled with his mother, stepfather and sister in Boston's Charleston
neighborhood. Whitey's grandparents had come from Newfoundland, a common first stop for the famine Irish because it was cheaper
than sailing directly to Boston or New York. The elder James Bulger
stood 5 feet 6 inches and set the physical standard for the men of the
family: slight and sinewy, but exceptionally strong. At age fifteen, he
walked some fifty miles to Rhode Island after being turned down
for an apprenticeship at a naval station. After spending the night
in a police station, the teen was attempting to jump a freight train
headed back to Boston when he fell beneath the wheels, mangling
his left arm so badly that it had to be amputated.[3] It was a devastating setback, particularly in that unforgiving era. He was working as
a seaman when he became a US citizen at age twenty-one, and then
he worked as a laborer. He moved to Boston's North End, which
for much of the second half of the nineteenth century was a prime
destination of the Irish fleeing starvation and poverty. James Bulger
had little formal education and there was scant demand for one-
armed laborers. He struggled for the rest of his life to find steady
work, though no one remembers him complaining about it.

James Bulger was fitted with a prosthetic arm, but it was crudely
made and he regularly stuck the wooden hand in his pocket.[4] Shy by
nature, a man of few words, his accident made him even more self-
conscious. Not so self-conscious, however, that he did not pursue
women. He was in his forties and had previously been married when
he met a young woman who lived in Charlestown, the neighborhood
on the northern edge of Boston, across the street from the Navy Yard,
where, no longer fit for physical labor, he had found a job as a clerk.
Her name was Jean McCarthy. She was a fair-skinned, blue-eyed brunette with a sunny disposition that belied a certain toughness. Jean was

the daughter of Irish immigrants, twenty-two years his junior, and very independent-minded. At some point, she decided she didn't like her given name, Jane, and, thinking her middle name, Veronica, too pretentious for a Charlestown girl, settled on Jean.[5] When James Bulger asked her out, she didn't seem to mind the age difference, or the missing arm.

They married and settled first in Everett, just north of Charlestown, and soon started a family. Everett was an industrial city, thick with factories and chemical and metal plants, and James Bulger scratched around for work as a watchman. The first two children were born in Everett: Jean, named for her mother, in 1928, followed sixteen months later by James, who was born on September 3, 1929, less than two months before the stock market crash that would send the nation spiraling into the Great Depression. He had his father's name but his mother's looks—light skin and sharp blue eyes. His mother took to calling him Sonny, even as he grew older and others called him Jimmy or, more rarely, Whitey, after his striking blond hair. It was a nickname he never liked much. As he got older, he asked people to call him Jimmy, and when those who didn't know him well called him Whitey, he would correct or sometimes berate them.

After a few years in Everett, the Bulgers moved back into Boston, to Dorchester, the largest and most populous neighborhood in the city, and St. Mark's parish. By the twentieth century, Irish and Italian immigration had turned Boston—for three centuries perhaps the most determinedly, and rigidly, Protestant city in the nation—into a Catholic haven, where the parish defined the social structure and the neighborhood. And within parishes, there was a social hierarchy based on when you'd arrived in town. St. Mark's was home to many recent immigrants, but it was also the parish and church of established families, the children and grandchildren of immigrants, including the former mayor John "Honey Fitz" Fitzgerald, whose daughter Rose taught Sunday school at St. Mark's. The Bulgers were newcomers and struggling, and their eldest son, Jim, didn't seem to hold much promise of elevating the family name. Whitey struggled in first grade at St. Mark's School. If the other kids tried to please the nuns, the Sisters of Notre Dame de Namur, an order founded to teach the poor, Whitey couldn't be bothered. He was restless, unable to sit for long periods of time. When he was seven, the family moved into a triple-decker on Crescent Avenue in St. Margaret's parish, the Dorchester neighborhood that bordered Southie. The Sisters of Charity who ran St. Margaret's Grammar School had the same problems with Whitey. He was clearly intelligent, but the routine and regimen of school didn't appeal to him. Sometimes he'd slip out unnoticed. Bill Bulger, in his memoir, said he believed his older brother was more naturally intelligent and a quicker thinker than him. "But he found school boring. His teachers, like my mother, often discovered that Jim was suddenly missing."[6]

Whitey was eight years old when, in 1938, the family moved to the neighboring parish of St. Monica's in South Boston. The family had no roots in Southie, no relatives or close friends there. They moved for one reason only. They had been one of 1,016 families lucky enough, and poor enough, to be awarded a place in one of the grand experiments of Franklin Delano Roosevelt's New Deal: public housing. The Old Harbor Village project, which opened that same year, was the first public housing development built in New England, and one of the first in the country. It consisted of one-, two-, and three-bedroom apartments in twenty-two squat, three-story brick buildings and one hundred fifty-two row houses, spread out over thirty-four acres in an area just south of Andrew Square. It was named for the body of water, sandwiched between Columbia Point and Castle Island, that surrounded much of Southie. The project bordered Southie's old Hooverville, one of the shantytowns named derisively after President Herbert Hoover, whose name had become identified, in the minds of many, with the collapse of the economy.[7] The new development felt, to those lucky enough to win a place there, like a piece of heaven. For the Bulgers, home had been a series of cramped cold-water flats with drafty windows. Their new apartment was a giant step up.

By May 1938, there were five children in the Bulger household—Jean, 10, Whitey, 8, Bill, 4, Carol, 1, and John (Jack), a month old—which qualified the family for a three-bedroom apartment, No. 756, on the top floor of 41 Logan Way. It was just around the corner from St. Monica's Church, a parish founded in 1907, mainly to absorb the overflow of immigrants who went to nearby St. Augustine's. For the Bulgers, as for most of their neighbors, church life and home life were fused, for while the government provided housing, the church provided almost everything else. Beyond the touchstones of Mass and ritual, the parish fielded baseball and football teams long before there was anything like Little League or Pop Warner. Jean Bulger became active in the women's sodality, or fellowship, at St. Monica's and sent her kids to join in the various activities organized by the parish. They went willingly, all but Whitey. He had little interest in such things.[8] St. Monica was the patron saint of difficult children, and from an early age Whitey showed that he could have used her intervention.

It was no accident that one of the nation's first public housing projects was built in South Boston. One of FDR's key allies in getting the New Deal through Congress was John McCormack, an ambitious congressman from the district. Indeed, South Boston had been one of the strongest votes anywhere for Roosevelt and, in those devastating times, looked to him for help. The Depression had not just thrown millions out of work; it had crushed the housing construction sector. In 1935, McCormack told the *Boston Globe* that the Roosevelt administration was determined to step in and fill the breach left by the private builders. "I have no hesitancy in insisting that Government in an emergency do everything that can be reasonably done to relieve human suffering and distress," McCormack said, as he helped sell the idea of public housing.

It was McCormack who told Roosevelt to consider not just the humanitarian but the political benefits of putting a housing project in Boston—where many Catholics, as the Depression wore on, were finding themselves drawn to the harsh xenophobia of Father Charles Coughlin, a Michigan priest who used his syndicated radio program to brand FDR his moral enemy and the nation's. It went without saying that McCormack believed the development should be built in South Boston. "McCormack pointed out the softening of the South Boston vote in 1936 to President Roosevelt, warning him that the 'sullen, discontented and bitter' people who had gone out of their way to support Father Coughlin's (preferred) candidates were obviously in need of greater federal assistance," wrote Thomas O'Connor, a professor of history at Boston College.

After the Old Harbor project was opened and another housing project broke ground right across from it, Roosevelt's popularity soared even higher in Southie. In 1940, he won more votes in the district than Al Smith, the first Catholic presidential candidate, had in 1928.[9] By 1940, McCormack was the House majority leader and he would later become the first Catholic Speaker of the House. Old Harbor was eventually renamed in honor of McCormack's mother, Mary Ellen.

South Boston's growing political influence, critical in winning Old Harbor, would be demonstrated repeatedly over the next quarter-century, until the neighborhood was home to two more housing projects and several subsidized apartment buildings for the elderly. For much of the second half of the twentieth century, South Boston had a little more than 5 percent of the city's population but 20 percent of the city's subsidized public housing stock.[10] It wasn't just McCormack; Southie's Irish ward bosses, and state representatives like Jimmy Condon and state senators like Johnny Powers, were expert at delivering votes for Democrats on local, state, and national ballots, although the neighborhood's resolute insularity made it hard to elect a native son citywide. Politicians won enduring loyalty by securing housing and jobs for their constituents, and Southie pols, if they wanted to survive, had to be skilled at delivering both.

In Old Harbor, everyone was poor—the average rent was twenty-six dollars a month—and everyone, it seemed, was Irish. In the Bulgers' building, there were six families—the Bulgers, the Pryors, the McCarthys, the Drinans, the McKeowns, and the Walshes—with twenty-seven kids among them.[11] In all, there were six thousand people living in Old Harbor, most of them children. There was always something to do. Games like tag and hide-and-seek started, and grew, spontaneously.

Unlike so many other desolate and isolated housing projects that would follow, in Boston and across the nation, many of the apartments at Old Harbor boasted ocean views, with Carson Beach just across the way. There was sprawling Columbus Park sandwiched between the project and the beach, where kids played baseball into the dusk on summer nights and football when those nights turned cool. On Saturdays, the maintenance building was converted into a cinema. For five cents, kids got to see a movie, a cartoon and one of the serials. Kids from the project would sneak into the storage yard of a barrel factory on nearby Dorchester Street and pull staves off used barrels returned by Baker's, a chocolate manufacturer. They'd eat the chocolate right off the staves, picking splinters from the hardened candy.[12]

During World War II, Italian POWs were housed at Camp McKay, at the end of Carson Beach. Kids from Old Harbor, many of them with brothers or uncles fighting overseas, would cross the fields to stare at the POWs behind the wire. Italians from the North End came, too, and the American guards did nothing to stop them from pushing a taste of home—Italian cheeses and cold cuts— through the fence to the POWs.[13]

After snowstorms, the kids from Old Harbor would run across Columbus Park up toward Dorchester Heights. They would block off Telegraph Street, a steep hill that rose to Dorchester Heights, and coast down on makeshift toboggans. Traffic wasn't an issue; there wasn't any.[14]

It was rare to see a car drive through or around Old Harbor during the war years. A car was a symbol of making it, and few here would reach that level. Whitey's younger brother Bill and his contemporaries remember the Old Harbor as something of a haven, a place where, for all the lack of wealth, it was considered rare and scandalous when a man walked out on his family. He, like many of his peers, remembers a neighborhood and a childhood that was idyllic. And he remembers that South Boston viewed itself as separate and distinct from the rest of the city. Indeed, when people from other neighborhoods took the trolley into the heart of the city, they said they were heading into town, just as in Southie people referred to their neighborhood as the Town.

Bill Bulger remembers the South Boston of his youth as a place where people swept their sidewalks and washed their windows, where the churches and schools were stable institutions, where divorce was rare. Southie had its share of bars and bookies, but it was also widely considered the safest neighborhood in the city. "And," he noted, "on the rare occasions when someone crossed the line into heavy felony, he alone was condemned. The neighborhood was wonderfully free of the star-chamber mentality that indicts or ostracizes entire families."[15]

It was, however, famously quick to distinguish outsiders from insiders and cherish its tradition of deciding for itself who belonged. "It takes a lot to incite South Boston people, but beware when that happens," said Patrick J. Loftus, a political opponent of Bill Bulger who nonetheless shared his view of Southie's essential character. "When Charlie Do Right or Mr. and Mrs. Nice Guy who know nothing about us come riding into South Boston from out of town and try to change us, our jobs, our neighborhood, and our traditions, without our accord, war is declared."[16]

For some, including the Bulgers, "outsider" was an elastic term. Bill Bulger says he never understood why his family escaped being labeled as outsiders.[17] In fact, the construction of public housing in the neighborhood introduced to Southie dozens of families who, like the Bulgers, had no previous or familial connection to the Town. It was a melting pot of the poor. The rest of the city, though put off or amused by Southie's preening pride, more or less bought into the view of the neighborhood as a place apart, and its physical isolation meant few outsiders passed through unless they had reason to.

Many outsiders saw Southie as a rough place with a disproportionate number of bars and the problems that accompanied them. But it
was more complex than that.

When Whitey Bulger was growing up, there were three distinctive parts of Southie: City Point, a leafy section on the east side,
bounded by the ocean; the hardscrabble Lower End, on the west side,
where tenements stood near factories and the fish warehouses that
stretched up from the waterfront; and the projects. While the projects were on the west side, they were considered distinct and apart
from the Lower End. Southie's population was about twenty-three
thousand during the Civil War, but it had nearly tripled in size by the
beginning of the twentieth century. From the apex of around eighty
thousand before World War I, the population steadily dwindled to
about fifty thousand in 1920 and remained fairly constant until 1980,
when it fell to today's roughly thirty thousand. It was an overwhelmingly blue-collar community, thick with tradesmen, laborers, and
longshoremen. Southie's lawyers and doctors and small businessmen peopled the brick town houses in City Point. A stretch of East
Broadway had so many doctors living in the brownstones that the
locals called it Pill Hill. The waterfront provided many jobs, legitimate ones to those who loaded and unloaded ships, illegitimate ones
to those who trafficked in the goods that were stolen off those ships.
If the waterfront gave James Bulger his only steady job, it would one
day give his first son and namesake his first crooked one. Not long
after the Old Harbor project opened, they dedicated a huge sculp-
ture in the project's courtyard showing three workingmen—a fisherman, a longshoreman, and a foundry worker—flanked by a boy and
girl at play. Those were the sorts of people who lived in Old Harbor.

The Cliffords of O'Callaghan Way, who were close to the Bulgers,
were considered almost royalty: Billy Clifford was the first priest
ordained out of the projects, while his sister Marilyn was the first
nun.[18] Such was the ideal for ambitious Catholic families, but it was

hardly the rule. It was not unusual—indeed, it was probably more common—for the same household in South Boston to produce a cop and a criminal, a priest and a politician, a firefighter and an arsonist. That duality left people less judgmental and more empathetic about those who went astray. When Whitey Bulger started getting into trouble as a young teenager, snatching and reselling stolen goods, no one suggested he came from a bad family; in fact, they knew just the opposite. The rest of the Bulger kids were well behaved and studious; Whitey was just the wild one, the black sheep, and there were few clans in Southie who could credibly claim their family tree never knew the backhand of a cop or the inside of a jail cell. It wasn't considered just poor form in Southie to hold a family accountable for its bad seed; it was considered hypocritical.

Jean Bulger, Whitey's mother, was infused with an optimism that defied a depression and a world war. Neat in appearance, invariably pleasant, she was a master at the art of stoop talking, by which news and gossip spread from one building to the next. She handed out freshly baked cookies to the neighborhood kids.[19] Viewed with great fondness by her neighbors, she was also a different person in different settings. In the presence of her husband, who was quiet, she was retiring and demure, even deferential. But on her own, she stepped forward. Her sometimes reticent demeanor hid a street-smart sagacity. You could not pull anything over on Jean Bulger, and she did not like phonies.[20] "When she put her mind to something," her son Bill said, "she usually got it."[21]

As the family patriarch, James Bulger cut something of a sad figure. He was self-conscious about his missing arm and eventually stopped wearing his prosthetic. No matter what the weather, he slung a coat over the missing appendage. But he liked a well-cut cigar and was a good conversationalist, a staunch New Dealer who believed that FDR saved the country, and especially the working-man. At the very least, FDR gave his family a good place to live for $29 a month, about a third of their monthly income.[22] In part because he never held a full-time job after losing his arm, in part because of his introverted nature, James Bulger was fond of long, solitary walks along the beach. When he did stop to talk, it was usually about politics. He was politically astute, and a staunch supporter of James Michael Curley, Boston's empathetic if ethically challenged mayor.

Curley's rise from poverty to power was a potent symbol to Boston's ethnic poor of what could be done, and what they could hope for. He personified a defiant, anything-is-possible ethos that resonated in Old Harbor. And while there is no evidence that Whitey paid much attention to Curley, Whitey's little brother Billy grew to idolize him, to want to be like him, first as a student, then as a politician. He patterned his rhetorical style and wit after the master.[23] Curley, who grew up poor but was a learned man, had been caught in the early 1900s taking a civil service exam for an Irish immigrant. This transgression landed him in jail briefly and marked him forever as a scoundrel to the ruling Protestant Brahmin establishment. But to the working-class ethnics he was a hero. They returned him to office despite repeated acts of graft and corruption. Curley turned his criminal record into a campaign slogan: He Did It for a Friend. He was shameless and savored hard-nosed tactics. When he found out that Boston mayor John "Honey Fitz" Fitzgerald had had an affair with a cigarette girl named Elizabeth "Toodles" Ryan, he announced that he would be giving a public lecture entitled "Great Lovers in History: From Cleopatra to Toodles." The public had never heard of Toodles but Honey Fitz had; he withdrew from the race, and Curley canceled his lecture and cruised to victory in the 1914 mayoral election.[24] He was Boston's most charismatic and resilient politician, and, in a career that stretched well beyond a half century, he served terms in the mayor's office, the governor's office, Congress, and a federal penitentiary. Long after the Irish became the most powerful force in Boston and Massachusetts politics, Curley exploited class divisions to create an us-versus-them narrative that helped sustain his wild popularity with his blue-collar base.

In places like Old Harbor, Curley was especially loved. During the Depression, he received constituents at his mansion, located on the main, winding tree-lined boulevard in Jamaica Plain. Its shutters were decorated with shamrocks. The line of supplicants formed early in the day, and Curley listened to stories of hardship and handed out cash or jobs. In the projects, his roguish ways engendered only affection. If he stole, many reasoned, he stole from the Brahmins and the banks—and what have they ever done for us? Curley was especially admired in Southie because he built the L Street Bathhouse on Carson Beach and greatly expanded City Hospital, which served the lower classes. He was known, with justice, as the Mayor of the Poor.

James Bulger, while a Curley loyalist, had no connections in City Hall, no political patron to wangle him a secure job, and so he struggled to keep his family out of poverty. It was an era, Bill Bulger recalled, when there were no special programs or opportunities for the disabled. His father had to work when others wouldn't. "If it were very, very cold, he would be the night watchman. If it were Christmas, or New Year's, when no one else wanted to work, he would take whatever jobs he could get. He wasn't a complainer, though. He was happy to get the job. It was a grind."[25]

World War II changed both the Bulgers and South Boston. For Southie, the war brought a sudden end to the Depression. Thousands of neighborhood men enlisted, and both men and women filled new jobs in factories and shipyards.[26] O'Connor, the Boston historian, argues that Southie came out of the war more unified than ever, more recognized as a special place than ever. The old vaudeville song "Southie Is My Home Town," which praised a neighborhood where "they'll take you and break you but they'll never forsake you," was ubiquitous. It was sung at military posts, PXs, "and barrooms from South Carolina to Georgia, Texas to California. . . . By the time the war had ended South Boston, for better or worse, had become the only one of the city's two dozen neighborhoods to epitomize the 'Boston Irish' at their open-hearted, ebullient best, or their brooding, belligerent worst," O'Connor said. "The single image of

'Beacon Hill' comes close to encapsulating the notions of the Yan-kee heritage, the Brahmin influence and the conservative Prot-estant tradition of Boston. In much the same way, 'South Boston' had come close to symbolizing, in a single community, the 'other' Boston—the immigrant spirit, the Irish character and the Catholic influence in the city."[27]

The war brought marked improvement to the Bulgers' finances. With so many men in the military, James Bulger got work at the Charlestown Navy Yard. The work remained steady until the war ended. James Bulger was philosophical about the end of the war and his job. "Look," he told his family, "even though it's better for me than it's been, I wouldn't want the thing to go on one extra day, because of what it would mean to other people."[28]

If finding work was a constant worry, so was his son Jim. Com-pared to his other siblings and most of his peers, Whitey was notably uncooperative and combative. By nature a nonconformist, he was constantly in trouble with his teachers for acting up or, just as often, for chronic apathy. He seemed ungovernable and unreachable. The nuns at St. Mark's and St. Margaret's in Dorchester had had little success in getting him to study. The public school teachers fared no better after the family moved to South Boston and Whitey enrolled in fifth grade at the Thomas N. Hart School, at the corner of H and East Fifth streets. Tommy Moakley, a contemporary of Whitey's, remembers the public schools and parochial schools as completely different worlds. Whitey didn't fit in either. In the Catholic schools, a rap on the knuckles was common when you acted up, and that kept outbursts to a minimum for most children. But it was looser in public school. "We went to the Hart School," Moakley said. In honor of its often unruly students, Moakley said, the kids called it the Nut House.[29]

Whitey went to the Hart School through eighth grade. A federal probation officer who much later reviewed his report cards and the less than glowing reviews written by nuns and teachers was harsh in his assessment. "His scholastic record was poor. He failed in all of his subjects, receiving poor marks in conduct and effort. The school report shows that he was surly, lazy and had no interest in school work."[30] But he kept getting advanced to the next grade. The available record offers no explanation for the lenient treatment.

Whitey also defied the rules and expectations at home, testing his father's patience and risking his hand. James Bulger Sr. was a man of solitary pursuits, and child rearing in those years was largely left to women. Still, like many parents of that era, James Bulger sometimes resorted to corporal punishment, especially with Whitey, who later told prison interviewers that his father beat him severely on occasion. The image of James Bulger beating his wayward son was contrary to his character, according to Bill Bulger, who described his father as "instinctively gentle." But if Whitey's claim about his father is accurate, the harsh discipline reflected James Bulger's utter frustration with his scapegrace son. Still, the one-armed beatings seem to have had little or no effect. At his father's insistence, Whitey gave school one last shot, at the Brandeis Vocational High School downtown, where there was hope he could pick up a trade. He lasted a year.

But he found a trade. It was not a coincidence that Whitey's last year in school coincided with his first recorded arrest, in 1943, for larceny and delinquency. He was thirteen years old. His sentence was suspended, and he was off probation by the next time he was arrested, two years later, as a wayward youth—a nebulous, catch-all charge reserved for the most incorrigible defendants in the juvenile system. Four more arrests followed, at fifteen and sixteen, on more serious charges, including assault and battery. He was found guilty on only one of the charges, and he won that on appeal; the rest were dismissed or he was found not guilty. He appeared before judges six times as a juvenile, twice for violent offenses, but was not incarcerated. He kept getting a break.[31] Perhaps he was the beneficiary of political influence through his Southie connections, or perhaps it was judicial sympathy for the bad apple in a good family; the court files are silent on why. Some who knew him well say some of

Whitey's early criminal forays were motivated by a desire to bring some money to a cash-poor household. He was the oldest boy and felt some obligation. But there were also offenses that don't fit that pattern at all.[32]

Trouble wasn't all that lured Whitey. The Ringling Bros. and Barnum & Bailey Circus came to town one year when he was a teenager, and he ran away with it. He didn't last long as a roustabout, but his willingness to try it betrayed his desire for something beyond the confines of Southie, the certainties of Old Harbor life that he valued but also felt suffocated by, and the scrutiny of his parents. His mother had just given birth to her sixth and last child, Sheila. Bill Bulger, five years younger than Whitey, recognized the itch, the frustration that in his brother's case was obvious. "I had seen him change from a blithe spirit to a rebel whose cause I could never discern. He was in a constant state of revolt against . . . I'm not sure what. He was restless as a claustrophobic in a dark closet."[33]

Whitey's rebelliousness was in stark contrast to the behavior and preoccupations of his siblings. They were studious. They strived to conform. His older sister, Jean, was voted the prettiest girl at South Boston High School.[34] His brothers and sisters followed the rules.

Not Whitey. Rules were a particular point of contention for him. He would defy them or rewrite them. One day, he came home with an ocelot, a small wildcat that looks like a miniature leopard. He named it Lancelot and kept it in the bedroom he shared with his brothers. Jean Bulger refused to enter her sons' room as long as Lancelot the Ocelot was there. Bill recalls that whenever his mother reminded Whitey that pets were forbidden in the project, Whitey cited the fine print, insisting that the rules specifically forbade only dogs and cats. "Read the rules," he told his mother. "Where does it say anything about ocelots?"[35] Lancelot the Ocelot grew to such a size that, eventually, even Whitey agreed it had to go to a zoo. He brought it there himself.

Throughout the projects and much of the Lower End, Whitey was known as a good-natured hellion who grew tougher with time and also grew into a figure of real charisma among his peers. Joe Quirk, who grew up across the courtyard from the Bulgers, remembers the teenage Whitey as a physical specimen with a washboard abdomen. "Hit me in the stomach," Whitey dared him. "Hard as you can." Quirk was just a kid, six years younger, and he punched as hard as he could. Whitey didn't flinch. "You can hit me harder than that," Whitey said.[36] He also began building a reputation as something of a gentleman among troublemakers. Sally Dame, who moved into Old Harbor across the street from the Bulgers when the project opened in 1938, remembers Whitey, whom she called Jimmy, as especially solicitous of his elders. If he saw her bumping her shopping carriage down the steps, Whitey would run up to her, saying, "Wait a minute, Mrs. Dame. Wait a minute." He would then gallantly carry the carriage down the steps for her.[37] Bobby Moakley, Whitey's classmate at the Hart School, said that whenever Whitey saw Moakley's mother walking home from the store, he would offer to help. When he was young, he offered to carry her grocery bags. When he was older and had a car, Whitey would pull alongside Mrs. Moakley and insist on driving her home. "He was always the perfect gentleman," said Moakley.[38]

Whitey also began to stand out for other reasons. Not long after World War II ended, he was a high school dropout without a legitimate job who somehow managed to have a car. Boston police intelligence reports in those years identified him as a tailgater, someone who stole goods and appliances from the trucks that loaded up from freighters on the waterfront. Whitey was hardly alone in this trade. Southie was full of tailgaters, who found willing buyers in the neighborhood for winter jackets or toasters or irons or whatever else they could get their hands on. His neighbors, knowing he didn't have a job, would doubtless have assumed that Whitey got his money through illegitimate means, but South Boston in general and Old Harbor in particular were not places where people asked questions about such things.

He was also, even as a nascent criminal, preoccupied with appearances, seemingly conscious of creating a public persona that belied his true profession. He dressed neatly, in sports shirts and slacks. The only sartorial nod to his criminal life was a fedora he'd often don while driving—the favored headgear of the hoods of his era. And Whitey, while he could swear like a sailor, was fastidious about not doing so in front of his elders. Sally Dame remembers Whitey asking a neighbor for permission to use a hose to wash his car. He let some of the younger kids help him, giving them a quarter for their trouble, a sizable amount for a young kid in postwar Southie. "One kid swore," Sally Dame said, "and he grabbed him by the ear, Jimmy did, and he said, 'Don't you ever, ever let me hear you swear again or I won't let you help me wash my car.'"[39]

After Ann McCarthy moved into Old Harbor in 1947, she noticed that Whitey had a way with animals. "All the dogs in the neighborhood loved him," she said. "They all ran for him. He always had goodies in his pockets."[40]

If Whitey's image, especially among his elders, was of an affable, gentlemanly teenager, he was seen quite differently by peers. Those his own age knew he was a fierce street fighter, someone not to be messed with. He was, one police officer recalled, the type of kid who would take two punches to land one. And he worked to maintain his chiseled, compact physique. Whitey played football with the Shamrocks, a Southie gang that played other neighborhoods in games where a punch was used as often as a block. But generally he wasn't drawn to team sports. Instead he lifted weights at home, rare in those days, and ran the beach to stay in shape. His regimen and self-discipline were intense. There was love and stability inside Apartment 756 at 41 Logan Way, but Whitey craved something else: the wild side. Still in his teens, he scandalized his mother when he began dating a burlesque dancer who used the stage name Tiger Lil.[41] Bill Bulger remembers his older brother being in search of something far beyond Southie. "'Where's Jim?' my mother was always asking. 'I turn my back for a second and he's out the door. He's always out the door. Where does he go?' I couldn't answer. I didn't know. I don't

think Jim knew where he was going most of the time—just out."[42]
Jean Bulger remained relentlessly optimistic about her oldest son.
He's going through a stage, she would say.[43]

But his restlessness didn't recede with time. It grew.

Johnny Connolly was sitting on his stoop on O'Callaghan Way, the
longest street in Old Harbor, which loops around the project. It was
the summer of 1946 and he was six years old. He looked up, shielding his eyes from the sun, and saw Whitey Bulger walking briskly
up the street. He knew it was the kid everybody called Whitey, just
by looking at him. In the Old Harbor projects, you learned about
Whitey Bulger quickly. He was only seventeen but his legend was
taking shape. He was the toughest kid, the wildest kid, in the neighborhood. Being tough meant something in all of Southie, but especially the projects.

From that stoop, Johnny Connolly watched Whitey stride across
the courtyard, his short-sleeve shirt revealing a bulging bicep, his
dungarees rolled up at the ankles. His hair was somewhere between
blond and white, shimmering in the afternoon sun. John Connolly
would never really let go of this romanticized image even years later
when he knew Whitey as a gangster and a murderer.

Two years later, eight-year-old Connolly and two of his playmates
were standing in a drugstore everybody called The Druggie, at the
corner of Mohawk Street and Devine Way. The boys had gone to
buy penny candy, but one of them spied nineteen-year-old Whitey
and another teenager standing at the soda fountain and whispered,
"There's Whitey Bulger." By that time, even prepubescent boys
knew he was a tough guy. Some of them might have even known he
was a budding hoodlum. "It was like meeting Ted Williams," Connolly said. "He was a legend in the project."[44]

Whitey noticed the boys staring, so he asked, "You guys want
an ice cream?" Connolly's companions nodded enthusiastically, but
Connolly hung back, remembering his mother's admonition not to

accept gifts from strangers. After the other boys had placed their orders, Whitey turned to Connolly and asked, "What kind of ice cream do you want?" Connolly was embarrassed and looked at the floor, but his buddy Robby wasn't as shy.

"His mom says he can't take anything from strangers," Robby blurted out between licks of his cone.

Whitey scrunched up his face.

"Strangers?" Whitey said. He looked down at Connolly.

"Kid," Whitey asked, "where do you live?"

Connolly pointed down the street, to O'Callaghan Way.

"Kid," Whitey Bulger said, bending over so his face was level with Connolly's. "I'm no stranger. Your mother and father are from Ireland. My mother and father are from Ireland. I'm no stranger. Now, what kind of ice cream do you want?"

The families' immigration history was somewhat truncated—it was Whitey's grandparents who were from Ireland—but the larger point was made.

"Vanilla," Johnny Connolly said.

And with that, Whitey Bulger reached down and lifted little Johnny Connolly up to the counter and bought him an ice cream cone.[45] It was the first encounter in a relationship that would span more than half a century and become mutually beneficial, though the vector of power would always remain, as it was that day, tilted toward Whitey.

A short time later, Connolly was walking through the courtyard when an older kid threw a ball at him. He instinctively picked it up and threw it back in anger, striking him in the face. Enraged, the other boy pounced on Connolly and began pounding him. He had thirty pounds on Connolly and it wasn't a fair fight. Whitey Bulger appeared and pulled the older boy off. "Go fight somebody your own size," Whitey told the kid.

The Connollys moved out of the project and a mile away to City Point when John was twelve years old. Other than buying him an ice cream cone and saving him from a beating, Whitey Bulger played no role in young Connolly's formative years. But those two acts of generosity and protectiveness were seared into Connolly's memory, and Whitey's brother Bill became Connolly's mentor. Bill Bulger was six years older than Connolly, but he saw something in the younger boy and was solicitous of him, walking him home from church on Sundays. They worked together as lifeguards at the L Street Bathhouse.

For many in the neighborhood, St. Monica's, the local parish, was more than a church. It was a youth center. Its pastor, Rev. Leo Dwyer, was more like a social worker than a priest. He could talk baseball with anybody. He took the kids on the trolley down to Mattapan Square, then on hikes in the Blue Hills. Sometimes he'd hitchhike with the kids to get out of town for the day.[46] Bing Crosby would have played him in a movie. But Dwyer never had a chance with Whitey, who stayed clear of the church, even as his brother Bill became an altar boy and a standout second baseman on the parish baseball team. Being an altar boy, not to mention a good ballplayer, carried a lot of status in the neighborhood, another reason John Connolly looked up to Bill Bulger. And even after Connolly's family moved out of Old Harbor, Bill Bulger remained a mentor, a constant, one of the most important people in Connolly's life, encouraging him to take the same route he took, to Boston College. "I didn't know a lot of people who went to college growing up," Connolly said. "Bill Bulger planted the idea. He knew education was the way up and out."[47]

It may have been the way up but it was not the way out. You never left South Boston. You might move away. But you never really left. Connolly only left for five years, cutting his teeth as a young FBI agent, and when he came back Whitey was already the biggest gangster in town. He decided to repay Bill Bulger's kindness by protecting Whitey, by protecting the Bulger family from scandal. It was an act of loyalty, of fealty, and of incredibly misguided priorities. It was the sort of blind devotion that puts family and friendship first, something that grows from allegiances born on the stoop of a housing project in Southie. It would be his undoing.

2

Stick-up Man

The wrong kind of fame came early to Whitey Bulger. Even as a teenager he was a figure of growing renown in the neighborhood, looked up to by the likes of the young John Connolly, feared by others for his toughness and temper. He also began drawing the attention of police. Whitey was just sixteen when, by his account, the cops dragged him into the back of the South Boston precinct house. They knew him as a notorious tailgater—gifted in the art of stealing valuables off delivery trucks and fencing them for cash on the streets—and they wanted names. Who were his associates? Who were his buyers? He gave them a smart answer instead, and they gave him a beating. His arm was throbbing; he thought it was broken. One of the cops jammed the barrel of a revolver into Whitey's mouth and drew so close that he could smell the booze on the officer's breath. "I thought I was dead," Whitey told a friend years later.[1]

But the moment passed and Whitey was released. He was proud of himself. Even expecting a bullet, he insisted he had given no one up. There would be other backroom episodes with police officers, though apparently none quite as dramatic. But Whitey's interactions with the law became increasingly adversarial, and with good reason. With every year that passed, he veered more deeply into trouble. The crimes he was accused of took on a more sordid edge.

In June of 1948, when he was eighteen years old, Whitey was charged with assault with intent to rape after the twenty-three-year-old wife of a marine got into a car with Whitey and two other young men. The woman told police she joined the men willingly after watching a movie downtown. But instead of driving her home, they took her to Malibu Beach in Dorchester, where she had to fight her way out of the car and flee. A month later, the charge was reduced to assault and battery. Whitey paid a fifty-dollar fine and walked out of court a free man. It was a considerable break. A few months later, he enlisted in the air force.

In Southie, men enlisted enthusiastically. There was a patriotic tradition of joining the service and a solemn sense of pride in the number killed or wounded in war. Whitey's older sister, Jean, had married a career army man from Southie, Joe Toomey. After graduating from West Point in 1949, Toomey was commissioned as a first lieutenant and sent into combat in Korea the following year.

Whitey's military career followed a less impressive trajectory. Not surprisingly, the boy who never had much patience for rules had a hard time taking orders from superiors. In the nearly four years he was in the air force, from January 1949 until August 1952, he worked as an aircraft mechanic and managed to get his high school degree, but he also kept getting in trouble. His rule breaking, however, proved both a blessing and a curse: He never got promoted, but neither was he deemed fit for combat in Korea. Whitey's brother-in-law was not so lucky. He was wounded and captured by Chinese troops in Korea in November 1950. Like other POWs, he endured harsh conditions, and Jean Bulger later received a letter from the army telling her that her husband had been starved to death by his captors. Whitey's sister was a widow at twenty-three. Her dead husband's body was never recovered. Joe Toomey is the last name of the twenty Southie natives listed on the Castle Island Korean War memorial that Whitey helped underwrite some forty years after Toomey's death.[2]

Joe Toomey's capture and horrific death traumatized the Bulger family. It also increased their concern that Whitey, too, might see combat in a conflict that would take the lives of more than thirty-six thousand US servicemen. But the Bulger family's worries proved misplaced; Whitey's disciplinary issues kept him comfortably stateside. "He wrote me often," his brother Bill said.

> It was clear he was enjoying himself. The Air Force apparently had more rules than planes, and he delighted in breaking or circumventing a great number of them. It appeared from his letters that he contrived a new system each week for being absent without leave and did so with impunity. His conduct was not from any lack of patriotism. He was just being Jim. I believed then, and I believe now, that he would have performed well in combat.[3]

The part about going AWOL was not hyperbole. In January of 1950, Whitey was arrested in Oklahoma City and charged with being absent without leave. A year later, while stationed at an airbase in Montana, he was charged with rape by police in Great Falls. The details of the alleged incident are unclear, but he was released to military authorities. The disposition of the case, while not specified in available records, favored Whitey. He left the air force with an honorable discharge. A prison report later recounted his adult arrest record and remarked on Whitey's charmed life: "He has been arrested on charges of unarmed robbery, investigation, AWOL, rape, grand larceny and vagrancy. However, in no case did he ever receive a sentence or serve any time."[4]

Whitey returned to Logan Way at the end of the summer of 1952 and picked right up where he'd left off, stealing and selling hot merchandise. This gave him cash and a certain cachet. Boys of a certain age would watch Whitey, sporting a pearl-gray fedora, drive by in his blue Oldsmobile with a buxom hairdresser named Jacquie McAuliffe beside him in the front seat. They wanted to be like him, but most of them couldn't imagine what that meant. He had begun by boosting goods off the back of trucks parked up and down Broadway. It was petty thievery, but it was profitable enough for Whitey to dress the way he wanted, to always have a car, to always have a girl.

A Boston police intelligence report noted that Whitey had become one of the city's preeminent tailgate thieves. "However," the report states, "sometime in 1955, it was reliably reported that he had stopped this activity and decided to go in for more serious crime." While he was never a drinker, police reports describe Whitey frequenting the myriad barrooms in Southie. In the bars a small-time thief, especially one with ambitions, could latch onto a group of like-minded criminals. Bank robbery in those days was considered the next step up the criminal ladder. It was also a team sport. A typical crew consisted of three men, one of them to drive the getaway car, another to vault the counter, the third to keep his gun drawn while his accomplice scooped the cash.[5] Whitey would, in time, master all three roles, though he proved especially good with the gun.

But even as he was moving on to bank robbery, or because he was, Whitey seemed unusually sensitive about his reputation within Old Harbor. George Pryor, whose family lived in the apartment beneath the Bulgers when he was a boy, remembers Whitey apologizing for not going out of his way to drive Pryor home. "I felt bad," Whitey told him, "because I didn't want you to think I drove by you."[6]

During the early to mid-1950s, Mickey McGonagle had the paper route in the Old Harbor project, and every day he delivered a paper to the Bulger apartment. The weekly bill was fifty cents. Whitey paid McGonagle every week, handing him a dollar and telling him to keep the change. Whitey was the biggest tipper in the

project by far.[7] He had begun cultivating the image of the benevolent wiseguy. Of course, as a bank robber, he had more disposable
income than just about anyone else. He later told his criminal associates that he robbed seventeen banks in all.[8] But it was for three
very specific heists that Whitey, for the first time, found himself
suddenly and very seriously wanted by the law.

Bank robbery was the sort of thing you fell into because of the people you had fallen in with. Whitey had been hanging in the taverns
on and off Broadway, where ex-cons and wannabes dreamed of big
scores. But he had to go downtown to find his first crew. He later
claimed to prison authorities that he came under the tutelage of
Carl Smith, an experienced bank robber from Indiana who used
Boston as one of his bases of operation.

In an interview with prison authorities in 1956, Whitey suggested he was duped into committing his first bank robbery. He said
he was introduced to Smith in May 1955 at the Stage Bar in Boston's
theater district by an ex-convict. Smith encouraged Whitey to drive
for him but was vague about what he had in mind, other than saying
it was easy money. Whitey's explanation for going along with a robbery sounds implausible—even at that young age his smarts and self-
awareness stood out—but it is also suggestive of the importance he
placed on his reputation among other criminals. He wasn't about to
retreat from the action, no matter what it might entail. "When he
learned that this deal concerned a bank robbery he wanted to back
out but did not want them to know he was afraid," a prison official
wrote. "He claims that he was even more afraid when he learned
he had to go into the bank since two persons who [were] involved
backed out. He stated that the bank robbery was successful and
afterwards he was in on three more bank robberies."[9]

In May of 1955, Whitey walked into the Darlington branch of
the Industrial National Bank in Pawtucket, Rhode Island, with
Smith and Ronnie Dermody, an ex-con from Cambridge, Massa-

chusetts. There were five customers and fourteen employees in the bank. Whitey pointed a .22-caliber revolver and forced two bank employees to lie on the floor. One of the customers, a Pawtucket housewife, closed her eyes and whispered a prayer, "Blessed Virgin, help us. Blessed Virgin, help us."[10]

There were some tense moments when a young man training as a teller lifted his head. "All right junior G-man," one of the robbers barked, "I said to lay down."

They were in and out in four minutes, then returned the getaway car to the nearby factory parking lot where they had stolen it and switched cars. If Whitey was somehow duped into his first bank robbery, as he claimed, he acquitted himself well. One of the tellers told police that Whitey "walked like a cowboy."[11] And it was a very good score for four minutes' work: $42,112.

A few months later, Whitey would show off his newfound affluence, taking his girlfriend Jacquie to Florida, staying at high-end hotels. Besides cutting hair, Jacquie had done some modeling, and Whitey had wooed her relentlessly, often stopping by the Broadway salon where she worked. When he told her he had money to burn, she left her young daughter with her mother and jumped in his Oldsmobile. They pretended to be husband and wife. It was an expensive con. In the year of living dangerously and robbing banks, Whitey estimated he spent twenty-five thousand dollars on clothes and hotels.[12] Jacquie, blonde and two years Whitey's senior, looked a lot like Jayne Mansfield, the pin-up icon of the 1950s. Jacquie was the first of the string of beautiful women who would become his companions. At some point, he started referring to her as his fiancé, but they never married.

In October 1955, Carl Smith told Whitey they had another potential bank job lined up, this one in Hammond, Indiana, where he had once lived. Smith had experience robbing banks in the Midwest and considered them easy touches compared to those on the East Coast. Whitey drove to Indiana with Smith and another member of the crew, Richard Barchard. They cased the Mercantile National Bank and agreed to rob it on October 29. On the appointed day, they stole a car from a shopping plaza and parked near the Mercantile. When they walked into the bank, however, they did not pull their guns; instead they abruptly turned around and walked out. There was a police officer inside. They drove the car back to the parking lot where they had stolen it, and, as they did so, Whitey and Barchard noticed the Woodmar branch of the Hoosier State Bank, unguarded and enticing.

Looks like a soft touch, Whitey said to himself.

A month later, Whitey and a bricklayer from Dorchester named Billy O'Brien robbed a bank in Melrose, a suburb north of Boston. While O'Brien held a gun on the customers and employees, Whitey vaulted the counter and scooped $5,035 out of the tellers' drawers. They split the money with Barchard, who had picked the bank out and cased it. Two days later, Whitey and Barchard agreed it was a good time to leave town, to let the heat die down. They remembered that little lonely bank they had seen from the parking lot in Indiana and thought two words: road trip.

Barchard took his wife, Dorothy; Whitey took Jacquie. It was a nine-hundred-mile double date. The boys left the women in a motel, cased the bank, and, the next day, the day before Thanksgiving, they returned in a 1954 Oldsmobile 88 with Illinois plates they had just stolen, parked on Indianapolis Boulevard right in front of the bank, and strolled in. They wore blue jeans, plaid work shirts, and hunting caps with the ear flaps pulled down, but no masks.

Whitey held a pistol in each hand, pointing them at the customers and tellers. He went to the nearest customer, stuck the gun in his chest, and pushed him down. "Everybody on the floor!" he shouted. "I'll shoot the first one who moves!"

There were five other customers, and they all hit the deck. Barchard vaulted the counter and grabbed fistfuls of cash from the tellers' cages and stuffed it into a bag. Whitey, meanwhile, tried to reassure the terrified customers. "We aren't going to hurt anyone," he said. "But we have to make a living. Dillinger did."

It was a great line, invoking the name of the Midwest's most famous and charismatic bank robber. It might not have played in Southie, but it played big in Hammond. The customers who were forced to lie on the floor later took to calling Bulger and Barchard "the two Dillingers."[13]

The two Dillingers almost hit a housewife in the parking lot of the shopping center as they made their getaway. Their haul was less than a third of what they got in Rhode Island—$12,612.28—but it was still about three times the yearly salary of a Boston firefighter living across the street in Logan Way.

Back in Southie, Whitey told Jacquie to pack: They were going to Miami for another romantic spree. They were only there a couple of days when they were both arrested for vagrancy—a pretext charge, evidently—by the Miami police, who had some reason to be suspicious of Whitey. When the police in Boston said they had no outstanding warrants on Whitey, the charges against him and Jacquie were dismissed after Whitey paid a fine of one hundred dollars.[14] The cops had no idea Whitey had just robbed a bank in Indiana. It was a different time. The technology now commonly used to trace bank robbers, or even to photograph them in the act, didn't yet exist. Whitey and Jacquie headed home for Christmas.

A few days after the New Year, authorities in Indiana issued a warrant for Whitey's arrest. He later told prison officials that Carl Smith "squealed on us" after Smith was arrested with two men from Tennessee robbing a bank. Whitey got wind of the warrant and drove cross-country to California. But he missed Jacquie, so he drove back to Southie and picked her up at her mother's house on Dorchester Street. They drove south, to Wilmington, Delaware, and spent the next two months on the road. They made stops in Reno, San Francisco, Salt Lake City, and Chicago. But Jacquie got homesick. She missed her six-year-old daughter and her life in Southie and begged Whitey to bring her home. Against his better judgment, Whitey turned the car around and headed east.

Back in town, he dyed his hair black, donned horn-rimmed

glasses, and tried to stay inside as much as possible. When he did walk around Southie, he had a cigar in his mouth, because it distorted his facial appearance.[15] But this proved useless when an informant called the FBI in Boston and said Whitey was back. The informant had spotted Whitey at a nightclub in Revere, a city north of Boston; the FBI and police pounced. His arrest was widely touted by the FBI. The special agent in charge of the Boston office, usually a desk jockey, turned up for the festivities and was prominently displayed in the photos splashed in the next day's paper, which showed Whitey being taken from the nightclub in handcuffs. The FBI field agent who put the cuffs on him was Paul Rico, an ambitious investigator who specialized in organized crime. More specifically, Rico was known for having an unrivaled array of underworld informants and was always on the lookout for more.

Because he considered everyone he arrested a potential informant, Rico treated Whitey with respect and Whitey in return answered his questions. He copped to robbing the three banks and named his two accomplices in the Rhode Island robbery.[16] He seems to have justified the betrayal on the premise that you can't rat on a rat: Whitey claimed it was Carl Smith who had dimed them all out. But Whitey also claims he admitted his role and implicated his accomplices to save Jacquie. The FBI had threatened to charge her as being a lookout for the Indiana bank job. He later told a friend that he had offered to plead guilty if the FBI would release Jacquie.[17]

He also cajoled Jacquie into cooperating with the FBI, and she identified Barchard as having been with Whitey on the Indiana job and said O'Brien had been with Whitey in Melrose. "Bulger orally admitted who his accomplices were in these bank robberies," FBI agent Herbert Briick wrote. This is the first known instance of Whitey, the prideful stand-up guy, acquiescing to the role of informer. But he was cute about it, as he would always be. In a slick move that foreshadowed their future relationship, Whitey and his FBI handlers purposely masked his role in implicating his fellow thieves. While Whitey only verbally identified his accomplices, he persuaded Jacquie to formally identify them. "As a result of her cooperation," Briick wrote, "process was obtained for Bulger's accomplices." Jacquie's cooperation won her a free pass on prosecution, and Whitey's role in snitching on his accomplices was never made public. Being labeled an informer was not just humiliating; in Whitey's business, it could easily get you killed.

Perhaps Whitey thought that his quickness to cooperate in the case, and his role in getting Jacquie to do so as well, would earn him a measure of leniency, such as he had enjoyed in his years as a juvenile offender. But this time the judge in the case took a much dimmer view of his character and prospects for rehabilitation, for Whitey's local image had changed. In the year that he was robbing banks, he had simply stopped going to Logan Way. He lived out of town, often out of state, to avoid the police. By cutting himself off from his parents and siblings, Whitey appeared to the court to be a more generic sort of scoundrel, a rootless criminal. The presentencing report that Judge George Sweeney reviewed painted him as having "very little to do with his parents. It may be noted that during his formative years his father was very strict with him and on occasions beat him severely. This, however, had very little effect on him as he continued to misbehave in the community. According to his parents he comes home occasionally but, for the most part, has been living elsewhere. His family would not be affected in any way if he were given a severe jail sentence."[18]

The report also indicated that Whitey's IQ was 118, "which indicates above average intelligence. He has always been a leader and knows the difference between right and wrong. His actions have been in accord with his own choosing. The prognosis for future behavior in society is poor."

Sweeney agreed and gave Whitey twenty years. The prosecutor had asked for twenty-five. But Whitey's lawyer, Ted Glynn, pleaded for some leniency, noting in court that Whitey had shown some remorse and had cooperated with authorities.[19]

As a kid, Whitey had had no time for clergy, even the much-admired Father Leo Dwyer at St. Monica's. But after he was locked up, he sought guidance and comfort from a priest, the Rev. Robert Drinan, a family friend whom Bill Bulger had met at Boston College. Bill Bulger had asked the Jesuit priest to help his brother.[20] Whitey and Drinan struck up a correspondence, and a friendship.

Two days after he was sentenced, while awaiting his transfer to a federal lockup for processing, Whitey sat on his bunk in Charles Street Jail in Boston. It was a foreboding, damp, Victorian prison, the city's oldest, where the rats were so big inmates said you could hear their footsteps in the dark. It had been, at various times, the holding tank for some famous lawbreakers—James Michael Curley, Sacco and Vanzetti, Malcolm X—and many of lesser note like Whitey.* But Whitey's mood didn't match his grim surroundings as he wrote to Drinan, who had just been appointed dean at Boston College Law School. Drinan had visited Whitey since his arrest and had vouched for the Bulger family in presentencing reports.

For a twenty-six-year-old man who had just gotten a twenty-year prison sentence, Whitey was remarkably lacking in self-pity and seemed almost ebullient. The certainty of twenty years in prison was preferable to the unknown risks and certain disgrace of the life he'd been living. He seemed determined to make the best of it. "I thank you from the bottom of my heart for all the help you have given me," he wrote to Drinan. Whitey pledged to put his time in prison to good use. He considered himself fortunate to be sent to a federal prison instead of a state penitentiary; the quality of life was said to be higher. "Things have turned out very well for me. The twenty year sentence pleases me. . . . I feel so much better now that I know I can look forward to getting out some day. These years will be put to good use. I'm eager to leave here and get settled down at the next place. I'm lucky to be going to a federal prison rather

---

*In 2007, the Charles Street Jail was converted into the Liberty Hotel, one of the most expensive in the city.

than a state prison. The conditions are supposed to be much better." Whitey said he'd had a chance to say farewell to his family and his girlfriend, and that he had gotten some books to read from his brother Bill; but he wished he'd had one more chance to see Drinan. "I can't think of anything else to say except I wish I could really let you know just how I do appreciate how things have turned out. I'm going to say goodnight and I do hope to see you again." He signed the letter, "Your friend, Jim."[21]

If the letter to Father Drinan was remarkable for its optimism and introspection, it was also notable in one other aspect: Whitey had noted on the top left corner the conditions under which it was written—in the dark. "Writing this after lights out," Whitey said. The lights would go out early for the next nine years. The one who always walked out—out of school, out of his home, out of the safe cocoon of Old Harbor—was now a guest of the Federal Bureau of Prisons. And he described it almost as a relief. For the restless boy from Logan Way, there was nowhere to go but up.

3

The University of Alcatraz

Whitey Bulger was standing on Pier 4 at Fort Mason, waiting to board the *Warden Johnston*, a sixty-five-foot boat that traveled between the mainland and a small island in the middle of San Francisco Bay. He remembered the city fondly and well, though it had been a while since he'd last visited, back when he was a bank robber on the run, with money in his pockets and a girlfriend at his side. Now he was in chains and federal marshals stood next to him. It was the second week of November 1959 and the air was chilly and slightly sweet from the nearby Ghirardelli Chocolate factory. The fading chime of cable car bells echoed over the dull hum of the *Warden Johnston*'s idling diesel engine. San Francisco rose majestically behind him. The Golden Gate Bridge was off to his left, but looming most vividly was that island in the bay, his new home: Alcatraz.

They called it The Rock, the island for incorrigibles. Whitey was three thousand miles away from the jail cell in Boston where he had pledged to Father Robert Drinan, the family friend and future congressman, that he would reinvent himself in prison. But now, staring out at The Rock, Whitey Bulger felt utterly cut off from Southie, from his family, from all he knew. He still meant to keep that pledge, though in this new, intimidating place, the question was how.

Alcatraz was his second stop in the federal corrections system. He had first entered prison in Atlanta in July 1956, twenty-six years old, taut and wiry at 5 feet 9½ and 148 pounds, still radiating self-confidence. He was a common criminal, of course, but an oddly impressive one, who began his twenty-year sentence for bank robbery with a plan, to read and take seriously the education he had spurned in his youth, all the while making himself eligible for parole as soon as possible. Instead, his impulsivity and the allure of trouble had gotten the better of him, as they had throughout his young life—he had always been the boy no one could quite understand or control. His plan to conform and sail through prison in the fastest possible time had gone badly awry. As he stepped onto the *Warden Johnston,* he was headed for the toughest prison in America.

Three years earlier, Whitey had arrived in Atlanta in the summer sun, and even with the prospect of two decades in prison ahead of him, the Beaux-Arts façade of the federal penitentiary had looked deceptively inviting. But that view was only for those on the outside. Whitey was driven to the back gate, where the new inmates were received, and reality quickly set in. He could see the sprawling, three-hundred-acre prison for what it was. Armed guards manned the looming watchtowers. Rows and rows of tiered cells, enough for more than a thousand inmates, were stacked in the middle of the main yard.

Whitey was shocked to find that he would have not one cellmate but seven. There were four bunk beds crammed in the cell. There was a toilet against the wall, one sink to wash your face in, and a smaller sink to brush your teeth. The humiliation of being forced to use the toilet in full view of seven other men was nothing, in Whitey's mind, compared to his inability to get away from the constant, banal chatter of his cellmates. It wasn't that he had no interest in the predictable subject matter—sex, cars, money—it was that they talked of nothing else. Many of them were short-timers, counting days and months, while Whitey was looking at years. He had goals and saw himself as a young man with prospects. All they had was their maddening, relentless, trivial talk. Whitey couldn't read; he couldn't think. The distraction was unnerving and then infuriating, and he began to worry that one day he'd punch someone and land in the hole, an isolation cell where there was no reading, no mail, nothing but walls.

In time, he did find some relief by taking a job in the prison's "education department," which meant he could spend a lot of time in the library. He lifted weights to relieve his nervous energy and to put some bulk on his frame. But there was something heavier than prison monotony weighing on Whitey. Almost as soon as he'd arrived in Atlanta, FBI agents turned up to question him about yet another crime: They said two of his bank robbery accomplices had implicated him in a murder in Indiana.[1] The robbers claimed that they had dumped the victim in a lake. Investigators dragged the lake and did not find a body, but still they considered the information credible and warned Whitey and Atlanta prison authorities that a murder charge was imminent. Whitey insisted he was innocent, that he didn't know anything about a murder—and he was telling the truth, in this case, although prison officials had no way to know that. "[Whitey] wrote an anxious letter to his brother about this charge but it was difficult to tell whether he was bragging or complaining," prison authorities wrote. "Under any circumstances he appears deeply concerned and such a warrant in all probability will affect his adjustment here."[2]

Distraught that he might be indicted for a crime that could turn his long sentence into life in prison, Whitey found his cellmates' chatter even more unbearable. He needed to think and had nowhere to do so. His patience was gone; he was about to snap. After just three months in the prison, he checked himself into the prison's psychiatric ward, complaining that "other men in his cell got on his nerves."[3] There was a method to his self-admitted madness; he wanted to be placed in a single cell permanently. As he sat in the ward, he wrote a two-page letter to Father Drinan in Boston, pleading for help. The priest wasn't just a friend and a spiritual adviser, he was also a lawyer, and Whitey was looking for legal advice.[4]

Whitey told the priest he was feeling mixed up. He thought he was doing all the right things. He was working in the library. He was going to chapel on Sundays. "I'm no angel but as you know I've got a twenty year sentence and I know if I don't help myself and put this time to good use I will have no future. I can only help myself by an education and forming good habits and sensible outlook on life," he wrote.

He told the priest that the distraction in his cell was so bad he couldn't read there. He was bottling up his emotions. He wondered if he had any grounds to demand a cell transfer, and asked Drinan to explain the situation to his brother Bill, who would update his family and Jacquie. Whitey's plea never reached the priest. The letter was confiscated by prison officials, who reviewed all outgoing mail and prohibited inmates from revealing details of their incarceration. Still, Whitey finally managed to persuade staff on his own that it was best to move him. His new, solitary cell was no panacea. He was still on edge, worried about the murder case, and feeling the distance from home. No one had visited him, and while he was writing to his family regularly, the return mail was spotty. Letters from home were being withheld or delivered weeks late. A few months after Whitey wrangled himself a single cell, he got into a fight with another inmate in the morning bath line. It was his first infraction and he was briefly put in segregation and lost ten days of "good time." The prison system rewarded model behavior by allowing inmates to shave up to ten days off their sentences each month by staying out of trouble.[5] It was a considerable incentive, one that Whitey had intended to make full use of.

Bill Bulger, ever the good son to Whitey's bad, graduated from Boston College Law School and became a state representative while his older brother was in prison. Insistent, organized, and able, Bill soon emerged as Whitey's principal advocate and protector. He frequently called and wrote prison officials complaining about how his brother was being treated and urging them to transfer him closer to home.[6] He found a powerful ally in a family friend from the neighborhood: US Congressman John W. McCormack, who rose from House Majority Leader to Speaker while Whitey was behind bars. Bill Bulger relied on McCormack's political influence to make sure his brother did not get lost in the system, and McCormack called the director of the Bureau of Prisons in Washington to request updates on Whitey's progress and to arrange prison visits by Whitey's family and several friends.[7] In describing his personal debt to McCormack, Bill Bulger said that the congressman kept his family apprised of Whitey's situation in prison. "I remembered his saying to my father, 'James made a mistake and is paying for it, but he can change if they give him a chance.'"[8]

Bill believed his brother wanted to change. He visited Whitey twice at the Atlanta prison and wrote to the warden before each trip, urging him to waive the customary seven-day waiting period between visits so he could see Whitey two days in a row.[9] "This visit to my brother can only be an annual trip for me due to the heavy expense and the time taken from work and school," Bill Bulger wrote, noting that his brother did not get very many visitors because he was so far from home. Whitey wasn't happy, but he and his family on the outside were gradually learning how to navigate the ins and outs of a sometimes infuriatingly unresponsive system. As Whitey eyed the calendar and calculated the good time he was earning each month, he signed up for another way to trim days off his sentence. It proved a bad bargain.

The Atlanta penitentiary's façade did more than mask the factory-like complex lurking behind it. It put a benign face on another unseemly facet of prison life in Whitey's day: the use of inmates as guinea pigs in medical studies and experiments.

With a 1963 parole date his entire focus, Whitey was preoccupied with earning as much good conduct time as possible, and so he was intrigued when he learned about a way to earn added credits not long after taking a job as an attendant in the prison hospital. Dr. Carl Pfeiffer, a noted pharmacologist and researcher from Emory University, told Whitey and other inmates that he was conducting a study looking for a cure to schizophrenia. He said volunteers would be injected with a hallucinogenic drug called LSD, which at the time meant nothing to them: Few people outside the research community had ever heard of lysergic acid diethylamide, or knew of its effects, in 1957. In exchange, inmates would receive small cash deposits in their prison savings accounts and a promise that they would be credited with enough good conduct time to shave months off their sentences.[10]

What they were not told is that the LSD injections were part of an effort, sponsored by the Central Intelligence Agency (CIA), to develop a mind-control weapon. Project MKUltra, the agency's secret program of research into behavior modification, mostly recruited college students and other doctors. The Atlanta prison was just one of eighty-six universities and institutions involved in the testing, which ran from 1953 to 1964.[11]

On August 6, 1957, Whitey signed a contract affirming that he understood "the hallucinatory effect of lysergic acid diethyl amide, LSD-25" and that "the potential benefits to humanity, and the risks to my health of participation in this study have been explained to me . . . and I hereby freely assume all such risks."[12] Six days later he reported to the psychiatric ward, a large, antiseptic room with bars and a locked steel door in the basement of the prison hospital, where he was injected with his first dose of LSD. It was a routine that would continue once a week for the next fifteen months. Whitey got three dollars for every injection, and fifty-four days off his sentence in total, but it was a devastating compact. The hallucinatory effects of the LSD would last a lifetime and Whitey would bitterly recall, years later, how he felt tricked into taking something that nearly drove him mad and would forever rob him of a good night's sleep.[13]

The hallucinations began within minutes of the injection. Suddenly, blood seemed to explode from the walls and drown him. The inmate sitting next to him turned into a skeleton. The bars on the windows morphed into writhing black snakes. He and the other test subjects became "raving . . . totally out of control mental and psychological animals." Whitey felt depressed and suicidal after the sessions. He said two inmates in the project became psychotic and were shipped off to the federal prison hospital in Missouri.[14]

Richard Sunday, an inmate who worked in the prison hospital with Whitey and became one of his closest friends, witnessed the effect of the experimental injections and was horrified. Whitey, he said, screamed wildly and babbled incoherently. His face was contorted. "He was one crazy individual when he was on those drugs," Sunday said.[15] "He was a lunatic."[16] Sunday urged Whitey to drop out, but Whitey trusted Dr. Pfeiffer and stuck with it. For someone who had shown little respect for authority before he got to prison, Bulger was surprisingly deferential to the doctor. Years later, he would threaten to hunt down and kill Pfeiffer, but his trust was implicit when he was in prison. Sunday speculated it was a manifestation of Whitey's sense of duty, an extension of his patriotism, that he saw the LSD project as a form of public service.[17]

This uncharacteristic bow to authority may have been an outgrowth of his upbringing in South Boston, where loyalty and pride in the blue-collar, working-class neighborhood fused, for most, with an unquestioning love of country. Young men felt a duty to join the military, and Southie has had a disproportionate share of soldiers killed in action over many generations. Street corners, parks, and schools are named in their honor. Despite his own very sketchy service record, Whitey prided himself on being a veteran. It rankled when other inmates went off on anti-American rants. "People in there talked about the country like a dog," said Sunday, a decorated US Army veteran who was sent to prison after a military court found him guilty of raping a woman when he served in Korea. "I was extremely patriotic . . . Jimmy [Bulger] was also patriotic. He did not want to hear any commie talk about the country."[18]

Plagued by persistent insomnia and nightmares after the injections, Whitey went to the infirmary, begging to be excused from work and left alone in his cell for a day while he recovered. "Shook up from LSD project," a medical staffer wrote on Whitey's medical chart after examining him one day.[19] After fifteen months, doctors dropped him from the study because he was "persistently noisy and boisterous to a rather extreme degree."[20] It's unclear whether they were running out of volunteers or Whitey settled down, but, still desperate to earn good conduct time, he rejoined the LSD study for six weeks the following summer. He also volunteered for a less grueling experiment, testing a vaccine for whooping cough. He was rewarded with one dollar for each vaccination, two dollars for each blood test, and three days' additional good conduct time each month.[21] Gradually and painfully, he was earning his way out.

When he first went to prison, Whitey made good on his vow to use this time to better himself. He took typing classes and completed correspondence courses in bookkeeping, salesmanship, and business law. He began reading in a serious way and discovered an interest in historical novels about war and politics, and in autobiographies, westerns, and poetry. He subscribed to *America*, a Jesuit magazine recommended to him by Father Drinan, whose writings appeared regularly in its pages. And he was a steady letter writer, allowed, under prison rules, to correspond with ten reputable people who had passed a background check. Initially, his list included his parents, brothers, sisters, Jacquie McAuliffe, Drinan, and another priest. When his girlfriend stopped writing, he replaced her on his list with another priest, and thus the boy who couldn't be bothered to walk the few minutes from Logan Way to St. Monica's Church in Southie was now corresponding in prison with three priests— and going to Mass regularly. He may have found a new spirituality, or perhaps he'd simply figured out that one way to impress a parole board is to find religion behind the walls—and to show that you had reputable allies on the outside.

Whatever his motives, his image in the prison began to shift. "This man is devoted to his mother," staff wrote on his annual review, noting that he corresponded regularly with her.[22] He earned a "meritorious award" for helping physical therapy patients in the infirmary, where he demonstrated "cooperative work habits and a cheerful personality." But for all his conscientious reputation building, Whitey still found it hard saying no to the temptation of trouble. A year after that glowing annual review, prison staff discovered he had slipped a hacksaw blade to four inmates who used it to saw their way out of the hospital. The men were captured on the roof over the prison's dining room and an inmate informant told authorities of Whitey's involvement.[23] That Whitey would risk his institutional record for a prison escape he wasn't even going to take part in seemed especially reckless, and prison authorities now viewed him as an escape risk, too. "Almost every time information is received about some escape plot, Bulger's name heads the list," Associate Warden W. H. York wrote, recommending to his boss that Whitey be transferred to Alcatraz, the nation's first super maximum security prison.

Bill Bulger, far away and busy with his own burgeoning career, had access to few of the day-to-day specifics of Whitey's prison life, but it was nevertheless plain to him that things weren't going well. He wrote to McCormack, then House Majority Leader, complaining that Whitey was in solitary confinement, cut off from communication with his family.[24] McCormack personally contacted Bureau of Prisons director James Bennett, urging him to investigate the complaints, and his intervention worked: Whitey was returned to the general population, and Bennett rejected the warden's transfer request, suggesting that the recent move to Alcatraz of two other inmates involved in the escape might work as a sufficient warning to Whitey and persuade him to behave.[25] Five months later, prison authorities uncovered an escape plot planned by Whitey and several other inmates, including Tom Devaney, an enforcer for notorious Irish American mobster Mickey Spillane in Hell's Kitchen, New York City,[26] and plans to ship Whitey to Alcatraz were revived. Once again, Bill Bulger rushed to his defense, writing to the warden: "Despite the supposed tangible evidence to the contrary, I am convinced that my brother has been doing all possible to make himself eligible for parole."[27]

Bill told the warden he would travel to Atlanta in the next few days and hoped for a personal meeting not just with Whitey but with the warden. Bill believed he could explain Whitey's demeanor and his plans. "Few things are as important to me as his eventual return to a decent life," Bill wrote.

The warden sent a reassuring letter back: "Your brother has been identified with some rather serious irregularities during the past few months here, but I am pleased to inform you that he has now emerged to full program participation and is seemingly again participating enthusiastically thereon."[28] He added, "Your writing him letters of a cheerful type and visiting him as frequently as you can reasonably do so will, no doubt, contribute to his progress."

Bill Bulger's next letter to Whitey did not pass the cheerfulness test and was sent back to him undelivered with a note from the warden: "Your letter to your brother James is being returned to you since the major portion of the letter concerns institutional affairs and happenings and is not a social letter in the true sense." A few days later, after receiving a letter from his brother indicating he was still in isolation, Bill Bulger accused the staff of mistreating Whitey and deliberately delaying his letters home so he couldn't get messages to his family. The angry back-and-forth escalated when the warden refused to deliver still another letter and accused Bill of deliberately backdating it to make it seem like the gaps in communication with Whitey were longer in fact than they were.[29] The accusation infuriated Bill Bulger, who prided himself on his moral upbringing and sense of propriety. Nothing made him so hot as to have his honor challenged. He fired back an indignant four-page, handwritten note, defending his integrity and proclaiming, "I don't lie."[30] A second-year law student at the time, Bill Bulger asked the warden to send any future letters to him at Boston College Law School in Newton, an upscale suburb west of Boston, an attempt, perhaps, to underscore that he was someone to be reckoned with.[31] But the warden was done writing about Whitey. In a letter supporting his recommendation to transfer Whitey to Alcatraz, the warden wrote that he was now "actively affiliated with his former, undesirable associates" and plotting to escape.[32] "Notwithstanding our patient efforts to counsel Bulger toward constructive program participation, he is becoming more sullen, resistive, and defiant by the day. We do not believe we can return him to the population here without inviting further serious trouble."

Bill Bulger showed up unexpectedly at Bennett's Washington office on November 12, 1959, hoping to make a personal appeal on his brother's behalf.[33] Bennett was not available and it was already too late. Whitey had just set off on the first leg of his trip to The Rock.

The only thing about Alcatraz that reminded Whitey Bulger of home was the name they gave the corridor near the row of cells where all newcomers were held. They called it Broadway. In this hard new world, his arrival drew no special notice. Al Capone, George "Machine Gun" Kelly, and "Birdman" Robert Stroud had been among the most notorious inmates to ever call Alcatraz home. Whitey Bulger was just another bank robber, inmate 1428—and he wasn't even the only Whitey in the place. There were two others with the nickname.

Jim Albright, who served as a correctional officer at Alcatraz from 1959 until it closed in 1963, recalled Whitey as a nondescript, "run-of-the-mill" convict who stayed out of trouble and didn't draw much attention.[34] "He'd mind his own business," Albright said. "He wasn't overly friendly, but if you asked him something he'd answer you. If you said, 'Good morning,' he'd say, 'Good morning.' He didn't stand out from anyone else."

Whitey was relieved to discover that every inmate had his own cell, even though each one was just five feet wide by nine feet long, with a seven-foot ceiling. Standing in the middle of his cell with both arms outstretched, he could touch the walls on each side. It was furnished with a bed, a toilet, a sink, a couple of bookshelves, and two metal planks that folded down from the wall and served as a seat and table. Whitey spent most of his time in Alcatraz in cell C-314, a unit located on the top of a three-story tier that faced a wall. That didn't give him much of a view, but it gave him privacy, which he wanted much more. No one across the way could peer in. If he stood with his face close to the bars, he could glimpse the library on the corridor to his left. Sunlight streamed through the windows on good days. The cells were wired with earphone jacks, which allowed inmates to listen to radio broadcasts approved by the warden. But if there were some amenities that hadn't been available in the Atlanta prison, the regime was familiarly strict: Inmates were required to work eight hours a day Monday through Friday unless they were ill or sent to "the hole," or segregation, for punishment.

Whitey went along with the work routine—his experience in Atlanta had convinced him that resisting the rules was counterproductive—but he figured out a way to game the system and earn an assignment to his liking. The man he played was Maurice Ordway, who, having joined the staff in 1934, was the longest-serving guard at Alcatraz. Ordway was ornery, with thick, beefy hands. The inmates called him Double Tough because he once told one of them, "You think you're tough? Well I'm double tough."[35]

Double Tough Ordway sidled up to the newly arrived Whitey and said, "You're working in the kitchen." The kitchen detail was considered one of the most taxing at Alcatraz.

"OK," Whitey replied. "Do they have meat cleavers and big knives?"

Ordway narrowed his eyes, went to see his superiors, and was soon back at Whitey's side with new orders: "You're working in the clothing room," he said.[36]

For all of Alcatraz's notoriety, Whitey felt more at ease there, even though Alcatraz was, by design, filled with volatile criminals. It was, after all, the last stop for the irredeemable. "At Alcatraz you had to watch your back and you had to have somebody watch your back," said Sunday, who was transferred to Alcatraz for fighting in Atlanta and arrived about a week after Whitey. "Jimmy watched my back and I watched his."

On weekends and holidays, prisoners were allowed into the recreation yard, where there was a baseball diamond and bleachers. They could play baseball, handball, horseshoes, chess, checkers, or dominoes, and they could lift weights. Whitey had never much liked team sports,[37] so he spent most of his time pumping iron and occasionally playing handball. Some days he would climb to the top of the cement bleachers and look longingly at the San Francisco skyline and the Golden Gate Bridge.[38] The sound of women's laughter could sometimes be heard coming from boats cruising by the island. And, when the wind was just right, the smell of chocolate baking across the bay at Ghirardelli's occasionally wafted past. The sights and smells, tantalizingly close and yet so far away, inspired hope even in those serving long sentences. "We'd talk about what we wanted to do when we got out," Sunday said.[39] "A lot of us were just dreamers."

Reading was a favorite pastime for many inmates, who had access to a library of fifteen thousand books and seventy-five popular magazine subscriptions.[40] Prisoners were not allowed inside the library but could order books from a catalogue. Whitey forged a close friendship with Clarence "The Choctaw Kid" Carnes, a Native American from Oklahoma who worked in the library and delivered books—sometimes with chewing gum or cigars tucked inside— to the cells on a pull cart. By the time Whitey arrived at Alcatraz, Carnes was already a legend. At eighteen, he became the youngest inmate ever sent to Alcatraz after he was convicted of murder and kidnapping and made a couple of escape attempts. In 1946, he was involved in a violent escape attempt in which three inmates and two guards were killed—resulting in an additional sentence of life in prison. The Choctaw Kid wasn't going anywhere soon.

Whitey considered many of his fellow inmates on Alcatraz intellectually superior to the domino-playing gossips in Atlanta, and there is evidence that they were. A Bureau of Prisons booklet published in 1960 reported that Alcatraz inmates "read more serious literature than does the ordinary person in the community. Philosophers such as Kant, Schopenhauer, Hegel, etc., are especially popular and their books have a wide circulation. Advanced mathematics and physics texts, too, are in great demand, as are other types of literature having to do with more profound aspects of our culture."[41]

The Rock proved a safe and quiet place for Whitey to grow into his intellect and hone his views. He read books about military history, war, philosophy, and politics and was fascinated by Machiavelli, the Italian political philosopher who espoused using brute force, deceit, and illicit means to achieve power.[42] They were lessons he would live by. He also studied Spanish, though without ever attaining much fluency. "He reads voraciously and his choice in reading is very good," an Alcatraz staffer noted.[43] "He composes some poetry also and these outlets he says afford him a means of escapism."

Whitey the poet—it is something remarkable to contemplate, but, sadly, none of his compositions has survived. He wasn't, Sunday recalled, serious about his writings, dismissing them as simple rhyming verses that weren't very good. But he knew what he liked in a poem, and was so impressed with one that Sunday wrote in prison called "The Ballad of Billy the Kid" that he asked for a copy and kept it tucked inside his Bible.[44]

Whitey was generally well liked by other inmates and was more sociable than he had been in Atlanta, but he did not get close to many people and seemed, to his prison acquaintances, always on guard.[45] "He was a very nice guy if he liked you," said Robert Schibline, a convicted bank robber who served time on Alcatraz with Whitey. "But he kind of kept a low profile like he was expecting people to fuck with him." Two months after his arrival, Whitey wrote a surprisingly upbeat letter to Rev. John O'Shea, a priest and South Boston native who had befriended him when Whitey was in the Atlanta penitentiary. Whitey told the priest his incarceration had been hard on his family and especially on his mother. She had expected him to be imprisoned somewhere closer to home. Whitey wrote her letters to cheer her up, but the anguish he caused his family left him bitter.[46]

Alcatraz changed his attitude. He liked his job, his single cell, the food. Eating, he said, had become a pleasure again. He was listening to classical music. He was reading as many books as he liked. He was lifting weights almost every day. He told the priest that the rules were "fair and sensible, and to break one would require going out of your way." He said his brothers and sisters were comforted by his description of life on The Rock and that eventually his mother would be, too. "We intend to make the best of things," Whitey wrote, "and hope that one day I'll be transferred closer to home."

Many inmates echoed Whitey's thoughts on the tone of life in Alcatraz, and especially the food. The prison staff prided itself on providing the best meals in the federal system, a deliberate strategy aimed at mollifying the hard men held there. Whitey spent three Christmases at Alcatraz, and the holiday menu was hardly hardship fare: roast young tom turkey, chestnut dressing, giblet gravy, fiesta salad, stuffed olives, snowflake potatoes, candied fresh yams, buttered June peas, baked young pearl onions, Parker House rolls, bread and butter, mincemeat pie, fruitcake, and coffee and cream.

He seemed as contented as a man spending much of his young life behind bars could be, but soon enough trouble found Whitey again, or he found it. Ironically, this time it was two of the things that Whitey liked most about Alcatraz—going to work every day and the institution's food—that snared him. A group of inmates with complaints about the food not being as good as it once had been orchestrated a work strike. The strike organizers urged other inmates to stay in their cells when the morning alarm sounded to report for work. The few who didn't go along with the plan were branded scabs and targeted for retaliation.

Whitey had no problems with the food, but he did have a problem with being considered a scab, so he joined the strike. After nearly two weeks most of the strikers gave in and returned to their jobs, but Whitey was among the eight on his cellblock who held out. He told prison staff it was unfair that Sunday and another inmate were singled out for punishment and sent to "The Hole," a dimly lit cell with a solid steel door, a toilet, a sink, and, at night, a mattress on the floor.[47] Prison officials had also heard rumors that Whitey and three other inmates were planning a knife attack on inmates who had worked on the dock during the strike.[48]

When he was called before a prison board poised to revoke some of his hard-earned good conduct time, Whitey seemed despondent but also proud. He said he acted not in self-interest but out of principle: "I felt bad about the guys in the hole I worked with. How could I face them? I have to live with them and I can't let them down, that is the reason I stayed in."[49] Tension over the strike lingered as guards wrote reports noting that Whitey, Sunday, and another inmate were seen talking intently in the recreation yard. "They are up to NO good—but what I don't know," the associate warden scribbled on a report.[50] In the dining room, Whitey and several other inmates moved their seats in what was seen as a deliberate attempt to "freeze out" those who had worked during the strike. In the end, Whitey forfeited two hundred days of good conduct time for his acts of defiance during the strike.[51] Years later, he bragged that he spent ten days in the hole for fighting, and Sunday agrees that he did. But there's no way to know if this story was true or a bit of legend building. There is no record in his prison file of Whitey's ever being sent to isolation.[52]

The loss of good conduct time hurt—badly. Every day lost meant one more behind bars. Whitey had been keeping close track of those days and wanted to make sure he got credit for them. He wrote to the Atlanta prison to see how much he had earned for joining the LSD study and was furious to learn he had been shorted by forty-five days. He took out his aggression with a punishing weight lifting session that sent him to the infirmary complaining of "heart pain."[53] He was assured his heart sounded normal and that it was likely muscular strain. But the decision to lash out at the weights, and his body, instead of prison authorities suggested that Whitey was beginning to appreciate that it was more effective to be calculating and agreeable than it was to be impulsive and aggressive. He wrote a solicitous letter to prison officials, politely asking what steps he needed to take to verify his claim that he was owed good conduct time for volunteering in the LSD experiment. "Hate to be of any bother but this good time was earned at the expense of physical and mental discomfort and is valuable to me," he wrote.[54] The Atlanta staff reviewed the medical records and acknowledged that Whitey was right. He was credited with the additional forty-five days.

Soon afterward, he got even better news. He had come face-to-face in Alcatraz with one of the bank robbery accomplices who had told the FBI that Whitey was involved in a 1955 murder in Indiana. That man, Richard Barchard, was now profusely apologetic, saying he had made the whole story up. What Barchard didn't know was that the betrayal had actually gone both ways; that Whitey had identified Barchard as an accomplice in the robbery and even convinced his girlfriend to give a written statement implicating him in the bank job.

The bank robbery was very real; the murder never happened. At Alcatraz, Barchard told Whitey he had concocted the wild story of the murder of a nonexistent person, implicating himself and Whitey, while he was in isolation at Alcatraz. He said he did so on the assumption that by offering an admission and giving up Whitey he would be shipped out to Indiana to do easier time and possibly win a reduction in his sentence. It was a harebrained idea, Barchard admitted, but he was desperate at the time. Whitey was furious; being accused of murder had put him under a whole different level of scrutiny in Atlanta, opening up his girlfriend to questioning and upsetting his family. But he also realized that getting mad at Barchard solved nothing. Instead Whitey persuaded him to publicly recant his story about the murder. Barchard wrote a four-page letter to authorities on November 3, 1960, saying, "This is an honest attempt on my part to right a wrong that was rash and an immature act."[55]

Whitey knew that a murder charge could keep him in prison for life. Now he hoped that his vindication would make prison officials view him more favorably, and that they would perhaps recommend that he be moved closer to home. The great distance from Southie meant he seldom had visitors; indeed, the last time his brother Bill had visited him was in the summer of 1958, when he was still in the Atlanta prison. But Bill remained Whitey's tireless advocate, lobbying prison officials for a favorable transfer and writing to him frequently.

Bill Bulger had also continued his rise as a lawyer and would-be public figure. He'd gained increasing notice in Boston for his wit and gifts in public speaking and debate—excellent arenas to display the classical passages he'd memorized. His ambition to leadership was obvious. In 1960, Whitey was thrilled to learn that Bill had been elected to the Massachusetts House of Representatives. "Wow, he won," Whitey said, after getting a letter from Bill about his election.[56] "When I get out I've got to keep straight for him." Whitey was proud of his younger brother's accomplishments and a bit sheepish when he confided to Sunday that back home they were known as "the good brother and the bad brother."

Bill's success boosted Whitey's morale. During his annual prison review several months later, he was commended for his "improved attitude."[57] He was conscientious in his job in the prison's massive laundry room, where he worked alongside Sunday, and was often assigned to operate the mangle, a large machine used to press bedsheets. Whitey was praised for being a dependable worker who got along with black and white inmates alike.[58] In that era of deep racial prejudice and growing civil rights unrest, it was a trait that stood out.

Still, Whitey was homesick. It was difficult for his family to make the long trip to Alcatraz, and he had only three visits while there: two from his sister Carol and her marine pilot husband, who lived in California, and one from a childhood friend on active duty nearby with the navy. About two weeks before he turned thirty-two, Whitey asked prison authorities to take a photograph of him and mail it to his parents. "I have been locked up for five and a half years and have only seen my parents once in this period," he wrote on his request form.[59] Bill Bulger and House Majority Leader McCormack continued to pressure prison officials, and the head of the Massachusetts state prison system, Department of Correction commissioner George F. McGrath, joined the chorus with a letter to Bennett, the Bureau of Prisons director, pushing for Whitey's return to his home state. McGrath had been the assistant dean at Boston College Law School under Father Drinan when Bill was a student. Few inmates could claim such a powerful corps of advocates, the fruit of political pull and Southie solidarity. And this time, it had an effect. In October 1961, Bennett ordered Alcatraz staff to conduct a special review of Whitey's progress. The detailed report said Whitey had avoided trouble since his involvement in the strike but still had trouble controlling his temper and was vain about his intelligence and character.[60] "He is an extremely nervous individual and it requires a great effort on his part to avoid serious conflict with other inmates," the report read. "He resents bitterly any disparaging remarks made by others about religion, Country and womanhood. He recently indicated he is very well pleased with the new four man tables [in the dining room] as it enables him to avoid listening to 'unsavory characters.' He uses no profanity and dislikes hearing others use it. He expresses great respect and love for his family and says he will never again cause them shame and humiliation by any of his deeds or actions. He blames no one for his present predicament and is not bitter towards any law enforcement officials. When asked why he does not attend church services he says too many inmates scoff, sneer and criticise [sic] the clergy after the service is over and he does not want to risk getting into trouble by expressing objection to their remarks."

Whitey began telling people in a position to help him that he owed it to his family to go straight once he got out. It became his mantra, and others echoed it. The laundry foreman who supervised Whitey predicted he was unlikely to return to a life of crime once freed:

> He has an urgent desire to be well thought of in all things; his ability to think things out, his physical prowess with weights and the ability to get along with his fellow inmates. He is extremely nervous and jumpy much of the time and seems to be "on guard" at all times. He has a high regard for his family members and considers himself to be the "black sheep" for which he seems to be ashamed. . . . His hopes are that he can go to school on his release and that he can someday redeem himself in the eyes of his family and friends. He seems entirely sincere in this regard.[61]

The officer in charge of the cell house was equally complimentary, describing Whitey as a neat, well-groomed man who kept a slightly better than average cell, seemed better educated than most, and enjoyed reading poetry.[62] He said Sunday was Bulger's closest friend and that "although some of his friends are known troublemakers Bulger seems to have a mind of his own and does not follow this group." The officer said, "To my knowledge he has never asked for any special favors of any kind and he is not the type to get on personal terms with the officers. He smiles a lot, as though he has some sort of a joke to himself. Although he is very strong he is not known to use strong arm tactics on other inmates."

But if Whitey didn't ask for any special favors, he was certainly the beneficiary of McCormack's political influence. The officer's report disclosed something quite unusual: Bureau of Prisons director Bennett personally interviewed Whitey during a visit to Alcatraz. The officer wrote that Whitey's overall attitude and conduct had been very good in the past, and then noted: "Since his interview with Mr. Bennett, when he last visited this institution, his conduct has been excellent." A prison committee found Whitey had "an ebullient personality," regretted being "suckered" into participating in the food strike, and deserved to be transferred to a less secure prison.[63] Prison officials restored one hundred days of good conduct time, and in April 1962 Bennett approved his transfer to the penitentiary in Leavenworth, Kansas.

While Whitey was still in Alcatraz waiting for his transfer, three inmates attempted a daring escape. On June 11, 1962, after several months of using stolen tools to chisel holes in the walls of their cells, Frank Morris and brothers John and Clarence Anglin squeezed through the openings, made their way to the roof, and disappeared into the bay on a makeshift raft made of raincoats. They left dummy heads in their beds to fool the guards during cell checks. The men were never found, leaving some to speculate that they drowned in the frigid water and were swept out to sea. Others believe they got away. It was one escape plot that Whitey, his long dreamed-of transfer now in the offing, was never implicated in. The following month he left Alcatraz still strong and trim at 176 pounds but a much changed person—more calculating, deliberative, and confident of his path.

Whitey spent the following year in Leavenworth, where he was assigned to the sanitation detail and worked as a rodent and pest controller, spraying insecticides and setting bait for mice and rats. The remaining hundred days of good conduct time he had lost at Alcatraz had been restored, paving the way for his possible parole. But the parole board was unimpressed with his initial request in February 1963 and turned him down.

In Kansas he received repeated visits from his father, his brother Jack, and Will McDonough, a friend from South Boston who became a renowned *Boston Globe* sportswriter and who had managed Bill Bulger's successful run for the Massachusetts House of Representatives. In each case, McCormack wrote on their behalf, vouching for them. Then on September 3, 1963, his thirty-fourth birthday, Whitey was transferred to the federal penitentiary in Lewisburg, Pennsylvania. His resemblance to his politician brother was so strong that, during his move, prison authorities confiscated two photographs of Bill, thinking they were of the inmate.[64] Whitey filed a report, indicating that he received one of the pictures when he was Alcatraz in 1960, the other in Leavenworth in 1962. "I'd like to have these pictures but if you rule against it would you please permit me to mail them home," he wrote. The photographs were mailed to Whitey's mother in South Boston.

At Lewisburg, Whitey was housed in a single cell and worked as a sanitation clerk. Now even closer to home, he received ten visits during his eighteen months at the Pennsylvania prison. On January 16, 1964, he saw his father for the last time when he showed up at the prison with Whitey's brother Jack.[65] Two months later, on the same day the parole board had rejected Whitey's second request to be freed, the prison's Catholic chaplain received a call at 5:00 p.m. from Bill Bulger, who told him his father, James Bulger Sr., had died of pneumonia the previous day at St. Elizabeth's Hospital in Brighton, Massachusetts. He'd been given last rites while surrounded by his family. The chaplain broke the news to Whitey a half hour later. Whitey's imprisonment had taken a huge toll on his father: Bill Bulger told a friend his father never had a good day after Whitey went to prison.[66] Whitey asked to go home for his father's funeral, which was to be held two days later at St. Monica's Church, but was told there wasn't enough time to make arrangements.[67] He had, the prison chaplain reported, "an excellent attitude despite some bitterness" and did not tell his mother about his parole denial when he was allowed to call her the next day. They spoke for five minutes about his father's death while the prison's Catholic chaplain listened in on the conversation at Whitey's request.[68]

Whitey seemed to be growing impatient with the parole board's reluctance and yearned for his freedom. Prison staff reported that he "maintains some questionable associates and is among the group who are always watching the rear gate and the towers and other vital parts of the institution."[69] Yet they also referenced the fact that he had influential friends, noting: "He seems to have a good outlook and to be quite proud of members of his family who are in politics. It is also noted his family have a very close relationship with the speaker of the House of Representatives [McCormack]."

Bill Bulger's persistent requests for McCormack's help, and McCormack's strategy of going over the heads of individual institutional authorities directly to the Federal Bureau of Prisons, were finally paying off. In a note to the Lewisburg warden that seemed sympathetic to Whitey, Bureau of Prisons assistant director H. G. Moeller wrote that Whitey's adjustment was good and "and he is trying very hard to make a good record in order to be granted parole."[70] For a third time, Whitey went before the parole board, telling them he had a job waiting for him, earning $1.50 an hour at Farnsworth Press, a graphic arts company on the waterfront in Boston. He planned to live with his mother in South Boston. His parole adviser would be Father Drinan. The third time was the charm, and the board finally relented.

Whitey had gone to prison with a plan to get educated, and one thing he had learned was that relying on your own wits and cunning was not enough; that it was important to have friends in high places. Having spent nine years in some of the most fearsome corners in America, he had come to realize that power, even just the perception of it, accomplished more than fear. On March 1, 1965, at 10:55 a.m., Whitey strolled out of Lewisburg prison with $64.27 in his pocket. He'd be back in Southie in plenty of time for St. Patrick's Day.

4

Becoming Untouchable

He had persuaded everyone—his family, his priest, his best friend in prison, and finally the parole board—that he would go straight when he was released. But if Whitey Bulger meant it, he didn't mean it for long. He got work in construction when he returned to Southie, but he also began looking for work of a more familiar kind. If timing is everything, Whitey's was impeccable. The nine years he'd spent in prison hadn't just served as a finishing school for his mind, they had dramatically improved his chances of thriving in the Boston underworld.

Whitey was still in Alcatraz in 1961 when the Irish mobsters in Boston turned on each other with unprecedented vengeance. The bloodletting would go on for years, and when it was over, just as Whitey was getting out of prison, some sixty gangsters lay dead. A few dozen others were serving long prison sentences for violence connected to the war. The city had never seen anything like it. On the street, Whitey would have been either a potential victim or a perpetrator or, more likely, both. Tucked away in prison, he moved closer to power without lifting a finger. The war had drastically remade the criminal landscape in Boston, creating a vacuum of power and a wealth of opportunity that Whitey, older now, less impetuous and more tactically savvy, would exploit.

Like many things involving Boston's Irish gangsters, the war was ignited by the combustible mix of alcohol, women, and a warped sense of loyalty. In sheer numbers, the Irish gangsters should have been the dominant ethnic organized crime group in the Boston area, but they tended to group themselves by neighborhood, and sometimes even within smaller neighborhood subsets, diluting their citywide power and causing fights, even desperately bloody ones, over small questions of territory and pride. The Italians, by contrast, benefited from having an organization, La Cosa Nostra, whose main requirement for membership—Italian heritage—cast a wider net and limited, at least in a smaller city like Boston, the risks of factionalism.

The Irish gangs also demonstrated a remarkable propensity for fratricide, posing a greater risk to each other than the Italians ever mustered. This paradigm for organized crime in Boston extended back to the era of Prohibition. Even the 1931 Mafia ambush of Frank Wallace, leader of Southie's then-dominant criminal group, the Gustin Gang, did not persuade the Irish to coalesce. Instead, they retreated to their respective ghettos, making pacts and alliances that almost invariably collapsed over personalities and peccadilloes.

The Boston gang war of the 1960s involved criminals of all stripes, but it had a disproportionate impact on the Irish and, not surprisingly, was started by them. By war's end, the Italians had increased their power and dominance, mainly by having held their fire and let the Irish go at each other. Not only did the devastating mayhem give Whitey Bulger an opening to rise through the depleted Irish underworld, it created an enduring illusion in Boston of Mafia omnipotence. The Mafia, with its national and international tentacles, was the most powerful criminal organization the city had ever seen when Whitey got out of prison. The FBI had a national mandate to take out La Cosa Nostra, and thus the bureau's Boston office went after the New England Mafia with great zeal. Pursuing Irish gangsters took a backseat. Whitey was able to cement his power precisely because the FBI considered the Mafia the only worthwhile organized crime target for law enforcement. Agents got commendations and promotions for developing informants against the Mafia, not for taking down murderous, small-time Irish thugs.

The war was a critical bend in Boston underworld history, and it all started because George McLaughlin couldn't keep his hands to himself.

George was the youngest of the three brothers who controlled the rackets in Charlestown. With just fifteen thousand residents, Charlestown is Boston's smallest "big" neighborhood, the site of one of the most important battles of the Revolutionary War, and the center of Boston's maritime industry. As in South Boston, the Charlestown shipyard docks provided jobs for longshoremen and opportunities for criminals, and the McLaughlins controlled not just all the gambling in town but the thievery along the docks. Their bookies walked the wharves like supervisors, taking bets from longshoremen who played "the number," an illegal lottery. Meanwhile, the mob enforcers behind the bookies were free to select the goods they wanted to steal and fence. The McLaughlins had a mostly peaceful relationship with their fellow mobsters on Winter Hill in the neighboring city of Somerville—Irish, most of them—but that was about to change.

Perhaps because he knew his big brothers would always have his back, George McLaughlin often started fights he couldn't finish, and he started a doozy during a liquor-soaked Labor Day weekend in Salisbury Beach, just south of the New Hampshire border. According to various accounts by gangsters and law enforcement officials of that era, George McLaughlin staggered up to the wife of a Winter Hill mobster from Somerville and grabbed her breast. The Somerville mobster and his friends took offense. George McLaughlin was beaten unconscious and had to be hospitalized.

Bernie McLaughlin, George's older brother and the leader of the Charlestown gang, wanted justice, so he sought out James

"Buddy" McLean, leader of the Winter Hill Gang. Bernie McLaughlin thought his demand was perfectly fair and reasonable: Whoever beat his little brother should be killed, and Bernie wanted McLean to set the guy up. But Buddy McLean shook his head. His men, he asserted, had acted nobly, while George McLaughlin had flagrantly insulted the honor of a woman, in front of men from both Somerville and Charlestown. George McLaughlin had gotten what he deserved.

Bernie McLaughlin drove back to Charlestown nursing a grudge, and an idea. He dispatched some men to put a bomb in McLean's car, but McLean caught them in the act and chased them off. Not long after, McLean approached Bernie McLaughlin outside the Morning Glory bar in Charlestown, in the middle of the afternoon, and this time it was not to discuss the niceties of gangland protocol. He pulled a gun and shot Bernie in the head.[1]

It was Game On.

Besides clearing the playing field for Whitey Bulger, the gang war of the 1960s brought into prominence, and into the welcoming arms of the FBI, the man who would become Whitey's closest associate: Stevie Flemmi. A wiry 5 feet 6 inches, Flemmi was never the tallest guy in the room, but he was usually the deadliest.

The son of Italian immigrants, Flemmi grew up in the Roxbury section of Boston and seemed born to be a criminal. At fifteen, he was arrested on a charge of "carnal abuse," a charge usually applied to juveniles who have underage sex, and was locked up briefly on assault charges.[2] Even when doing the noblest thing in his life, signing up with the army in January 1952, he wasn't on the level: as a seventeen-year-old high school kid, he was too young to enlist, so he stole the identity of a childhood friend. With the Korean War on, army officials apparently didn't notice or didn't care. Flemmi, serving in the 187th Airborne, displayed a prowess with firearms. He claims to have killed five Chinese soldiers during his first taste of combat,[3] and his crack shooting led his Airborne buddies to dub him "The Rifleman," a moniker that stuck. His battlefield stardom also gave him the opportunity to tell his commanding officers what his real name was; Flemmi said he revealed the deception so his parents would get survivor's benefits if he was killed during the war.

Flemmi went on to kill many more Chinese and North Korean soldiers, and thus, in addition to his high school equivalency diploma and a nickname, he took home from Korea an identity he valued more than being a criminal: military veteran. Proud of his service, he would raise money for veterans' memorials and regularly attend Airborne reunions and functions as he rose in criminal eminence. He also discovered he was really good at, and seemed to enjoy, shooting people. This was the extent of his professional training when he returned to Boston in 1955. For what he had in mind, it would be enough.[4]

Back in town, he opened a convenience store, Jay's Spa, in Dudley Square, the main commercial district in Roxbury, and soon met Edward "Wimpy" Bennett, a racketeer who used a nearby storefront as a cover for his extensive gambling operation. Bennett asked Flemmi if some customers he had loaned money to could leave repayments off at his store. In gratitude, Bennett later staked him to some money that Flemmi used to extend credit, on steep terms, to gamblers, launching his career as a loanshark.

By 1958, Flemmi was already drawing notice from local law enforcement as an up-and-coming wiseguy. He was approached by Paul Rico, the FBI's prime local cultivator of confidential criminal informants and the agent who two years earlier had arrested Whitey Bulger after an informant spotted him in a nightclub. Rico showed up at Flemmi's store out of the blue and asked him if he had been involved in a recent bank robbery. Flemmi was stunned. He denied he was robbing banks—in fact, bank robbery was one of the few criminal activities Flemmi wasn't engaged in at the time. Rico took his word for it, but not long after, Rico was back, this time accusing Flemmi of driving a Roxbury bank robber to Los Angeles. This time Rico had it right; Flemmi had, in fact, made the drive in the company of the bank robber, and it was suddenly clear to him that the agent must be talking to Wimpy Bennett, who knew about the cross-country road trip. Flemmi also surmised, correctly, that Rico was trying to recruit him as an informant, letting him know how vulnerable he was to arrest, that others whom Flemmi had trusted were talking about him, and that his best hope for protection might come from the FBI itself.

Rico started visiting Flemmi's store every day, pumping him about the Mafia in the North End, where Flemmi was a frequent and respected presence. He'd come to know many local Mafia figures, including those who dropped by an after-hours club he'd opened in Roxbury. But if Rico and his FBI partner, Dennis Condon, irritated Flemmi at first, they became an asset after the Somerville-Charlestown gang war erupted. It was obvious to Flemmi that these guys weren't on the level, that they were up to their own game, even if at that stage he couldn't quite discern what the game was. The agents were playing favorites, trying to dictate not only who would win the war but who would die in it.[5]

Flemmi wanted to be counted among the winners, and so, at the urging of Rico and Condon, he changed sides, aligning himself with Somerville's Winter Hill organization. He did so gladly, for he had grown to scorn the McLaughlins. He considered them arrogant, undisciplined in their drinking, and unreliable allies. It was a critical turning point for him and for the city. Flemmi would survive the wars and go on to team up with Whitey Bulger in a match made by the FBI.

Watching the way Rico and Condon schemed to tip the balance of power in the gang war was Flemmi's first lesson in how deeply intertwined the FBI was in Boston underworld doings, and how blurred the line was between crime and crime fighters. It would not be his last. In 1965, Flemmi met Buddy McLean at the Winter Hill leader's hangout, Pal Joey's, a bar in Somerville, and mentioned what he'd learned. McLean surprised Flemmi by acknowledging that he talked to Paul Rico and Dennis Condon all the time. This wasn't a dread secret; it was an open alliance.

Rico and Condon hated the McLaughlins. But they also had calculated that Winter Hill could win the war, especially with their help. The agents' motives were then, and remain, a puzzle, a source of uneasy speculation among Boston mobsters. But the connection was clearly rooted in something personal.

Frank Salemme, who later became the head of the Mafia in Boston, grew up with Flemmi and was his partner in crime before Flemmi teamed up with Whitey Bulger. Salemme thought Condon, a Charlestown native, wanted to get rid of the McLaughlins because they had threatened his brother in a barroom dispute. But he also thought that Rico had an even more personal vendetta. Salemme claims Rico's animosity toward the McLaughlin gang stemmed from the McLaughlins' typically careless and insulting ways—specifically their bawdy claims that Rico and FBI director J. Edgar Hoover were lovers. Insinuations about Hoover were rife at the time, and linking the rumored scandal to Rico became a running joke for the McLaughlins.

Rico ignored the taunts, but he got even by helping Winter Hill pick off the McLaughlin gang, one by one. He helped Winter Hill set up the 1964 murder of Ronnie Dermody, who had robbed a bank with Whitey Bulger in 1955. Dermody was also one of Rico's informants, but when Rico found out that Winter Hill had Dermody on a hit list, he ingratiated himself with Buddy McLean and assisted with the disposal of Dermody, a far less significant player.

Rico arranged to meet Dermody about a mile from Rico's house. It was supposed to be a routine meeting between an agent and his informant, but Rico didn't show up; Buddy McLean did, with a gun. Rico picked McLean up after the hit and let McLean stay at his house for couple of days.[6]

But Dermody was small change. Rico and Condon wanted George and Edward "Punchy" McLaughlin to join Brother Bernie McLaughlin in the grave. They decided to get Winter Hill to do their dirty work.

As his name suggested, Punchy McLaughlin was a boxer, quick on his feet. He'd dodged two assassination attempts in the mid-

1960s. Rico meant to ensure he wouldn't survive the third. George McLaughlin was on trial for murder, and Punchy was dutifully attending the court proceedings in Suffolk Superior Court every day. Rico followed Punchy to find out how he was getting to court, then drove to Dudley Square and told Flemmi that Punchy was taking the bus from a stop in West Roxbury to the courthouse downtown every morning. Flemmi disguised himself and went to the bus stop. He covered a .38-caliber long barrel revolver with a newspaper and fired six times into Punchy's chest as he was boarding the bus. The next time Flemmi saw Rico, the FBI agent told him, "Nice shooting."[7]

The gang war that started in 1961 gradually petered out in the mid-1960s, but not before Flemmi had killed McLaughlin loyalists Wimpy Bennett and his two brothers. Wimpy Bennett had given Flemmi his start in the underworld, but he had also given Flemmi up to Rico. Flemmi had put down a marker; this was how he would deal with informers.

The McLaughlin gang got a bit of revenge before it was over. In October 1965, they ambushed the Winter Hill leader Buddy McLean as he walked out of Pal Joey's—a hit that was eerily reminiscent of McLean's shooting of Bernie McLaughlin outside the Morning Glory four years before. The assassinations of the gang leaders bookended the war, but taking out McLean proved a Pyrrhic victory for the Charlestown gangsters. He was replaced by Howie Winter, who was even more cunning, ruthless, and efficient. With Winter at the helm, the Somerville gangsters mopped up what was left of their Charlestown rivals.

With the McLaughlins vanquished, Paul Rico formalized what had been an unwritten arrangement for seven years: In 1965, Steve Flemmi became an official informant for the FBI.

Whitey left Lewisburg Penitentiary in 1965 and moved back in with his mother at 41 Logan Way. He was a skinny twenty-six-year-old when he went into prison; he came out a man of middle age at thirty-five, more muscular after all those years hitting the weights but, more important, with a sturdier sense of himself—he was older, wiser, harder. His famously light locks were slightly darker, robbed of years of sunlight. And the post-incarceration plan of employment he had provided to the parole board changed almost the moment he was free. The $1.50-an-hour job his brother Bill had arranged at Farnsworth Press, a graphic arts company on the waterfront, never materialized. Instead, a family friend who was head of the compressed air workers union got him his first job out of prison as a laborer at construction sites. One of his first tasks was working at St. Mary's, the residence hall for Jesuits at Boston College. Among those who lived in the spartan dormitory was, coincidentally, Father Drinan, Whitey's prison pen pal and parole adviser. The work at BC would also bring him into contact with another acquaintance from his Old Harbor days: John Connolly.

In 1961, Connolly had taken Bill Bulger's advice and gone to Boston College. Closing in on graduation day, he was walking across campus with John Cunniff, the BC hockey star from Southie, when Cunniff suddenly waved and went over to a guy who was carrying slabs of granite outside St. Mary's.

"Johnny," Cunniff said, motioning Connolly over, "you know Jimmy Bulger?"

John Connolly shook the hand of the guy who had bought him an ice cream cone all those years before at The Druggie.

"Sure," Connolly said. "We grew up in Old Harbor."

The skinny teenager Connolly remembered was now an ex-con, his physique bulked-up and toned. "I'm good friends with your brother Bill," Connolly said. There was a little more small talk and some handshakes, and then Cunniff and Connolly walked away and Whitey went back to work.

"How do you know him?" Connolly asked.

"We worked construction together," Cunniff replied.[8]

Connolly looked back over his shoulder. He wouldn't see Whitey

Bulger again for some ten years, by which time he was an FBI agent, looking to make a deal.

Whitey liked the construction work only because it kept him in shape. He was hoping for something else, and his brother Bill, by now a three-term state representative, was able to arrange for him to work as a janitor in the Suffolk County Courthouse.[9] It was an odd place for an ex-con to find work, but politics trumped security concerns in 1960s Boston. Luckily for Bill, Whitey's hiring did not draw attention, but the risk that his brother could cause him political embarrassment was a lurking concern.

Whitey was fiercely proud of Bill's political success, and when his brother ran for state senate in 1970, he volunteered for the campaign. He ferried people and campaign literature all over Southie. One day, when campaign workers were standing in the rain at the rotary across from St. Monica's, holding campaign signs, Whitey showed up with a bunch of umbrellas he had bought on impulse.[10] No one remembers Whitey doing anything overtly to help his brother's political career after that first senate campaign. His apparent disappearance from the campaign trail coincided with his reemergence in the criminal world. Whether his lowered profile was a matter of plan or coincidence remains unclear. There was always the risk that his temper, and passionate loyalty to Bill, could lead to an embarrassing incident. Politics was a contact sport in Southie, but at some point during that senate campaign, Whitey went too far. Pat Nee, who has spent most of his life as, by turns, Whitey's rival and criminal associate, says Whitey took it upon himself to intervene on behalf of his politician brother, often intimidating people perceived as political enemies. One of them, Patrick Loftus, was more than a perceived enemy. In 1970, he challenged Bill Bulger for the open state senate seat. Loftus, a fraud investigator for the state, and later the author of a rose-colored memoir about Southie, had a gift for piercing oratorical flourish. He was Bill Bulger's match in rhetoric and enjoyed sparring with him. After one heated debate, Whitey marched down to the Loftus campaign headquarters and lit into the candidate, accusing him of insulting his family. Whitey was more than vaguely threatening, and when Bill Bulger found out, he was appalled. He later told a congressional committee that it was the one instance of his brother's having taken on a political opponent, and that he had urged Whitey to refrain from such partisanship. "Billy told him to stop," Nee said. "Whitey hated the Loftus family because they had challenged Billy. Billy told him to knock it off. I don't think Billy asked him to do this stuff. Whitey did it on his own."[11]

In winning parole two years after becoming eligible and eleven years before his sentence officially ended, Whitey had convinced the parole board that he was going to leave crime behind him. But he didn't abide by the conditions of his parole for very long. As late as March 1969, his parole officer reported that Whitey was quite happy working as a custodian. "He remains on the job and seems to enjoy this type of work as a custodian," the parole officer wrote. "James is still working and not being involved in any difficulty so far."[12] But none of that was true. Whitey had stopped showing up for work at the courthouse. He was hanging in Southie's myriad taverns, not to drink but to network. He was reconnecting with the sort of men he had associated with before he went to prison. Players. People who made their money in the rackets. It was only a matter of time before he came to the attention of the Killeen brothers.

Donnie and Kenny Killeen were, at the time, the preeminent gangsters in South Boston, and they had taken a liking to Whitey, with his smarts and prison-honed toughness. His time in Alcatraz, which shut so many doors elsewhere, opened a door at the Transit Cafe, the seedy bar on Southie's West Broadway that served as headquarters for the Killeen gang.

The Killeens made most of their money off a lucrative gambling and loansharking business that was patronized by longshoremen and factory workers and warehousemen on the waterfront. It was a trade not without its risks. George Killeen was gunned down in

the North End in 1950. Eddie Killeen was shot dead in 1968. That
same year, the surviving brothers, Donnie and Kenny, decided to
add Whitey to their roster of enforcers. The Killeens were products
of Southie's rougher and poorer west side, and Whitey's reputation
preceded him in the Lower End and the projects, where many of
the Killeens' customers hung their hats. Donnie Killeen led the
group and saw to it that Whitey came under the tutelage of his top
enforcer, Billy O'Sullivan.

Billy O, as he was known, was an ex-marine, someone who was
quick with his fists and quicker with a gun. As would soon be the
case with his protégé, whenever someone ended up dead in Southie
the collective, if not always accurate, wisdom was that Billy O had
done it. The truth of such talk was irrelevant; a reputation for ruthlessness was very good for business. Billy O was also a gifted teacher.
He taught Whitey how to follow his prey unobserved and, just as
important, how to lose a tail. His military skills were invaluable,
and Whitey would in later years profess a debt for all that Billy O
had taught him.[13] But in another way, O'Sullivan set an example to
avoid, for if he had a vice, it was his fondness for drink. One of the
conditions of Whitey's parole was that he not consume alcohol to
excess. That was never an issue, because he didn't drink heavily, and
considered those who did weak and unreliable. The streets of South
Boston and Charlestown were littered with the corpses of men too
drunk to avoid or elude their assassins.

The Somerville-Charlestown gang war had been over for just a
few years when a smaller but similarly lethal conflict broke out in
July 1969. This war would be limited to Southie, and like the earlier upwelling of Irish fratricide, it began after copious amounts of
alcohol had been consumed. There had been a long, simmering feud
between the Killeen gang and the Mullens, a group of South Boston toughs who took their name from a street corner in City Point
named for a World War I hero. Mullen Square was hardly a square.
It was just a corner, with Mullen's name adorning a sign attached to
a black pole.

Pat Nee was with the Mullens. Born in Ireland, he moved to Southie when he was eight years old and had an accent, not to mention a stutter that made him stand out. He was picked on but responded by attacking his tormenters, which was the surest way to gain respect in South Boston. By his teens, he had cast his lot with the Mullens, which, in the beginning, was more Our Gang than a real gang. They stole donuts from the corner store, collected bottles they could turn in for money, searched for junk they could sell. But as they grew older they began stealing things off the trucks that left the docks near Castle Island. Scrap metal, especially tin, was a favorite and lucrative target.[14]

In 1962, Nee joined the marines. By the time he returned to Southie in 1966, after seeing combat in Vietnam, he noticed that the Mullens had become less deferential to the Killeens, who were, at the time, the only really organized criminals in Southie. "I think part of it was so many of us had been in the service," Nee said. "A lot of Mullens had been in Vietnam and were like, 'We just fought the Viet Cong in the fucking jungle. Why should we take shit from Donnie Killeen in Southie?'"

The war was a generational feud as much as anything. In the late 1960s, young Americans had begun to question the establishment, and it was no different in the criminal milieu. The Mullens considered the Killeens the establishment, The Man, the disdained status quo. Their taste ran to more freewheeling mayhem. "We were just criminal opportunists, wharf rats. The Killeens had a hierarchical structure, and we had just a loose federation," Nee said. "We saw something we wanted and we'd steal it. They were organized crime. We were disorganized crime. We robbed anything and everything. We weren't very respectful of them, and that eventually led to serious conflict. We ran up debts with them. We'd bet on everything and tell the Killeens, 'Oh, we'll pay you back as soon as we get the money.' But we had no intention of ever paying them back. That aggravated them. So a war was inevitable."[15]

Tensions between the two groups had escalated, so that by the summer of 1969, the littlest thing could launch a war, and the littlest thing turned out to be Mickey Dwyer's nose. Dwyer, a Mullens member, was drinking in the Transit Cafe, which was asking for trouble. He was also popping off, talking of how the Mullens weren't afraid of the Killeens anymore, which was begging for it.

Tired of such insolence, Kenny Killeen jumped Dwyer. Dwyer was a boxer, but he was also drunk, and Killeen was much bigger. At some point, as they tussled on the barroom floor, Killeen bit off a chunk of Dwyer's nose. Then he pulled a gun and shot him in the arm.

Mickey Dwyer's humiliation at the Transit was the final straw for the Mullens, who'd previously been known as brawlers, not shooters. That changed after the maiming of Dwyer. The Mullens started arming themselves, and the war was on. "Up to that point, we used our fists and maybe a baseball bat," Pat Nee said. "We didn't have shooters. But that had to change."

Few gave the Mullens a chance. There were only about twenty of them, and none were known as killers. The Killeens enforcement team boasted Billy O'Sullivan and Whitey Bulger, who were considered stone-cold killers. It was a reputation they deserved, and soon they offered a vivid reminder why. Whitey and O'Sullivan were hunting for members of the rival gang one night when Whitey saw the Mullens leader Paulie McGonagle alone in a car, driving up East Seventh Street in City Point. McGonagle parked in front of his house, and Whitey pulled right alongside him going in the other direction.

"Hey Paulie!" he called.

When McGonagle turned, Whitey shot him in the face. As soon as he fired, he realized his mistake.[16] It wasn't Paulie McGonagle but his brother Donnie, who looked a lot like him. Donnie McGonagle had two kids and was not involved in criminal activity. Whitey, aghast, raced away to O'Sullivan's house a couple of miles away. O'Sullivan led Whitey to the kitchen, where Whitey slumped in a chair. If he was expecting a reprimand, he got something else.

O'Sullivan pulled some pork chops from the refrigerator and threw them into a frying pan.

"I shot the wrong one," Whitey said, almost in disbelief. "I shot Donald."

Whitey prided himself on doing his job right, of never drinking when he needed to be shooting. He had patience, and he had no problem with passing on a potential target if something didn't feel right. Everything had felt right, until the moment he'd squeezed the trigger and killed the wrong man. O'Sullivan was blasé about the whole thing, telling Whitey to forget about it, because Donnie McGonagle was a heavy smoker and was going to die anyway. "Now," O'Sullivan said, rubbing his hands together, "how do you want your pork chops?"[17]

In 1971, the Mullens-Killeen war escalated dramatically, both in its malevolence and in its pointlessness. One day Buddy Roache, a Mullens member, approached O'Sullivan and Whitey in a bar on Broadway. Buddy said he didn't have a beef with them, but that he was going to kill Donnie Killeen and end the war once and for all. It was a remarkable thing to say, especially given that there were no other Mullens present to watch his back. Buddy Roache must have assumed that O'Sullivan and Whitey were too smart to do something stupid in a crowded barroom.

Buddy's brother Mickey was a cop and a decade later would become Boston police commissioner. But Buddy Roache was alone and unprotected when O'Sullivan pulled a .22 from his pocket. The shot struck Buddy Roache's spine and paralyzed him. Even with Buddy's brother a police officer, there were no arrests: While Buddy couldn't walk, neither would he speak, at least to the cops. The bar was crowded, but in typical Southie fashion, no one saw the shooter.

The war then took a turn that Whitey wasn't ready for. He was in New York, visiting an old friend from prison in Atlanta, Tommy Devaney, an enforcer with the Westies gang on Manhattan's West

Side, when he got the phone call: The Mullens had shot Billy O'Sullivan in front of his house. O'Sullivan's murder rattled Whitey; if his mentor, the craftiest killer around, was vulnerable, what of him? At Whitey's urging, Devaney traveled to Southie and drove around with him. The word spread quickly: the Westies were with the Killeens. But if this display was meant to intimidate the Mullens, it didn't work. O'Sullivan's murder had convinced them that they were winning.

"We weren't afraid of them," Pat Nee said, "and they knew it."

Nee, by his own account, came close to killing Whitey twice. Both times he had him in his crosshairs but held his fire, fearing he'd hit innocent bystanders. His first chance came one afternoon when Nee was sitting in a bar across from South Station, the main commuter train station on the city's south side. It was rush hour and Nee looked out the window as traffic inched along and horns blared.

"Shit," he said to Paul McGonagle. "It's Whitey."

Whitey was sitting in the driver's seat of a blue LTD, little more than a hundred feet away. He was trapped—by traffic, and now by the Mullens.

"Give me your gun," Nee whispered.

McGonagle slid a .32 under the table and Nee slipped it into his jacket. He walked out the bar door and broke into a gallop. Jack Curran, a Killeen enforcer, and another guy were in the backseat. They usually carried, but Nee had them cornered. Or thought he did. Whitey, who prided himself on his evasive driving techniques, simply pulled the car onto a median strip and plowed into the opposing lane, sending sparks flying from the undercarriage. Nee stopped and took aim. Whitey was careening away and there were innocent passersby everywhere, so Nee let his arm fall to his side and melted into the crowd.

Nee walked back into the bar and found that McGonagle had bought a beer to console him. "I found out something," Pat Nee said. "They weren't carrying. If they were, they would have drawn on me."

The next day, Nee went down to the Mullens clubhouse and sat at the bar next to Jimmy "The Weasel" Mantville. Mantville was one of the Mullens who had enthusiastically embraced the transformation from brawlers to shooters. "Weasel," Pat Nee said, sliding an arm around his shoulder, "we're going hunting."

They made a lovely couple, Nee and Mantville. Nee wore a dark wig and mustache. Mantville squeezed into one of his girlfriend's dresses and donned a woman's blonde wig. Nee took a baby doll and bundled it up in a child's car seat. But their prey proved elusive. Whitey was nowhere to be found, and Donnie Killeen was hard to find alone. Whenever he wasn't in his house or at the Transit, holding court, he walked on Broadway with his young son. "We had standards in Southie, and no one would shoot a guy if the guy was with his kid," Nee said. "If you did that, you'd end up dead."

The courtesy went both ways, Pat Nee found out. Like most of the other high-profile Mullens, Nee had moved out of his home in Southie during the war and was staying at a girlfriend's house in the Bunker Hill housing project in Charlestown. He kept his .45 with him at all times, and as he watched TV with his girlfriend's young daughter, Nee had the gun hidden under a dish towel on the coffee table.

"The light from the TV lit up the window to the apartment, and I could see a rifle barrel pointed at the window. Actually, at me," Nee said. "I saw Whitey's face. I knew it was him. He had the drop on me."

Nee went for his gun, and his sudden motion startled his girlfriend's daughter. The little girl jumped up. "She was right in the line of fire," Nee said. "She was between me and the window. I looked right over her at Whitey. He lowered the gun and smiled at me. And then he just disappeared."

Nee grabbed a rifle and gave chase. He saw Whitey running across the courtyard, holding a rifle. Nee knelt down and tried to focus on Whitey in his scope. There were people sitting on stoops and walking in the courtyard, and they kept coming into Nee's view.

Before he could draw a bead, Whitey was in the passenger-side seat of a car whose door had swung open. The tires squealed and Pat Nee cursed. "I never regretted not shooting in those circumstances, because I could have hit anybody, even though I'm pretty sure I would have got Whitey, too," Nee said. "And if I had, a lot of other people would still be alive."[18]

As adroit as Whitey was at dodging assassination attempts, he knew some day his luck might run out. So he planned ahead for his own death. He bought a fine suit and hung it in a girlfriend's closet. "In case I was gunned down in gang war," he explained to a friend years later. "For [my] funeral, if open casket, [I] wanted to make good appearance."[19]

Like a lot of people, Nee believes the credit for ending the Southie gang war goes to Jimmy Mantville and Tommy King. While the Mullens had abided by the rule of not shooting Donnie Killeen as he walked on Broadway with his son, there was nothing that said they couldn't shoot him outside his suburban home after the boy's birthday party.

It was a Saturday night, May 13, 1972, and the Killeen family had just finished dinner and were about to cut the cake for Killeen's four-year-old son when Donnie told his wife he had to get something outside. As soon as he climbed into the driver's-side seat of his car, Mantville and King ran up with a submachine gun. They had been lying in wait, hidden in a nearby aqueduct, for hours. The medical examiner took fifteen slugs from Killeen's body. The .38 revolver Killeen grabbed from the glove compartment hadn't been fired.[20]

The Mullens were exultant. They sent a bouquet of flowers to Donnie Killeen's wake with an "Au Revoir" ribbon stripped across the front. There was one final insult: the flowers were sent COD.[21]

Chandler's nightclub in Boston's South End was a living, breathing stereotype, the Hollywood image of a gangster hangout. The polished mahogany bar was lined with hard men, many of them wearing leather jackets, and garishly painted women. Everybody wore loud clothes and everybody was loud. A cacophony of profane conversation bounced off the walls, and a cloud of smoke hovered above the bar. Chandler's looked exactly as a mob bar should. But on this morning in 1972, the only noise was a vacuum cleaner moaning in the far reaches of the dining room and the clinking of spoons in coffee cups, as a dozen gangsters huddled in a couple of booths. The Southie gang war had to end, and it would end over breakfast at Chandler's.

Since the end of the Somerville-Charlestown gang war in the 1960s, Chandler's had emerged as something of a United Nations for gangsters. Ostensibly owned and operated by Winter Hill Gang leader Howie Winter and some of his partners, the nightclub was a gathering spot that attracted criminals of all ethnic groups. Mafia figures socialized with Winter Hill mobsters. In a city known for its racial segregation, even black criminals were welcome. So it was appropriate that Chandler's became the Versailles of the Southie gang war. Both sides knew the killing couldn't go on. It brought heat from the police; it was bad for business.

Donnie Killeen was dead. Kenny Killeen had no intention of meeting his brother's fate and had suddenly retired. That left Whitey Bulger as the de facto leader of what was left of the Killeen gang. And it was Whitey who sought out Howie Winter to mediate the truce with the Mullens. Winter presided over the biggest, most powerful Irish mob in metropolitan Boston. He had the respect of both sides. "Whitey walked into Chandler's," Winter recalled. "I never knew him before that. He knew I was friendly with the Mullens gang. He asked if I would intercede. I said, 'Are you serious about this? I don't want to intercede if you're not going to abide by it.' He said he would."[22]

The word went out, and on the appointed morning, Howie Winter stood in the aisle between the two booths of Southie rivals, proposing an end to their war. "Instead of fighting each other, why not join forces and make some money?" Winter suggested. The Southie guys eyed each other suspiciously, but as Winter kept talking they began nodding. He even offered to bankroll a bookmaking operation in Southie that they could share. "Why don't you start booking some horses and dogs and sports and make money that way?" Winter said.[23]

Whitey Bulger got the wiseguy equivalent of stock options in the transaction. Howie Winter anointed him the leader of the Southie faction, and, as a result, Whitey became partners with Howie Winter, Joe McDonald, Jimmy Sims and John Martorano—the real muscle of Winter Hill. Howie Winter liked Whitey, whose hard time in Alcatraz impressed him, as did Whitey's purported alliance with the Westies in New York.[24] And now with his blessing, Whitey would lord it over Southie for the Hill.

Needless to say, this didn't sit well with Paulie McGonagle, Pat Nee, Tommy King, and the rest of the Mullens. They thought they had won. It was, after all, the hit on Donnie Killeen, which Nee called "The Hiroshima" of the Mullens-Killeen war, that had ended it. The Killeens had sued for peace almost immediately after Donnie was buried. The Mullens thought they were being magnanimous to even consider the requested armistice, and they expected to reap the rewards. But Winter Hill was institutionally biased toward the more traditional organized crime outfits, and the Mullens were too unstructured, too wild, for their tastes. The Mullens might have ended the war, but the bookies who had worked for the Killeens were proven moneymakers. It came down to who could put more loanshark money on the street and take more gambling action off it. Howie Winter decided that man was Whitey.

At one point in the discussions, Tommy King took Pat Nee aside. "I don't like this," King said. "We shoulda killed Whitey before we settled this. We're going to live to regret this."[25] King was considered a hothead, a loose cannon, and not the smartest of the Mullens. But he was prescient about the threat posed by the newly formidable Whitey Bulger.

————

In just a few short post-prison years, Whitey had made the transition from small-time troublemaker to a major player, well positioned to rise toward the top. He had as well, in the Mullens-Killeen war, gained a kind of graduate education in the ways of the Irish underworld, in the strengths and weaknesses of the players, in the blood sports of attack, reprisal, and revenge, in the uproarious randomness of so much of it, and in the fine art of survival. Nothing he had learned contradicted what he had long thought of himself—that he was smarter than most hoods, more cunning and careful, and completely at ease in the use of violence as a tool in his chosen trade. There was also something about Whitey that drew people to him and made him stand out as a leader, something strangely charismatic in his ferocity, his self-mastery, and his obvious ambition.

His aura—not to mention the trim physique and penetrating eyes—was also a powerful draw for women, and, after his years in prison, Whitey had a lot of catching up to do on that front as well. Even before he reestablished himself as a criminal, he was aggressively reestablishing himself as a ladies' man. After nine years of no physical contact with women, he set out to bed as many as possible. The vast majority of these encounters were flings that, beyond the sex, meant little, if anything, to Whitey. But one of them was more than a one-night stand and produced his only known child.

He had been out of prison a year when he started working a jackhammer at a construction site in Quincy, just south of Southie. He noticed a young waitress leaving a diner across from the construction site. Her name was Lindsey Cyr, and she worked mornings at the diner and afternoons at a law office. Auburn-haired and buxom, she was a younger, darker version of his blonde former paramour Jacquie McAuliffe.

Whitey began showing up at the diner for breakfast before work. He flirted with Cyr, who at twenty-one was fifteen years younger than Whitey and was flattered by the attention of an older man. "God," Cyr recalled, "he was good-looking." He was also polite and well mannered and shockingly honest, telling Cyr he had been in prison and why. That wasn't the reason Cyr kept turning him down when he asked for a date. She was trying to get out of a bad relationship and wasn't ready for a new one. But Whitey would not be deterred.

Her former boyfriend showed up at the diner one morning while Whitey was having his breakfast. The man grabbed Cyr by her blouse and began screaming at her about some perceived slight. It was a perfect opportunity for Whitey to step in as her white knight. He pushed the man outside to the sidewalk, hit him quickly with four punches, and left him crumpled on the ground. Whitey then calmly walked back to his seat, picked up his coffee mug and said, "He won't be a problem anymore."[26]

Whitey's brutal gallantry worked; she agreed to go out with him. After a few dates, however, Whitey was frustrated because Cyr kept turning him down for sex. "I'm tired of taking you out and going some place else for what I want," he told her. "You know where to find me. It's put up or shut up."[27] Cyr didn't see him for six weeks, but she had fallen for him, and his absence weighed on her. Six weeks after Whitey's ultimatum, she strolled into the Transit Cafe. "I'm ready," Lindsey told him.

So was Whitey. But not before he took her to a department store in Dorchester to buy some new sheets. He had learned how to strip and make a bed quickly in prison, a skill he enthusiastically employed after bringing Cyr back to the Transit bartender's apartment in Southie. Cyr found Whitey to be hypersexual. He wanted it all the time, and at the oddest times. Driving her through Southie, he would suddenly pull down an alley and pull down his pants. Another time, Cyr was working in an office building downtown, and Whitey showed up unannounced. "Follow me," he said. She did, right into the ladies' room, where they had sex in one of the stalls.

The sex was spontaneous, furtive, and frequent. It was also unprotected, and a few months into their relationship Cyr discovered she was pregnant. Whitey wasn't pleased. He didn't want a child. The Killeens had taken him aboard and he was getting some action in their bookmaking and loansharking operation. The last thing he needed was a kid. He told Cyr she should get an abortion, but she refused. They argued, and when it became clear that she wouldn't do it, Whitey agreed to support their child. His only stipulation was that his name not appear on the birth certificate.[28] A man in his business couldn't afford known heirs; they gave his enemies a target, for extortion or kidnap or murder. Cyr listed her old boyfriend, the one she says Whitey beat up, as the father.

Cyr had a difficult labor, giving birth to a boy she named Douglas on May 22, 1967. She woke up in the hospital and found Whitey sitting by the bed. She remembers the gangster, who had little experience with babies, holding the newborn "like he was holding a time bomb." The boy had his father's blue eyes and blond hair, and Whitey doted on him when he was around. He visited Cyr and their son in her suburban home in Weymouth, south of Boston, at least twice a week. He helped pay for child care and showered Douglas with toys. He bought young Douglas a piano and paid for lessons. He took the boy on boating trips and family cookouts. Cyr and Douglas were welcomed at Bill Bulger's home in Southie when Whitey brought them over on occasion.

It was an almost ordinary domestic interlude in Whitey's life, one which coexisted in strange syncopation with his criminal doings. When Douglas was three, Cyr called Whitey in a panic. Douglas had gone to a carnival with a babysitter and had somehow wandered away. Whitey and the Killeens were, at the time, still at war with the Mullens gang, and Whitey showed up at the carnival with three other men, believing the boy had been kidnapped by his rivals. The explanation was far less dramatic. Douglas was soon found at a nearby donut shop, where a neighborhood girl had taken him without telling the babysitter.

In the fall of 1973, after Whitey had become top dog in Southie and a valued member of the Winter Hill Gang, six-year-old Douglas was rushed to Massachusetts General Hospital with a fever and nausea. The boy was diagnosed with Reye's Syndrome, a severe, often deadly, reaction to aspirin. Whitey was one the city's most powerful criminals, but he could do nothing about this. He maintained a vigil at the boy's side for three days. "When he died, Jimmy was out of his mind," Cyr said. "Tears were streaming down Jimmy's face."[29]

The open emotion in the aftermath of Douglas's death was quickly replaced by a new frigidity. Whitey walked into the garage in Somerville where his partners in the Winter Hill Gang congregated and told them that his son—the son they didn't know he had—had just died. He asked them not to send flowers or go to the wake or the funeral. That's the way he wanted it.[30]

Whitey paid for the boy's funeral and accompanied Cyr to the church and burial, but if Douglas was dead, so was their relationship. Whitey swore off more children, and he swore off visiting Cyr. He didn't want to be in the house in which Douglas had played the piano. He would meet her for sex and insist they not talk. The fun and the romance were gone. The boy's death had changed him. "He was colder," Cyr said.[31]

He had always been cold, but love had inured Cyr to it. The truth was that Whitey had never been straight with her, and even while Cyr was pregnant with his child, he'd begun a relationship with a woman named Teresa Stanley that would last almost thirty years.

Whitey had spent much of his youth trying to escape the suffocation of his family's three-bedroom apartment on Logan Way. But even as he rebuilt his criminal career, he found in life with Stanley the sort of stable domesticity he had fled as a kid. He had been out of prison nineteen months when he walked into a bar in Southie and saw Stanley sitting on a stool. He would never have guessed that she had given birth to her fourth child just three months earlier. Stanley was a natural beauty, with sparkling blue eyes, high cheekbones, sensuous lips, and Marilyn Monroe curves. Despite being a brunette, not a blonde, she was a variation of the theme.

Aside from being stunningly attractive, Stanley was an unusual choice as a partner for an up-and-coming gangster. She had divorced her husband and was living in the Old Colony housing project, a twenty-five-year-old single mother with four kids, the oldest of whom was seven. But Whitey pursued Stanley, and she considered herself lucky. He told her that he was in the construction trade but that she'd never want for anything. He would provide the money she needed to raise her children. She would be his companion. He never called her a common-law wife, but that's what she came to be.

From her point of view, he was a catch—a good-looking guy who always had money. What wasn't there to like? When they walked into a bar or a restaurant, people noticed. Stanley had gone from being a single mom in the projects to something of a Southie celebrity overnight.[32]

Whitey said he didn't want kids, but he treated Stanley's like his own. He had firm, deeply traditional views about what constituted a family and how a family should behave. He insisted on the children sitting down for dinner as a family every night. He told the kids to tell their friends: no phone calls between 5:00 and 7:00 p.m., and if the phone rang during dinner, Whitey fumed and the kids averted their eyes. He lectured them on the importance of things he had ignored in his own early life—of doing homework, of working hard and saving money, of not hanging around with the wrong people.

But Whitey's paternal presence, and financial support, came at a price. Stanley was by nature docile and easygoing, but Whitey expected her to be submissive. He expected her not to question him on anything. And he was frequently short and condescending.

One Christmas Eve, Stanley stood over a coffee table holding a bowl of nuts.

"I'm going to put these here," she said, bending down.

Whitey wrinkled his brow. "Why can't you say, 'I'm going to place these here'?"

Stanley knew little of Whitey's business, though she had an inkling that he made his money in gambling. On the few occasions

Stanley asked the wrong question, about where Whitey had been or what he was doing, his answer was always the same: "None of your fucking business." So she stopped asking.

"He expected perfection from everybody," she said.

Whitey was generous to Stanley and her children. He took Stanley on vacation regularly. They traveled to Europe, to San Francisco, and very regularly to Provincetown, a resort town on the tip of Cape Cod.

Provincetown has a large and long-established gay community, and Whitey's regular visits fueled rumors in some quarters that he was gay or bisexual. Stanley scoffed at suggestions that Whitey was anything but heterosexual. She says they went to Provincetown for the restaurants and the people watching. Despite the denials by Stanley and others who were close to Whitey, the rumors that Whitey was gay persisted. Most of them were spread by his criminal associates, for many of whom the worst insult is to be accused of being homosexual.

Whitey never took Stanley, or any woman, into his confidence, but she gave him something he would always value—a stable domestic corner in his world. It helped ground him through the brutal years of the Southie gang war and the tumult that preceded his emergence as the neighborhood's premier criminal. She helped him, even if she didn't know what she was helping him with.

5

Just Don't Clip Anyone

For every criminal Southie produced, it produced many more cops. At about the same time a teenaged Whitey Bulger started tailgating trucks on the Southie waterfront and along Broadway, John Connolly was in short pants, playing cops and robbers with his cousins, the Doohers, in the courtyard on O'Callaghan Way in the Old Harbor project. Connolly never deviated, in whatever game they played: he wanted to be one of the good guys.[1] Law enforcement was a proud tradition in the neighborhood, going back to the turn of the century, when it was one of the few jobs for which being Irish was considered a winning attribute.

Connolly's parents had immigrated to Boston from Galway, in Ireland's rural, rocky west, settling into Old Harbor not long after the Bulgers. His father was an amiable, reserved man known around Southie as Galway John. Galway John was an usher at St. Monica's Church and worked as a bookkeeper for fifty years at the Gillette shaving products factory, Southie's biggest employer. Connolly's mother, a homemaker, died relatively young, at fifty-four.

Galway John's son wanted a badge in the worst way, but from the start he had aimed higher than becoming a Boston cop. Like

Bill Bulger, young John Connolly left Southie for a more challenging school, Christopher Columbus High in the North End, the city's Italian neighborhood and Mafia stronghold, where he walked among the bookies and sidewalk men who would later become his informants. He took Bill Bulger's advice and enrolled at Boston College, working his way through school. After graduating, Connolly spent three years as a substitute teacher in the Boston public schools. His sister was a schoolteacher. But he had his eye on the FBI, and in true Southie fashion he made it happen through political contacts.

He was an excellent candidate for the bureau, with an engaging manner and winning blend of school smarts and street smarts. But an old sports injury to his hip prevented the twenty-eight-year-old Connolly from passing a required FBI physical. Desperate to find a way around the unexpected obstacle, he sent a letter to his father's old friend from the neighborhood, House Speaker John McCormack, looking for help. He also called his Old Harbor friend and mentor Bill Bulger, then a South Boston state representative, asking for support.

McCormack wrote a glowing recommendation to J. Edgar Hoover. Bulger also vouched for him. But the chief of orthopedics at the US Naval Hospital in Bethesda, Maryland, who reviewed Connolly's physical, "felt Connolly would be a poor risk for the Special Agent position" because of his hip, according to an FBI memo from Connolly's personnel file. That same FBI memo, however, concluded that Connolly should be given another chance to apply. And it made clear that the Speaker of the House carried more clout in such matters than the navy's chief of orthopedics. "Speaker of the House John W. McCormack subsequently advised that Connolly's father is a close and valued friend of his and applicant's doctor submitted a statement indicating that normal motion has now been restored in Connolly's hip and that he is in excellent physical condition. The Director [Hoover] approved the recommendation that Connolly be afforded a complete physical examination, including orthopedic consultation, at a Government facility to determine whether he is physically qualified for the Special Agent position."[2]

This time, no surprise, Connolly passed. He was appointed as an agent in November 1968 and was assigned to the Baltimore office. In early 1970 he was transferred to San Francisco and then soon after to New York, a plum assignment for a young agent just three years out of the academy. He was closing in quickly on his goal.

Connolly's plan always was to get back home, to make his name in the Boston office, and in 1972 Steve Flemmi played an unwitting role in making that happen. Flemmi had been out of town since 1969, after he and his then partner, Frank Salemme, bombed a car and seriously injured a lawyer who had represented a witness against the Mafia. Tipped off by his old handler, Paul Rico, that he was about to be charged with the bombing, Flemmi had gone on the lam, winding up in Montreal, where he worked as a photographer and printer. He stayed in touch with Rico, however, and with Rico's partner, Dennis Condon, as well.

Condon had taken a run at recruiting Whitey in 1971. The war with the Mullens was in full swing, and Condon thought Whitey might be willing to trade information. In a moment of optimism, he opened, or formally listed, Whitey as an informant in May 1971, but it was clear that Whitey was not ready to be much help. "Contact with this informant on this occasion was not overly productive and it is felt that he still has some inhibitions about furnishing information," Condon wrote on July 7, 1971. "Additional contacts will be had with him and if his productivity does not increase, consideration will be given to closing him out."[3] Whitey was, in fact, closed out just three months after Condon opened him, and it is unclear whether Whitey even knew he was considered an informant for that brief time. Either way, he wouldn't play ball. Condon was from Charlestown. That was enough for Whitey not to trust him.

But Flemmi did. He let Rico and Condon know Salemme was still in New York. Shortly after, in December 1972, Salemme was walking down a sidewalk in Manhattan when Connolly picked him out of the crowd and arrested him. The collar was worthy of a com-mendation and a coveted transfer home. It is widely believed, if never entirely proven, that Rico and Condon told Connolly where he could find Salemme. Connolly denies it, and Flemmi insists it was a Providence mobster who offered the tip. But Salemme didn't buy it; he still doesn't. He believes it was Flemmi who gave him up, and the chain of events makes his case a persuasive one.[4]

If the story behind the Salemme arrest remained unclear, what happened next was not: Connolly was transferred to Boston, where he was soon given a job that would allow him to follow in the footsteps of Rico and Condon: rolling gangsters into informants. Cultivating informants was the primary job of FBI agents at the time, and Connolly was made for it. He was gregarious and charismatic, a back-slapping raconteur with a ready smile. He dressed more like a wiseguy than a cop. His suits were tailored, flashier than the button-down agents' suits. His lapels were wide, his ties wider. Like many of the men he was trying to cajole, Connolly wore a pinky ring—again, an anomaly among FBI agents. And he liked to have his nails manicured. He also wore his thick black hair in a pompadour, leading Whitey to bestow one of the several nicknames he had for Connolly: Elvis.

Connolly carried himself with a cockiness bordering on arrogance that was common in Southie, and he was as popular in his new office as he was in his old neighborhood. Other agents, many of whom didn't grow up in Boston, marveled at his array of friends and contacts, from big-shot politicians to the sort of guys who could get tickets to the most sought-after Red Sox, Bruins, and Celtics games. Connolly's accent and his mannerisms, not to mention his local knowledge, opened doors and gave him credibility with people on both sides of the law. Growing up in Old Harbor made him streetwise; going to Boston College provided access to the city's biggest politicians and businessmen. His irrepressible friendliness made him a natural gatherer of intelligence. He was good at what he did.

The Salemme pinch not only got Connolly transferred back

home; it brought Flemmi back, too. Salemme was convicted of bombing the lawyer's car and sentenced to thirty years. The witness who testified against Salemme conveniently recanted his testimony against Flemmi. The message from Paul Rico, his old FBI handler, was plain: It is safe to come home.[5]

After the charges were dropped, the Mafia threw a party for Flemmi. It was really an excuse to recruit him. They held it at Giro's, a restaurant in the North End. Larry Baione, the No. 2 man in the local Mafia, buttonholed Flemmi alone in a corner of the restaurant and said it was time Flemmi was made. Baione offered to be his sponsor.

Baione, spreading his arms with delight at the thought of having his own mole in the middle of a gang that was simultaneously the Mafia's biggest ally and its most formidable competitor, suggested that Flemmi could be the Mafia's "eyes and ears" on Winter Hill. Flemmi shook his head. He appreciated the offer, but it wasn't for him. Later, Flemmi went up to the garage on Marshall Street in Somerville and told his friends about Baione's offer.

They all had a good laugh.[6]

Whitey was spending more and more time in that garage in Somerville. Marshall Motors was a working auto body shop with service bays for ten cars, but it was really the headquarters of the Winter Hill Gang. Gamblers who owed the gang money were marched into Howie Winter's office in the middle of the garage, where, after admiring the cheesy wood paneling, they would inevitably notice a trap door open on the floor. Howie sat at his desk and, against the backdrop of mechanics' drills, explained the virtues of paying one's debts. Howie's powers of persuasion were legendary, and he never had to make good on the implied threat to throw anyone through the trap door.[7]

Whitey, during his daily visits, would shoot the breeze with Howie Winter and his partners. Whatever money Whitey had made presiding over the rackets in Southie was dwarfed by the potential haul he could share in by working with Winter Hill. The gang's tentacles stretched across much of the metropolitan area, and all the way north to Lowell, an industrial city thirty miles outside Boston.

Business at the garage consisted mostly of dealing with bookies and gamblers who had borrowed money and were dropping off cash. But the garage was also something of a social mecca for the crooked set. The wives and girlfriends of the assembled gangsters took turns cooking and dropping off food. One day, after the women dropped by with a batch of spaghetti and meatballs, Whitey tied one of them to a chair in Howie Winter's office and, just for sport, repeatedly threw a knife into the wall behind her, like a circus act. "I remember saying, 'What the hell is with this guy?' He thought it was funny," Winter said. "Everybody was rolling their eyes, saying, 'What is this guy doing?'"[8]

Between 1972 and 1975, business was good. In 1975, however, the talk inside the garage began to circle around the uneasy alliance between Winter Hill and the Mafia. Whitey along with the others sensed that things had begun to fray; the conversation turned to the likelihood of war. Like the rest of Winter Hill, Whitey wasn't afraid of the Mafia's guns as much as its connections: The Italian mob had many more police and politicians in its pockets, the kind of allies who could tip the balance.

On one level, Whitey knew he was insulated from any future mayhem: The South Boston territory he ruled for Winter Hill was never going to be taken over by the Mafia. There were just too many Irish and too few Italians in Southie to make that a possibility. But Whitey had grown up hearing the cautionary tale of Frank Wallace and the Gustin Gang being ambushed by the Italians in the North End. The memory of that treachery was deeply embedded in Southie's subculture.

Winter Hill and the Mafia had long tried to make nice with each other because there was so much money to be made, and peace was better for business than war. But on occasion the sides clashed when they were going after the same money. The beef in 1975 started over vending machines. A vending company was paying the Mafia fifty thousand dollars a month to keep its machines in the bars in and around Boston. The Hill wanted the Mafia-controlled machines out of their bars in Somerville, Charlestown, Southie, Roxbury, and Dorchester so they could install their own.

Jerry Angiulo, who ran the Mafia in Boston as underboss of the Rhode Island–based Patriarca family, was livid when he found out that Howie Winter and his crew were driving the vending company out. In the Boston FBI office, the news of Angiulo's fury stirred worry but also a sense of possibility, a chance to cultivate ties with one side or both. One of Connolly's informants who was close to Whitey told Connolly that Winter Hill was planning to kill a group of Mafiosi. That would start a war, a war maybe worse than the one in the 1960s that killed sixty men. Connolly went to his supervisor, Jim Scanlan, and proposed taking a run at turning Whitey. Why not, Scanlan replied.[9]

Connolly got word to Whitey through a mutual friend that he wanted to talk to him. Word came back that it couldn't be in Southie. And it couldn't be in public. A date and a time were set, and then the place: at the far end of Wollaston Beach in Quincy, just a few miles down the coast.

"What's he driving?" Whitey asked. He'd find the car in the dark.

It was September 18, 1975, a Thursday night. Whitey Bulger always listened to the car radio, and as he drove to the meeting the news was full of reports that Patty Hearst, the newspaper heiress, had just been arrested in San Francisco. She was charged with bank robbery, just like Whitey had been twenty years before.

It was almost 10:00 p.m. when John Connolly backed his car into a parking space on the far end of Wollaston Beach. The Boston skyline twinkled in the distance. The moon was nearly full, and its yellowish glow filled the car. There was only one other car nearby. When Connolly looked over he saw what appeared to be two men having a tryst in the backseat, so he moved his car further down the beach, again backing in, so he'd be able to see Whitey's approach.[10]

Like Paul Rico before him, Connolly considered himself especially adept at developing informants. It was, he believed, a science and an art. Like Rico, he killed them with kindness, earning respect by showing respect, even to wiseguys. Especially to wiseguys. One day, for example, when Connolly went to arrest a mob associate named Richie Floramo, the gangster's kids came to the door. Connolly said he was a lawyer and needed to talk to their dad. Then he led Richie out to the car, eschewing bureau rules in not handcuffing him. Years later, when Connolly walked into Floramo's restaurant, Floramo greeted him warmly and introduced him to his now-grown kids at the bar. Floramo had never forgotten, and greatly appreciated, that Connolly had not humiliated him in front of his children.[11]

"You get more bees with honey," Johnny Connolly always said.

Connolly was lost in thought when the passenger door swung open and Whitey plopped himself in the front seat. His recollection of the conversation that followed remains vivid.

"What the hell did you do? Parachute in?" Connolly said, still startled.

Whitey shrugged.

"I was waiting for you by the water," Whitey said. "I just walked up."

Whitey had parked his car on a side street, not even chancing that someone might see it parked in one of the lined spots on the beach.

"I just want you to hear me out," Connolly said.

"I know who you are," Whitey said. "You're a friend of my brother's."

Connolly nodded.

Whitey wanted to let him know just how much he knew, so he

referred to Connolly's arrest of Frank Salemme three years earlier. "That was a good pinch in New York," Whitey said. "You'll endear yourself to Jerry with that."

Connolly was glad that Whitey brought up Jerry Angiulo, because it was the simmering feud between Angiulo's Mafia faction and Winter Hill that was at the heart of his pitch. Connolly said his sources claimed that Angiulo's right-hand man, Larry Baione, was telling people Winter Hill was willing to go to war with the Mafia over the vending machines. Whitey replied that if Baione opened his mouth, Winter Hill would take him out. He didn't trust Jerry Angiulo, or any of the Italians, for that matter.

"I hear Jerry is feeding information to law enforcement to get you pinched," Connolly told Whitey. "I don't think it's a good idea to go to war with the Mafia."

Whitey turned sharply.

"You don't think we'd win?" Whitey asked.

"Oh, you could win," Connolly replied. "But I don't think they have any intention of taking you people on."

Connolly explained his theory: Angiulo was too cute to get into a shooting war with a bunch of crazy Irishmen, not to mention Flemmi and his fellow Winter Hill hit man Johnny Martorano. Instead, Angiulo would "whittle you down," using his police contacts to "send you all to the can." Whitey agreed that that was the real risk. Angiulo had cops in his pocket, and he was using them to go after any outfit that cut into the Mafia's turf. Whitey was particularly worried that Angiulo had been able to plant a gun in the car of Joe Barboza, a hood who used to carry out hits for the Mafia but had become an unpredictable renegade. The planted gun forced Barboza, desperate for clemency, to become a government witness, the ultimate humiliation for a criminal. Whitey worried that Jerry Angiulo would use his corrupt allies in law enforcement and put him in a compromised position like Barboza.

"What if three cops stop me at night and say there was a machine gun in my car," Whitey said. "Who is a judge going to believe? Me? Or the three cops?"

Whitey shook his head. Connolly nodded, commiserating, and let Whitey talk on.

"Jerry pried the lid off a very dangerous pot," Whitey said. But Whitey reluctantly admired Angiulo's ability.

"You can't survive without friends in law enforcement," Whitey said, almost wistfully.

Connolly saw his opening.

"I have a proposal," he said. "Why don't you use us to do what they're doing to you? Fight fire with fire."

Whitey said nothing.

"Why not use the same tactics," Connolly went on. "You take out a Mafia family and you would be the talk of the country."[12]

Whitey was intrigued. He said he had to run the offer by his Winter Hill partners. "I know you know my brother," he said. "But I don't believe you owe me. I'm a big boy. I chose this business." He opened the door and left as quickly as he'd arrived, walking in the moonlight.

In his bid to recruit Whitey, Connolly had a distinct advantage. He not only was a Southie guy, he was an Old Harbor guy. He not only knew the Bulger family, he was considered a family friend. And he told anybody and everybody who would listen that he wouldn't be where he was without Bill Bulger, who was not only Whitey's little brother but Whitey's biggest hero.

Whitey knew that even being seen talking with an FBI agent could trigger fears that he was a rat. The story he took back to his Winter Hill partners was that Connolly was working for him, not the other way around. He told them the agent offered to leak him information and protect him from prosecution as a favor to Whitey's brother Bill, who had guided him on the path to college and helped him make something of himself.[13]

Whitey said Connolly told him he had asked Bill Bulger, "What can I do to help you in return?" and Bulger had responded, "Just keep my brother out of trouble."

Two weeks later, Whitey sent word for Connolly: same time, same place.

"They went for it," Whitey said of his meeting with his Winter Hill partners.

Connolly smiled, but Whitey put his hand up, as if to say he wasn't finished.

"Here's the deal. I don't want your money," Whitey said. "I'm no fucking informant. I'm the liaison for Winter Hill. We're not going to hurt any of our friends. Any discussion of the IRA [Irish Republican Army] is off the table."[14]

But he was willing to hurt the Mafia, and that's all that mattered to Connolly, because the FBI's national policy was to take down La Cosa Nostra. "I'll only consult with you on these fucking people," Whitey said. "They're enemies."

It was an extraordinary soliloquy. Whitey had essentially signed up for tribal warfare, the Irish vs. the Italians. He would not only be protecting himself and his friends in Winter Hill, he would be avenging the Italian-driven demise of the Gustin Gang a half century earlier. And an FBI agent had sat there and let a gangster dictate the conditions of the FBI's relationship with him.

Whitey's conditional embrace of his role with the bureau, even his preference for the word *liaison* instead of *informant*, underscored that, from the very beginning, he was calling the shots. His criminal activities would go unimpeded; indeed, only one ground-rule condition would be set, halfheartedly and not for some years: Just don't clip anyone.[15] He was never cautioned or told to thank his lucky stars the FBI was reaching out to him. His conditions were accepted, no questions asked.

And Whitey had one final condition. His brother Bill couldn't know.[16]

Whitey had probably always intended to kill Tommy King, the brawler who had been his onetime counterpart and rival. Once Whitey became an FBI informant, it was just a matter of time. He didn't need a reason to kill King, but King gave him one. And his new role with the FBI helped him get away with it.

Tommy King's clenched fist never left his side. But Whitey saw it. They were having words at the far end of the old Transit Cafe, which had been reinvented as Triple O's. The Killeens were gone: Donnie dead, Kenny retired. Whitey Bulger held court now, and his throne was at the back of Triple O's. King, a former Mullens guy who had become a combustible member of Whitey's emerging group, always said too much when he drank too much, and he always drank too much. He had fists the size of toasters and was known for his sucker punches—wild, looping haymakers that came out of nowhere and left their targets unconscious. Whitey glanced at King's right hand and saw it balled up, ready to fire. "Knock it off, Tommy," he said.

King unclenched his fist and picked up the longneck Budweiser in front of him. But it was too late. He was as good as dead. Whitey had seen the fist, and he knew it wouldn't be the last one, so it would have to be the last one.[17]

The fist wasn't the only issue. King had been talking about killing Eddie Walsh, a cop from Southie who kept pulling Whitey and his boys over, looking into their car, taking mental notes of who was who and who was with whom. Walsh wasn't good at taking notes and writing up reports, but he remembered faces and names with uncanny precision. He was also Connolly's liaison in the Boston Police Department, the one to whom Connolly gave his informant reports known as 302s. After that agreement in the car on Wollaston Beach, almost every 302 about criminal activity in South Boston that Connolly gave to Walsh was based on the uncorroborated, and often blatantly untruthful, words of Whitey Bulger.

King's animosity boiled over one day when Walsh pulled Whitey's car over near Carson Beach.

"What are you boys up to?" Walsh said, leaning over, looking into the back of Whitey's Malibu, taking a mental inventory of the passengers, nodding at Whitey in the driver's seat.

"Fuck off!" King barked, and Whitey turned to cast a cold, hard look at him.

"That's no way to talk to a police officer, Tommy," Walsh said.

Later, as they drove away, King went off in the backseat. "We don't need to take that kind of shit," he said. "I'm going to kill that fuckin' bastard. I'm gonna fuckin' kill him."

"Hey!" Whitey snapped glaring at King in the rearview mirror. "You're not fuckin' killing anyone. And you're not killing a fuckin' cop any time."[18]

The night after the clenched fist at Triple O's, King showed up at the front door of Whitey's mother's apartment in the project. He was hung over, his hair more tousled than usual, his tongue sandpaper.

"I'm sorry, Jimmy," he said, as soon as Whitey opened the door. "I was out of line last night. Out of line."

Whitey looked back over his shoulder, stepped into the hallway, and closed the door behind him. King was not coming into his mother's place.

"Forget about it, Tommy," Whitey said, knowing more than ever he would kill him. "It's done. It's over."[19]

They shook hands.

Tommy King would be dead in a week.

Pat Nee and Howie Winter believe Whitey had always intended to kill as many Mullens as he could after the truce Winter negotiated between the Mullens and the Killeens ended the gang war.[20] And the way Whitey went about setting King up was ingenious and cynical. He used King, blaming him for the murder of the Mullens' titular leader, Paul McGonagle, a murder Whitey had made his priority. "It was deviously clever," Nee said. "Because not only did Whitey get rid of Paulie, but the rest of us Mullens never looked at Tommy the same way again. Whitey isolated Tommy. And after it was clear that he was cut off from the rest of us, at least in our minds, he took out Tommy."

For Whitey, killing Paulie McGonagle had been unfinished business. In a perverse way, he blamed Paulie for his having killed Donald McGonagle by mistake in the middle of the gang war. Whitey figured that eventually Paulie was going to avenge his brother's murder, so he made a preemptive strike.

According to Flemmi, Whitey tricked Paulie into getting into the back of a car with him by saying he had a suitcase of counterfeit money to show him. Tommy King set him up, telling Paulie it was a good score. Paulie climbed into the back of the car outside the Mullens clubhouse. Whitey opened the suitcase, pulled out a gun, and shot him.[21]

Up to that point, it had been the underworld's calling card to leave bodies where they fell or to stuff them in trunks. It was the rule of the jungle, to humiliate the vanquished and display the trophy of the hunter. But after he killed Paul McGonagle, Whitey turned that rule on its head. Paulie would go into the ground. There would be no funeral, no mourning, no absolute proof he was even dead. In the absence of the ritual of death, the chance of retaliation by the dead man's friends was greatly reduced. With the absence of a body, the chance of a criminal charge was almost entirely eliminated.

They took Paulie to Tenean Beach, a couple of miles away in Dorchester, and dug a grave in the moonlight. King refused to take part in the burial. That didn't stop Whitey from telling all the Mullens that King had killed McGonagle.[22] King was such a hothead that they believed him.

Whitey let a year go by with Paulie's body in the Dorchester sand before moving on King. The Mullens had been stewing over Paulie's murder, and King was growing ever more erratic and isolated. It wasn't any one thing. Whitey told the Winter Hill crew that King had to go because he had said something inappropriate to a little girl.[23] He told the Mullens that King's threatening Eddie Walsh was going to get them all locked up. Even Howie Winter, who liked King, agreed that threatening a cop was stupid and bound to bring heat.[24] And, in the back of Whitey's mind, there was that clenched fist in the back of Triple O's.

Whitey pulled up outside of the Mullens club one afternoon and King walked over. "We need you," Whitey said. "We're looking for Suitcase. We'll be back in a couple of hours. Be at the nursing home."

It would be entirely plausible that they were going to kill Alan "Suitcase" Fidler, a rival gangster. But in fact they weren't hunting

Suitcase. It was a ruse, an excuse to get King in the car. A couple of hours later, when Whitey pulled into the parking lot in back of a nursing home on Columbia Road, King willingly hopped in the front passenger seat.

Johnny Martorano was in the back, directly behind King. Sitting with your back to Martorano, anytime, anywhere, was dangerous, but King sensed nothing. Flemmi was driving a backup car and nodded to King. Whitey took some guns and walkie-talkies out of a duffel bag and handed them out. The gun Whitey handed King was loaded with blanks. As Whitey drove down Day Boulevard, past Carson Beach, King started talking excitedly.

"Where we lookin'?" King asked.

"Everywhere," Whitey replied. "We'll head over to Savin Hill first."

"If we can't find Suitcase, we can always test this out," King said, rapping his knuckles on the bulletproof vest he was wearing.

Whitey smirked, and Martorano leaned forward and put the muzzle of his gun a few inches from the back of King's skull and fired. He then reached from behind, grabbed King's shoulders, and slid him over, so that King's right shoulder was propped against the door. He placed a baseball cap on King's head and tilted the visor down a bit. It looked like King was sleeping.

Whitey slowed, about to make a U-turn at the causeway that heads out to Squantum, an isolated part of Quincy, but Martorano asked him to pull into the Dunkin' Donuts on the other side of the road. "I've got to check a race," Martorano said, as if leaving a dead body in the front seat of a car while he made a call from the phone booth outside the Dunkin' Donuts was the most normal thing in the world.

"Hurry up," Whitey called after him, throwing the car into park.

They buried Tommy King not far from the Dunkin' Donuts, in the tidal banks of the Neponset River.[25]

Later that night, Whitey went looking for and found Buddy Leonard, another Mullens gang member. Leonard might have taken revenge for King's murder, and Whitey wasn't going to give him a chance. But Leonard's murder was more than a preemptive strike. It was also a diversion. After the shooting, Whitey told John Connolly that Tommy King had killed Buddy Leonard.*

Whitey had only been an informant for a little more than a month when he killed Tommy King and Buddy Leonard, and he quickly realized how useful his new arrangement with the FBI could be. He had been feeding Connolly mostly gangland gossip, but he was able to use Connolly to disseminate reports to the FBI and Boston police that kept the focus of the investigation of the King and Leonard murders away from him.

Four days after Leonard's body was found in King's car, Connolly quoted his unnamed informant, who was Whitey, saying that King had killed Leonard after a violent argument. "Source stated that King would probably face some reprimand from the Mullin [sic] gang for killing Leonard in that manner although it would probably not be anything severe as Leonard was disliked by almost all of the Mullin crew, and himself had been responsible for a few murders."

Eleven days later, Whitey went back to Connolly with a new story.

Source advised that Tommy King, who recently murdered Francis X. "Buddy" Leonard, was told by the Mullin [sic] gang that he is to remain out of the Boston area on a permanent basis. According to source, King was forced to accept the decision but agreed that it would be best if he never came back in light of speculation that the police are believed to have a couple of witnesses to the Leonard murder. Both the Mullin [sic] gang and the Winter Hill people made the decision and, according to the source, they plan to support King while he is away.

Sometime around New Year's Eve, Whitey decided to alter the story for a third and final time. He could write his own history and he was starting to enjoy it. "Source stated that the word is out

---

*A jury in US District Court in Boston found on August 12, 2013, that prosecutors failed to prove that Whitey had participated in Leonard's murder.

that Tommy King has been 'taken out.' Source stated that various rumors are flying about as to whether or not he is actually gone and the reasons for it," Connolly wrote. "Source heard that King had gone 'kill crazy' and was placing people's lives in jeopardy in that he was talking crazy about killing various people including police officers. Source stated that King gave them no alternative but to make a move on him."[26]

When Whitey fed John Connolly those stories, they were sitting in a car less than a mile from Tommy King's body.

6

Southie Is His Hometown

Night had fallen on September 8, 1975, as Whitey slid into his green Chevrolet Impala and set off across town. The cool rush of air filled the car as he cruised through Franklin Park, down to Forest Hills, bound for Brookline, a prosperous town and liberal stronghold on the other side of the city, fifteen minutes, five miles, and a world away from South Boston. He was angry—seething, in fact—and had a mission in mind, something to shake up the city.

It wasn't the usual sort of thing that was testing Whitey's temper—not a betrayal by a criminal associate, or a bookie slow to pay. No, what had him upset was the silence. The Boston public schools had opened that morning, and the day had passed quietly, especially compared to the year before, when court-ordered school integration had gone into effect and the first buses carrying black kids climbed the hill on G Street to South Boston High School. The black students were greeted by a wave of rocks and slurs. To Whitey, the comparative peace smacked of complacency or at least an end to forceful resistance to the busing plan, a plan that he, like most residents of Southie, saw as a mortal threat to the neighborhood as they knew it and the high school that bore its name. An incorrigi-

ble student, Whitey had never managed to enroll at South Boston
High, but he recognized it as a symbol of the neighborhood's sov-
ereignty and resolve. With Southie gone silent, he decided to make
some noise of his own. He had everything he needed close at hand—
a bottle full of gasoline, a lighter in his pocket, a can of spray paint
in the backseat, and an accomplice up front.[1]

It was sometime after ten when Whitey parked on Stedman
Street, which runs parallel to Beals Street, in a leafy part of Brookline. As he later described it to an associate, Whitey grabbed the
Molotov cocktail and the paint can, cut through a backyard, and
jumped a fence. He walked down a narrow lane and found himself standing next to an old-fashioned gaslight in front of a three-
storey green clapboard house at 83 Beals St.[2] It was the house where
John F. Kennedy was born. A national historic site, it was usually
full of tourists during the day, but empty and unguarded at night.
Whitey had been in Alcatraz when Jack Kennedy was elected president. Like just about every other Irish Catholic in America, he'd
felt a surge of ethnic, religious, and cultural pride at the time. But
the Kennedys were no longer heroes; they were enemies, the political patrons of W. Arthur Garrity Jr., the federal judge who had just
turned Southie upside down. Jack Kennedy had appointed Garrity
US Attorney in Massachusetts, and Garrity had worked for Bobby
Kennedy. After the president's assassination, Senator Edward Kennedy became Garrity's chief patron, pushing his appointment to the
federal bench. The senator remained Garrity's most influential supporter, and a leading advocate for busing as an imperfect but necessary remedy for the long-running shame of Boston's schools—their
stark racial divide in educational opportunity and quality. The Kennedys, who had once symbolized the unlimited upward mobility of
Irish Catholics in America, now were seen in Southie as rich, out-of-
touch scolds, sitting in smug, liberal judgment of their own tribe. To
Whitey, the Kennedys had become something worse than enemies.
They were traitors.

Whitey bent down and aimed the spray-paint can at the sidewalk. He stood up and admired his handiwork, big looping letters in black paint: *Bus Teddy.* Then he slipped around back and peered through the darkened hallway into the kitchen. Whitey lit the rag he had stuffed into the bottle's neck and smashed the backdoor window.[3] The bottle exploded on the gold carpet and flames were licking the kitchen walls by the time Whitey and another man vaulted the fence behind a house on Stedman Street owned by someone named Marvin Feil. Feil noticed that they wore dark shirts but could say little else about them.[4]

Feil and other neighbors called the police, and firefighters quickly extinguished the blaze. But the police couldn't find the car, identified as a green Impala, that had been parked in front of the home of a man named Robert Novak, at 82 Stedman St.[5] By the time the fire was out, the kitchen was gutted and Whitey and his accomplice were back in Southie, the car stashed in a garage. Whitey boasted to friends that he had personally shut the Kennedy house down for three months.[6]

Whitey's trip to Brookline came just ten days before his September 18 meeting with John Connolly, when the agent first broached the idea of Whitey becoming Winter Hill's "liaison" to the FBI. It was a time when Whitey was sitting pretty and had been since the summer before.

He had not only survived the war with the Mullens gang, he had managed to fill the leadership vacuum left by the assassination of his former boss in the South Boston rackets, Donnie Killeen. He was a full-fledged member of the Winter Hill Gang, controlling South Boston for the Somerville-based crime group. The money was rolling in from his gambling and loansharking operations in Southie. But outside forces, the bane of the proud residents of South Boston, were conspiring to insult their honor and encroach on their territory. A federal judge was, in 1974, about to make Southie a prisoner of its reputation as a racist stronghold—a reputation unfair to many, perhaps most, who lived there—with a ruling that would have a profound impact on Whitey's world. Judge Garrity's plan was meant to be an exercise in achieving racial equality but quickly devolved into an ugly battle over identity and power, and the resulting tremors threw Boston into a period of instability and polarization that lasted more than a decade.

In South Boston, residents cherished the ethos of neighborhood cohesion. Parents were outraged that their teenagers would be forced out of their own neighborhood to attend a high school miles away. They were particularly horrified that Southie students were slated to be shipped to Roxbury, a neighborhood that was mostly black, with higher crime rates and a high school that the judge himself had deemed inferior. Just as unthinkable was the idea that outsiders would be coming in. This challenged the neighborhood's basic sense of self-governance. The court-ordered disruption also threatened the separate criminal and political empires the two Bulger power brokers had built. The status quo before Garrity's order had served the brothers well, albeit in starkly different ways. Neither saw an upside to changing it. And they'd be damned if outsiders were going to tell them or anybody else in Southie what to do.

As South Boston's state senator, Bill Bulger quickly emerged as busing's most articulate foe. He denounced the judge who issued the court order and the mayor who acquiesced to it. He confronted the police who enforced it, accusing them of heavy-handed tactics against ordinary citizens with legitimate grievances. He savaged suburban liberals, with some justice, as phonies who would never allow their own children to be bused to faraway, inferior schools in high-crime neighborhoods. And he blasted the media for playing up racism and downplaying the concerns Southie residents had about their children being used as human guinea pigs in a social experiment.

The oft-repeated guinea pig analogy might well have resonated with Whitey, taking him back to his experience in prison when he volunteered for the government program testing the effects of LSD. But his major focus was on a side effect of the turmoil in his home neighborhood—the army of police that flooded the city to enforce the court order posed a problem for someone in a business like his. Whitey came to see the situation as requiring a tactical shift. With police so preoccupied with public order, and most police resources deployed during the day, he figured he had to do most of his work at night. More than ever, he used the cover of darkness to take care of personal business, picking off his rivals—and making his way to Brookline with a Molotov cocktail in hand.

The school busing crisis thus cemented the brothers' positions in the neighborhood: Bill, the elected defender of Southie, visible, on the streets and at the podium; Whitey working from the shadows, engaging in symbolic, rear-guard gestures that thrust a communal middle finger in the face of those who would presume to push South Boston around. To borrow an analogy from Irish Republicanism: If Billy was the leader of the anti-busing movement's political wing, Whitey, in effect, commanded its stealth military wing.

The hard fact confronting Judge Garrity in 1974 was that because Boston's neighborhoods had long been segregated, as much by ethnicity as by race, its schools were largely one color or the other, black or white. After the great Depression-era migration to the north of southern blacks, and the post–World War II migration of white ethnics, especially Jews, from Boston to the city's suburbs, the neighborhoods of Roxbury, the South End, and parts of Dorchester became overwhelmingly African American. Southie, Charlestown, East Boston, Hyde Park, the North End, and West Roxbury remained, as they had been, overwhelmingly white. The 1970 census showed that more than 98 percent of Southie's 38,489 residents were white.[7]

Boston had been the capital of the abolitionist movement during the decades before the Civil War era, and throughout the nineteenth century the city's public schools were, at least officially, not segregated. But Boston students had always attended the school nearest their home, and those schools reflected the demographics of the neighborhoods. If they were racially separate largely by accident of history, the blatant gap in quality between schools serving whites and those serving blacks was a matter of political choice by the white establishment.

After the US Supreme Court ruled, in 1954, that de facto segregation was unconstitutional, the Boston School Committee had taken its usual course in the face of the obvious school segregation—it did nothing. Boston came to be seen as among the least tolerant of northern cities. The abolitionist movement may have been led by the Brahmin establishment, but the immigrants from Europe who flooded into Boston in the latter half of the nineteenth century, especially the Irish, were less concerned with the fate of slaves and their descendants. In many cases, they saw blacks as rivals for jobs and public housing.

The Boston School Committee brusquely denied any suggestion that its policies perpetuated segregated schools. But that posturing would soon be seen for what it was, in part because of the efforts of Whitey Bulger's spiritual adviser and Bill Bulger's law school dean: Father Robert Drinan.

In 1964, the same year he was signing letters accepting a role as Whitey's parole adviser and sponsor, Drinan began preparing a report on Boston's schools as chairman of the Massachusetts State Advisory Committee to the US Commission on Civil Rights. He emerged as a leading intellectual force in Massachusetts not only because of his support for desegregation but because he believed that busing schoolchildren across neighborhood lines was the most practical remedy for generations of institutionalized segregation. He wrote regularly about the need to advance the civil rights of blacks in *America*, the Jesuit magazine that Whitey had subscribed to in prison at Drinan's suggestion. Drinan's seminal report for the US Commission on Civil Rights found that Boston's schools were segregated and that the ones black children attended had inferior books, buildings, and educational results.[8]

Drinan wrote that the segregation of Boston's schools had damaged the self-confidence of black children, reinforced "the prejudices of children regardless of their color," and created "a gap in the quality of education facilities among schools."[9] The report was ignored by the Boston School Committee, but it helped inspire passage of a 1965 state law that required schools to be racially balanced. The Boston School Committee ignored the new law, too.

In 1972, frustrated at the city's inaction, the National Association for the Advancement of Colored People (NAACP) filed suit on behalf of a group of black parents. Judge Garrity was assigned the case, and in June 1974 he ruled in favor of the black parents. That fall, South Boston High's entire junior class, which was all white, was sent to Roxbury High School, and Roxbury High's sophomore class, which was mostly black, was sent to South Boston High. Some eighty-five members of South Boston High's senior class who lived in neighboring Savin Hill were bused to a predominantly black school in Dorchester. Other schools in predominantly white neighborhoods were likewise affected by the first phase of busing, including Roslindale, West Roxbury, and Hyde Park. There were angry protests and outbreaks of violence throughout the city, with whites attacking blacks and blacks attacking whites. But Southie produced a more sustained and volatile reaction. Residents of South Boston viewed Garrity's order as punitive and greeted it with guffaws and defiance. If some parents in the other neighborhoods vowed resistance, Southie promised outright revolt.

Signs and bumper stickers appeared overnight. Southie Won't Go. Southie Says No. No Forced Busing. A grassroots anti-busing group, the South Boston Information Center, appeared suddenly in a previously vacant storefront. The young men who staffed the office were aggressive and, to outsiders at least, intimidating. Anti-busing rallies were quickly organized by South Boston residents, many of whom vowed to never let their children be bused out of the neighborhood. Some sent their children to parochial schools. Others later formed a private academy. Busing was Southie's ultimate nightmare, but it was also a powerful unifying issue for a neighborhood that tended to downplay its own ethnic and class divisions.

Bill Bulger especially bristled at suggestions that, for all the talk of neighborhood integrity, a good number of his constituents simply did not want black kids coming into Southie. He insisted it wasn't about race but about government overreach and class. "The promised quick fix of busing—busing of poor urban children only—enjoyed noisy support from millions who lived in the all-white citadels in the suburbs," Bill Bulger said. "It was endorsed by affluent citizens of Boston who could afford to send their children to private schools, and who did so. None of them was affected. Only the intended victims resisted—only those in the targeted communities, primarily urban ethnic Catholics with thin pocketbooks."[10]

Bulger, with such remarks, was borrowing a page from the playbook of his political hero, James Michael Curley, portraying the city's biggest ethnic group, the Catholic Irish, as being put-upon by the moneyed classes. But he had a point: Many of busing's staunchest defenders did not have to live with its consequences. Under state law, a school where more than 50 percent of the students were minority was deemed racially imbalanced. The suburbs simply didn't have enough nonwhite pupils to trigger the law's tough remedies. In Southie, that seemed like an arbitrary and convenient distinction, and the resentment against the white suburbs of Boston ran deep. Which is why, a few days before the first buses carrying black students arrived at South Boston High in September 1974, Whitey Bulger drove under the cover of darkness to Wellesley, an affluent suburb west of Boston, and Judge Garrity's hometown.

Wellesley and Southie had long stood on opposite sides of the class divide that busing exacerbated. In Southie, they derisively called it Swellesley. With its stately homes and manicured lawns, it represented everything Southie was not, and Whitey had felt that way long before busing. He had once urged two Southie hoodlums who had broken into a South Boston home to move their burglary business to Wellesley.[11] Whitey was furious that Southie students were being shipped to worse schools in a high-crime neighborhood. "Social Engineering by a bunch of politicians . . . and [a] federal judge from rich Wellesley," he later wrote to a friend.[12]

Whitey's analysis, thick with class envy and Southie Pride, was ironic on the matter of crime, coming from someone who had used murder and menace to become the kingpin of his neighborhood rackets. But it also was shrouded in prejudice, infused by his belief that he was a fair-minded gangster who presided over an underworld where there were rules—that Southie criminals had scruples that were lacking in other, especially black, neighborhoods. Whitey used the word "nigger" liberally, and he frequently denigrated blacks in conversation. Some of those who knew him well considered him racist.[13] Whitey believed he was striking a blow for Southie when he drove to Wellesley that night, just a few days before busing became a reality. His mission was to send a message to Judge Garrity, but if Whitey was angry, he wasn't stupid. He knew the judge's house in the Wellesley Hills neighborhood was under twenty-four-hour guard, so he chose a proxy target, an elementary school a half mile from the judge's house. Whitey approached the Kingsbury Elementary School with a Molotov cocktail in hand. He broke a window and tossed the firebomb in.[14] Two classrooms were destroyed before firefighters doused the blaze. The next day, he called the Wellesley fire station. He didn't say who he was, but he did say where they could find the gasoline can he used to fill the Molotov cocktail. "I'm gonna burn down every school in Wellesley," Whitey said. "Even if it takes me thirty years."[15] Wellesley Fire lieutenant Joseph Keough said investigators never identified the arsonist, but the caller made his motive clear. "He said if the kids in Southie had to be bused, then the kids in Wellesley were going to have to be bused," Keough recalled.[16] There was talk all over Southie that Whitey had done it, but the police couldn't prove it. Whitey got his wish, at least temporarily. About forty Wellesley students were bused to nearby schools for a couple of months while construction workers fixed their two fire-damaged classrooms.

Ground zero of the busing controversy was South Boston High School, a three-story, yellow brick building next to Dorchester Heights, where the colonists had used cannon to scare off the British fleet in 1776. Because it sat on a hill, the high school looked like a citadel, and in September 1974 it became one. Southie High had about two thousand students, and between 1964 and 1974 only three black students attended, two of them sisters.[17]

Jim Miara was working for the Social Security Administration in downtown Boston when his boss announced that they were looking for volunteers to ride the school buses as monitors when desegregation began. On the morning of September 12, 1974, Miara boarded a bus in Roxbury, headed for Southie. He and the driver were white; all the children were black. "The bus was about half full," Miara said. "It was mostly little girls, ninth graders. Almost no boys. They all looked scared. They all were nervous. None of us knew what to expect, but we didn't expect to be welcomed, that's for sure." The bus cruised past Carson Beach before turning on to G Street for the short ride up the hill to the high school. The bus crept past the signature three-deckers and sidewalks choked with people shaking their fists.

"Right in the middle of the street, someone had painted 'Niggers Go Home' in huge letters," Miara said. "At some point, there was a backup at the high school so we were stopped on G Street, waiting to move. The street was lined with people, and they moved toward the bus. There were all these middle-aged people, men and women, beating on the bus, yelling, 'Nigger' and 'Niggers go home.' They were pounding on the bus. There were cops all over the place but they didn't do anything. They never intervened. The kids had this look on their faces, like, What's happening? We're not going to get killed, are we? The kids weren't crying. They were silent. They were cowed. As was I. I will never forget the look of the people who were pounding on the bus. Their faces were contorted in anger and hatred. The hatred on that street was palpable."[18]

Whatever moral high ground Southie had gained as a neighborhood suffering under judicial fiat was lost as the scenes around the high school were broadcast on national TV. Southie was soon widely derided as a racist Boston backwater. Those images infuriated Bill Bulger, because he considered them cruelly unrepresentative, and he thought the show of anger, while unfortunate, was a predictable by-product of Garrity's heavy-handed order. He regularly stood with his constituents outside the high school, and he prided himself on never losing his cool. But he lost it one day when he confronted Boston police commissioner Robert diGrazia outside Southie High. The Tactical Patrol Force (TPF), a special mounted unit formed to contend with the busing disturbances, lined the streets, ordering residents back to their houses.

"Get this Gestapo out of here," Bulger yelled, according to diGrazia.[19]

DiGrazia saw Bulger as one of the politicians who had helped make the busing crisis inevitable by obdurately refusing to act, even after the schools were found in violation of the state's racial imbalance law.

"Bulger," diGrazia fired back, "if you had any fucking balls we wouldn't be in this position. If you did your job we wouldn't be here. You had ten years. If you had any guts, you'd tell these people to get their kids into school."[20]

Bill Bulger felt the veins pulse in his neck. He was walking away, but he wheeled and strode up to diGrazia, leaning in so that their faces almost touched. "The community has a message for you, Commissioner," Bill Bulger hissed. "Go fuck yourself." Then he stormed off, regretting what he had said before he got to the bottom of G Street.

Bill Bulger accused diGrazia in particular and police in general of cooking up grand conspiracy theories involving the people of

South Boston and what they were plotting. He believed the police had floated a rumor that his brother Whitey wanted to kill Mayor Kevin White, who had steadfastly promised to implement the integration order.[21] But if Bill Bulger considered that a malicious rumor, the mayor himself considered it a very real possibility. The mayor told many of his friends that he believed Whitey was looking to kill him, and he became paranoid about it. One night after playing a few sets of tennis, the mayor was suddenly gripped with fear as he was about to leave his South Boston health club. The club was on the edge of Southie's gritty industrial waterfront, and the mayor imagined Whitey lying outside with a gun, waiting to ambush him.[22]

The mayor believed not only that Whitey shared the neighborhood's vehement opposition to forced integration but also that busing was cutting into Whitey's racketeering profits by causing so much disruption. During the campaign the following year, the mayor was more worried about losing his life than losing the election. "In the '75 fight, everybody knew the mob was out to get me," the mayor told the journalist Christopher Lydon in 1978 during an off-camera conversation after filming an interview for public television. "Whitey takes me out, and they win all the marbles."[23]

Whitey, the mayor insisted, was just crazy enough to do it. But Whitey knew killing the mayor of Boston would have brought unrelenting heat on him and every other criminal in Southie. As much as he may have wished the worst on White and the other busing supporters, he had to know that killing him would ruin him.

DiGrazia and other law enforcement officials of that era claim, in fact, that Whitey did his best to keep the violent opposition to busing controlled, because the disruption was indeed costing him money. It was largely a myth, part of the "good Whitey" image the gangster had begun to cultivate. Whitey was doing more than the police commissioner could have imagined, and none of it had anything to do with keeping the peace. He used the police preoccupation with busing to settle some old business. Two months after the first phase of busing started, he had shot and secretly buried Paul

McGonagle, the old Mullens gang leader. A year later, as the second phase of busing was implemented, he had lured Tommy King, another Mullens rival, to his death. But that was after John Connolly and the FBI had entered the picture. For now, the police were so distracted by the turmoil on the streets and in the schools that they barely took note of stray gangland disappearances.

Bill Bulger considered Judge Garrity, Senator Kennedy, and the *Boston Globe* hypocrites—for the court order and the defense of it, and for the way the crisis was covered in the pages of the city's dominant daily newspaper. "As a parent, I felt it was the natural right of the parent to make these decisions," Bill Bulger said. "I never saw anyone from the [*Boston*] *Globe*, in all that time, I never saw anybody from the United States Senate, I never saw anyone, no clergyman, no priest, no minister, no rabbi, not one of those critics who came in heavy on us from the outside ever said to their congregation, ever say to their children, 'Now, we are going to put you at the disposal of a federal judge.'"[24]

The way the press covered busing fueled a persecution complex that was widespread in Southie, where people believed the media deliberately overemphasized the intolerance of whites while downplaying retaliatory violence by blacks against whites. After a black student stabbed and nearly killed a white student in Southie High in December 1974, many in South Boston complained that the media, especially the *Globe*, underplayed the stabbing, and claimed it would have been a bigger story if the roles had been reversed.[25] Bill Bulger complained that the *Globe* was relentless in its search for bad news about South Boston, that Southie was portrayed simplistically as a home to bigots, and that he was regularly singled out as chief bogeyman.[26] But Bill could only aim tough words at the *Globe*. A month after busing started, Whitey decided to take direct action. In a letter to a friend explaining why he attacked the newspaper, he complained that the *Globe* was hostile to Southie and had labeled its people as racists. He claimed that most of the newspaper's journalists enrolled their children in private schools. And for Whitey, it wasn't just his home neighborhood that was unfairly tarnished, it was the treatment of his brother that riled him the most. "The *Globe* has always savaged my brother through its editorials," Whitey wrote.[27]

The *Globe* building on Dorchester's Morrissey Boulevard is just a mile away from the streets where Whitey grew up. Historically, the newspaper had been the champion of the poor and immigrants. Many people from Southie worked at the *Globe*, but few were reporters. More often they printed and delivered the papers or worked as secretaries, custodians, and other support staff. In Southie, the *Globe*'s owners, part of an old New England Yankee clan, were viewed with suspicion, which grew into full-blown hostility after the paper editorialized in favor of busing.

Whitey had little trouble talking Pat Nee into being his wingman on an attack against the newspaper. Nee had briefly worked at the *Globe* after returning from the Vietnam War. He left his job after smashing a custodial supervisor with a mop. Like Whitey, Nee hated the *Globe*, seeing it as deeply biased against South Boston. Some people in Southie had taken to using their cars to block *Globe* delivery trucks from distributing the newspaper. But Whitey wanted to up the ante. He loaded a 12-gauge shotgun with deer shot and climbed behind the wheel. It took Whitey and Nee five minutes to drive from the Mullens clubhouse in City Point to the *Globe*. It was after midnight when Whitey stopped his car on Morrissey Boulevard, directly in front of the newspaper. They stepped from the car and opened fire.

A security guard sitting in a booth at the entrance to the newspaper's parking lot made eye contact with Whitey and hit the ground when he saw him level the shotgun.[28] But Whitey wasn't aiming his way. Instead, he fired toward the glass doors of the *Globe*'s front lobby, narrowly missing an eighteen-year-old security guard sitting behind a desk. Whitey says he missed on purpose, firing above the guard's head.[29] Three more shots pierced the plate glass windows in the press room. The next night, as police stood guard out front, Whitey and Nee returned and went to the other side of the *Globe* building, shooting at the newspaper plant from a car on the Southeast Expressway. Whitey bragged that he tracked in his sights a man running through the *Globe* newsroom, purposely firing in back of him as he ran.[30] And he took great satisfaction in learning that the *Globe* spent tens of thousands of dollars to replace the plate glass windows in its building with bulletproof glass. "Globe knew it was me," wrote Whitey, boasting that his handiwork had "created jobs"—that the *Globe* was forced to hire twenty-four-hour security and put in surveillance cameras. "Those bastards spent a fortune because of me."[31]

Whitey considered each of his busing-era attacks carefully. He sought to maximize the symbolic expression of his neighborhood's anger while minimizing the risk to himself. He knew that directly attacking Garrity or Garrity's house would have invited an unrelenting response from law enforcement, so he had attacked a school nearby. He knew the same logic of risk and reward applied to taking on Ted Kennedy, so he had attacked the Kennedy birthplace, not the senator himself. And as much as he wanted to attack the police who were such an intimidating presence during the busing years, he knew it would be madness to charge at them directly. Whitey finally settled on a way to get even after the Tactical Patrol Force burst into a Southie bar, The Rabbit Inn, and beat patrons they held responsible for orchestrating anti-busing violence. DiGrazia, the police commissioner, contends Whitey was one of those patrons, but Whitey wasn't in the bar when the police burst in, though he was friendly with some who were.[32] Whitey knew that any physical attack on a police officer would bring a disproportionate response from law enforcement, so he decided to hit the TPF indirectly. "They love their horses," Whitey said. "Let's kill their horses."[33]

Whitey's wild idea was to poison apples with cyanide and scatter them in a grassy area at the bottom of G Street where the riot police kept the horses when they weren't up at the high school. He carved out the cores of a bunch of apples, filled them with poison, then replaced the cores. Long before dawn, he spread them in the grass at the bottom of the hill. But the plan was thwarted when a police officer picked up one of the apples and saw that the core had been tampered with.[34] Cops scrambled to move the horses and collect the poisoned apples.

Whitey's oddest anti-busing protest took place far from South Boston, forty miles south at another symbolic site. In 1976, Whitey gave dynamite to a South Boston man and instructed him to place it on historic Plymouth Rock, where the Pilgrims are said to have waded ashore in the seventeenth century. The explosion chipped the rock slightly and blew a hole in the sand, but the rock survived mostly unscathed.[35] "The symbolism, the way Jimmy saw it, was to aim this at the original settlers, because it was the Yankees, the Brahmins, who were pushing the busing on us," said Kevin Weeks, Whitey's longtime associate. It was dubious logic at best, but logic did not predominate when busing was the subject in Southie. "Jimmy hated busing. Hated what it did to Southie," Weeks said. "We all did. So he did what he had to do. We all did."[36]

Unlike some of the haters who stood on street corners hurling rocks and epithets, Bill Bulger had a history of supporting civil rights. In the 1960s, he brought a Boston College Law School classmate, David Nelson, to speak on interracial justice at St. Monica's Church. Nelson, who would later become the first black to sit as a district judge in Boston's federal court, was a lawyer and a member of the Catholic Interracial Council, a civil rights advocacy group. Nelson said his remarks were well received, and he considered Bill Bulger a progressive on civil rights. But his opinion changed after watching how Bulger comported himself during the busing crisis. "I know he has loyalties," Nelson said. "I know he has a strong sense of family. But I hold Billy responsible as a leader. He came to the conclusion that desegregation was a bad idea, that busing was an atrocious idea, so I can allow that on an intellectual basis. On the other hand, he really preferred no response to, 'What then, if not busing? What then, if not desegregation?' Billy, in my view, had more power and influence than anyone to at least assuage, and ultimately do away with the kind of hatred and anger and regressiveness, by reason of his strength and leadership. I don't think he did much to do that."

Nelson saw Bill as very much a product of Southie's self-image as a place apart. "But it's that kind of notion that can't work. You can't have a city or any large entity viewed as pockets, as separate countries."[37] Nelson came to judge Bill Bulger as much for his limitations as for his strengths. What he didn't know, couldn't know, is that, in the midst of the racial turmoil of busing, another Bulger—Whitey— had quietly intervened on his behalf.

Nelson was a law partner of Joe Oteri, a lawyer whose powerful courtroom skills had attracted as clients several of Whitey Bulger's criminal associates. One night, in the middle of the busing crisis, Oteri brought Nelson to his mother's house in South Boston for dinner. The two were out on the sidewalk, outside the house, when they were surrounded by a group of teenagers. "We don't want niggers around here," one of the teens snarled. "Get outta here."

Oteri stood in front of Nelson to protect him. An ex-marine, he was more angry than scared. "Hey, I grew up here. This is my mother's house," Oteri said, and as soon as he said it, he regretted it. The teens grew more agitated and closed in. Oteri's elderly uncle sprang from the house, telling the kids to scatter. Eventually they left, leaving a trail of profanity and racial insults.

Oteri feared he had exposed his mother to retaliation. At the least, he worried that the young men would return and vandalize the house. He had an idea of how to avoid that—he called Steve Flemmi, who had done some business with Oteri's firm. He explained the situation to Flemmi before broaching the real reason for his call. "Stevie," Oteri said, "do you think you could ask Jimmy Bulger to make sure nothing happens here?"

A week later, Oteri was in his law office when he got a phone call from someone who identified himself as one of the teenagers that accosted him on the sidewalk. The kid apologized for his loutish behavior outside Mrs. Oteri's house. "We were out of line," the kid said, sheepishly. "It won't happen again."[38] Joe Oteri put the phone down, knowing two things: No one would ever bother his mother on account of David Nelson's visit for dinner, and Whitey Bulger controlled more than just the rackets in Southie.

Whitey's response to busing was visceral but at the same time carefully calibrated. He stepped in at times, as he did with Oteri, conscious of not letting things get completely out of hand. More than looking after his own interests, Whitey was looking after those of his politician brother.

As winter turned to spring in 1975, the busing crisis had left Mayor Kevin White politically vulnerable in the white working-class sections of the city, which traditionally had the highest voter turnout in Boston. In South Boston, many people called for one of their own to challenge Mayor White. The two leading politicians in the neighborhood, Bill Bulger and Ray Flynn, were testing the waters, trying to figure out whether they had a shot. Bill Bulger was the state senator, and Flynn was the state representative. Their supporters were growing more enthusiastic about their prospects, and there was a lot of talk going around the town about who had the best shot. In the bars and restaurants, there was a lot of trash talking, too. "It got a little nasty," recalls Brian Wallace, Flynn's top aide. "I think there was a sense on both sides that our guy could do it if they tried. And I think there was a sense that only one could run. If both of them did, they'd split the Southie vote and the rest of the anti-busing vote in the city. So there was a lot of jockeying for position, not by Billy and Ray so much as people who wanted them to run."

Wallace had just returned to his family's house one afternoon when the phone rang. His father answered.

"Brian," his father called out. "It's for you."

"Who is it?"

"Some guy named Jim," his father said.

Wallace took the phone and said hello.

"Brian," the voice on the other end said, "this is Jimmy Bulger."

Like everybody else in Southie, Brian Wallace knew who Whitey Bulger was, but he had never spoken to him before.

"What's wrong?" Wallace asked.

"Nothing," Whitey replied. "I'd just like to talk to you about something."

"Where are you?" Wallace asked.

"I'll be right outside," Whitey said. "In a blue car."

Wallace gulped. "Okay," he said, "I'll be right out."

His father, who had been standing there listening to the conversation, took the phone and hung it up.

"It's Whitey Bulger," Wallace told his father. "He wants to talk to me."

"I don't want you going out there," his father said.

"Dad," Wallace replied, "I've got to. It's Whitey Bulger. I've got to see what he wants."

For about twenty minutes, the gangster didn't appear to want anything; he just drove Wallace around town. They drove past the high school, quiet after the school buses had left. They drove past the lines of double-parked cars on East Broadway, all the way to City Point, then down along the water, past the yacht clubs and Carson Beach. Wallace didn't dare speak. Whitey eventually broke the ice. "I was going to hit you last night," Whitey said. "I followed you."

Whitey named each of the bars Wallace and a group of his friends had been in the night before. How long they had stayed. What they were wearing. Where they had gone next. Wallace realized that Whitey had followed him for hours. He sat quietly as Whitey drove slowly through the projects where he grew up. Wallace was twenty-five years old, a low-level political operative whom everybody remembered as a good basketball player at Southie High.

He was, as they'd say in Southie, harmless. "Why would you hit me?" Wallace asked, almost in a whisper.

"This is a small town, Brian," Whitey replied. "There's a lot of nasty things being said about my brother."

"I love your brother Billy," Wallace interjected.

Whitey turned and glared at him, and Wallace didn't say anything else.

"You know who I mean. You know who they are, what they're saying, and I can't have them talking about my family, disrespecting my family. You're right in the middle of this. You are tolerating this. You are encouraging this. These are people who are with you. They are Ray Flynn's people. And you're going to have to get them to stop. Or else."

He told Wallace he decided to let him live, in part, because Wallace was dating the daughter of a man who worked for Whitey's bookmaking network. "I gave you a pass," Whitey told Wallace. "But that's your only pass. I can't kill Ray Flynn. But I can kill you. I could walk into the Bayview [pub] and put one behind your ear and no one would say anything."

As they idled at a traffic light, Whitey turned to Wallace and Wallace found himself staring into the cold, blue eyes he had heard others talk about all those years. "Brian," Whitey said, "I've killed twenty-six people in my life. Killing you would be easy."

They talked for a half hour, as Whitey continued to snake his car around Southie. Wallace said little, but piped up when Whitey accused him of backing Kevin White. "I'd never be with White," Wallace said. "I'd never be with anybody who supports busing."

Whitey smiled and the menace was suddenly gone, evaporated. They started talking about mutual acquaintances, Southie stories and characters. It was like flipping a light switch. The intimidating face was now beaming. The ominous voice was pitched higher, almost a lilt. When Whitey dropped him off at his house, Wallace felt dizzy. The conversation had begun with Whitey saying he had spent the previous night picking a spot to shoot him. It ended with a handshake, with Whitey as friendly as could be. All in the course of an hour.

Wallace spent the next few weeks exhorting Flynn loyalists to tone down the rhetoric. And in the end, neither Bill Bulger nor Ray Flynn challenged Kevin White.

Sometime after his long drive and talk with Whitey, Brian Wallace met some friends at Triple O's and a waitress came over and handed him a beer.

"What's this?" he said. "I didn't order this."

"It's on him," the waitress said, using a thumb to indicate Whitey, who was standing at the back of the bar, his back to the wall.

"I really don't want it," Wallace said.

The waitress stared at Wallace, then tossed her hair and said, as she turned on her heel, "Then you go fuckin' tell him."

Wallace thought about it for a few moments. Then he grabbed the beer and held it aloft toward Whitey in a show of appreciation. Whitey didn't even look over.[39]

The Bulger brothers defended their town the way they knew best: Bill with eloquence, Whitey with menace. But the fallout from the busing controversy had deep implications for both of them. After the schools were desegregated, so were the housing projects in the late 1980s, including the one where Whitey had grown up and lived occasionally with his mother until she died in 1980. Whitey's power was based in part on the perception of his ruthlessness; that he controlled the whole neighborhood as an unseen but all-seeing force. It was a perception that didn't resonate with outsiders who moved in from neighborhoods in which the name Whitey Bulger meant nothing. As South Boston became less racially homogeneous and more economically diverse, Whitey Bulger's reputation and power ebbed.

Busing changed the town in other ways, too. Many of the natives who moved to the suburbs to escape busing were replaced by younger, more affluent outsiders. Three-deckers that had been rented for generations were sold, floor by floor, as condominiums. The seedy bars that had served generations of longshoremen and factory workers were replaced by gleaming pubs with polished wood and French doors. Whitey's gambling business suffered, especially as the legal, state-run lottery grew. The 1980s saw him turn to other ways to make money. Extorting the growing number of drug dealers in Southie became his most lucrative business.

The busing crisis affected Billy's prospects to an even greater extent. His impassioned defense of his neighborhood made him more popular than ever in South Boston. But if he was the political pope of Southie, his defiant stance against busing carried with it a perception of intolerance that made him unelectable outside of his own district. His stance, however, did not affect his popularity with peers in the state senate. He became the body's president in 1978 and held the position for eighteen years, longer than anyone in state history. But his opposition to busing had defined him to an outside world, and his ambitions were permanently circumscribed.

In contrast, Ray Flynn was able to move his political career beyond the confines of South Boston, despite being as closely associated with the anti-busing movement as Bill Bulger had ever been. Flynn was elected mayor of Boston in 1983, during a campaign against a black candidate that was notable for its conciliatory tone. Bill Bulger accused Flynn of abandoning the neighborhood for political gain. That didn't, however, stop him from asking Flynn to make John Connolly, Billy's old friend and Whitey's FBI handler, the police commissioner of Boston. Flynn declined to do so, as he had his own preferred candidate: Mickey Roache, whose brother had been shot and paralyzed during the Southie gang war and who would focus as commissioner on racial reconciliation. Flynn's snub of Connolly earned him Bill Bulger's lasting enmity. Whitey also hated Flynn. His man, Kevin Weeks, bragged of punching the future mayor when Flynn dropped into Triple O's for a drink in the 1970s.

Busing also changed, irrevocably, the Bulger brothers' relationship with their old friend Father Drinan. The priest had been an active booster of Whitey's rehabilitation, and even served as his parole adviser, a gesture that facilitated Whitey's release. But Drinan, who served in Congress from 1971 to 1981 and filed the first impeachment resolution against President Nixon in 1974, had also been the driving force, and legal mind, behind Massachusetts' efforts to desegregate its schools. After busing, Bill Bulger's and Drinan's relationship was strained, at best.

Drinan died in 2007, and his sister-in-law, Helen Drinan, said he sometimes lamented that his efforts on Whitey's behalf had come to so little. Helen Drinan was married to Father Drinan's brother, a doctor, and it was over Sunday dinner at their Newton home, not far from the Boston College campus, that Father Drinan would sometimes talk about his lost sheep, Whitey Bulger. Father Drinan corresponded with, and intervened on behalf of, many convicts, but Whitey stood out because of his supportive family and because of his intelligence. Whitey's letters from prison, Father Drinan told his family, were written with almost perfect grammar. Father Drinan "kept track of people who came to him for advice. And he took it personally when they failed," Helen Drinan said. "He invested a lot of his personal time in Bulger. He knew the family, and when Whitey Bulger went to prison, Bob wrote to him very regularly. Bob said he [Whitey] was very intelligent, and that he could have been anything he wanted to be, but apparently he wanted to be a criminal."

"Bob was very sad," Helen Drinan said. "He spent a lot of time trying to keep him straight. And at one point, he thought the man had gone straight. But it all changed. He felt he was a flop."

Father Drinan's outspoken support for busing alienated more than the Bulgers. "There were many people in Boston who disagreed with Bob about that," she said. "The Bulgers might have been more outspoken, but they weren't alone."[40] And the ranks of the critics of the integration experiment, and Garrity's order, would only grow, for if the intention behind busing was noble, its implementation was an utter disaster. Thousands of white families moved out of Boston for the suburbs, so that within a few years of busing's introduction the schools were more segregated than ever. Even the *Boston Globe*, busing's leading media champion, admitted as much. "Busing has been a failure in Boston," the paper editorialized on the twentieth anniversary of Judge Garrity's order. "It achieved neither integration nor better schooling."

Twenty years after Whitey firebombed JFK's birthplace, FBI agents searching Whitey's home office in Southie seized a stash of books and papers. One of the books was *Southie Won't Go*, a diary of a teacher at South Boston High during the first two years of busing. Whitey had circled a paragraph on page 117 of the book that describes news accounts of the firebombing of the kitchen of John F. Kennedy's birthplace and the spray painting of "Bus Teddy" on the front sidewalk. In the book's margin were the neatly printed words: *Mary Jo K. wishes Teddy was in the kitchen having coffee that evening—so do others.*

Mary Jo Kopechne was the passenger in Ted Kennedy's car who drowned when he drove off a bridge on Chappaquiddick Island in 1969. In Whitey's world, Ted Kennedy's death would have avenged her. And Southie, too.

PART TWO

THE REIGN

7

A Beautiful Friendship

When Steve Flemmi finally came home in 1974 after five years on the lam, it was time for hoodlums of a certain standing in town to celebrate the prodigal's return. And that meant at Chandler's. The party that night at the South End bar where peace had been brokered in the Southie gang war a few years back attracted a particularly rich cross-section of Boston's underworld, a mix of Flemmi's old partners from Winter Hill and a bevy of local Mafiosi. Loud men in loud shirts slapped Flemmi on the back. Made guys in leather jackets kissed him on both cheeks. Women in tight dresses kissed him on the mouth. As at a political function or high-society event, it was important to be there, to be counted in that number. In the dim light of the room, Flemmi noticed someone standing off to the side, leaning against the mahogany bar set on an antique brick base. It was a face he hadn't seen for years: Whitey Bulger.[1] They shook hands. Whitey said they should talk soon. Flemmi said he'd like that. They agreed to meet at the Marshall Street garage.

In Flemmi's absence, Whitey had become a core member of the Winter Hill Gang. He was now, with Flemmi's return, one of six partners in a lawless firm—a senior partner, in fact. In addition to the proceeds from the Killeens' territory, he was getting a cut of Winter Hill's extensive gambling and loansharking business. Some gangsters would have been jealous; Flemmi was impressed, not only that Whitey had survived the war with the Mullens but that he had emerged as the leader of the merged Southie gangs, handpicked by Howie Winter, the Winter Hill boss. If Howie thought Whitey was the most capable of the Southie gangsters, that was good enough for Steve Flemmi.[2]

He had met Whitey only a couple of times before the encounter in Chandler's, but Flemmi remembered him as an ambitious guy who, while still on parole, used to drop by his after-hours club on Dudley Street in Roxbury. Flemmi's club was more than a spot to get booze after the bars closed; it was something of a recruiting stall for gangsters, a place to find criminal partnerships and broker opportunities. When Flemmi first met him, Whitey had been trolling for a partner. Now, back in town after five years, it was Flemmi who was looking. He had to reestablish himself not only within Winter Hill but beyond it.

Not long after the welcome-home party, Flemmi bumped into Paul Rico's old FBI partner, Dennis Condon. Rico was now posted in Miami, but Condon told Flemmi he had nothing to worry about. Condon had removed the old federal fugitive warrants for the murder of Billy Bennett and the car bombing that maimed John Fitzgerald, the lawyer—the crimes that had forced Flemmi to flee town.[3] Flemmi knew that Condon's assurances implied a quid pro quo. He was expected to resume providing information to the FBI. What he didn't know was that the FBI wanted to pair him with Whitey.

While the Winter Hill Gang had dozens of associates and scores of bookies working for it, the hardcore membership was small: Howie Winter, the leader, plus Jimmy Sims, Joe McDonald, John Martorano, Whitey Bulger, and Steve Flemmi. Within the gang itself, there was no rigid hierarchy of capos and soldiers after the fashion of the Mafia; members were free to break off and make separate partnerships as long as common interests weren't impaired. In the mid-1970s, Winter Hill began extorting independent bookmakers, shaking them down for the privilege of taking bets on Winter Hill's sprawling turf. Whitey and Flemmi volunteered to take on this new front, to go out as a team and squeeze the bookies.

They were kindred spirits, their instincts and their taste for brutality remarkably in sync. One day early in their dealings, Flemmi looked on approvingly as Whitey threatened a bookie named Bernie Weisman with an ax. Weisman collapsed, clutching his chest. But he recovered, and he started paying.[4] And they were alike in other ways. Loners in a dangerous trade, they were men with an incongruous need for domestic tranquillity who could yet never settle for one woman. And they were men who considered themselves principled and patriotic, even as they murdered with equanimity and corrupted law enforcement. Over time, they became partners who trusted no one but each other.

As kids, they had both floundered at school, not from lack of intelligence but lack of interest; both got their GEDs in the military. As criminals, they were wary of affiliating with big groups, preferring to maximize their profits while minimizing the risk of being cheated or informed on. For all their troubles at school and in large organizations like the military, they were clearly smarter, and wilier, than most of their criminal associates.

Together, they represented the two main ethnic strands of organized crime in Boston in the twentieth century, which made them an attractive tandem for an FBI that needed eyes and ears in both camps. Bulger's parents were the children of Irish immigrants, while Flemmi was the oldest son of Italian immigrants who settled in the Roxbury section of Boston. Unlike Southie, where the Irish formed a substantial majority, and the North End, which was almost exclusively Italian in those years, Roxbury was a hodgepodge of ethnic groups and races. Italians, Irish, and Jews shared the neighborhood throughout the first half of the twentieth century, and then, as African Americans began to move north in great numbers, Roxbury evolved into the city's most populous black neighborhood. Some

Italian kids from Roxbury, including Flemmi's first criminal partner, Frank Salemme, hoped, like their North End peers, to join the
Mafia. But Flemmi didn't share that aspiration. He was more comfortable with the ethnic blend and freedom of maneuver he knew in
Roxbury, without the restrictions of the relatively stratified Mafia
hierarchy. His after-hours club drew a noticeably integrated crowd
in a starkly segregated city. Some of the bookies who paid him to
operate were black, and many of the gamblers were, too. He was an
enthusiastically equal opportunity gangster and extortionist.

Flemmi's father Giovanni was a bricklayer and also owned a
pushcart from which he sold costume jewelry and quahogs. Anything to make a buck. Giovanni was also famously frugal. When
he died in 1991 at the age of ninety-eight, his sons were stunned to
learn that he had amassed from his humble labor seventy thousand
dollars in savings.[5]

The Flemmi boys were living proof that in the working-class
neighborhoods of Boston, the same household could produce a cop
and a criminal. Flemmi and his younger brother Jimmy "The Bear"
were prolific killers, while their younger brother Michael joined the
Boston police. Stevie was, in matters of business, far more circum-
spect than Jimmy. A few days after Christmas in 1964, Jimmy got
into an argument with a smalltime hood named George Ashe, and
he wasn't one to end an argument just with words. As Ashe remon-
strated from the front seat of his car, Jimmy pulled a gun and shot
him through the open window. Two police officers watched the
whole episode, but instead of arresting Jimmy, they went directly
to Steve Flemmi's store and told him what had happened. Flemmi
handed the cops a thousand dollars, a late Christmas present, then
went and chastised his brother, saying he was lucky to have shot
Ashe in front of two cops on the take.[6]

But it was Jimmy who introduced Flemmi to the world where
the interests of cops and criminals intersect, where the two sides
could happily coexist for mutual benefit. Jimmy had worked as an
informant for Rico and Condon in the 1960s, and not only had the

agents turned a blind eye to his many murders, they had framed four men, two of them Mafia leaders, for one of his killings.* Steve Flemmi would come to know this dark, compromised side of the FBI—its blinding fixation on the Mafia—better than Jimmy could have imagined.

Whitey and Stevie mirrored each other in still other ways. They stood out from other gangsters in being obsessed with eating healthy food and with keeping themselves in top physical condition. They worked out daily, and while they spent inordinate amounts of time in bars—Whitey at Triple O's in Southie, Flemmi at the Marconi Club in Roxbury—they drank very little. Too vain to let booze make them puffy, they were fonder of wine with meals than beer, the favored beverage of many criminal comrades who had gone to fat. Their fastidiousness did more than set them apart: they viewed other gangsters as their inferiors, weak-willed, prone to mistakes, more likely to cheat their partners, statistically more likely to get caught. "The rest of the guys were kind of party-type guys. We liked to party also," Flemmi said, noting that he and Bulger were hardly teetotalers. "We weren't square. But we weren't extreme."[7]

While many of their associates read, at most, the racing section of a newspaper, Whitey and Flemmi read books. They were intrigued by military history and were students of Machiavelli. While their associates considered long-distance travel a flight to Miami or Vegas, Whitey and Flemmi were more likely to jet off to Europe, touring old battlefields. But in the end, what really made their partnership unique in town, what brought them together and kept them together for twenty years, was their relationship with the FBI. Their informant status conferred on them a belief that they could do anything as long as they weren't sloppy—and they prided themselves on not being sloppy.

FBI agents Paul Rico and Dennis Condon had put Flemmi on

---

*The framed men—Peter Limone, Henry Tameleo, Louis Greco, and Joseph Salvati—were formally cleared of the 1965 murder of Teddy Deegan, and the Justice Department was ordered to pay them $102 million. Greco and Tameleo died in prison before they were cleared.

the winning side in the Somerville-Charlestown gang war. They had also helped set up rival gangsters, potential competitors, to be murdered. Whitey had risen and prospered without the FBI's assistance but had quickly taken advantage of his newfound status as an FBI informant to engage in a self-serving propaganda effort, giving information about his rivals and covering his own tracks as he killed off what was left of the Mullens gang. And all the FBI wanted in return was for Whitey and Flemmi to tell them whatever they knew about the Mafia.

When the two men got together at the garage after that spirited evening at Chandler's, Whitey took Flemmi aside and, out of earshot of the other Winter Hill members, explained how John Connolly had recruited him and why. It was a stunning disclosure, not to mention a potentially deadly one, but Whitey had a specific purpose. Flemmi read between the lines, and got it: Connolly must have told Bulger that Flemmi, too, was an informant, and that the FBI wanted him and Whitey to join forces. It would be their little secret, and their huge advantage. Theirs was a partnership envisioned, encouraged, and sanctioned by the FBI.[8] It would make them unstoppable.

Unlike other Boston criminals, the Winter Hill Gang was not afraid of the Mafia. There was an uneasy alliance between the two organizations. The Mafia had all the trappings of power, and they had popular culture cachet, but the Winter Hill boys were not much impressed. They knew their Mafia counterparts and considered them soft and spoiled, living on their reputations. In New York, the Mafia was unrivaled. In Boston, the Irish gangsters' wild, unpredictable violence, and their superior numbers, forced the Italian organization to appease or even employ them. "If we had a competition with the Mafia, we would absolutely, positively destroy them and they knew it," Flemmi said.[9]

Because he was Italian, and because of his reputation as a moneymaker who could handle a gun, Flemmi was frequently courted by the Mafia. But he always demurred. He told Whitey his anti-Mafia attitude could be traced to the late 1950s, when Larry Baione, a Mafia leader, refused to honor a three-thousand-dollar winning number one of Flemmi's gambling customers had picked. Baione contended that because the bookie carrying the slip was arrested before depositing the wagers with the North End, the bet was technically never made.[10] Flemmi concluded then and there that, if the likes of Baione would chisel him on such a small matter, the Mafia's claim to prestige and to being "men of honor" was nonsense, a finely constructed myth. He humored Mafiosi like Baione when they tried to recruit him, and whatever they told him went straight to the FBI.

Not long after he agreed to be an informant for John Connolly in September 1975, and had intimated to Flemmi that he knew of his arrangement with Dennis Condon, Whitey suggested that Flemmi meet with Connolly. "All of us?" Flemmi asked.[11] No, Whitey replied. Go alone. Get your own read on Connolly. Whitey put the meeting together like a social secretary, picking a coffee shop in Newton, believing it unlikely that other gangsters would be anywhere nearby.

There had been a changing of the guard at the FBI office in Boston. Rico, who had developed Flemmi as an informant, had retired. Condon, Rico's partner, who had inherited Flemmi as an informant, was about to retire, too. Connolly was the new sheriff in town, the FBI agent who handled the top-echelon informants, gangsters who provided information to the FBI even as they remained criminally active. When Flemmi arrived at the coffee shop, he saw that Condon and Connolly were there, waiting for him. Their pitch to him was noticeably similar to the justification that Whitey had given Flemmi when he had divulged his relationship with Connolly: They could save themselves by giving up the Mafia. Flemmi was friendly with Gennaro "Jerry" Angiulo, who led the Mafia in Boston but reported to the boss of the New England Mafia family based in Rhode Island. Flemmi also knew Baione, the Mafia's consigliere. His access was unmatched. But as he sat there, stirring his coffee,

Flemmi quickly grasped that the new deal would be different from the one he'd had in the 1960s. He was going to be part of a team with Whitey, something new and strange for both of them.[12]

Flemmi said he'd think it over, but he didn't really think he had any options. He couldn't very well go back and tell his Winter Hill partners that Whitey wasn't just getting information from Connolly but giving it; Whitey could simply out him as an informant as well, and neither of their lives would be worth much. The risk was less in joining forces with Whitey than in defying him. Flemmi was in, and Connolly would be his handler, too. It was two for the price of one. While the rest of Winter Hill knew that Whitey was talking to Connolly, they had no idea that now Flemmi was, too, at least a couple of times a month. Whitey and Flemmi kept their secret close. Connolly's arrangement, to have two gangsters working in concert with each other, was highly unusual for the FBI. He even admitted that, when he sat down to type up reports, he would sometimes confuse and conflate the contributions of the two.[13] But it was not an innocent mistake; it was a conscious effort by Connolly to make Whitey appear Flemmi's equal as a source of information on the Mafia, when the truth was that Whitey had little to give. He didn't trust the Italian mob, and the feeling was mutual. Mafia leaders respected Whitey, but they didn't like him because he was violent and independent, which made him unpredictable, a man to be feared more than welcomed.[14]

In what would become a pattern, Connolly falsified reports and credited Whitey with detailed information about the activities of a Mafia leg breaker. But eight months later, in a memo that justified keeping Flemmi on as an informant, Connolly credited Flemmi for the same information. It was Flemmi, not Whitey, who associated with the Mafia figures on a regular basis.[15]

Connolly not only allowed Whitey and Flemmi to believe they were, as Whitey put it, strategists and not snitches, thus avoiding in their minds the stigma of the rat; he bought into it, adopting the language they used. "These guys were not informants, they were strategists," Connolly insisted. "They were never paid and we could never ask them to hurt their friends. Their deal was, if the Mafia wants to play checkers, we'll play chess."[16]

Connolly also insisted that neither he personally nor the FBI as an agency gave Whitey and Flemmi the green light to commit murders to enhance their cover. But he acknowledged that they were killers, and that they were encouraged to do everything short of murder. To Connolly, it seemed naïve in the extreme to imagine you could recruit top-level criminals as sources and then expect them to mend their ways. If they were to be of any use at all and remain credible with the mobsters they mixed with, Whitey and Flemmi had to stay their brutal selves. "They were like Mafia members," Connolly said. "You're dealing with stone killers. That's who you're trying to recruit. Then you're supposed to tell them you can't do that anymore? Are you shitting me?"[17]

Whitey and Flemmi were anything but shy about playing this two-sided game. They became in fact, the epitome of lethal hypocrisy, and would spend a decade killing people who were, for the most part, actual or potential informants for law enforcement. And whenever they went out on a hit, Whitey and Flemmi preferred the company of their friend and Winter Hill partner John Martorano.

Martorano had grown up in a well-to-do family in Milton, an affluent suburb just south of Boston. His father ran a restaurant and successful after-hours club that attracted a gangster clientele. Martorano attended a prestigious Catholic prep school in Rhode Island; among his well-heeled classmates was a poor kid on scholarship who would grow up to be the CBS newsman Ed Bradley. Like a lot of well-off suburban kids, Martorano went to summer camps in the Berkshires. But he found himself drawn more to the hit men who drank at his father's bar in downtown Boston than to his classmates who went on to the Ivy League. He started working at his father's place right out of high school, learning things they didn't teach in college.

Unlike Whitey and Flemmi, Johnny Martorano didn't watch what he ate, didn't count his drinks, and had trouble keeping count of how many people he had shot. While Whitey and Flemmi were discreet with their cash, Martorano was flashy. He wore a huge Rolex on his wrist and drove a big Mercedes-Benz. But whatever Martorano lacked in self-discipline he more than made up for in his utter and complete willingness to kill anyone, anywhere, especially at the behest of a friend. And Whitey and Flemmi were his friends. He committed his first murder in 1965, when he was twenty-four, at Flemmi's request. There was a guy named Bobby Palladino who Flemmi thought might implicate his brother Jimmy in a murder. Martorano shot Palladino before he could give up Jimmy Flemmi.[18] Killing snitches, or potential snitches, became his forte. He had no idea that the two men who most often put him up to this were snitches themselves.

Flemmi was on the lam in Canada when Whitey and Martorano first went hunting together, dispatching various enemies of Winter Hill. In December of 1973, they went gunning for a rival gangster named James "Spike" O'Toole. O'Toole was one of the last living members of the McLaughlin gang from Charlestown. One night, O'Toole was drinking at Bulldogs, a bar in the Savin Hill section of Dorchester. Eddie Connors, a former boxer who owned Bulldogs, knew O'Toole was on the Winter Hill hit list, and he made a phone call. Before O'Toole had finished his drink, Whitey and Martorano were parked outside the bar. O'Toole had walked a few blocks away from the bar when Whitey pulled the car alongside of him. O'Toole scampered behind a mailbox but Martorano just fired through it.[19]

By Martorano's account, he and Whitey had done a half-dozen murders together by the time they set off with Flemmi on the first of what would be many hits by the trio. It was 1975, and their prey was Eddie Connors, the bar owner, who was himself a marked man, and for more than one reason. There were claims that he had bragged openly about helping Winter Hill kill O'Toole. Howie Winter, meanwhile, worried that Connors could implicate him in an armored car robbery for which Connors was awaiting trial.[20] Connors was a former New England middleweight champion, and that toughness was sometimes useful, but he was also considered a risk to talk if facing a long prison stretch. And so he had to go.

Connors was told that Winter wanted to talk to him. He was instructed to go to a pay phone at the corner of Morrissey Boulevard and Freeport Street, about a half mile from Bulldogs. Shortly after 9:00 p.m. on a rainy June night, Connors pulled his black Lincoln Continental up next to the phone booth and left the car door open and the motor running as he stepped in and waited for the call. A police van parked a few hundred feet away had left moments before, lured away by a phony report of a bad accident nearby. The call Eddie Connors was waiting for never came, but Whitey and Flemmi did, running out of the shadows toward their cornered victim. Whitey fired a sawed-off shotgun, bringing Connors down, then pulled a .38 revolver and emptied it into him as Flemmi raked him with bullets from a carbine.[21]

Connors slumped to the floor of the phone booth. One of his legs protruded through the smashed glass panel. The phone dangled by its cord.[22]

Martorano usually did the shooting, but this time he was the getaway driver. Whitey and Flemmi jumped into the car, adrenaline pumping, and Martorano drove away from the scene at a leisurely speed. They were less than a half mile away when an impatient Whitey ordered Martorano to pull over. Whitey said he knew the area better. They switched places and Whitey pushed his foot to the floor. They were in Somerville fifteen minutes later.[23]

Despite the occasional petty dispute, the three proved a most effective hit team. Flemmi said he and Martorano helped Whitey pick off some of his remaining Mullens gang rivals. And in 1976, the three men got together again to kill Richie Castucci, a bookmaker who doubled as a professional gambler. It was a bad combination, as potentially destructive as an alcoholic owning a barroom; there was always the temptation to sample the product. Flemmi says they killed Castucci because John Connolly had told Whitey that the bookie was, in fact, an FBI informant. More precisely, Castucci had compromised the New York City hiding place of some Winter Hill fugitives. That would have been enough to get him killed, but there was a secondary motive—money. If Winter Hill got rid of Castucci, they wouldn't have to pay two hundred thirty thousand dollars they owed him in gambling debts.[24]

Castucci was called to the garage on Marshall Street on the premise that Winter Hill was going to hand over the first installment of the debt. Martorano told him it was sixty thousand dollars and that they had it at a nearby apartment, where Castucci was welcome to count it. Whitey led Castucci to the apartment and even went so far as to let him start counting a large stack of cash in small bills. Martorano came to the apartment minutes later. Castucci was trying to keep the numbers in his head when Martorano put a snub-nosed .38 revolver to his ear and fired.[25] They stuffed him in a sleeping bag and put him in the trunk of his car.

Richie Castucci, a forty-eight-year-old father of four, was dead, but Winter Hill's gambling debts were not. A good chunk of the two hundred thirty thousand dollars due Castucci was actually owed, through him, to the Mafia in New York. When a few New York Mafiosi came north for a meeting at the Somerville garage to collect, Whitey recognized one of them as someone he had been in prison with.[26] The Mafiosi noticed that the garage was crowded with far more people than cars; Martorano had arranged for fifty local gangsters to be on hand as a show of force.[27] They stood around in wary clusters in the service bays. The New York Mafiosi were chaperoned by Sonny Mercurio, a Mafia soldier in Boston who later became John Connolly's informant on the recommendation of Whitey and Flemmi.[28] The Mafia men started shaking their heads when Martorano told them Winter Hill wouldn't pay because Castucci had been a snitch and so had his bookie partner.[29] It was a standoff rich with irony: one FBI informant outed, another killed, all at the behest of another FBI snitch named Whitey Bulger. But Winter Hill's ploy worked. The Mafia men walked away empty-handed.

Still, Whitey and Flemmi weren't satisfied with taking Castucci's life and wiping out the gambling debt. They also wanted Castucci's financial interest in The Squire, a popular and highly profitable strip club in Revere. Castucci's widow, Sandra, was terrified when Flemmi showed up unexpectedly at her Revere Beach home a year after her husband's slaying. He asked about the stake in the club and suggested he should handle it for her. She had never met Flemmi but knew of his reputation. She reported the visit to her husband's partner. The Mafia quickly got involved, and this time they won. New England Mafia boss Raymond L. S. Patriarca summoned Sandra Castucci to a meeting in a back room of a store in Providence, Rhode Island. The Don told her that he was seizing her husband's share of the club because he had died owing him money. Sandra Castucci was left with nothing, but she was too frightened to go to the police. And the FBI, which knew she had been fleeced, looked the other way.[30]

The murder of Richie Castucci demonstrated to Whitey and Flemmi that the FBI would protect them no matter what. Whitey and Flemmi knew they could even kill other informants and it would be excused by the bureau as the cost of doing business with dangerous people. Years later, Castucci's handler, FBI agent Tom Daly, was asked, "What, if anything, did you do to investigate the murder of your own informant?"

"Nothing," Daly replied.[31]

Sometime in the mid-1970s, Joe Oteri's law office in downtown Boston became Whitey's and Flemmi's favored meeting spot. It was much plusher than the garage in Somerville and contained exercise equipment of the sort the mobsters enjoyed. Health clubs were the craze at the time, but Whitey and Flemmi couldn't be bothered paying for memberships or mixing with strangers. They used the law office's state-of-the-art gym instead. The office was typically thick with Winter Hill gangsters; Oteri's firm represented a number of them. Whitey and Oteri knew each other well, going back to elementary school days. One of the most successful criminal defense lawyers in town, Oteri was also a Southie guy, and a marine. He had attended the Hart School in South Boston with Whitey. Oteri remembered Whitey as the kid who just walked out of school.

As the son of Italian immigrants, Oteri had a different perspective on the clannishness of South Boston. The Irish, so dominant in numbers, dominated the Italians. "I never knew I was Italian," Oteri said. "I thought I was a guinea, because that's all I was ever called." In those days, there was a matter-of-factness about the bigotry in Southie, an air of innocence about—or was it indifference to?—the invidious ethnic divides. Because a large number of Italian families clustered around Emmet Street in South Boston, the locals called it "Guinea Emmett," almost with fondness. Almost. "We had a fight a week," Oteri said. "The Irish kids would call us guineas until someone fought."

The animosity was the product of immigration patterns and a change in the fortunes of the various groups. The Irish were treated poorly by the Brahmins when they filled Boston during the second half of the nineteenth century. By the time the Italians began arriving in great numbers in the early part of the twentieth century, the Irish had been able to make serious inroads in politics and filled the police and fire departments and other municipal jobs with their own. The Italians were on the lower rung, and the Irish wouldn't let them forget it. "Ethnicity was terribly important in the city, but nowhere more so than Southie," said Oteri. "And especially down around Andrew Square and the projects, so Whitey would have grown up in that."

But Oteri was not surprised that when it came to picking a business partner, Whitey chose Flemmi. "My best friend growing up was an Irish kid," Oteri said. "On a personal basis, everything was fine. But in a group, we were all guineas. It was groupthink, not individual think. Whitey and Stevie were very similar as persons, that's why they teamed up. The Irish-Italian thing didn't have anything to do with it, except that the FBI wanted to go after the Mafia and Whitey and Stevie knew what was good for them."

Oteri's office was in Post Office Square, right across from the federal courthouse where more than a few of his clients had regular appointments. Whitey and Flemmi started dropping by the office every other day, mainly to use the gym. "They liked the free weights," Oteri said. "They were very competitive, trying to lift more than each other." After a workout, they would sit around, having lunch and shooting the breeze. Whitey would pick at his salad and sneer as Oteri bit into a hamburger. "That stuff'll kill ya," Whitey told him.

When they discussed cases, Whitey was anxious to impress. One day, as Oteri debated the option of taking a plea or going to trial in the case of a Winter Hill associate, Whitey said, "Joe, that is a Scylla and Charybdis."

Oteri laughed out loud, and Whitey looked at him with dead eyes.

"Jimmy," Oteri said, holding his hands out, trying to explain his reaction. "I'm not laughing at you. I'm laughing because there's only three guys in Massachusetts who know what you mean: you, me and Alan Dershowitz."

That explanation, an exaggeration meant to flatter, didn't appease Whitey. He looked at Oteri and said, "Yeah, well, I spent nine years in prison and I read a book a day."

Whitey seems to have resented Oteri. Among the tips Whitey was credited with passing along to John Connolly were repeated and unsubstantiated claims that Oteri's law office was being used to traffic cocaine. Oteri said that the claims were nonsense. But on more than one occasion, Connolly's reports cited Whitey as the source of claims that Oteri was not just representing drug traffickers Michael Caruana and Kevin Dailey but that he was in business with them. A report from November 25, 1980, quotes Whitey as claiming that Oteri and other Boston lawyers were snorting cocaine at a fund-raiser for then Norfolk District Attorney William Delahunt at Anthony's Pier 4 restaurant on the South Boston waterfront.

How Whitey Bulger, a convicted felon and, at the time, a notorious hit man, could have known of this is not mentioned in Connolly's report. A political fund-raiser like that would more likely have been the domain of Bill Bulger or his Beacon Hill peers, not his gangster brother.

Oteri doesn't believe Whitey Bulger implicated him in drug trafficking or cocaine use. He believes John Connolly did this on his own, as part of a vendetta Connolly held against some defense lawyers. Connolly, he said, had long been rude to him, in court and in public, addressing him, in Southie fashion, as Guinea Oteri. "There was no reason for Jimmy to do this to me," Oteri said. "I wasn't that close to him, and he knew I was his brother's friend."[32]

But Whitey's need to stay engaged and useful as an informant may have been reason enough. He had to regularly come across with tips, whether true or not. And the information went both ways. In 1978, after five men were gunned down during an after-hours drug robbery at a Boston nightclub called Blackfriars, Whitey asked Connolly to give him a copy of the crime scene photos. Connolly got the photos from contacts in the Boston Police Department and handed them to Whitey, who then brought them to a guy who owed one of the Blackfriars victims, Vincent Solomonte, sixty thousand dollars. Whitey said he was there to collect on behalf of Solomonte's family.

"You remember Vinny, don't you?" Whitey asked, showing the man a photo of the slaughtered Solomonte. The man paid up. Whitey split the money with Flemmi and John Martorano.[33] It was the first, but hardly the last, act of extortion Whitey would commit with the FBI's tacit or active assistance.

In 1979, John Connolly asked his supervisor, John Morris, to meet Whitey Bulger and Steve Flemmi. That wasn't so unusual. The next part of the request was. We should do it at your house, Connolly suggested. Out of the city. Morris lived in Lexington, an upscale suburb.[34]

Morris just nodded and said yeah, yeah. Connolly looked him in the eye. This was serious. Connolly asked Morris to treat Whitey and Flemmi not like criminals but with respect. They weren't just informants; they were analysts, partners, on the same team.

Bringing gangsters to an agent's home was against protocol. It was foolhardy, and dangerous, to expose one's family to criminals who might be able to exploit that knowledge. But Connolly sensed something in Morris even before he asked. Morris had been complaining about the administrative side of his job; he envied the life of a field agent. And he especially envied Connolly, who was a man about town. He knew politicians. He knew everybody. He had respect. Connolly sensed that Morris, in his restlessness and his weakness, could become a useful ally at the bureau.

Morris's wife, Rebecca, with whom he already had a strained relationship, didn't like the idea of having criminals in her house. She refused to cook for them and left the dinner to Morris. He made steak, and as they sat around the table Morris kept filling his own wine glass. Whitey regaled him with stories about Alcatraz, and Flemmi talked about life on the run in Montreal.

Both men noticed how many glasses of wine Morris drank.

They were always looking for a weakness.

Whitey and Flemmi were, however, sympathetic to Morris on one point: They appreciated the difficulty of balancing business and a home life. They seemed to spend as much time juggling their multiple and multilayered domestic situations as they did their booming criminal enterprise. Whitey had been with Teresa Stanley for a decade when, in 1976, he moved her and her children from the projects into a two-story, brick-front colonial house he purchased on Silver Street in South Boston, just a couple of doors down from her mother's home. Whitey moved in, too, sharing the eight-room house, located on a narrow street on Telegraph Hill, around the corner from South Boston High School and the historic Dorchester Heights monument. He was a father to her children, but they never called him Dad. Their nickname for him was Charlie. As much as he loved them, Whitey was quickly overwhelmed by the daily chaos of a house teeming with kids, four of them ages ten to seventeen. There was a part of it that Whitey liked—the nightly family meals, holiday gatherings, and Teresa's unquestioning devotion. But his business kept him out late at night, and Stanley and her children had to tip-toe around the house in the morning so they wouldn't wake him. He moved out, telling Stanley he needed more solitude.[35] Whitey had actually started seeing another woman a year earlier and was getting more serious about her. Catherine Greig was twenty-four when they met and ten years younger than Stanley. By the late 1970s, Whitey began a new routine. He dined at Stanley's nearly every night, then slept elsewhere, usually at Greig's apartment in Quincy.

Theirs was an unlikely pairing. Cathy Greig, who is twenty-two years younger than Whitey, had grown up in City Point, surrounded by the Mullens gang. Her father was a Scottish-born machinist and her mother, a Canadian housewife. It was a dysfunctional house-hold; her father was an alcoholic. Greig, who had a twin sister and a much younger sister and brother, spent most afternoons with her grandmother.[36] The family lived in a three-decker on East Fourth Street, a block from the McGonagles, a huge clan that included Pau-lie McGonagle, the leader of the Mullens, and his brother Bobby, a Boston firefighter.

Many of Greig's classmates at South Boston High School were happy to go into the military or get a civil service job, something safe and secure with a good pension. Her twin sister, Margaret, aspired to be a secretary. But Greig, voted the prettiest girl in her class, declared in the 1969 Southie High yearbook that her personal ambition was "to have a medical career."

She was, like Whitey, a devoted animal lover, and flirted with the idea of going to veterinary school. But after high school she enrolled in a two-year program at the Forsyth School for Dental Hygien-ists, then affiliated with Northeastern University. She proved very good at it; in her second year, Dr. Sigmund Socransky, a prominent periodontist and research scientist, chose Greig to work in his lab. While Greig had previously vowed not to end up a young, married housewife without a career, she nevertheless married Bobby McGonagle, her first serious boyfriend, when she was twenty. When they got back from their honeymoon, McGonagle complained that Greig had sat on the beach and read books the whole time.[37] Greig was caught in the riptide of Southie, saying she aspired to a life outside its confines but married into a large, extended family that was Southie through and through.

The marriage was troubled from the start. McGonagle wanted to go out every night; Greig wanted to stay at home. When McGonagle was caught in a compromising position with Greig's twin sister, he joked to family members that he had confused the two. Greig was heartbroken by her husband and sister's betrayal. McGonagle moved out and resumed the relationship with Margaret. Greig was left with the couple's two miniature Schnauzers. They split up in 1973, but the divorce wasn't finalized until 1977.

Even before the divorce, Greig had begun dating Whitey Bulger. Either she didn't know that Whitey had killed two of her brothers-in-law—Donnie McGonagle by mistake, Paulie McGonagle very much on purpose—or she didn't care. Given her feelings toward the man she married, it may have been the latter, though the circumstances surrounding Donnie McGonagle's murder had not been revealed in the mid-1970s. Paulie McGonagle, meanwhile, had just disappeared, his body secretly buried by Whitey on the other side of Dorchester Bay.

Charles "Chip" Fleming, one of the Boston police detectives who chased Whitey for years, says Cathy Greig pursued Whitey with purpose, seeking him out at the Triple O's. "She did it to get back at her husband," said Fleming. "It was a Southie thing."[38] Even if it was Greig who initiated the romance, Whitey was the one who controlled it.[39] He could be charming and charismatic when he wanted to be, and that was the side he showed to Greig. She worked long hours, taking night classes at Northeastern University while teaching in the Forsyth program during the day, ultimately earning her bachelor's degree. Greig soon started showing off the spoils of dating a gangster. Her co-workers at the dental research facility noticed the new jewels and even a fur coat. "After all she had been through with her ex-husband, I think she just wanted to be loved," said Linda Hanlon, the former dean at Forsyth and a friend of Greig's. "And Jimmy was very good to her. Certainly, in a material way he was."[40]

Greig's colleagues wanted to meet her boyfriend and regularly suggested dinners or meetings for drinks, but Greig always demurred, citing some previous engagement. She did, however, constantly sing Whitey's praises, describing him to colleagues as a generous benefactor of strangers. He paid to fix someone's teeth. He bought someone else a car. Greig knew that some of her colleagues thought Whitey must be a gangster—he had tons of money, but Greig couldn't or wouldn't say much about what he did for a living. She tried to provide an alternative narrative, that he was a Robin Hood figure unfairly maligned by police. Either she was kidding herself or she really believed it. Probably it was a little bit of both.[41]

Steve Flemmi's domestic arrangement resembled Whitey's: He had children with Marion Hussey; the family had dinner together at home most nights; after dinner, he left the house for a younger lover. Marion Hussey was a nineteen-year-old with a baby daughter, Deborah, when she left her husband for Flemmi, then twenty-five and married with two young daughters. Flemmi had separated from his wife and had moved in with Marion and her daughter. Flemmi and Marion Hussey had three children together—Billy, Stephanie, and Stephen—but Flemmi insisted that they take Hussey's last name. He figured, as Whitey had with his son, Douglas, that kids with his name would have a target on their backs. In 1969, when Flemmi fled to evade murder charges, Hussey worked to support her kids. She waited tables and groomed dogs.

In the summer of 1970, while Flemmi was still hiding from the law, he rented a beachfront house for the family in Montauk, on Long Island. It was his attempt to hold the family together as he figured out his new life. They spent the days on the beach. His nine-year-old son, Billy, got caught in a riptide and was being dragged out to sea when Deborah Hussey, now twelve and a strong swimmer, raced out to save him.[42] Deborah had grown up fast: Even before she was in her teens, she had had to look after her siblings while Flemmi was in Canada and Hussey was working. She had also grown into a beauty.

After Flemmi returned to Boston and rejoined the Winter Hill Gang, the family moved into a sprawling mansion in Milton, just south of Boston. Flemmi's cash bought a swimming pool and tennis courts. The family gathered every Sunday for Italian meals cooked by his mother, Mary. They were often joined by Whitey and Teresa Stanley and other gangsters and their girlfriends. Sometimes, Whitey tucked twenty-dollar bills into the kids' pockets.

But the wife and kids and the whole domestic tableau did only so much for Flemmi. He always had girlfriends on the side, and they were always much younger. Debra Davis was the one he kept around the longest. She might have stayed around longer had she not found out about Flemmi and Whitey's relationship with John Connolly and the FBI.

They first met in 1972, when Flemmi, looking for something for one of his girls, dropped into a jewelry store in Brookline. He scanned the display case but was drawn to the young salesgirl standing behind it. Debra Davis was seventeen but seemed older. She was a teenage bride, with her young husband already in jail. And as far as she was concerned, the marriage had ended the moment they'd shut the cell door.

Davis had a bikini model's figure, deep blue eyes, and a dazzling smile. She feathered her blonde hair in a way that, in the 1970s, reminded people of Farrah Fawcett. She'd grown up in a house with nine brothers and sisters. She got married to escape the chaos at home. But that was over, and now there was this older guy named Stevie flirting with her in the store, and so she flirted back.

Flemmi was always attracted to younger women, and Davis was twenty-one years his junior. He was smitten, and Davis knew he could provide a lot more than her jailbird husband. Soon she was living in a high-rise apartment with Flemmi. He gave her clothes and cars—a Jaguar, then a Mercedes, then a Corvette—and took her to the Caribbean. When Davis wanted a proper divorce, Flemmi paid for it. When her husband complained about it from jail, Flemmi sent word that his cooperation was expected. The young man signed the divorce papers and never bothered her again.[43]

Davis's father, Ed, objected to his daughter's dating a middle-aged gangster and took a sledgehammer to one of the cars Flemmi had given her to underscore his displeasure.[44] Ed Davis fell overboard in Boston Harbor and drowned in 1975 while boating with some friends. Flemmi swore he had nothing to do with it, and the death was ruled accidental, but Davis's family remains unconvinced.

Davis talked about marriage. Flemmi talked about divorce. In a bid to impress Davis, he flew to Haiti to get a quickie divorce from his wife. Flemmi brought Davis's brother Mickey with him to be a witness, so Mickey could report back to Davis on his noble gesture. But even after going through all that trouble, Flemmi wouldn't marry Davis and maintained a relationship with Marion Hussey. As the years passed, Davis realized she wanted something more than a free apartment, a free car, and all the money she could spend. She wanted a house, a picket fence, some kids—a normal life. Exactly the things Flemmi couldn't, or wouldn't, give her.[45]

In early 1981, Davis went to Acapulco on a vacation Flemmi paid for but didn't want to go on himself. Davis took her mother, Olga, instead and met a Mexican guy named Gustav. Gustav had made a fortune in the olive oil and poultry business. He was everything Flemmi wasn't: a legitimate businessman, a romantic, an aspiring dad. Gustav talked about kids. He didn't want a mistress; he wanted a wife. Davis and her mother went on and on about Gustav, right in front of Flemmi, thinking maybe it would change his attitude. Instead, Flemmi and Whitey flew down to Mexico, looking for Gustav. They couldn't find him. Whitey, as Flemmi recounted it, believed that if they couldn't kill Gustav, they had better kill Davis; she couldn't be trusted if she wandered out of Flemmi's control. Flemmi said that Whitey was the prime mover in Davis's murder. In letters and in conversations with friends, Whitey has insisted that he didn't kill Davis—indeed, that he has never killed a woman.

Flemmi would later suggest that what got Davis killed was jealousy—not his but Whitey's. Whitey got irked when he called or paged Flemmi and his partner didn't answer because he was with her. To Whitey, this wasn't personal, it was business. He told Flemmi he was going soft, that Davis was taking his edge. They were losing money because Flemmi was preoccupied with his high-maintenance girlfriend. "Bulger kind of resented the fact that I didn't spend enough time with him and our business," Flemmi would later testify.[46]

Flemmi always insisted he loved Davis, but he did two things that got her killed: He told her that he and Whitey had an FBI agent named John Connolly in their pocket, and then he told Whitey that she knew.[47] It wasn't something he intended to do but rather something he blurted out one night when he and Davis were having a romantic dinner in the Bay Tower Room, which afforded panoramic views of Boston from the thirty-third floor of a downtown office building. This was the kind of night that Davis wanted more of, and she was making that very point when Flemmi's pager went off. It was Connolly, asking to meet. Davis was furious; she was also suspicious. Flemmi was always rushing off to meetings and never explaining why. Flemmi tried to assuage her, insisting that it wasn't another woman; that it was Whitey. In fact, he said, it wasn't just Whitey but John Connolly, an FBI agent who'd given Whitey and Flemmi a license to operate as they pleased. Everything he had been able to give Davis was because he and Whitey had an FBI agent on the inside.[48]

It was the one thing about his life that he was never supposed to share, and as soon as Flemmi told Whitey, Davis was as good as dead. Flemmi tried to make a case to let it go—after all, Whitey's closest girlfriends knew John Connolly, too. Flemmi believed they knew Whitey was an informant.[49] But Whitey's girls were Southie girls. They knew the rules. They would stand up. They'd go to jail before they'd talk to the cops. Davis wasn't anything like them. She was a kid, really. She didn't understand the life. She wouldn't stand up. Whitey insisted she had to go. And if Flemmi wouldn't do it, he would.[50]

On September 17, 1981, Flemmi called Davis and said he wanted to see her. She was glad, because she wanted to talk to him anyway, to tell him she wanted to break up. She had gone back to Acapulco, this time for a month, and was more sure of Gustav than ever. "She loved him," her brother Victor said of Gustav. "She was going to marry him. She was preparing to leave Stevie Flemmi, but she was afraid."[51]

Flemmi told Davis he wanted to show her a house on East Third Street in South Boston, saying he had just bought it for his parents. Davis had an eye for design and decorations, and Flemmi said he wanted her to see the house and tell him what she thought. Pat Nee was walking to the old Mullens clubhouse at O and Third, just down the street, when Flemmi pulled over on the way to the house. Flemmi said hello and introduced Davis. Pat Nee took one look at Davis and read her body language: She was pressed against the passenger door, as if she was trying to stay as far away from Flemmi as possible.[52]

Flemmi pulled the car a little further down East Third Street, parked, and walked with Davis toward the property he was buying his parents. It was a nice house with important neighbors. Whitey's brother Bill, now president of the Massachusetts senate, lived next door. Whitey visited his brother's home often. But this time he was hiding in the house Flemmi had bought, waiting for his partner and Davis. After Flemmi led Davis in, Whitey, by Flemmi's account, approached from behind. Davis didn't know he was there until his hands wrapped around her throat. Whitey wouldn't use a weapon to kill a woman. He used his bare hands. It took a few minutes for Whitey to choke the life out of her, and as he did she was looking right into Flemmi's face.*

---

*Steve Flemmi testified on several occasions about the circumstances of Debra Davis's murder, but Whitey has told friends he did not kill her. The authors also viewed letters Whitey has written from jail insisting he did not kill Davis or Deborah Hussey. A jury in US District Court in Boston could not reach a verdict in August 2013 on whether Whitey had killed Davis but found that he had participated in Hussey's slaying.

Whitey was still throttling her as he dragged her toward the cellar stairs. Flemmi did nothing except watch, and then he followed them down to the cellar. Davis was unconscious or maybe already dead. "Let her pray," Flemmi said, as Whitey laid her body on the cellar floor. If Whitey heard him, he ignored him.[53] Flemmi bent down and kissed her on the forehead. "You're going to a better place," he said.

Suddenly, Flemmi was gripped with remorse, and for a moment he thought about killing Whitey right then and there. But that thought passed quickly. Instead, he took out a pair of pliers, knelt down, and started yanking Davis's teeth, to make it harder to identify the body if it was found. Whitey stripped her clothes and wrapped her body in plastic.[54]

Whitey and Flemmi had been in on at least a half-dozen murders together before. But their victims had been men, almost all of them involved in the underworld. The murder of Debra Davis was different, and the decision to kill her strained their partnership. It was the one murder in their many years together in which the only witnesses, by Flemmi's account, were him and Whitey. And they would each blame the other. In the moment, however, the flare-up was swiftly set aside, and they went back into mission mode, preparing to dispose of her body without a word between them.

Just minutes after he'd wrapped Debra Davis in plastic, Whitey walked into the Mullens club and sat next to Pat Nee.

"We need some help," Whitey said. "Stevie's up the street doing Debbie."

"What do you mean, 'doing her'?" Nee asked.

"He's killing her," Whitey replied.[55]

They waited for it to get dark, then put her body in a trunk and drove a few miles over the bridge into Quincy. They buried her in some marshland, next to a train bridge, a few hundred yards away from the busiest road in Boston.[56]

Olga Davis knew something was wrong. Debra wouldn't just disappear without calling her. But Flemmi went to Olga's house and

told her he was on top of it. Debra had gone to Texas, and Flemmi
had sent some people down there to find her. He needed some photos of Davis, he said, to give to the people looking for her. "I'll find
her," Steve Flemmi told Olga Davis. "I'll never stop looking."[57]

Later, Flemmi called a friend and asked him to go to Davis's dentist in Brookline and pull her dental records. As soon as Flemmi got
the records, he destroyed them.[58] He had already torn out her teeth,
but he was obsessed with making sure there was no way Davis would
ever be found and identified. His remorse, if he felt any, was short-
lived. Not long after Flemmi buried Davis, he started having sex
with her thirteen-year-old sister, Michelle, who had been living with
Debra when she vanished.[59] Debra was gone without a trace, and
the two men who killed her were confident her body would never
be found.

There was a perfunctory investigation. FBI agents visited Olga
Davis. She and her sons told the agents they were sure that Flemmi
was behind Debra's disappearance. The FBI men nodded and took
notes, but neither Flemmi nor Whitey was ever interviewed about
Davis. Olga Davis reported her daughter's disappearance to local
police, who entered a missing persons report in the FBI's national
computer database, the National Crime Information Center
(NCIC). Six months after Davis vanished, someone secretly tapped
into the FBI's database and removed the missing persons alert,
falsely claiming she had been spotted in Houston.[60]

Even as some FBI agents were actively engaged in protecting Whitey
and Flemmi, other agents were building a race-fixing case against the
Winter Hill Gang. In the mid-1970s, a Boston-born gangster named
Tony Ciulla had been sent to prison in New Jersey for orchestrating a scam at various racetracks on the East Coast. Given the size
of the conspiracy, Ciulla's sentence of four to six years in New Jersey was relatively light, but even so he offered to give up others for
reduced time. The New Jersey state cops didn't know who he was

talking about when he started throwing around names like Howie and Whitey and Flemmi and Martorano, so the FBI was brought in. Even before the Boston office of the FBI could weigh in, the feds in New Jersey had opened a case and put Ciulla before a grand jury.

In New Jersey, it was a good case. In Boston, it was a massive headache, because among the targets of the investigation were Whitey and Flemmi. John Connolly caught wind of the probe and reached out to Whitey. They met in Connolly's town house in Southie, and Connolly told Whitey he'd meet with his supervisor, John Morris, and the federal prosecutor in Boston who had taken over the New Jersey case, Jeremiah O'Sullivan. Surely, he thought, they would see the folly of losing two informants in the battle against the Mafia because of a two-bit race-fixing case where a few jockeys got beat up. It was 1979, and the FBI was gearing up to take down the local Mafia. Connolly and Morris told O'Sullivan they couldn't afford to lose any of their eyes and ears inside the Italian mob. According to Flemmi, O'Sullivan's response to Connolly and Morris was that he had to consult the case agent, Tom Daly, who was handling Tony Ciulla. If Daly harbored any ill will for his informant Richie Castucci's having been murdered by Whitey only a couple of years earlier, he didn't show it. He signed off, and Whitey and Flemmi skated.

Connolly did elicit a promise from them, however. "We had to give our word we wouldn't kill Tony Ciulla," Flemmi testified.[61] Connolly's stipulation was significant. At no other time when he was identifying informants or potential informants to Whitey and Flemmi did he extract such a promise.

It probably should have dawned on the other members of Winter Hill how odd it was that, of all those who made money from the race-fixing scam, only Whitey and Flemmi avoided being indicted. But Winter and Martorano and Jimmy Sims and Joe McDonald were so relieved that somebody would be left on the outside to watch the gang's interests that they never stopped to consider why. Instead, the gang held a breakup dinner. Johnny Martorano took the sports betting operation and offered a piece to Whitey and Flemmi. Winter, McDonald, and Sims kept the numbers and the loansharking operation.

Johnny Martorano also suggested they start rounding up the independent bookies and force them to pay rent, the way it was done in New York. Whitey and Flemmi were all for that.[62] They did some quick calculations: If they charged a couple of dozen bookies a thousand dollars a month each for the privilege of staying in business and staying alive, they could pull in almost twenty-five thousand dollars a month. The possibilities were tantalizing. Near the dinner's end, Johnny Martorano announced he was going on the lam to avoid the impending indictment. His destination was not exactly imaginative for a wiseguy: Florida. He had barely settled into his digs in Miami when John Connolly pulled Whitey and Flemmi aside. Martorano had been spotted in Miami, Connolly told them.

Whitey and Flemmi scrambled to get word to Martorano: move. They later sat down with Connolly and talked about the benefits of keeping Martorano out of town for a while. It was Connolly, Flemmi said, who went a step further: Martorano should stay on the lam for good. As long as he was out there in the ether, the Mafia wouldn't move on either Flemmi or Whitey, because they knew Johnny would avenge them. Martorano was the most prolific hit man in Boston; and now he was, in a way, even more dangerous, on ice, in Florida.

But the flashy Martorano was a lousy fugitive. Your guy is in Fort Lauderdale, Connolly told Whitey and Flemmi. One of the problems was that so many people from Southie and the rest of the Boston area who knew him routinely traveled to Fort Lauderdale. "He's gotta move again," Whitey said. But when Flemmi called him, Martorano said he couldn't move: He had just gotten new furniture.[63] After a while, he relented. He headed to Boca Raton. The FBI would later insist they were hot on his tail from the moment Martorano went on the run. Connolly was doing all he could to keep him from being nabbed, because Martorano had killed too many people. If he got locked up, he might be tempted to talk and cut a deal. He had to stay out there.

Sometime after the Winter Hill breakup meeting, Flemmi drove out to the state prison in Shirley, in central Massachusetts, where Howie Winter had been incarcerated in another extortion case. He explained to Winter how things had been split up and assured him his share would be taken care of. Winter understood. He only had one request. "You guys gotta leave the garage," he said. "I'm gonna rent it out."[64]

So the gangsters cleared out of the garage on Marshall Street, the seedy headquarters for so much plotting and mayhem. Years later, Howie Winter's old stomping ground, where Whitey Bulger first grasped the reins of power in Boston, would be transformed into an evangelical church.

8

Lancaster Street

With the garage on Marshall Street on the rental market, and
their Winter Hill partners either locked up or on the run,
Whitey and Flemmi needed a new base of operations. They found it
on one of the narrow side streets near the Boston Garden, where the
Boston Bruins and Boston Celtics play. Lancaster Street was perfect
because it was within walking distance of the North End, where the
Mafia had its headquarters, and where Whitey and Flemmi were
expected to gather useful information for the FBI. The street was
also one-way and didn't connect to major thoroughfares, as surrounding streets did. There were few businesses on the block. If you
didn't belong there, you stood out. They set the place up as a working car repair shop. Like the one in Somerville, it had the look of
a legitimate business. It became the meeting place of men whose
business was anything but on the level.

It was also soon a target for surveillance. If the FBI, or a faction within it, was dedicated to protecting Bulger and Flemmi, the
Massachusetts State Police was hell-bent on nailing them. The relationship between the FBI and the state police had long been tense,
mirroring, in a way, the wary ties between the Mafia and Winter

Hill: Both groups were ostensibly in the same business, and supposedly on the same side, but institutional and personality differences created divisions and sometimes open hostility. For years, the two agencies had attempted to make a common cause when it came to investigating and prosecuting organized crime in the Boston area, but the FBI's insistence on leading any and every investigation, and its refusal to share information with colleagues, had engendered considerable friction and undercut progress. Part of the problem was cultural: The state police pride themselves on being a paramilitary force; getting through their academy is akin to a marine surviving Parris Island. They looked down on many FBI agents as soft, and resented what they considered the FBI's unearned superiority complex. They felt patronized, disrespected. But it was more than that. It was about Whitey. The Staties had watched Whitey and Flemmi rise in power and malevolence, untouched by the FBI, and they thought they knew why.

Col. Jack O'Donovan, who for years led the state police detectives who specialized in organized crime, was the first to publicly articulate the unspoken tension between the two agencies. A legend on the force, O'Donovan was a former marine who had taken a bullet in the mid-1960s while chasing a fugitive across a rooftop and later tackled a shotgun-toting man who had taken hostages in a drugstore. O'D, as O'Donovan was known, was deeply respected for his clear thinking and gruff candor, and he displayed some of both in 1979 at the FBI Academy in Quantico, Virginia, as a student in a class being taught by an FBI agent named Bob Fitzpatrick. Fitzpatrick's eyes widened as he listened to O'Donovan talk about how Whitey Bulger, Boston's preeminent gangster, was getting away with murder because he was an FBI informant.[1] He couldn't prove it, of course, because the FBI denied it, but O'Donovan and a cadre of his detectives had begun pursuing Whitey in spite of the FBI.

It was that resourceful mentality that led Rick Fraelick, a state police detective, to walk into the dilapidated office of a flophouse on Merrimac Street in the spring of 1980. The building was known as a rooming house for older gay men, so Fraelick pretended that he was gay and asked to rent a room, preferably one that faced out toward Lancaster Street. "It's quieter," he told the guy with the keys.[2]

The Staties had known something was up when Whitey stopped showing up at Howie Winter's old hangout in Somerville, but they'd found Whitey's new base of operations quite by accident: A tip came in about a stolen car ring using an auto body shop on Lancaster Street, near the Boston Garden. Fraelick, who was accomplished at undercover surveillance, had driven over to check out the garage. He saw Whitey and Flemmi, the only members of Winter Hill not in jail or on the run, standing outside, and realized they had abandoned Marshall Street for this place. "Bob," he said, walking into the office of his supervisor, Sergeant Bob Long, "you're not going to believe this." In fact, Long didn't believe it until he saw it with his own eyes, sitting next to Fraelick in their unmarked cruiser. "Holy shit," Long said, almost to himself. "They're all there."

The rooming house was to be their surveillance perch, so when Fraelick walked into the room and saw that it provided a clear vantage point, he said, "I'll take it." He set up a camera and started taking photos: Whitey Bulger standing outside like a guard dog, sunning himself. Whitey meeting with Larry Baione, now the local Mafia's consigliere, and Danny Angiulo, brother of the Mafia underboss Jerry Angiulo. Whitey with Frank Lepere, one of the biggest drug dealers in Boston, who showed up regularly. It was a Who's Who of the Boston underworld. Anybody who was anybody dropped by to shoot the breeze, or deliver tribute to Whitey and Flemmi. Sometimes the men went into the garage's office and briefcases of money changed hands. It didn't take long for the Staties to gather enough visual evidence to justify electronic surveillance—a bug.

Whitey and Flemmi liked to strut outside, checking themselves out in the reflective windows of cars parked out front. When the state cops weren't chuckling at the blatant vanity of the two hoodlums, they were killing mouse-sized cockroaches that lumbered across the grimy floors of the flophouse. They noted the time of death and the size of their prey, and they mounted the dead bugs on the wall like big game hunters. It relieved the boredom of the stakeout.

Nicky Femia, a hulking hit man, served as Whitey and Flemmi's bodyguard at the time and was left to prowl the sidewalk. Femia was as slovenly as Whitey was fit. One afternoon, he put a spread of McDonald's burgers and fries on top of Whitey's shining black Chevy. Whitey sprang from the garage in a rage, snatched the fast food off the car, and began pelting Femia with it.

The troopers in the room across the way watched it all. Bob Long, as the commanding officer of the state police team investigating the garage, met regularly with Jeremiah O'Sullivan, the prosecutor in charge of the Justice Department's Organized Crime Strike Force. Long had no idea it was O'Sullivan who had acceded to John Connolly and John Morris's requests to keep Whitey and Flemmi out of the race-fixing indictments. O'Sullivan was committed to using them in an elaborate plan to bug the Mafia headquarters in the North End, just a ten-minute walk from the Lancaster Street garage. Recognizing that he couldn't keep the state police entirely away from Whitey, O'Sullivan said that the feds would pay for the Lancaster Street operation but that the Staties were on their own beyond that. That was fine with Long. Jack O'Donovan was Long's mentor, and, like O'D, Long believed the FBI was protecting Whitey and Flemmi; the less the Staties had to do with them the better.

They nicknamed their first try at planting a bug Trojan Horse. They created a false bottom in a van, and a trooper named Jack O'Malley got in it. Fraelick dropped the van off at the garage for service just before closing time. But O'Malley never got a chance to get out and plant the bug after a local wino deposited himself outside the garage, making a racket and drawing attention. Long thought the commotion made the operation too risky, so O'Malley slipped out of the garage and the Staties regrouped. The next time, the troopers simply broke into the garage and planted the bugs. One of the devices was crushed when Vincent "Fat Vinnie" Roberto, a four-hundred-pound mobster, plopped himself down on the chair where it had been hidden. Another didn't function. But a third did pick up conversation, even though it was sometimes interrupted by radio transmissions from the city's ambulance fleet. By purposely keeping the FBI out of the investigation, the state police had been forced to improvise their bugging operation; they did not have access to the FBI's state-of-the-art technology. The Staties, in fact, bought some of the microphones they used at Radio Shack.[3]

But none of that mattered in the end, because Whitey and Flemmi suddenly, unexpectedly stopped doing business in the open. They climbed into cars when they needed to talk. Then they simply stopped coming to the garage. For more than three months, the Staties had watched Whitey and Flemmi take few to no precautions when meeting other gangsters. But as soon as their bug became operational, the garage ceased to function as the new clubhouse. "They were tipped," Bob Long said, staring out the window. "Somebody tipped them."

The initial blame fell on John Morris. "Do you guys have something going on Lancaster Street?" Morris had asked Bob Ryan, a Boston police detective. Morris had a glass of wine in his hand and it was a law enforcement party, and Ryan didn't know what to say. Ryan was one of the chief investigators in the Suffolk County district attorney's office, which had obtained the court authorization for the bugs to be installed. He feigned ignorance but called Bob Long. Long went to O'Donovan, who demanded a big sit-down with the FBI.

They met at a downtown hotel on an August morning. There had been a leak, and O'Donovan made it clear he believed the source was inside the FBI. In fact, he said, he believed it was Morris. Oh, and another thing, Jack O'Donovan said: We know that Bulger and Flemmi are FBI informants.[4] The FBI guys promised to get to the bottom of it. Instead Connolly and Morris began to spread various stories, muddying the waters: The state police team was inexperienced in bugging (which was true) and had relied on someone with dubious skill for technical assistance (which was also true). The Staties were just trying to cover their asses, the FBI said.

John Connolly later said it was Jerry O'Sullivan, the strike force chief, who told him about the Lancaster Street bugging. Clearly, O'Sullivan knew about it, and Connolly said O'Sullivan told him to tip off Whitey and Flemmi. But Connolly said he startled O'Sullivan when he told him that there was no need to warn them because they already knew about it. "In the middle of the Lancaster Street case, Stevie told me the garage was being wired up," Connolly said.[5] For his part, Whitey told the FBI that they found out about the bug from a crooked state cop. And he had it right. The leak came from a Statie named Richard Schneiderhan, whom Flemmi had been paying for years.

Even though the FBI was not to blame, O'Donovan's complaints about the leak caused havoc internally. The new special agent in charge of the Boston office of the FBI, Larry Sarhatt, called Morris in and told him to close down Whitey and Flemmi as informants and target them for prosecution. "I thought it was insanity," Connolly said. "We were in striking distance of the Angiulos." He and Morris went to see Whitey and Flemmi. "I think this whole business is over because of Lancaster Street," Connolly told them. "I won't be able to meet you anymore."[6]

Then Connolly and Morris launched a final attempt to persuade Sarhatt to see the light. They told Whitey he needed to go see someone in the North End. And so, on a cool, late fall afternoon in 1980, Whitey stood on the sidewalk outside a nondescript apartment building at 98 Prince Street, waiting for the door to open. Flemmi stood next to him, having just knocked on the door. Their presence that day recalled a similar occasion a half-century before, when Whitey's predecessor as Southie's most powerful gangster, Frankie Wallace, had stood outside a door in the same neighborhood, paying a call on his Italian mob rivals. He was greeted by a hail of gunfire blasting through the door. That audacious ambush allowed the Mafia to push aside the Irish gangsters from the Gustin Gang and to dominate local bootlegging for years, establishing Italian gang-land dominance in a city where the Irish, by dint of numbers, should have been as much in control of crime as they were of politics.

This time, the door opened and Whitey was greeted not with gunfire but with quizzical looks. The Mafia leader Jerry Angiulo and the rest of the men gathered inside the apartment that served as La Cosa Nostra headquarters in Boston didn't expect to see Whitey walk in behind Flemmi. Flemmi was a regular visitor, but this was the first and only time Whitey would enter Angiulo's lair. It was, though the Italian mob boss couldn't know it, Frankie Wallace's revenge: Whitey had been sent by the FBI to scope out the place as the bureau prepared to seek court authorization to bug the Mafia's headquarters, a historic step toward dismantling the Italian crime syndicate.

That headquarters was a glorified bachelor's pad on the bottom floor of a four-story brick apartment building where Angiulo, a compact man with thick glasses, a booming voice, and a shock of white hair, dressed down bookies. Whitey wasn't there because FBI agents needed his help to get a judge to authorize the bugging operation—they had more than they needed from the aggrieved bookies who chafed under Angiulo. And the fruits of the visit, a crudely drawn sketch by Flemmi of the L-shaped room, with the TV by the windows and the kitchen where the Angiulos cooked many of their meals, wouldn't have been of much use anyway. No, Whitey was there because Connolly and Morris sent him, to make Whitey seem more useful than he actually was and to make the Lancaster Street controversy seem trivial next to his value as a source. The FBI in Boston was preparing to launch its most ambitious effort ever—the bugging of Angiulo's headquarters—so if Whitey was going to remain a protected informant, he had to get some credit for it.

Connolly understood the colliding cultures of the FBI and the state police, and as he scrambled to keep Whitey onboard he sought to exploit the historical animosities and biases of both. Connolly painted the Staties as inept finger-pointers, jealous of the FBI; the

FBI were professionals, the Staties just a bunch of cowboys. Connolly wrote Sarhatt a memo, based on a conversation with Whitey, that tried to paint the state police in general, and O'Donovan in particular, as paranoid. "State Police hierarchy speculate that SA Connolly possibly tipped off Whitey Bulger through his brother, Senate President William Bulger. Source advised that they are very upset that their investigation was blown and they are looking to hang it on someone. Source added that Agent Connolly would be a prime target due to his involvement [in a murder case] in which the State Police were embarrassed."[7]

Sarhatt pushed for a meeting with Whitey to satisfy himself that he was worth the trouble. Perhaps because Whitey's charisma had won them over so thoroughly, Connolly and Morris were certain that if Sarhatt met him, he would be suitably impressed. The meeting was highly unusual. Special agents in charge rarely sit down with informants. They met, two days before Thanksgiving, 1980, at the Hilton at Logan Airport. Connolly paid thirty-seven dollars for the room. The meeting lasted four hours. Whitey was his usual confident self, plopping his cowboy boots up on a table. Sarhatt's account of the meeting is extraordinary in that he seems to have accepted Whitey Bulger's self-serving narrative without challenge. In it, Whitey insists he became an informant because his family was treated so well by FBI agent Paul Rico, who arrested him for robbing banks in 1956. "His family indicated to him that SA Rico was such a gentleman and was so helpful that he, informant, changed his mind about his hate for all law enforcement," Sarhatt wrote. "Additionally, he has a close feeling towards SA John Connolly because they both grew up in the same neighborhood in Boston and had the mutual childhood problems, as well as his deep hatred for La Cosa Nostra."

Whitey told Sarhatt that he knew the state police believed he was an FBI informant but that he wasn't worried about his safety because, as Sarhatt described it in a follow-up memo, "no one would dare believe that he is an informant. It would be too incredible."

More incredible still was Sarhatt's acceptance of Whitey's rationale for not naming the Massachusetts State Police mole who tipped him off. "Informant was asked whether he would divulge the identity of the State Police source that has been furnishing information to him and he stated that he would not because this source is not doing it for monetary benefit but as a favor to him because of his close association with him."[8]

And that was as far as it went. The head of the FBI in Boston allowed Whitey to keep his secret. And Whitey had demonstrated again how adroit he was at stroking the FBI. "With respect to his association with Colonel O'Donovan," Sarhatt said of Whitey, "he stated that he has met him on some occasions especially one in which [O'Donovan] made very disparaging and derogatory statements about the professionalism of FBI personnel to which [Whitey] took great umbrage inasmuch as his association with the FBI has been nothing but the most professional in every respect."[9]

The week after the hotel meeting, Connolly wrote, at Sarhatt's request, a justification memo, a response to the Lancaster Street controversy that embellished Whitey's importance as an informant and gave Sarhatt plenty of cover to keep Whitey on the books. He gave Whitey credit for saving the lives of two undercover FBI agents in separate investigations, claims that were deeply suspect. He also gave Whitey credit for providing the names of those who took part in a high-profile bank robbery in Medford, just outside Boston, in 1980—again, a dubious claim because those names were known to police almost immediately.[10] But the pièce de résistance was this: Whitey, he said, was helping them get inside the Mafia headquarters in the North End.

This was fiction—the browbeaten bookies were the crucial source—but Sarhatt couldn't know that. He was not from Boston. Like all the supervisors who rotated in from out of town, he had to rely on field agents like Connolly. And Connolly knew exactly what to say and how to say it. The FBI, as a national organization, was in the midst of building cases against La Cosa Nostra families across the United States. Sarhatt was sensitive to any suggestion that shedding an informant might compromise the FBI's ability to build a case against the Mafia. Measured against Mafiosi, Whitey was small game.

Connolly and Morris were successful in getting their boss to back off the idea of closing out Whitey, and they had managed to ride out the nearly disastrous fallout of the Lancaster Street garage investigation. But the FBI's blatant protection of Whitey had inflamed members of the Massachusetts State Police. The Staties were more determined than ever to get Whitey. To do so, they now knew with even greater certainty that they would have to work around, not with, the FBI. The war against organized crime in Boston was reaching its climax, and, through it all, the FBI and the state police were at war with each other. Whitey had not orchestrated this war, but he was, for now, the main beneficiary of it.

A month after Connolly and Morris persuaded Sarhatt to keep Whitey on as an informant, the FBI bug planted inside Jerry Angiulo's office began picking up conversations that did more than expose Mafia crimes. Angiulo and his henchmen spoke glowingly about Whitey and Flemmi, placing them firmly in the highest echelons of criminality.

"Whitey's got the whole of Southie," Angiulo was recorded saying. "Stevie has got the whole of the South End."

Angiulo implied that Whitey and Flemmi worked as subcontractors for the Mafia.

"I'll tell you right now," Angiulo told the assembled Mafiosi, "if I called these guys right now they'd kill any fuckin' body we tell 'em to."

Larry Baione, the consigliere, also gushed, praising them as lethal problem solvers.

"These are nice people," Baione said. "These are the kind of people that straighten a thing out."[11]

The recordings would not be played in court for another four years. When the tapes were heard, state police investigators said they proved that the FBI had been protecting killers.

By then, the US Drug Enforcement Administration (DEA) had formed an alliance with the state police, as well as the police in Boston and Quincy, to target Whitey for his most lucrative trade, extorting money from drug dealers. The posse chasing Whitey was getting larger and smarter, all because of the Lancaster Street garage investigation.

The great irony in all this is that the person who compromised the entire operation was a state police officer, not an FBI man like Connolly or Morris. But the scandal the leak touched off reordered the law enforcement landscape in Boston, so that within a few years every agency wanted to put Whitey in prison. Every agency but one, the FBI.

9

Circles Within Circles

In the fall of 1982, Whitey Bulger strolled into the Dining Room at the Ritz, which overlooked the finely manicured Public Garden in Boston's Back Bay. Gone today, it was then the most elegant dining room in the city, playing host to the rich, the beautiful, and the powerful. Whitey felt he belonged there. He was as much a captain of his industry as were the financiers and lawyers who sat at the tables draped in crisp white linen. He had brought along his protégé, Kevin Weeks, a boxer he had groomed to be his man Friday. Their women stood a step behind them as they waited to be seated. Weeks hailed from the housing project in Southie across the street from the one where Whitey grew up. Project rats didn't eat dinner at the Ritz. But they weren't project rats anymore. They were princes of the city.

"Look at this," Whitey said, almost to himself.

Chandeliers glistened overhead. Exquisite pale blue draperies framed the wide plate glass windows that afforded one of Boston's most sumptuous views. From the best tables, diners could see Beacon Hill rising beyond the garden where a bronze George Washington presided on horseback and the famous swan boats offered rides through a man-made lagoon. The dining party was led to their table and Whitey took the seat next to Teresa Stanley. Weeks sat with his wife, Pam.

"We'll start with the Dom Perignon," Whitey told the tuxedo-clad waiter. He ordered for the table. Caviar. Lobster. Filet mignon. He made a selection of French wine, instructing the sommelier to decant the reds and to put the whites in an ice bucket. Whitey's dining companions sat back and breathed in the extravagance.

"Who deserves this more than us?" Whitey said, turning to Weeks.

Whitey pointed at the next table.

"Does that guy deserve it? Why shouldn't we have the better things in life? Why should that guy have this and we don't?" Whitey said.

It sounded like a soliloquy, or the start of one, on his hard road from poverty and obscurity to wealth and infamy. The women didn't get it and just laughed. But Weeks nodded. He had heard this speech before. He also knew what it meant that he, Kevin Weeks, had come to live in Whitey's world.

When the bill came, Whitey picked it up. Weeks glanced over and saw it had been rounded off to twenty-seven hundred dollars.[1]

Whitey left a good tip, too.

He paid for everything in cash.

As the 1970s melted into the 1980s, Whitey was an undisputed power in the Boston underworld. He and Steve Flemmi had the Winter Hill empire to themselves, with their partners on the run or in jail. John Connolly and the FBI had their back, and their main competition, the Mafia, was about to talk themselves into prison. Whitey's gambling business in Southie was still robust. But he and Flemmi were not content with their monthly collections from bookies. And they were preparing to launch their most lucrative business venture yet: extorting rent from drug dealers who operated in and around Southie.

One of the keys to Whitey's long-running success, and survival, had been his ability to keep his profile relatively low, to stay within his limits. Whitey's world stretched just a few miles, from the hidden graves of the Neponset River in Quincy to Southie, where he held court at Triple O's. During the day he would visit Castle Island at Southie's seaside tip to talk business out of electronic earshot. Most nights he ate dinner with Teresa Stanley and her kids at her house on Silver Street before retiring to the place he shared with Cathy Greig in Quincy. While he was widely known and feared in Southie, word of mouth rarely carried his reputation beyond its borders. His name was seldom in the newspapers, even after his brother Bill became the president of the Massachusetts Senate in 1978. Whitey kept a small circle of trusted friends and associates. Some were criminals, some were FBI agents. Some were family, some were lovers. All were in his thrall, caught up in his intoxicating, intimidating aura. He was the tough guy they wanted to be. Or the rich man who provided the lifestyle they dreamed of. Being in his circle was a vicarious thrill, though there were also some very tangible benefits. For the criminals, it was money. For the women, it was money and his charisma, his handsome bad-boy looks, his undeniable power. For the FBI agents, it was the proximity to that power, not to mention the institutional status and merit raises and promotions that came from being the bearer of tips from a top-echelon informant. But it was also, in some cases, money. They were all corrupted, to one degree or another, by him.

Whitey's inner circle was a set of concentric circles. He self-consciously compartmentalized his life as a way to control its complexities, and understanding him requires understanding how he stitched his world together, what he demanded of himself, and others, in friendship, and where he drew the line in his loyalties. His family, especially his brothers Bill and Jack, occupied one of those circles, offering unconditional love and support and getting it in return. His family looked the other way when it came to Whitey's day job. Bill, in particular, took the most abjectly benign view of his older brother's criminal exploits. He saw Jimmy as the man who stood with the FBI in bringing down the Italian mob, not as a casual and ruthless killer. The women most constant in Whitey's life, Stanley and Greig, occupied separate circles, close to the core, though there were other women kept at a more distant remove, welcomed into his bed but never into his confidence. The men with whom Whitey served prison time were part of another distinct circle. Whitey stayed in contact with some of them, especially those from Alcatraz.

Besides Flemmi, no one was closer to Whitey than Kevin Weeks. If Weeks looked up to Whitey as the man he wanted to be, deeply feared and utterly respected, Whitey looked at Weeks as the one-punch wonder he had aspired to be in his youth. Weeks was born to be a fighter. His father, a professional boxer, trained him, if you can call smacking a little boy in the face training. Sometimes his father beat Weeks for blinking too often. He thought that he was doing his son a favor. Southie was rough; the Old Colony projects Weeks grew up in were rougher. If you could fight, you could survive. "My father was the kind of guy who would take two punches to land one," said Weeks.[2] That's exactly how a Boston police officer once described a teenaged Whitey.

Like Whitey, Weeks was one of six siblings, in a family where only one became a criminal. They both had humble beginnings and had brothers who had prospered professionally without the help of a gun. Weeks's two brothers went to Harvard; one became a lawyer, the other a respected political operative who played a key role in Massachusetts governor Michael Dukakis's failed campaign for president in 1988.* Whitey saw the common thread in their lives, and his relationship with Weeks was almost familial. When Weeks's father died, Whitey paid for the funeral, but, as was his pattern, he

*Jack Weeks was blamed, fairly or unfairly, for the idea of having Dukakis take a drive in an army tank in front of the campaign press corps. Meant to boost Dukakis's reputation among military backers, the resulting image of the presidential candidate wearing a jumpsuit and too-large helmet backfired and was used by Republicans in commercials to demean Dukakis.

didn't attend. He was never one for such public rituals, though he made an exception when his mother died in 1980. Even then, however, he filtered into the funeral home after the wake was over to pay his final respects. Whitey avoided events like funerals because he worried about being photographed, something he always assumed was just another way for the newspapers to embarrass his politician brother.

Weeks went to Boston College High School for ninth grade, just as Bill Bulger had. But where Bill Bulger had succeeded at BC High, Weeks only lasted a year. He missed the last week of school after he was suspended for punching a kid who referred to his mother, Peg, whose arthritis forced her to use crutches, as Peg Leg. He left BC High for Southie High, graduating in the spring of 1974, the year before court-ordered busing began and the school descended into chaos. Weeks would nevertheless wind up in the middle of the integration drama, not as a student but as a security aide at the high school. His reputation for toughness preceded him, and school officials hoped his presence alone would make some troublemakers think twice. Almost inevitably, given his Southie roots, Weeks got caught up in the running disputes in the classrooms and hallways between black and white students. Black students accused him of favoring the whites, and one of them accused Weeks of punching him. Weeks denied it, but he was fired. He was also charged with assault and battery after he slugged the father of a black student, and it was while waiting for his case to be called at South Boston District Court that Weeks got talking to Billy O'Neil, who was in court for beating up a black taxi driver. O'Neil and his two brothers owned Triple O's. He and Weeks commiserated, and O'Neil offered Weeks a job as a bouncer at the bar.

Triple O's was typical of Southie dives: longer than it was wide, dimly lit, smoke hovering like a low cloud, with booths on one side, stools and the bar on the other. The O'Neils had some local artists paint the walls with images of the Seven Dwarfs and other Disney characters, an incongruous choice given the type of people who drank there. One St. Patrick's Day, Weeks put down some beer and ice he had carried up from the basement and knocked out, with two punches in quick succession, a pair of men who were fighting. It was the first time Whitey, a regular at Triple O's, had taken notice of the burly bouncer. "I didn't know it at the time, but Jimmy was sizing me up," said Weeks, who always called his boss Jimmy. "He wanted to see if I was capable, how I handled myself."

Triple O's provided many opportunities for such demonstrations. Fights were common, especially on weekends, when some people would come in just to see who might start something. Weeks was known for ending the scuffling before anything in the bar got damaged. Whitey had a favorite spot, at the end of the bar, his back to the wall. He could see everything and everyone, and could slip out the back door if he saw trouble coming in the front. He was usually clad in denim jeans and cowboy boots and, when it wasn't summer, a leather jacket. Whitey started engaging Weeks in small talk, exhorting him to stay out of trouble, to read books, to stay away from booze. "Boozers are losers," Weeks remembers Whitey telling him.

There was a fight outside the bar one night, and a biker got stabbed. When Weeks came outside to see what was going on, someone handed him a bloodied knife. He took it wordlessly and walked back into the bar with it. Kevin O'Neil, who managed the bar, flipped out. "You bring that knife in here?" O'Neil bellowed. "I'm gonna lose my fucking license."[3] Weeks said nothing, and Kevin O'Neil continued to ride him about his stupidity. A few weeks later, Billy O'Neil told his older brother to lay off Weeks. Billy said it was he who had stabbed the biker; he had handed Weeks the knife to get rid of it.

Whitey, standing at the end of the bar, heard the whole exchange and was impressed that Weeks had kept his mouth shut despite being falsely accused. He would watch Weeks for almost three years before he approached him and said, "Let's take a ride." They weren't in the car for more than a few minutes before Whitey pulled over outside a bar on East Broadway and a man in his twenties whom Weeks didn't know climbed in. It looked to Weeks like it was all prearranged. Whitey started screaming at the guy, accusing him of smacking his niece, and then he pulled over to the curb at M Street Park and continued his harangue. Whitey searched the guy, found a knife on him, and dragged the blunt side of it across his neck. It didn't draw blood, but the guy thought his throat had been slashed. His eyes were wide with panic. Whitey looked at Weeks, who had been sitting there wondering what was going on. Without a word, Weeks started punching the guy. His first punch broke his nose. His second broke some teeth. Whitey pulled out a sap and started beating him with it. Then they drove him back to the bar where they had picked him up and dumped him on the sidewalk. The guy stumbled into the bar and a group of his friends ran outside. Weeks was waiting for them and knocked the first one out with one punch. The others stopped dead in their tracks. "Anyone else want to bother my niece?" Whitey asked.

There were no takers. A couple of days later, Whitey told Weeks he had made a mistake. The young guy they had so savagely beaten had, in fact, slapped a girl, but it wasn't Whitey's niece. That was, to Whitey, a distinction without a difference. The guy had beaten up a girl, Whitey explained to Weeks, so he deserved what he got. Whitey praised Weeks for breaking the guy's face and handed him a thousand dollars in cash. It was official: Kevin Weeks was in.[4]

Some people around town assumed Weeks was Whitey's driver, but Whitey drove himself everywhere; he didn't trust anybody else at the wheel. Weeks always sat in the passenger seat as they motored around the Town. Whitey liked Lincoln Continentals. He had a four-door and a two-door in midnight blue. He liked Chevys, too; Malibus, especially, and Impalas. He had a few of them. Whitey also had a forest-green Jaguar XJS, a luxury sedan he seldom drove. When Weeks bought it from him some years later, it had only two thousand miles on the odometer. The Jaguar didn't exactly match the image Whitey was trying to maintain in Southie, as a man who had risen without losing track of his roots.

With thick forearms and huge hands, Weeks was Whitey's pit bull. Whitey sicced him on anyone who displeased him, and Weeks obligingly punched, no questions asked. Whitey urged him to reserve his fighting for business and to avoid barroom brawls. He told Weeks he didn't realize how lethal his fists were. "You're one punch away from jail," he warned him once. One day, a teenager whose car blocked their path on a narrow Southie street ignored Whitey's plea to move. Worse, the kid told Whitey to go fuck himself. "Kevin," Whitey said, and that's all he needed to say. Weeks got out of the car, walked to the driver's side and punched the kid in the teeth, breaking a number of them. The kid's father was a police officer, his mother a crossing guard. They complained and demanded compensation. Whitey handed over sixteen hundred dollars to pay for the dental work. He then admonished Weeks.

"Why did you hit him so hard?"

"You told me to hit him," Weeks replied.

"Yeah, well, I didn't tell you to hit him that hard," Whitey replied.[5]

When a guy sitting in a car near the Triple O's was dumb enough to give Whitey the finger, Weeks walked over and punched him through his open window. Later, Weeks noticed that the punch had dislodged a diamond on his pinky ring. Whitey bought him a new one. "It was the only time he gave me jewelry," Weeks said. "The ring had a solitaire five-carat diamond. It was worth more than $100,000."

Weeks, in his rough fashion, was also crucial to Whitey's efforts to create a persona as a benevolent wiseguy. If you did something in Southie that Whitey disapproved of, there was the chance of a beating or worse. But Weeks insisted he and his boss performed a public service, too. He compared Whitey to a rogue sheriff in a lawless town, using vigilantism to create equal measures of fear and security. Southie had the reputation for being among the safest of neighborhoods in Boston in terms of street crime. It was comparatively safe because it was so dangerous. If you stepped out of line, there was a chance you'd have to deal with Whitey, which meant you'd make acquaintance with Weeks's fist. Weeks claims that he and Whitey chased heroin dealers out of Southie, and that Whitey gave money to families down on their luck. He admits it was a combination of a public relations pose and genuine philanthropy. "Jimmy really was a good bad guy," Weeks said.

The good bad guy. That was how Whitey described himself, even to law enforcement agents. In 1985, the DEA succeeded in planting a bug inside the door of Whitey's car. It picked up snippets of conversations Whitey had with Flemmi and Weeks, but not enough to bring charges. Weeks did routine sweeps of Whitey's cars with a device that could detect bugs, and after he got a high reading on the device, he and Whitey brought the car to a garage near their liquor store in Southie. The mechanic pulled the door panel out, and Weeks removed some wires. The DEA agents who had been monitoring the bug from a van parked nearby rushed to the garage to retrieve their electronic equipment. Whitey tried to put the agents at ease. "We're all good guys here," he said. "You're the good good guys, and we're the bad good guys."

Growing up poor had had a profound impact on Whitey. Not long after Weeks joined him full-time, Whitey steered his blue Lincoln Continental slowly down a narrow street in Dorchester and pointed up at one of the three-deckers. From the passenger's seat, Weeks craned his neck to see.

"There," Whitey said. "We lived there."

He didn't stop the car. The house the Bulger family had called home before they moved to Logan Way in Southie held only faded memories, none of them fond.

"We didn't have hot water," Whitey said. "It was always cold."[6]

Whitey hated being poor, he told Weeks. But he was also conscious of being seen as too obviously rich, though he liked to splurge occasionally on jewelry and clothes. The ring he gave Weeks was almost identical to the diamond pinky ring Whitey wore on his right hand. Around his neck, he wore a gold Jesus Christ medallion. On his wrist, he wore a gold Patek Philippe watch that his buddies in Winter Hill had given him. On his left pinky, he wore a diamond claddagh ring, the traditional Irish token of friendship or love. His key chain was emblazoned with the words "Born to Raise Hell."[7] Whitey preferred cowboy boots with an ample heel. Some suggested this was because he was self-conscious about his height, which he was, but the boots also helped hide the knife he kept in a sheath strapped to his calf. He insisted on R. J. Foley boots, a premium brand. In the mid-1980s, Weeks watched him pay twenty-five hundred dollars in cash for a pair of black alligator-skin Foleys at the El Paso store on Newbury Street, Boston's most fashionable shopping district. Whitey bought his suits, and was friendly with the staff, at Louis, the most expensive men's shop in Boston. Everything Whitey bought was with cash. Nothing was in his name. The cars he drove were owned by straws. He also spent a lot of money on good food, in fine restaurants, and at home. He'd send Teresa Stanley across the Charles River to Cambridge, to Bread & Circus, a natural foods supermarket, gladly paying much more than he would at Flanagan's, the neighborhood supermarket on East Broadway.[8]

Weeks spent more time with Whitey than Flemmi did. He was, for all intents and purposes, his shadow. But while Weeks was twenty-four and Whitey was fifty-one when they began working together on a daily basis, he bristles at suggestions that they were like father and son, or even mentor and protégé. "Jimmy treated me like a partner, an associate," Weeks said.

They had a routine, and it was, by Weeks's admission, mundane. Whitey stayed up most of the night and slept late in the day. He drove into Southie in the middle of the afternoon to pick up Weeks, and they would drive around and do their business: collecting rent from bookies and drug dealers, handing out money to their loansharks. They met Flemmi every day at one of the various fronts they used—a bar, a furniture store, a liquor store—but they never talked business there; they assumed those places were bugged. Anything criminal was discussed outdoors. On most days, Whitey and Weeks walked around Castle Island, a scenic, twenty-two-acre park at the easternmost extremity of the Southie peninsula. They met there even in the dead of winter when it was numbingly cold and wind whipped off the water, bundling themselves in thick air force jackets to keep warm. Their daily constitutional served more than one purpose. First, it was good exercise in a beautiful setting: The looping waterfront walkway circled the imposing pentagon-shaped Fort Independence. Walking around the fort afforded spectacular views of Boston Harbor on one side, the docks and the skyscrapers of downtown on the other. When they were on the Sugar Bowl, the walkway that connects Castle Island to the beach at Pleasure Bay, they could look across the water and see the faint outlines of the shoreline in Quincy where the bodies of Debra Davis and Tommy King lay buried. Castle Island's physical isolation, and the huge edifice of Fort Independence, also allowed Whitey and Weeks to discuss business without the fear of electronic surveillance. Not that law enforcement didn't try. DEA agents and Boston police at one point buried a listening device in a patch of dirt where Whitey and Weeks regularly stopped on their jaunts around Castle Island, but the bug malfunctioned, picking up the frequency of a local all-news radio station.[9] The huge granite walls of the fort also made it impossible for police, parked in unmarked cars nearby, to use long-distance microphones to listen in.

On most days, Whitey and Flemmi rarely spent more than an hour together. Weeks, however, spent what amounted to shifts with Whitey. Every night, usually around five or six, Whitey retired to Teresa Stanley's house for dinner with her and her kids. Then he picked up Weeks and they drove around, usually in silence, listening to police activity on a radio tuned to the various law enforcement frequencies. Sometimes when they noticed an undercover police tail on them, Whitey would turn the car around and follow the cops, just for fun.[10] Whitey and Weeks had a nightly habit of stopping at the Store 24 convenience store on West Broadway around midnight to pick up the first editions of the *Boston Globe* and the *Boston Herald*, and they went straight for the crime stories, offering critiques that were rarely complimentary of the Boston press corps. "Jimmy always said the press never let the facts get in the way of a good story," Weeks said.

After catching up on the news, Whitey would drop Weeks off and drive the ten to fifteen minutes it took to get to Cathy Greig's place in Quincy, where he spent the night. The routine—broken up by the occasional burst of violence—was always about the same, six days a week. "Jimmy took Sundays off," Weeks said. "He was very traditional like that."[11]

Whitey trusted his gut on who came within his favored circles and how close they got. If Weeks and Flemmi were trusted inherently, others were not. Pat Nee was a classic case. Whitey and Nee began as rivals: Whitey as an enforcer for the Killeen gang, Nee as a gunman for the Mullens. They tried to kill each other several times, but they put that animosity aside after the Killeens and the Mullens called a truce and became a subsidiary of Winter Hill. There was a grudging mutual respect, but there was also an unmistakable mistrust between the two. Whitey called Nee "cement head" behind his back.[12] Nee constantly tried to embarrass Whitey around other gangsters, poking fun at his idiosyncrasies. Once, when Whitey dropped by a cottage on Cape Cod where Nee and a group of gangsters from Charlestown were drinking and playing cards, Nee instructed his friends to make a point of smoking cigarettes and shaking Whitey's hand when he came and left. Whitey hated cigarette smoke and rarely shook hands, even with his close associates, as he had a phobia about germs. "I knew it would drive him crazy," Nee said.[13]

Nee believes Whitey was jealous of his combat record as a marine in Vietnam. When he was in the air force, Whitey never left the United States. Nee also believes that Whitey resented his status among Irish Republican Army operatives who came to Boston, either to hide out or secure weapons. Nee was born in Ireland, and the IRA men took to him easily. When Whitey traveled to Ireland in 1986, he tried to meet with IRA operatives. "They blew him off," Nee said. "They thought he was too full of himself." While most of Whitey's criminal associates deferred to his intellect, Nee would not. Once, sitting around the old Mullens clubhouse, Whitey held up a book written by Sun Tzu, the ancient Chinese military strategist.

"*The Art of War*," Nee said. "I've read it."

Whitey mentioned Machiavelli.

"*The Prince*," Nee said. "I've read it."

Whitey figured he could stump him by mentioning the martial arts title *A Book of Five Rings*. Nee told him that the author, Miyamoto Musashi, was the greatest samurai.

Whitey just glared. And yet, despite the friction at the edges of their relationship, Whitey entrusted Nee with sensitive assignments that ranged from shooting to grave digging. "I can't explain it," Nee admitted. "We worked with each other even as we didn't trust each other. He knew I was capable. I knew he was capable. That's how it worked in the criminal world." Nee knew he was in the circle just outside the one that included Whitey, Flemmi, and Weeks. That meant, among other things, that whenever he was summoned to a meeting, he always assumed they might kill him. If Weeks called him and buzzed like a mosquito, that was code to meet them at a small park on East Fourth Street. If Weeks croaked like a frog, that was code to meet in back of the Tynan Elementary School, where outdoor tables are held up by supports shaped like frog legs. Nee always went armed. But they never made a move on him.

Not that Whitey didn't consider it. In the mid-1980s, without citing a reason, he abruptly urged Weeks to kill Nee. Weeks was stunned by the suddenness and specificity of the request. Whitey suggested that Weeks drop in on Nee and ask for a cup of tea. Nee would always offer guests a cup of Irish tea. When Nee turned his back to brew it, Whitey said, Weeks could pull a gun and shoot him. Weeks liked Nee and had gone to martial arts competitions with him. He was relieved when Whitey dropped the idea of killing Nee as suddenly as he had raised it.[14]

Unlike Nee, Weeks saw much to admire in Whitey. He found him a fascinating boss, a student of the human condition. Whitey routinely struck up conversations with strangers he was sure neither knew nor cared about him. One of his favorite spots was the Public Garden near Boston Common. "He'd sit on a park bench and talk to people for three hours," said Weeks. "He had two different personalities. Business was one thing and everything else he was just a regular guy. He was always trying to figure out what made people tick. It was more than curiosity. It was so he could be a step ahead."

He was, as well, a student of the art of crime. Whitey listened to weather forecasts closely, especially when planning a move that carried with it an above-average risk of being observed. When it came to moving guns, hurting someone, or meeting somebody who might attract law enforcement attention, Whitey preferred to do it when it was raining or snowing. People had their heads down, or they were in a rush when it was wet—much less likely to notice the hoodlum nearby.

Whitey's apologists, including his brother Bill, would sometimes cite the lasting after-effects of the LSD experiments in prison when defending him. His experience with LSD had altered his mind, they said, and was one of the reasons Whitey was so opposed to drugs, and why he worked to keep narcotics out of Southie. This was pure mythmaking. Drugs were everywhere in South Boston; epidemiological studies in the 1980s showed that the neighborhood had a disproportionate number of young abusers. And Whitey was hip-deep in the trade. Weeks estimated that Whitey made about thirty million dollars over the nearly twenty years he was with him, most of it from shaking down drug dealers to let them do business on his turf. Only rarely did they get more directly involved in the trade. One day, Flemmi was upset when he climbed into a car with Whitey and Weeks, only to learn that they were delivering a kilogram of cocaine to a dealer near one of Southie's housing projects. Whitey was sanguine, even though he knew he was being targeted by the DEA at the time, because he felt "exceptionally comfortable" in his home-town.[15] Weeks said it was the only time they ever personally deliv-ered drugs. Weeks says Whitey made distinctions between types of narcotics. He insists that they regularly chased heroin dealers out of South Boston, even as they tithed local cocaine and marijuana dis-tributors. Weeks said the heroin dealers usually left after the first warning. Whitey hit one slow learner with his car, putting him in the hospital. "He left after he got out of the hospital," Weeks said.

Federal drug agents scoff at the notion that Whitey distin-guished among drugs and drug dealers. "Whitey took money from people no matter what they sold," said Paul Brown, who was sec-ond in command of the US Drug Enforcement Administration in Boston and who oversaw a DEA targeting of drug dealers who paid Whitey tribute. "The idea that he kept drugs out of Southie is a joke. He allowed it and he made money off it."[16]

Whitey's family occupied a special circle that he defended fero-ciously, especially when it came to his brother Bill, who had been such a loyal advocate while Whitey was in prison. Bill's success as a politician and his reputation as an erudite spokesman for Southie were sources of family pride. Whitey took it upon himself to be a defender and avenger of that reputation. For example, while Bill Bulger was busy promoting the 1990 gubernatorial bid of his friend John Silber, the president of Boston University, Whitey worked to muddy the name of Silber's Democratic rival, Frank Bellotti, the former Massachusetts attorney general. Whitey hated Bellotti because Bellotti had once sent his prosecutors after him—an effort, in Whitey's mind, to soil the family name and humiliate his brother Bill.[17] There was no evidence that Bellotti ever got close to indicting Whitey while he was attorney general, but there was plenty of evi-dence that Bill Bulger didn't like Bellotti and especially didn't like Bellotti challenging his friend Silber. He took special offense at Bel-lotti political ads that drew parallels between Silber's authoritarian

rule at Boston University and Bulger's iron-fist leadership style as
senate president.

Whitey decided to counter Bellotti's ads with some "ads" of his
own, which harkened back to long-ago controversy. Years earlier, a
state tax official named John Coady killed himself just hours after he
learned he was going to have to testify before a grand jury Bellotti had
convened as part of a corruption investigation. Critics accused Bellotti
of leading a politically motivated probe and using Coady as a pawn to
get at others, and the suicide reflected badly on Bellotti's office. Eight
years later, Whitey and Weeks drove around spray-painting "Remember John Coady" on sidewalks, walls, and highway bridges. The van-
dalism was noticed, and it inspired news stories.[18] Bellotti ended up
losing the primary, and Whitey boasted to Weeks that they had cost
Bellotti the election—a dubious claim. "He was as proud of that as any
crime that made him money," said Weeks. "He had helped a friend
of his brother's."[19] Bellotti believes Whitey cost him votes not just
by reminding people of John Coady. "Whitey and Weeks were going
around town, tearing my signs down," Bellotti said.[20]

Bill Bulger also had a long-running feud with a state senator
named Alan Sisitsky, who, in the early 1980s, began acting erratically and publicly accusing Bulger of corruption. At one point, Sisitsky rose in the senate and proclaimed that the senate president's
brother, Whitey, was eavesdropping and knew all that was being
said.[21] After Sisitsky's behavior became more extreme and unsettling, Bill Bulger expelled him from the senate chambers, and Sisitsky's family hospitalized him. But Whitey had a different sort of
intervention in mind. He instructed Weeks to call Sisitsky on the
phone. "I know where you live," Weeks hissed. "I'm gonna kill you."[22]

Weeks believes Whitey wouldn't have stopped harassing Bill's
political enemies even if Bill had asked. But Bill Bulger told a congressional committee that he did press his brother to back off once,
when Whitey confronted Patrick Loftus, Bill Bulger's challenger
for an open senate seat in 1970. "Jimmy took it as a personal affront
to him when someone went after Billy," Weeks said. "But he didn't

make a big deal about it. He called it a hobby. He had hobbies. This was one of them."

Another of Whitey's favored pastimes was giving gifts to his friends in the FBI, particularly at Christmas. Those friends occupied a circle that Whitey considered both personal and professional. Blurring those lines enabled him to conduct his criminal business without fear of prosecution and to remain an FBI informant long after any reasonable justification had expired.

The gift giving was a holiday tradition, carried out at the kitchen table at Teresa Stanley's house on Silver Street. Whitey kept the gift list on a small piece of paper. There were symbols and nicknames. Vino was John Morris, because of his fondness for wine. Pipe was FBI supervisor Jim Ring because he smoked one. Nicky was FBI Agent Nicholas Gianturco. Agent Orange was FBI Agent John Newton because Whitey believed he had served in the Vietnam War. As Whitey chose a gift for each of them—cash or Lalique crystal or a Chelsea clock—he'd cross off a name.[23] "Christmas," Whitey told Weeks, as he stuffed the envelopes, "is for cops and kids." The gifts were delivered by John Connolly, whom Whitey gave three nicknames: Zip, because they grew up in the same zip code; Neighbor, because they lived near each other; and Elvis, because of the way Connolly combed his thick black hair. And the gift giving was reciprocal. Whitey was especially fond of a belt that FBI Agent Nick Gianturco gave him. The buckle was emblazoned with "Alcatraz 1934–1963"—the active lifespan of the federal prison on The Rock.[24]

Gianturco first met Whitey in 1979, after being told by Connolly that the gangster had saved his life. As Connolly told the story, Whitey warned him that truck hijackers whom an undercover Gianturco was working with had figured out he was an agent and were going to kill him. The claim was almost certainly specious—the supposed threat was never forwarded to Gianturco's supervisors, and the gangster who allegedly made the threat was never charged with making it—but it enhanced Whitey's value as an informant. One evening, Gianturco was invited along when John Morris, at Connolly's urging, held a celebratory dinner for Whitey and Flemmi at the FBI supervisor's home in suburban Lexington. Connolly had urged Morris to hold the dinner so Morris and other agents could get to know Whitey and Flemmi. The dinner party itself was extraordinary: gangsters and G-men, sitting around the table, pouring each other wine, praising the steaks and their company. It was at that dinner, Flemmi says, that Morris told him and Whitey that they could do anything they want, with one caveat: Just don't clip anyone.

Gianturco liked Whitey and Flemmi so much that on four separate occasions he hosted dinners for them and his colleagues at his own home in Peabody, north of Boston. He admitted that they regularly exchanged small gifts. At one dinner, Whitey gave Gianturco a toy truck, a not so subtle reminder of how Whitey supposedly had saved his life from the truck hijacker.[25] The gifts Whitey gave Morris and Connolly were more substantial. Whitey knew his wine and frequently gave Morris bottles and even cases of it. As they were leaving one of their dinners at Morris's girlfriend's apartment, Whitey handed him five thousand dollars.[26] Morris was keeping a family at home and a mistress on the side. Whitey understood the pressures, financial and otherwise. He was keeping two mistresses himself.

There were other dinners: at the Flemmi house in South Boston where Mary Flemmi made her son proud by cooking up an Italian feed for Whitey, Flemmi, and a table of FBI men. At one of them, in 1983, the plates had been cleared and the gangsters and FBI agents were enjoying after-dinner drinks when Bill Bulger walked in from next door. Jim Ring, who had just succeeded Morris as the organized crime squad's supervisor, was stunned to see the senate president pull out photographs from a recent trip to Ireland and begin showing them to the dinner guests.[27] Bill Bulger's presence seemed like a postdinner benediction, a tacit blessing from one of the most powerful politicians in Massachusetts of the unholy alliance between gangsters and federal agents. The social dinners, the exchange of gifts, the friendly banter, and even his brother's witness—all were confirmation to Whitey that he and his FBI handlers were on equal footing. They were partners in an enterprise that served their mutual interests. In Whitey's mind, they also kept the world a safer place by making the underworld a more orderly place.

Weeks found out how seriously Whitey took the relationship with Connolly and the FBI when, one day in 1984, Connolly drove up to the liquor store that Whitey had begun using as his headquarters. The South Boston Liquor Mart was a squat, one-story building standing between the two housing projects where Whitey and Weeks had grown up. The sign over the entrance featured a shamrock, and there was another, much larger, shamrock painted on the whitewashed cinderblock exterior. The store was crammed with narrow rows of wine racks, and cases of beer were piled to one side. Weeks was standing behind the counter when Connolly walked in. He viewed Connolly dyspeptically—just another corrupt agent, with his hand out—and offered no greeting. "What's up?" Connolly asked Weeks. "What's going on?" Connolly was looking for "the other guy"—Whitey—but the gangster wasn't there. When Whitey returned to the store, Weeks relayed the story. "He has some fuckin' nerve," Weeks told Whitey, "coming in and saying, 'What's going on?' Like I'm going to fuckin' tell him what's going on." Weeks expected to be praised for his discretion, but Whitey was furious. "Shut the fuck up!" he hissed. "Don't ever talk about that guy like that. He's a friend of ours."[28] It was a telling phrase. Calling someone "a friend of ours" was what a Mafia wiseguy would say about another made guy.

Connolly insisted to other agents, and even to his supervisors, Morris and Ring, that Whitey and Flemmi were to be treated not as criminals but, as he put it, associates. Connolly's relationship with Whitey was as much social as professional. They took vacations together and occasionally traveled to Provincetown. During a particularly snowy winter in 1978, Whitey and Connolly vacationed together in Mexico. They got into an accident while Whitey was driving, leaving Connolly with a black eye he had to explain back at the

FBI office.[29] Connolly enjoyed traveling with a guy who dispensed cash like an ATM. For Whitey, there were perks as well. Once, when they confronted long lines at an airport in Mexico, Connolly and Whitey walked to the front of the line. Connolly flashed his badge and introduced Whitey as a fellow FBI agent. They were escorted onto the plane together without having to wait in line.[30] But for all the conspicuous camaraderie, there was a built-in imbalance in their bond. "I got the sense that Connolly envied us. One day he said to me and Jimmy and Stevie, 'You guys have all the fun.' He would have been indebted to Billy for getting him into college and all that. But Jimmy was the guy he wished he was," Weeks said.

Sometimes Connolly, who was a divorced bachelor in the early 1980s and maintained an active social life, displayed the perks of the partnership too openly. His flashy suits and pinky ring, his vacation home on Cape Cod with the twenty-seven-foot boat, didn't match his modest FBI salary. "He's gotta tone it down," Whitey told Weeks. "You can't call attention to yourself." Flemmi says Whitey convinced Connolly to sell the boat that Connolly had bought with cash they'd given him.[31] Whitey was also upset when Connolly bought a condo in the same six-unit complex on West Fourth Street in which Whitey and Weeks had bought units. Whitey worried that it would draw unwanted scrutiny. "Stupid," Whitey said.[32] But, more often, Connolly and Whitey worked together seamlessly, and their meetings produced a large number of thick reports. Connolly did more than pad Whitey's informant files. He also often acted as Whitey's public relations consultant, propagating Whitey's own view of himself as a disciplined criminal who did not engage in gratuitous violence, a neighborhood vigilante using force for the greater good. Connolly cultivated contacts throughout the Boston media and invariably emphasized the image of Whitey as the good bad guy to reporters. Sometimes, too, Connolly worked to burnish Bulger's name by tapping him for help on high-profile cases. After a nine-year-old girl was abducted and disappeared from an affluent Boston suburb in 1985, the FBI agent handling the case, Dick Baker, told Connolly that they had identified a suspect in the disappearance, a twenty-two-year-old man from South Boston. Connolly asked Whitey to smoke the suspect out—to visit the young man in the jail in which he was being held on unrelated charges and get him to reveal where the girl's body was buried. The young man was terrified to find Whitey Bulger's emissary, Kevin Weeks, waiting for him in the visiting area, and he convincingly denied having had anything to do with the crime. Whitey had long fancied himself as having been deputized by the FBI. In this case he essentially was. He reported back, telling Connolly and Baker, "I do not believe this guy did it."[33] The FBI's investigation into the disappearance and presumed murder of a nine-year-old girl was, in this instance, directed by the gut feelings of Whitey Bulger. The woman who initially led investigators to the twenty-two-year-old man later admitted she had made up the whole story.

Connolly was more than Whitey's chief handler; he was his chief apologist. He insisted that Whitey and Flemmi "were an extension of the police department, the difference between anarchy" and normality. Connolly didn't deny that Whitey and Flemmi were killers. "I don't think they ever killed anyone who wasn't trying to kill them or wasn't going to rat them out," he said.[34] And Connolly never accepted the premise that it had been a mistake to let a Southie agent work with a Southie wiseguy. It wasn't a conflict of interest, he would say, it was a convergence of them. "I liked him. I liked him a lot," Connolly said. "We came from similar circumstances. But I never lost sight of who he was and what he was. Some people say you shouldn't put the hometown boy in charge of the hometown guy. Who the hell else is going to talk to the hometown guy? He wouldn't talk to anyone else."

Connolly looked at the whole uncommon arrangement as one of priorities and numbers. The FBI's priority was taking out the Mafia. Whitey and Flemmi delivered Italians. "It was a brilliant business decision," Connolly said. "We got forty-two stone criminals by giving up two stone criminals. What's your return on investment there? Show me a businessman who wouldn't do that."[35] That wasn't just Connolly's opinion. It was the opinion of the FBI leadership in Boston and Washington, who rewarded him for recruiting and maintaining a top-echelon informant like Whitey Bulger. During the 1980s, Connolly's FBI salary grew from $45,000 to $65,000.[36] But during that time, he would let his desk drawer fill with paychecks. An FBI assistant was astonished when Connolly called her at the office and asked her to leave his check in his desk drawer; she opened the drawer and counted ten others lying there.[37] He was living beyond his means and still left his checks uncashed. Something didn't add up.

There was another money stream. Flemmi says he and Whitey gave Connolly about $235,000 over the years. Whitey usually handed Connolly large lump sums twice a year: $5,000 when Connolly was going on vacation and $10,000 for Christmas. When they made a particularly big score, such as extorting a major drug dealer, Connolly was occasionally given a share. According to Flemmi, after Connolly accepted a $25,000 kickback that came from the shakedown of a drug dealer in 1983, Connolly joked, "Hey, I'm one of the gang."[38]

Connolly insists he never accepted money from Whitey or Flemmi.

Whitey's peculiar zeal for relationships, and his loyalty in friendships, was never more apparent than in his efforts to keep track of his old prison mates. In some deep place, he stayed connected to those people and those years. While he had vowed never to go back to prison, he couldn't resist the draw of Alcatraz when it was converted to a national park and opened to visitors. In 1977, with Teresa Stanley by his side, he blended in with hundreds of other tourists as he walked through the old cellblock, the dining hall, and the recreation yard. He breathed in the sights and smells and sounds that reminded him of the three years the island prison was his home.[39] He tugged at Stanley during the tour, pointing out his old cell across from the library. He confided to a park ranger that he was a former inmate, which gave him instant celebrity status. The ranger pulled him from the group tour and gave him a private one. The ranger led Whitey up some stairs to the third level of the cellblock, cranked a large lever, and the heavy metal bars of cell C-314 slid open. Whitey stepped inside the tiny cell he had lived in for nearly three years, stretching his arms out and touching the familiar cold concrete.

Whitey returned to Alcatraz at least two more times. He hated prison but he loved The Rock, or at least the idea of being part of a fraternity that had lived in America's most notorious prison. On Broadway, the central walkway between the B and C blocks, he had forged bonds and loyalties as strong as those along Broadway in Southie. Whitey's 1977 visit to Alcatraz triggered a nostalgia that led him to begin tracking down friends who had done time with him. He yearned to talk about the prison years with other Alcatraz alumni, and he wanted to know what had happened to them. Richard Sunday, who had followed Whitey from the Atlanta penitentiary out to Alcatraz, was a property manager in Virginia when Whitey called him out of the blue in the early 1980s. The two hadn't spoken since Sunday had left Alcatraz in 1961.

"Sunday!" Whitey said warmly. He was calling from Boston but hoped to come visit sometime soon and take his old friend to dinner. Sunday was grieving the death of his thirteen-year-old son. He was married, working a legitimate job, and didn't want any trouble. "How are you doing?" Sunday asked. "Are you going straight?" Whitey said he was working construction—a lie, of course—and that he was being unfairly targeted by the FBI. "Don't say nothing," Whitey said. "My phone might be tapped."[40]

Whitey told Sunday that he was trying to find some old friends from prison and, in particular, that he was looking for a friend he had served time with in Atlanta named David Comeaux. Sunday knew that Comeaux was living in Biloxi, Mississippi, so Whitey grabbed Teresa Stanley and they flew south. When they found Comeaux, he was poor and sickly, struggling to pay his bills while undergoing dialysis treatments. Whitey gave Comeaux money to pay his rent and buy some clothes. He gave Comeaux a small car to drive to and from his treatments, and he took him to dinner. On another of their cross-country trips, Whitey and Stanley went to visit Comeaux again but found he had died in 1986 at age fifty-four.[41] Whitey called Comeaux's sister, saying he wanted to drop by and visit Comeaux's mother and place some flowers on his old comrade's grave. She told him not to and abruptly hung up. He was miffed.[42]

When Whitey found out that another friend from Alcatraz, Clarence "The Choctaw Kid" Carnes, had died and been buried in a pauper's grave, he resolved to do something about it.[43] Whitey had looked up to Carnes and considered him a victim of government connivance. Carnes, a Native American from Oklahoma, had been convicted of murder at sixteen after his accomplice had killed an attendant while they were robbing a gas station. Carnes had tried to escape from prison a couple of times, earning a transfer to Alcatraz when he was just eighteen. In 1973 he was paroled, and, like Whitey, he returned to Alcatraz a free man, serving as a technical adviser on a film about his eighteen years in the prison. He got a job as a counselor at a halfway house in Kansas City, Missouri, but couldn't stop drinking and was sent back to prison for violating his parole.

Whitey was fond of Carnes. During their prison days, while delivering books to Whitey on the library cart he pushed around Alcatraz, Carnes had shared with Whitey lore about the Native American afterlife and his desire to be buried on Choctaw land in Oklahoma. Whitey was eager to help and rented him an apartment in Kansas City just before Carnes was scheduled to be released.[44] But Carnes never got to move in. The sixty-one-year-old died in federal prison in Missouri on October 3, 1988. Prison authorities could not locate any of his relatives and buried him without ceremony. Whitey was furious, believing that Carnes had been wrongly treated in life and in death. He paid ten thousand dollars to have Carnes exhumed and given a proper Choctaw burial in his hometown, Daisy, Oklahoma.[45]

Whitey called from Boston to make the arrangements and told the funeral director to spare no expense on the graveside service at the small Indian cemetery in which Carnes was buried alongside his relatives. He bought a four-thousand-dollar top-of-the-line bronze casket and a headstone of Texas rose granite with a bronze plaque. He and Teresa Stanley flew to Dallas, where they rented a Lincoln Continental and drove 153 miles for the service in Daisy on November 17, 1988. Shortly after arriving, Whitey discovered that Carnes had a great-nephew in jail in Tulsa. He raced to bail him out and brought him back for the burial. Whitey had given his old Indian friend his wish to come home. He paid for everything in cash, raising eyebrows when he pulled out a roll of bills "thick enough to choke a horse," said former Atoke Funeral Home director Robert Embry. He tipped the preacher and singers fifty dollars each and gave Embry a hundred dollars for making the arrangements and a few hundred more for picking out the headstone. "If you ever hear I'm Irish Mafia don't believe it," Whitey told Embry.[46] "I own a couple of liquor stores." Whitey told Embry that if he'd ever like to relocate to Boston, he'd buy him his own funeral home. Embry politely declined.

When Whitey learned that another former inmate of Alcatraz, Leon Thompson, had written a book and was trying to get it published, he looked up his number and called him in California. Their years on Alcatraz overlapped, but Whitey couldn't remember Thompson, a bank robber, even though his nickname was also Whitey. When Thompson started relating names and events, Whitey began correcting him, offering his own version. He noticed that Thompson had grown quiet. Annoyed, Whitey accused him of taking notes on the conversation.[47]

Thompson changed the subject and talked about his wife, a native of England. She had left after World War II and never got back, and Thompson said he hoped to be able to afford to send her for a visit if his book sold well. Whitey asked to speak to her. He immediately took a liking to Helen Thompson, who shared his love of animals and had a charming accent. He offered to pay for her trip home and told her to check the price of a round-trip ticket and he'd call back in a couple of hours. "Don't forget twenty dollars for the book!" Leon Thompson shouted in the background. Whitey kept his promise. He sent Helen Thompson the airfare and twelve hundred dollars in spending money. He confided to some of his friends that he also sent Leon Thompson a significant amount of money to help publish his book.[48]

In the summer of 1988, Thompson sent Whitey an autographed copy of his biography, *Last Train to Alcatraz*, and tucked a note inside: "If and when you get out to the west coast, be sure to get in touch with Helen and I. It would be a real pleasure to see you. Take care now. Best wishes! Leon and Helen."[49] Whitey, however, was livid when he read Thompson's account, which he thought was full of distortions and errors. He was particularly upset at the portrayal of some of his old Alcatraz pals. "The author has done a disservice to the guys who were on the Rock by lying about individuals, conditions, events, etc." Whitey scribbled on the front of the book, underneath an inscription Thompson had written wishing him well. "This book is strictly fiction." Thompson had quickly gone from friend to foe. Whitey never received a thank-you note from Thompson's wife and was convinced Leon Thompson had pocketed the money meant for her trip to England.[50]

He decided to pay Thompson a visit, but not a friendly one. Whitey and Teresa Stanley traveled to San Francisco twice looking for him. "Intended to confront him and call him a liar and maybe give him a broken jaw," Whitey wrote.[51] Like other former Alcatraz inmates and guards who had gone on to write books about their time at the prison, Thompson was in demand for book signings on Alcatraz. Whitey lurked around Pier 41, where the ferries left for Alcatraz, hoping to confront him. "He came here five days straight looking for him," said Peter Dracopoulos, who has been selling books and souvenirs from a small shack on the pier since the 1970s. "He wanted to beat the crap out of him. I believe he was so angry he would have knocked him out right on the pier."[52]

Once expelled from one of Whitey's circles, you were never allowed back in.

The last and in many ways the smallest of Whitey's circles was the one reserved for his women. He took much from them in the way of domestic life and companionship, and gave them much in return, but they were never entrusted with the concerns and details of his violent business. All were astonishingly blind to his dark side and professional activities.

Teresa Stanley and Cathy Greig were the principals, Whitey's most enduring mistresses, even though he had frequent flings with other women. But they were very different people. Greig was from South Boston but not completely of it. She was better educated and more worldly than Stanley. Greig, who never had children, preferred the company of animals, especially dogs. That was fine by Whitey, who often said he liked animals better than people.[53]

Greig fought constantly with Whitey over his relationship with Stanley; Stanley was entirely unaware of Greig's existence and of Whitey's domestic partnership with her. Stanley had no idea that when he left her house he drove six miles to Quincy, where he and Greig lived together. But Stanley provided Whitey with a level of domestic normalcy that balanced out his stressful work as a criminal and FBI informant. He treated her children as his own, even walking Stanley's daughter Karen down the aisle and paying for her lavish wedding to professional hockey player Chris Nilan—a man famous for his on-ice brawling. Whitey took a shine to his surrogate son-in-law. He had never been much of a sports fan, but when Nilan played for the Montreal Canadiens, Whitey frequently traveled to Montreal with Stanley to attend games. After the Canadiens won the Stanley Cup in 1986, a smiling Whitey proudly posed for a photo with Nilan and the Cup.

Even though she hated sharing Whitey, Greig was tolerant of his infidelties. When she and Whitey shared a condominium at Louisburg Square in Quincy, he brought another woman back one night when Greig wasn't home. The next morning, Greig arrived and was in the kitchen making breakfast when the other woman walked in and asked, "Are you the maid?" Greig replied, "No. You've been fucking my boyfriend all night."[54]

Greig's response to Whitey's wandering eye was to make herself more attractive. She worked out daily. She got her teeth cleaned monthly. She had breast implants, a facelift, liposuction, and eyelid surgery.[55] The girl who had been voted best-looking in the Southie High class of 1969 had a complete makeover, all of it paid for by Whitey.

And despite all, she doted on Whitey. He would show up in Quincy at all hours of the night and early morning, and she would get up to cook for him. He became increasingly devoted to Greig, who gave up her dental career to take care of him. Her decision to stop working was heavily influenced by the 1984 suicide of her twenty-six-year-old brother, David, who had struggled with drugs. David Greig shot himself at the family's South Boston home, a deeply traumatizing event for Cathy. Whitey told her she didn't have to go back to her job; he'd take care of her. In 1986, Whitey bought her a split-level ranch house in Squantum.

With Stanley, Whitey was a family man. But when he was with Greig he expected her undivided attention, and he didn't like it when Greig put her beloved French poodles before him. Once when DEA agents were listening in on a wiretap on his cell phone, they overheard him screaming at Greig, "You care more about the fucking dogs than you do about me!" Like Stanley, Greig never wanted for anything when Whitey was around; he paid all the bills. He kept a globe in the middle of the dining room of Greig's home. It was designed to hold liquor, but Whitey used it as an ATM, stuffing it with hundred-, fifty-, and twenty-dollar bills. When Greig wanted anything, she'd open the globe and help herself. Greig's twin sister, Margaret McCusker, was amazed when she watched Greig open the globe one day and peel off bills. "Oh my God, do you know how much you're spending?" McCusker asked her. "Do you even know?"[56]

It didn't matter. The money was rolling in, and Whitey was in control. He had many balls in the air, balancing two ongoing domestic relationships even as he eliminated rivals either with his gun or his informant reports. It was complicated, but he was managing it. As long as Whitey stayed inside Whitey's world and kept each circle in its place, his empire seemed as solid as the walls of Fort Independence on Castle Island. But once he stepped outside the careful choreography of his life and started to break his own rules, he was asking for trouble. And found it.

10

Overreach

The pitch came in the spring of 1981 from John Callahan, a sly and successful executive who, like his gangster friends, was always on the lookout for a score. Callahan asked Whitey and Stevie Flemmi to kill a businessman who was getting in his way—a legitimate guy, as the wiseguys say. It was something they had never done. Their victims had always been tied somehow to the underworld. But this was a reach. An overreach, it would turn out. But Whitey and Flemmi listened because what Callahan was dangling sounded so lucrative, so easy.

Callahan was an accountant who preferred the company of assassins. He rubbed shoulders with the gangsters he met at Chandler's, the South End nightclub controlled by the Winter Hill Gang. He was generous with rounds; the wiseguys liked that. They also liked the fact that, despite his own legitimate job, Callahan was a rogue, willing to engage in various moneymaking and money-laundering schemes with criminals.

Callahan grew up in Medford, a blue-collar city where upwardly mobile crooks from neighboring Somerville liked to install their families. His father ran a wholesale produce company in Charlestown, a neighborhood where gangsters were almost as common as longshoremen. Callahan, with his thick build and hearty laugh, knew the life and was attracted to it. More studious than most of his peers, he joined the air force right out of high school, determined to have the military pay for his college education. The air force sent him to Yale to learn Chinese. He left the service after one tour and studied accounting at Bentley College while working for his father in Charlestown. In time he landed a job with the accounting firm Ernst & Ernst. He became a CPA and joined a bigger firm with a national profile, Arthur Andersen. A gifted schmoozer, Callahan made partner at Arthur Andersen in 1970. But it didn't last. He liked the nightlife too much to be much good at early-morning client meetings. He often showed up hungover and unkempt, if he showed up at all, and in 1972, he left the firm to set up his own consulting business. His contacts in the banking and finance worlds rivaled his contacts in the underworld, and he would use both.

In 1974, he was hired by World Jai Alai, a Miami-based company founded in the 1930s and one of the first to turn the Basque sport of jai alai—in which a curved basket is used to catch and hurl a ball at startling velocity—into a game that could be wagered on. Betting on the sport was legal only in a few states, including Florida and Connecticut, and World Jai Alai was looking to expand.[1] To do so, it hired Callahan to help the company find a new president. After reviewing the firm's robust cash flow, the opportunistic Callahan recommended himself. The board of directors hired him on the slimmest of majority votes. Callahan's backers pointed to his accounting skills and the banking contacts he had who could help the company get needed financing. His detractors said he knew nothing about gaming. Both sides were wrong. His contacts were less in banking than in crime, and he knew more about the gambling business than they could have imagined.

The board might have voted the other way had it known that, at the same time that they were considering hiring him, Callahan was in Boston, drinking with a Winter Hill Gang leg breaker named Brian Halloran. In the course of the evening, Halloran got into a fight with an off-duty police officer. The cop was badly beaten and Halloran wound up in jail, even after Callahan testified on his behalf. Without knowing it, World Jai Alai had hired a magnet for trouble.

Callahan's decisions in his new job came under scrutiny almost immediately. The Boston man he hired to run the jai alai arena's food and beverage concessions had no previous experience in the field and was known mainly as a boxer and boxing manager. The man was barely on the job when, in a fit of frustration, he kicked the freezer door in the stadium's kitchen off its hinges.[2] Callahan redeemed himself by bringing in as head of security a recently retired FBI agent who specialized in organized crime: Paul Rico. Rico seemed like a savvy hire. He had come to Callahan with the highest recommendations—from criminals. Rico, during his Boston years, had facilitated the rise of the Winter Hill Gang by helping it eliminate its rivals in Charlestown. Much like his successor in the Boston office, John Connolly, he was an agent who had grown fascinated by the underworld and then been swallowed by it. The board of directors, however, saw him only as a veteran FBI agent who would win them brownie points with jai alai's overseers in law enforcement.

But Callahan's taste in after-work companions, his yen for the reckless, riotous, ever-scheming side of underworld society, would eventually get him fired from World Jai Alai. In 1976, as the company was seeking to expand its operation, opening an arena in Connecticut, the board of directors asked Callahan to resign because police had complained about his open association with gangland figures. Notable among those associations were the Martorano brothers, Jimmy and Johnny, and Howie Winter, head of the Winter Hill Gang. Callahan couldn't exactly plead innocent. On March 1, 1976, he'd spent the afternoon in a meeting with Connecticut investigators who were vetting World Jai Alai, and when the conversation drifted to the sort of people he socialized with after work

As a teenager, Whitey Bulger was one of the toughest kids in his neighborhood. He was a dedicated physical fitness buff, running on nearby Carson Beach and lifting weights in his family's apartment in the Old Harbor Village housing project. (Courtesy of Teresa Stanley)

By the time Whitey was in his twenties, he had graduated to bank robbery and the lifestyle it afforded. He estimated that he spent twenty-five thousand dollars in one year on stylish clothes, sumptuous food, and fancy hotels for him and his girlfriend. (Courtesy of Teresa Stanley)

William "Bill" Bulger in 1988 in his office at the Massachusetts State House, where he presided as president of the senate from 1978 to 1996. He was fiercely protective of his older brother, Whitey, advocating for him during the nine years Whitey was in prison. (*Boston Globe* / Mark Wilson)

Above left: After Whitey's discharge from the air force, he was arrested repeatedly in 1953 on minor charges. (Courtesy of the Boston Police Department) *Above right*: In 1956, he was sentenced to twenty years for bank robbery and sent to the Atlanta penitentiary, where he participated in an LSD experiment that left him with nightmares for the rest of his life. *Below left*: After being linked to escape plots, Whitey was banished to the notorious Alcatraz prison in 1959. *Below right*: Whitey's father died in 1964 while he was in Lewisburg Penitentiary, Pennsylvania, and Whitey wasn't allowed to attend the funeral. (Courtesy of the National Archives in San Bruno, California)

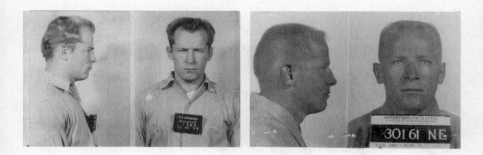

Lindsey Cyr, mother of Whitey's only known child, and their four-year-old son, Douglas, in 1971. Whitey, a doting father, was deeply shaken when the boy died at age six. (Courtesy of Lindsey Cyr)

Whitey firebombed John F. Kennedy's birthplace in 1975 to protest busing of Southie students during desegregation. He spray-painted "Bus Teddy" outside because Senator Edward "Ted" Kennedy was a staunch defender of busing. (*Boston Globe* / George Rizer)

Triple O's in South Boston became Whitey's hangout. He used the bar's private upstairs room to plot mayhem, extort money, and meet with the founder of the Provisional Irish Republican Army. (*Boston Globe* / Pam Berry)

John Connolly, Whitey's FBI handler, in 1998, nine years after his retirement. He grew up in the same housing project as the Bulgers, and Whitey's brother Bill was a mentor. Connolly returned the favor by becoming Whitey's protector. (*Boston Globe* / George Rizer)

Connolly, in 1983, at the time considered a model agent, escorting Mafia bookkeeper Frankie Angiulo to court after his arrest on federal racketeering charges. (*Boston Globe* / Ted Dully)

Whitey and Teresa Stanley during a trip to Europe in the 1980s. Whitey began dating Stanley in 1966, when she was a single mother with four young children. He insisted on nightly family dinners and lectured her kids about studying hard and staying away from bad influences. (Courtesy of Teresa Stanley)

John Morris in 1987. Morris, who supervised the Boston FBI organized crime squad, took gifts and money from Whitey and leaked him information. He avoided prison by cooperating against Whitey and John Connolly. (*Boston Globe* / Tom Herde)

Whitey and Teresa Stanley at a wedding in the 1980s. Whitey paid for the wedding of Stanley's daughter Karen and Chris Nilan, who played hockey for the Montreal Canadiens and the Boston Bruins. (Courtesy of Teresa Stanley)

Whitey and his protégé, Kevin Weeks, in 1994 on Castle Island in South Boston. Whitey groomed Weeks, a champion amateur boxer, to be his go-to guy. They walked the island daily, avoiding electronic surveillance as they talked. Weeks helped Whitey in his early days on the run, before he knew Whitey was an informant. He cooperated with investigators after his arrest and led them to the secret graves of Whitey's victims. (*Boston Globe* / John Tlumacki)

Cathy Greig in an undated photo with her poodles, Nikki and Gigi. Whitey once accused Greig of caring more about the poodles than him. She complained about being second fiddle to Whitey's other longtime girlfriend, Teresa Stanley. (Courtesy of the FBI)

Kevin Weeks in 2006 on Castle Island. After just five years in prison, Weeks emerged to write a memoir about his life with Whitey and continued to testify, in a plethora of criminal and civil trials, about the deeds of Whitey and Steve Flemmi. (*Boston Globe* / John Tlumacki)

Boston Mafia chief Gennaro "Jerry" Angiulo in 1987, a year after he was convicted of racketeering. The FBI credited Whitey with helping plant a bug inside Angiulo's headquarters, but there is little evidence that Whitey was needed to get the court authorization. (*Boston Globe* / Jim Wilson)

Steve Flemmi and Debra Davis in an undated photo. Twenty-six-year-old Davis tried to end her nine-year romance with Flemmi after falling in love with another man. Flemmi said he and Whitey strangled her because she knew they were FBI informants. Whitey denies killing her. (Courtesy of Bill St. Croix)

Richard Sunday served time with Whitey Bulger in both Atlanta and Alcatraz and became one of his closest friends. Whitey liked Sunday's poetry so much that he kept a copy of his poem "The Ballad of Billy the Kid" tucked in his Bible. (Courtesy of the National Archives in San Bruno, California)

Boston accountant John Callahan, 1975. He paid his Winter Hill Gang friends to kill Roger Wheeler. The gangsters killed Callahan in Florida in 1982 to keep him from cooperating against them. (Associated Press)

Roger Wheeler in an undated photo. The World Jai Alai owner was gunned down in Tulsa in 1981 after refusing to sell his business to John Callahan, a Boston business consultant with Winter Hill Gang ties. (Associated Press)

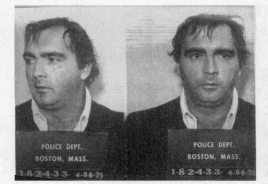

Brian Halloran in a 1975 mugshot. Halloran, a Winter Hill Gang associate, was gunned down by Whitey in Boston in 1982 after telling the FBI that Whitey and Steve Flemmi killed Roger Wheeler. (Courtesy of the Boston Police Department)

Michael Donahue in a family photo from 1977. A truck driver and unintended target, Donahue was giving Halloran a ride home when Whitey opened fire, killing both of them. (Courtesy of the Donahue family)

Deborah Hussey in an undated photo. Steve Flemmi said that in 1985 he and Whitey killed Hussey, the daughter of Flemmi's longtime companion, and buried her in a basement. Whitey denies it. (Courtesy of Tom Hussey)

John McIntyre in an undated photo. A member of the crew
that delivered a Whitey-sponsored weapons shipment to the
IRA, McIntyre was killed by Whitey and Steve Flemmi in 1984
after they learned he was cooperating against them. (Courtesy of
the McIntyre family)

Cathy Greig and Whitey walking Nikki and Gigi in the summer of 1988 at a
Dorchester playground, not far from the condominium in Quincy where they lived at
the time. Whitey, who rarely drank, picked up a discarded beer can and tossed it in
the trash. (*Boston Globe* / John Tlumacki)

The *Valhalla* in 1984, shortly after returning to port in Boston from a rendezvous off the coast of Ireland. The fishing trawler ferried seven tons of weapons to the Irish Republican Army after the founder of the IRA visited Whitey in Southie, saying that the organization needed guns. (*Boston Globe* / George Rizer)

Pat Nee in his native Ireland in 1984, awaiting arrival of weapons on the *Valhalla*. A onetime rival of Whitey turned criminal confederate, Nee broke with Whitey when he suspected he was an informant. He wrote a memoir that was bitterly critical of Whitey. (Courtesy of Pat Nee)

The Donahues in 2008. *From left*: Shawn, Patricia, Michael Jr., and Tom. The government was ordered to pay them $6.3 million for the wrongful death of Michael Donahue. An appeals court overturned the award. (*Boston Globe* / Pat Greenhouse)

Steve Flemmi testifying at Connolly's murder trial in Miami in 2008. He said that he and Whitey paid kickbacks totaling around $235,000 to Connolly, who once joked that he was one of the gang. (Associated Press / J. Pat Carter)

John Connolly in 2008, at a hearing on the eve of his trial in Miami for the 1982 murder of John Callahan. He was convicted and sentenced to forty years. (Associated Press / Wilfredo Lee)

John Martorano in an undated photo. He served twelve years for twenty murders after agreeing to testify against Whitey, Steve Flemmi, and John Connolly. (Courtesy of the Martorano family)

Anna Bjornsdottir playing with her cat outside her home in Reykjavík, Iceland, in 2011. The former Miss Iceland was paid two million dollars by the FBI for her tip leading to Whitey's capture (*Boston Globe* / Bill Greene)

The Princess Eugenia, the Santa Monica complex where Whitey and Cathy Greig lived for fifteen years, hours after their arrest in June 2011. Their apartment is on the top floor, farthest to the right. (Associated Press / David Zentz)

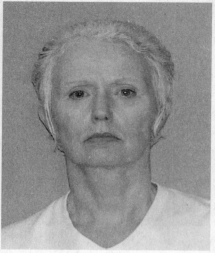

Whitey, in booking photo, shortly after his arrest in Santa Monica in June 2011. (Courtesy of the US Marshals Service)

Cathy Greig, in booking photo, shortly after her arrest in Santa Monica in June 2011. (Courtesy of the US Marshals Service)

Whitey, at Logan Airport in 2011, being led by US deputy marshals from a US Coast Guard helicopter that brought him from a Plymouth, Massachusetts, jail to federal court in Boston. (Courtesy of Bill Converse)

he'd abruptly left, telling Connecticut State Police he had to fly to Miami. They didn't believe him and followed behind as he drove from Hartford to Boston and then went drinking with Jimmy Martorano at the Playboy Club. Boston police later gave Connecticut State Police a series of surveillance photos showing Callahan to be a regular at Chandler's, the Winter Hill Gang's bar of choice.

Callahan had been exposed. He told the board he'd depart willingly if they agreed to let his friend Richard Donovan succeed him and also let Rico stay in place. The board had no idea why this was so important to him, didn't know that Callahan and Rico had been skimming money from the company, up to a million dollars a year, mostly cash from the food and parking concessions and bets that weren't being reported. Within two months Callahan was back with a surprising proposition—to buy the company himself for thirty-five million dollars. The board declined the offer. Next, in what should have been a tip-off, Rico proposed that Jack Cooper, a Miami Beach associate of the gangster Meyer Lansky, buy the company. Again, the board, though open to the notion of selling, demurred.[3]

Callahan then had what he considered an inspired idea: If an established businessman, a white knight, bought the company, the board would be pacified, law enforcement attention would be diverted, and he could still quietly skim off his share. Callahan used his business contacts in Boston to recruit Roger Wheeler, an Oklahoma entrepreneur who had made his fortune with a computer company called Telex Corp. and was in the market for investment opportunities. Wheeler was unlikely company for gamblers, and even less likely to associate with mobsters. Born in Boston, he grew up in Reading, a suburb north of the city. He attended MIT, served in the navy, then went to Notre Dame and Rice University, where he graduated with a degree in electrical engineering in 1946. He worked in the oil industry before founding companies of his own, making chemicals and metals. In 1965, he took over the then failing Telex Corporation in Tulsa and turned it into a moneymaker. Wheeler did very well but wanted more; he wanted to get rich enough to fulfill a dream and buy a home on Nantucket, the pricey, exclusive island off the coast of Massachusetts. He'd looked at the obscene profit margins of the legalized gaming industry and wanted in.[4] A devout Presbyterian, Wheeler said that he opposed gambling personally but that, as long as it was legal, it was better if it were run by responsible businessmen—people like him.[5]

Wheeler's subsequent failed attempts to buy racetracks, a slot machine business, and even a Las Vegas casino signaled his interest, which led to an approach by Callahan's business contact at the First National Bank of Boston, David McKown. A loan officer with the bank, McKown had done business and was friendly with Wheeler, and told him that the jai alai company could be had for fifty million dollars. In 1977, the last year World Jai Alai was a publicly owned company, it reported net profits of five million dollars on revenues of thirty-one million dollars.[6] The margins were irresistible. Wheeler said he could put up seventeen million. McKown said the bank would front the remaining thirty-three million on favorable terms. Deal.

One of Wheeler's first moves as owner was to send his sons to Miami to audit the company's finances. That made Callahan extremely nervous, and well it should have. A million-dollar-a-year skim would be hard to miss. He had to find a way to pry the business away from Wheeler before Wheeler found him out, and he had an idea who could help. He called his old drinking buddy from Chandler's, Johnny Martorano. When Martorano went on the run from the horse race–fixing indictment in 1979, it was Callahan who helped set him up with an apartment and a car in Florida. When Martorano needed cash, Callahan ferried it down to him from Boston. Now Callahan was looking for a favor. He was going to make a move on World Jai Alai, but before he did he wanted to secure Winter Hill's muscle to protect his investment. "He was trying to buy the [business] for a lot of money," Martorano said. "He said if the deal goes through, we'll give you $10,000 a week, cash, through the company, parking lot, vending, whatever."[7]

Once Callahan was at the helm, Winter Hill would make sure nobody, especially other criminals, bothered him. It seemed like easy money; it *was* easy money—as much in a week as Winter Hill collected in tribute from a dozen bookies in a month. Martorano ran it by the only two Winter Hill partners who still mattered—Whitey and Flemmi—and they agreed it was a no-brainer. They probably wouldn't have to lift a finger for ten grand a week. There was only one problem. Roger Wheeler. "Callahan offered $60, $80, $100 million and the guy refused it," Martorano said. "Roger Wheeler refused to sell." Callahan told Martorano that Wheeler would have to go. He asked Martorano to kill him. Martorano's first instinct was always to help a friend, and Callahan was a friend, but then he paused. Whitey and Flemmi had to approve any hit, and they were wary—not about the deal but about killing the likes of Wheeler. But Callahan was a confident man, or maybe a desperate one: He said he'd talk to Whitey and Flemmi himself.[8]

They met on a warm spring night at the Black Rose, an Irish pub next to Faneuil Hall Marketplace, a collection of restaurants and shops on Boston's tourist trail. Like Whitey, Callahan styled himself an Irishman. Like Whitey, he gave money to the Irish Republican Army regularly. There was always loud live music at the Black Rose, and this night was no different. Above the din of Irish rebel songs, Callahan leaned into Whitey and Flemmi. "Listen," Callahan told them, "Wheeler is being unreasonable." He explained that he and Rico had decided that the only way to get the company back was to eliminate him. He was sure that Wheeler's wife would want to sell if her husband was dead. And he said that Johnny Martorano was willing to do the hit, but only if Whitey and Flemmi were on board.[9] The gangsters said they'd think about it, but as they left the raucous bar, Whitey told Flemmi he had serious reservations. For one thing, Callahan drank too much and Whitey never liked that in his partners. And as much as he liked to hang around gangsters, and as fluently as he talked the game, Callahan was a civilian, a member of no gang. Now, suddenly, he's looking to arrange a murder?

Flemmi called Rico, his old FBI handler.

"Are you with this?" Flemmi asked.

"Yeah, I want it to happen," Rico replied. "We want you to be part of this."[10]

The hit was to take place in Tulsa, where Wheeler lived and would be most vulnerable; Rico had begun working on Wheeler's routine, watching his patterns as he came and went from work and home, looking to find the best place and time to shoot him. But Whitey still didn't like it. "He's a legitimate guy," Whitey said, pacing back and forth in Broadway Furniture, the appliance store in Southie they were using as a meeting spot. Whitey had killed a lot of people, but all of them had been criminal competitors, and Boston guys. He had survived this long in a hazardous trade by being smarter and more careful than most. This was something new and unsettling, though the money was undeniably enticing.

For days, Whitey and Flemmi went back and forth, as in a tennis, or maybe a jai-alai, match. "The guy's a zillionaire," Whitey said. "His family is politically connected. We'll never survive it."[11]

"This is easy, steady money," Flemmi replied.[12] Besides, their old friend Paul Rico was their insurance policy. Rico, with his FBI connections, will deflect the heat, Flemmi said. He could make anything go away. "Johnny's gonna do this whether we're involved or not," Flemmi said. "He's our partner. We've got to be part of this."[13]

Whitey could be obstinate, but he also was susceptible to the peer pressure of criminal partnerships. When he asked his partners to do a murder, he didn't expect a debate. He expected them to follow him unquestioningly. In the end, Flemmi wore Whitey down. He was probably the only one who could.[14] But even after Flemmi had won him over, Whitey second-guessed himself. "We're all gonna go to jail," he told Flemmi. "This will never go away. Never."[15]

It was never a good idea to do a hit alone, especially in unfamiliar territory. Even a legendary killer like Martorano needed help, and Rico asked the old Winter Hill hit man Joe McDonald to be the accomplice. McDonald was already on the run but agreed to do it, saying he owed Rico a favor from years ago.[16] Martorano and McDonald flew out to Oklahoma City and rented a car. They drove a hundred miles east toward Tulsa, checking into a series of cheap motels, the last being the Trade Winds West. Martorano liked the tiki bar there.

Whitey and Flemmi had prepared the hit kit: a .38 revolver, a machine gun with a silencer, a slim jim to pop a car lock, a dent puller to yank out the ignition of the stolen car that would be used for the hit. They'd wrapped the kit up and put it in a suitcase, surrounded by clothes, and sent it on a Greyhound bus to Tulsa. Martorano and McDonald, meanwhile, spent their days assessing the best place to kill Roger Wheeler. They cased his mansion on East Forty-first Street and decided it was too wide-open. By the looks of it, the property had security cameras. They drove to the Telex Corporation's office building and saw a camera on the building pointed right at Wheeler's parking space.[17]

Martorano told Callahan that they were having trouble finding an advantageous spot for the hit. Callahan quickly sent along a note with some new information he'd obtained, courtesy of Rico. Wheeler played golf every Wednesday at the Southern Hills Country Club. As Martorano unfolded the piece of paper, he marveled at Rico. The retired FBI agent was crooked, but he was, as ever, meticulous. Besides the address of the country club, Rico had sent Wheeler's usual Wednesday tee time: Assuming a round would take about four hours, Wheeler would be off the course sometime around four in the afternoon.[18]

As his weekly golf game suggested, Roger Wheeler was a man of routines. At fifty-five, he ran three and a half miles every day. He was fit and trim, still the same weight he had been in his twenties. After his Wednesday game, he would shower, have a Scotch, then wash that down with a chocolate chip milk shake. Wheeler lost a friendly golf wager on May 27, 1981, and lamented, as he left the club locker room, that his 12-handicap was too low. He was giving away too many strokes and kept losing bets. "See you Saturday," he called out to the manager at the club's golf shop as he left. "Be sure to get my handicap up. These boys are killing me."[19]

It was after 4:00 p.m. when Martorano spotted a man who resembled Wheeler walking across the parking lot. Martorano got out of a Pontiac that McDonald had stolen earlier that day and walked briskly in back of Wheeler. He wanted to make sure the guy was going for Wheeler's Cadillac. Wheeler opened the driver's-side door and tossed his leather gym bag onto the passenger seat. He climbed behind the wheel and tried to pull the door shut.

Two little girls were standing on the diving board of the country club's pool next to the parking lot. They saw a heavyset man wearing a baseball cap and what turned out to be a fake beard walk quickly up to the Cadillac and hold the door open. The man in the cap, Johnny Martorano, dropped a white towel that had been draped over a snub-nose revolver in his hand and pulled the trigger. The gun exploded and five bullets fell to the pavement, but the one shot Martorano managed to get off went straight into Wheeler's forehead and killed him. McDonald slid the Pontiac to a halt just long enough for Martorano to climb into the passenger's seat and they were gone in seconds, out the back gate. The little girls on the diving board couldn't make out the license plate.[20]

When the news of Wheeler's murder reached Boston, John Connolly, nervous about the possible fallout for his No. 1 informant, called Whitey at Teresa Stanley's house. Connolly knew he'd be there because it was just after dinnertime. "If anybody asks, you were talking to me when this happened," Connolly said.[21] Whitey had been right to be wary and wrong to go along. Wheeler's murder caused more consternation within law enforcement than the average gangland hit. A millionaire businessman getting gunned down in the parking lot of a country clubs attracts a sort of attention that doesn't easily dissipate. Callahan had given Johnny Martorano fifty thousand dollars for the hit, a little more than usual given the risks of the out-of-state assignment. Martorano split the money with McDonald and then gave Whitey and Flemmi a cut of his share. Whitey pocketed the money, knowing it was more trouble than it was worth.

Back in Tulsa, Mike Huff, the detective who first leaned over Wheeler's body, had some good leads right away. It was, he found, common knowledge inside World Jai Alai that John Callahan had been angling to take the company over and that he was thick with the Winter Hill Gang. But when, at Huff's request, the Tulsa FBI asked the Boston FBI office for help, they received a terse reply that Boston had ruled out a Winter Hill connection. It was a scam, of course. Morris had dispatched Connolly to interview Callahan, who obligingly said that he had nothing to do with those Winter Hill characters. Connolly reported that his informants, Whitey and Flemmi, had had no role in Roger Wheeler's demise and that they, too, vouched for Callahan.

It was the kind of circle of lies that had, in the past, so often and easily fended off trouble. And it seemed like it would do so again, even though Callahan and Rico had badly misjudged Wheeler's widow. She refused to sell the jai alai company, and Wheeler's sons, Larry and David, were convinced that their father's murder had something to do with Callahan and his underworld connections. They were absolutely right, but with the FBI in Boston actively undermining the investigation, Mike Huff and the Tulsa cops got nowhere. Huff was so frustrated he overstepped protocol and went right to Connolly, asking for help. He was unaware that Whitey and Flemmi were informants and that Connolly was their handler. Huff's appeal ran into a wall. He said that Connolly told him "that his job was to 'take down the [Mafia]' and not investigate 'his Irish.'"[22]

Whitey and Flemmi, thankful for the support, sent a case of fine wine to Morris.[23] When Connolly delivered the gift in the garage of the FBI's Boston office, Morris urged him to return it. "You need to take this," Connolly insisted. "If you don't take it, they're going to think you don't trust them."[24] Morris nodded in understanding and took the wine.

For Whitey, an unsettling chapter appeared to be over at last. But it would have a sequel.

Only the extremely intoxicated or the uninitiated went to the Four Seas in Boston's Chinatown for the food. The menu was outdated, the spareribs greasy, the chicken fingers greasier. The laughing porcelain Buddha in the restaurant's ground-level window presided over a subterranean, garishly lit Chinese speakeasy. The Four Seas didn't have a liquor license but it had liquor, and it was open until four in the morning, attracting an eclectic mix: politicians from Beacon Hill, cops from headquarters, strippers from the nearby Combat Zone, gangsters from all over.

It was October 1981, and there were three men sitting at a round table inside the otherwise deserted restaurant. George Pappas, a cocaine dealer, sat between Brian Halloran, John Callahan's friend and a fringe player in the Winter Hill Gang, and Jackie Salemme, a Mafioso. Pappas was about to report to prison to begin a five-year sentence for dealing cocaine. A judge had given him a month to get his affairs in order. Part of that, in his line of work, was meeting Jackie Salemme and Brian Halloran at the Four Seas at four in the morning.

Jerry Angiulo, the Mafia leader, had accused Pappas of holding back on tribute he owed the mob and had dispatched Salemme to sort it out. Salemme brought the hulking Halloran along for some muscle.[25] The waiter, Soon Yen Chin, served Halloran and Salemme cans of Sprite. Pappas ordered a steak to go. The three men were chatting amiably. Chin put the takeout order in front of Pappas and left a check. Then, from the kitchen, Chin heard a single gunshot. He ran upstairs and hid with two cooks. By the time the police arrived, Halloran and Salemme were gone. George Pappas was facedown on the table. Blood poured from the hole above his right eye, congealing around the brown paper bag that contained his cooling steak.*[26]

Salemme ran to his Mafia friends, who had a plan for him to go underground for a while—to go, as the wiseguys called it, to the mattress. Halloran wasn't so lucky. He was on his own, or thought he was. He didn't know it, but for the previous seven weeks he had been under surveillance by a federal Bureau of Alcohol, Tobacco and Firearms agent named Bill Murphy, who was checking out a tip that Halloran had been carrying a weapon without a license. Murphy had been sitting for hours in his beat-up Chevy Impala, drinking bad coffee, following Halloran from one dive bar to the next. The radio was broken so he'd had no distractions. On Columbus Day weekend, he followed Halloran back to his apartment in Quincy around 2:00 a.m. and then finally called it a night. It was bad luck for Murphy, because not long after he ended the surveillance Halloran jumped into his car and went back out, arriving at the Four Seas shortly after 3:00 a.m.

When Murphy walked into the office the next morning, another ATF agent said, "Hey, did you hear about that hit in Chinatown?" Murphy had a feeling. He called the Boston police homicide unit and the detective on the case got on the phone and explained what they had: a dead body at the table, a set of keys underneath. The car key was matched to a white Buick Regal, rented from National Car Rental, that the cops had found parked near the restaurant. "It was Brian Halloran," Bill Murphy told the stunned detective, Steve Murphy. "That was the car I was following. There's a kid's car seat in the back, isn't there?"

A short time later, the two Murphys and a prosecutor were standing outside the Quincy apartment Bill Murphy had been sitting on for weeks. They had a search warrant that said that if the key fit the apartment door they could get an arrest warrant for Brian Halloran.

---

*In 1985, the Supreme Judicial Court of Massachusetts threw out Salemme's conviction for the murder of George Pappas.

Steve Murphy inserted one of the keys found under the table where George Pappas had ordered his last meal and the lock turned.[27] Seventeen days after Pappas was shot, Halloran turned himself in. He made bail, but all that did was release him to the wild. He had put the target on his own back—he couldn't really count on Jackie Salemme's friends to believe he would keep his mouth shut. A few months after Pappas was shot dead, and three days after Halloran's wife gave birth to their second son, on Christmas Day, Halloran reached out to FBI agent Leo Brunnick and said he wanted to talk. He wanted to trade information for protection. "I know who killed Roger Wheeler," Halloran told Brunnick and his partner, Gerry Montanari.

And so the aftershocks of Whitey's overreach continued.

Halloran told an intriguing story, recalling the day he went to Callahan's apartment, above Callahan's office, on a wharf overlooking Boston Harbor, and found Whitey and Flemmi there. They talked about taking out Wheeler, to ward off his audit of the jai alai company, which was sure to turn up the skim. Halloran said Callahan asked him, right there in front of Whitey and Flemmi, to kill Wheeler.

He had a reputation as a tough guy, but Halloran told the agents that he'd asked if there was some other way to get rid of Wheeler short of killing him, and that Whitey had sneered. Whitey didn't like Halloran, and the feeling was mutual. Callahan asked Halloran to think it over and said he'd be back in touch. Two weeks later, Callahan asked Halloran to meet him at his office. When he arrived he handed him twenty thousand dollars in cash, saying he wasn't needed on Wheeler anymore. "I shouldn't have involved you in the first place," Callahan said.[28]

After Wheeler was murdered, Halloran told the agents, he had met Callahan for drinks at the Pier, a restaurant and bar on the Southie waterfront, and Callahan had told him how it had gone down: that Johnny Martorano had done the shooting, Steve Flemmi had driven the getaway car, and Whitey Bulger had driven a backup car. Montanari and Brunnick were skeptical of his account and were right to be. It was a blend of fact—Martorano's role—and embellishment, bringing Whitey and Flemmi directly into the hit. And while Halloran had a reputation as a heavy, a leg breaker who collected debts, he wasn't known as a shooter. Why would Callahan and the Winter Hill boys ever have turned to him for such a complicated, risky job? Still, they thought, Halloran knew too much about the Wheeler hit to just brush him off; Callahan must have told him something. And here he was, implicating not just Whitey and Flemmi but his good friend John Callahan in a contract killing.

Halloran had nothing to lose, and everything to gain, by giving up Whitey and Flemmi. He knew the Mafia wouldn't think twice about taking him out to protect a made guy like Salemme. But it wasn't just the Mafia. Halloran could barely keep track of everybody who wanted to kill him. He told Brunnick and Montanari that he would testify but that he wanted to go into the Witness Protection Program. He had survived two assassination attempts in the months before he was charged with the Pappas murder. His wife was nursing a newborn and he had to get off the street before he made her a widow. He assumed the FBI would jump at the chance to take out the two biggest gangsters in town. What he couldn't know is that the guys he was shopping to the FBI were two of its most valued informants.

Brunnick and Montanari were working the labor racketeering side of organized crime, so they went to the office of the organized crime squad supervisor, John Morris, and asked him if he thought Halloran was telling the truth. "He's a coke head," Morris told them. "Unstable."[29] But, even as he fended off their query, Morris was worried. Brunnick and Montanari were not with the program. They were working their own cases. They weren't invested in Whitey and Flemmi in the least. Morris walked down the hallway to Connolly's office. "Would Bulger and Flemmi trust Halloran to do something for them?" he asked John Connolly.

"No," Connolly replied. "You know better than that. They don't trust him at all."[30]

Connolly eyed Morris suspiciously.

"What's going on?" Connolly asked. "If someone's saying something about my informants, I have a right to know."[31]

Morris explained and Connolly was concerned. Halloran might be a liar and a lowlife, but even a liar and a lowlife could tell a story that might be believed. Connolly went to see Whitey and Flemmi to tell them that Halloran was shopping them for Wheeler's murder. When he got back to the office, Connolly lied to Morris. "They already know," he told him.[32]

Connolly theorized that Halloran was offering Whitey and Flemmi up so he could later shake them down in exchange for recanting his story. It was a considerable stretch. The idea that Whitey and Flemmi would pay off somebody who was shopping them to the law made no sense at all. It was far more likely they would kill him. Brunnick and Montanari were understandably skeptical of Halloran and pleaded with him to take a polygraph. Halloran refused. Then they put a wire on him and sent him out fishing. When Connolly found out, he called Whitey.

"Brian Halloran's wearing a wire," Connolly told Whitey.[33]

In the end, it was Jerry O'Sullivan's call. O'Sullivan, chief of the Organized Crime Strike Force in Boston, was preparing the biggest case of his life, going through the tapes the FBI had recorded of Jerry Angiulo and the rest of the Boston Mafia talking about business in their North End headquarters. Now Brunnick and Montanari wanted protection for a hoodlum who had implicated two of the informants at the heart of the Mafia case in the murder of a Tulsa businessman. O'Sullivan decided that Halloran's credibility, or lack of it, made him a lousy witness. He had no corroboration for his claims. People said he was a drug user. A drunk. O'Sullivan ruled out the witness protection program. Then Bob Fitzpatrick, the assistant special agent in charge of the FBI in Boston, made a special appeal to O'Sullivan, asking him to reconsider. Brunnick and Montanari had put Halloran and his family in a safe house in Falmouth, on Cape Cod. They told Fitzpatrick they didn't think Halloran would last on the street very long, but O'Sullivan wouldn't budge.

Halloran was bored to tears in the safe house. He was stuck there with his wife and their two sons, twenty-two months and five months old. He was going stir-crazy. He told his wife that the FBI was stringing him along, that he was going to Boston to get a car, and that they would then leave Massachusetts. On Tuesday, May 11, 1982, he took the bus up from Falmouth. He got off at South Station and started walking toward the Topside Lounge, a bar at the Pier restaurant he knew well.

It opened around four in the afternoon. Halloran pulled up a stool right next to the plate glass window that looked out onto Northern Avenue, the cobblestone street that was the main thoroughfare on the grimy South Boston waterfront. At 4:30, he got up to use the pay phone. He called the FBI office looking for Leo Brunnick, but Gerry Montanari got on the line.

"Gerry, it's Brian Halloran."

"Where are you?"

"Downtown," Brian Halloran lied. "Leo's looking for me."

He left a number and within minutes Leo Brunnick called him back.

"What's up?" Brian Halloran said. "I hear you've been looking for me."

Brunnick said he wasn't and that it was crazy for him to be running around Boston. "Go back to your family," Brunnick said. "Stop bouncing around."

Halloran said he had to go, and he hung up.

He went back to the bar. It was his round.[34] And he needed a ride home.

That same morning, Patricia Donahue was getting ready to leave for work at a small salon in Fields Corner, a half mile from her house on Roseland Street in Dorchester. She usually worked downtown, but she helped out at a friend's Fields Corner salon once in a while. "You need a haircut," she said to her husband, Michael, over breakfast. "Why don't you come by this afternoon? I'm just up the street today."

As she cut his hair, Pat Donahue went over all the things they had to get done that day. Michael was heading down to the Fish Pier to see someone about some bakery racks they needed for the shop he and his wife were about to open. He was also planning to pick up bait for the overnight fishing trip to Maine that he had promised his eight-year-old son, Tommy, as a present for his First Holy Communion. Tommy was going to be allowed to miss a day of classes at St. Mark's School to go fishing, making him the envy of his older brothers, Shawn, 11, and Michael Jr., 13. Michael Donahue looked in the mirror, turning from side to side, before pronouncing his verdict on his wife's hairstyling skills.

"You're an artist," he said. He kissed her and was out the door. "I'll call you," he yelled over his shoulder, and he was gone.[35]

As Halloran drank and the Donahues went about their day, Whitey and Kevin Weeks were in Broadway Furniture in Southie, waiting for Flemmi to join them, when John Hurley walked in. Hurley, a squat, balding man with Popeye forearms and a bulbous nose, was a survivor of the Charlestown-Somerville gang war and had become the IRA's biggest fund-raiser in Boston. Like everyone else in the underworld, Hurley knew Halloran was a dead man walking. And he knew that what he was about to say would endear him to Whitey Bulger. "Brian Halloran is down by the Pier restaurant," Hurley said.[36]

The Pier was popular with fishermen, longshoremen, and truck drivers. It was the spot where Callahan had confided to Halloran the particulars of the Wheeler hit. In that instant, Whitey decided that it would be where Brian Halloran would die. "Thanks, John," Whitey said, smiling. "Thanks a lot."[37]

Hurley's news put Whitey in mission mode; he began looking

for Flemmi, then Pat Nee.[38] He told Weeks to go to the old Mullens clubhouse on O Street and wait for him there. Twenty minutes later, Whitey pulled up in the Tow Truck, their nickname for a car purposely built for hits. The blue Chevrolet Malibu had been fashioned into a James Bond–like gadget vehicle, complete with devices that dispensed an oil slick and smokescreen to aid getaways. The car had been souped up so that it could go as fast as 200 mph.

Whitey climbed out of the Tow Truck wearing a dirty-blond wig and floppy mustache. Flemmi hadn't answered his beeper.

"Go to Jimmy's Harborside and wait for me," Whitey told Weeks.[39]

Weeks climbed into his car, an Oldsmobile Delta 88, and made the five-minute drive to the popular restaurant, which was just up the street from the Pier. Whitey pulled up in the Tow Truck and handed Weeks a walkie-talkie. A man in the backseat, his face covered by a ski mask, sat up and waved.

"Go to Anthony's," Whitey said, referring to Anthony's Pier 4, the biggest seafood restaurant in the city, across the street from the Pier. "Just park there, and when Balloonhead gets up, let me know."[40] Balloonhead was Whitey's nickname for Halloran, a reference to his unusually large head, puffy from years of booze.

It was getting close to dinnertime, and Pat Donahue wondered when Michael was going to call. At 6:00, the phone rang in the kitchen of the Donahue three-decker on Roseland Street.

"I'm just leaving," Michael Donahue said. "I'll be home in ten minutes."

Pat had the phone tucked between her shoulder and cheek as she stood over the stove.

"We're having pork chops," she said. "We're just waiting for you."

"Ten minutes," he repeated, which was a bit of a fib, given that he was almost six miles away on the waterfront.

Besides, he had agreed to give Brian Halloran a ride home, and Halloran was taking his sweet time. Halloran's father lived right around the corner from the Donahues, in the house where Halloran had grown up. Donahue thought he was giving a ride to an old friend from the neighborhood, not a marked man. Other people in the bar recall that Michael Donahue was antsy, waiting for Halloran to drink up. He was pacing. He wanted to get home for dinner.

Weeks wasn't in his surveillance spot for long before he saw one of the people who had been sitting with Halloran get up and walk out to the sidewalk. It was Michael Donahue, on his way to the small blue Datsun he had borrowed from his father for the day. Halloran had asked Donahue for a ride back to Dorchester, reasoning that those who wanted to kill him would not risk killing somebody else. He knew that was one of the rules of the road for gangsters—leave the innocents out of it. He couldn't know that Whitey and his comrades were breaking their own rules these days; that their trademark circumspection had been replaced with arrogance and now, with Halloran spreading his story, a certain desperation. As Donahue pulled the Datsun in front of the bar, Weeks saw Halloran rise from the table inside.

"The balloon is rising," Weeks said into the walkie-talkie. "The balloon is in the air."

Halloran had just climbed into the passenger's seat when Whitey pulled alongside in the Tow Truck and leaned out the driver's-side window with a carbine rifle.

"Hey, Brian!" Whitey yelled.

He didn't wait for an answer, unleashing a volley. Whitey had turned off the automatic mechanism, allowing him to aim and place shots.[41] The masked man in the backseat started firing, too, but his shotgun jammed quickly. Donahue's car, stuck in neutral, drifted slowly across Northern Avenue and came to rest against a parked car. Whitey made a U-turn on the wide street. Halloran had climbed from the car and was lying in the middle of the street. Whitey leveled his gun out the window and fired some more. From across the street, Weeks could see Halloran's body twitch as the bullets entered him. The Tow Truck then raced away, one of its shiny hubcaps bouncing off on the viaduct that led from the waterfront to Summer Street, the main road into Southie.

A judge would later conclude that Whitey had purposely fired at Halloran's extremities, in an attempt to cause maximum suffering before death. An autopsy showed that Halloran was shot twenty-two times: five in his legs, four in his arms, four in his groin and abdomen. A headshot only grazed him.[42] Donahue was gone, mortally wounded. But when police arrived minutes later, they found that Halloran was somehow, improbably, still alive. "Get me the fuck out of here!" he yelled at the first two police officers who arrived. "I don't want to die! Get me to a fucking hospital!"[43] Halloran was delirious, fighting with the EMTs who tried to put him on a stretcher. Sergeant William "Bo" Mullane of the Boston police was a Southie guy, and he knew all the wiseguys. He recognized Halloran, lying in the ambulance, the blood and the life draining out of him. Mullane climbed into the ambulance.

"Brian," Mullane said, "who did this to you?"

Mullane leaned down so he could hear Halloran's raspy last words.

"Jimmy Flynn," Halloran said.

It made sense. Halloran had told the FBI that Jimmy Flynn, a Winter Hill associate, was looking for him, believing correctly that Halloran was talking to the FBI about him.[44] The blond hair, the thick mustache he'd seen on the shooter looked just like Flynn's. Whitey hadn't purposely tried to impersonate Flynn. It was just his good fortune that Halloran thought that that's who his killer was.[45]

After the shooting, Whitey was euphoric. And hungry. He went to Teresa Stanley's house for dinner. As Stanley cooked dinner for her kids, Whitey was still wondering why Flemmi hadn't shown up for the hit. He sent out another voice message to Flemmi's pager: "The balloon has burst."[46] As soon as he heard it, Flemmi knew Halloran was dead, and he started cursing: he had missed out on all the fun.[47]

Around 9:00 p.m., a few hours after the murders, Weeks picked up Whitey at Stanley's house and they drove over the viaduct to look for the hubcap that had fallen off the Tow Truck. They found it by the curb. Then they went to meet Flemmi at Flemmi's mother's house, right next to Bill Bulger's house. While Mary Flemmi stirred her tomato sauce in the kitchen, Whitey regaled his partner with all the gory details in the living room: how Halloran turned when Whitey called him, how the first shots blew out the windows, how Halloran's body bounced as the rounds hit him on the street.

"Shit, I wish I was there," Flemmi kept saying. "I wish I was there."[48]

They sat down in the kitchen for a late dinner—spaghetti and veal and eggplant parmesan—and Whitey kept telling Mary Flemmi how good her cooking was.[49] After dinner, Whitey, Flemmi, and Weeks went for a long walk down to Castle Island, talking about the murders like it was an unforgettable baseball game, the memory of a lifetime.

Pat Donahue had turned down the heat on the pork chops, waiting for Michael. The six o'clock news was on TV in the other room, and she could hear the anchor excitedly talking about a shooting on the waterfront. The anchor said it was a gangland shooting. She wondered if Michael had heard anything.[50]

"Where the hell is Michael?" she said aloud, as she turned down the heat even more so the pork chops wouldn't dry out. Then she heard, from the TV, that they had pictures of the car the men who were shot on the waterfront were driving. She stood in the doorway of the kitchen, holding a spatula in her hand, looking at the TV in the living room, and said, "That's Michael."

Her husband had borrowed his father's car, and there it was on the TV screen, its windows blown out, its side pockmarked with bullet holes. She went to the second floor, where Michael's father, a police officer, was sitting in a chair. "Michael's been shot," she told him, and the old cop sat there, dumbfounded.

The TV said that one of the men was dead and the other was in the hospital. She went to the phone and methodically called every hospital in Boston. No one could tell her anything. No one said they had Michael. Word spread in the neighborhood, and soon the house was a beehive. Neighbors brought food and tried to shield the three boys from the news because nobody knew what was going on. Was Michael dead or alive?

The police didn't show up until 10:00, four hours after the shooting. They drove her to Massachusetts General Hospital but wouldn't tell her whether Michael was dead or alive. Then one of the doctors said, "I'm sorry, Mrs. Donahue," and she knew. They asked her to go into a room, to make a formal identification, and she stood at the doorway, summoning the nerve. She went over in her head what she would do: She would sit down and talk to Mike, say some final words. When she went into the room, her husband's body was propped up; he looked like he was sitting up. His head was bandaged, his eyes closed. It almost looked like he was sleeping. Pat Donahue looked at her dead husband, and all her plans to tell him how much she loved him went out the window. Pat quickly left the room. She couldn't bear to see him like that.

A half-hour later she was back in the house on Roseland Street and called the boys down from the third floor. They had been on the landing for hours, listening to the adults speaking in hushed tones downstairs, and they knew something was wrong. Some of the women were crying, and Michael, the oldest, knew in his heart what had happened. If his younger brothers couldn't comprehend what was going on, thirteen-year-old Michael did.

Pat Donahue cleared the living room of everybody else and asked her boys to sit on the couch. "Dad died and he's not coming back," she said, and eight-year-old Tommy was crying before she got the last words out.

The waterfront rubout was right out of the movies, and it dominated the news. Law enforcement agents were everywhere, trying to find Jimmy Flynn and the unknown second gunman. If Whitey was concerned about the heat, he didn't show it. A couple of days after the murders, he drove Flemmi and Weeks down to the tow lot in Southie where Donahue's Datsun had been impounded. They found it and saw that it was riddled with bullet holes. Whitey pointed to his handiwork on the driver's-side headrest: strands of hair, scalp, and tissue.[51]

About ten days after the murders, John Morris dropped by Whitey's condo in Quincy with John Connolly. The agents were concerned that their informants were being mentioned as suspects in the killings. Whitey plied Morris with beers as Morris filled him in on what various law enforcement agencies were saying. Morris told Whitey that an FBI agent had been doing a stakeout, trying to keep an eye on Halloran, and had gotten the license plate number of the hit car.

The next day, Whitey told Weeks to make sure the Tow Truck stayed out of sight in a garage on K Street until they could chop it up. Whitey said Morris had been forthcoming the night before, the beer eventually serving as a truth serum. "Thank God for Beck's," Whitey said.[52]

Not long after that talkative evening at Whitey's place, Morris had to fly down to Georgia for a two-week training session on narcotics investigations. He called Connolly with a delicate sort of request. Morris had been carrying on an open affair with his secretary, and he knew Connolly had left his own wife and was a ladies' man. So Morris felt comfortable in asking him for some help. Morris reminded Connolly that Whitey and Flemmi were always volunteering to help him. "Do you think they could arrange for an airline ticket?" Morris asked.[53]

Not long after, Connolly handed Morris's girlfriend a white envelope, saying that what was inside had come from Morris. It was a thousand dollars in cash, more than enough for a ticket to Georgia. Connolly smiled and lied to her: He said Morris had been saving the money, little by little, just for this occasion. She put in for a few days off and rushed to Logan Airport, waiting for a flight that was a gift from a pair of murderers.[54] Morris was now compromised to the point that he wasn't just protecting Whitey and Flemmi, he was protecting himself. He was on the payroll. They had given John Morris wine and women. The only thing left was song.

Two weeks after the Halloran hit, there was a big meeting at FBI headquarters in Washington. Headquarters staff and agents from Boston, Miami, and Oklahoma City crowded around a conference table. There was a problem: two key informants, Whitey and Flemmi, were suspects in the Wheeler hit and in the waterfront ambush that killed Halloran and Donahue. Bob Fitzpatrick, the assistant special agent in charge of the Boston office, recommended that they be closed as informants. But Sean McWeeney, the organized crime section chief in Washington, noted that headquarters remained impressed that "they were extremely valuable assets" in the FBI's war against the Mafia.[55]

It wasn't just the Boston office that had Whitey and Flemmi's back; headquarters in Washington did, too. FBI brass were willing to cover for a pair of suspected murderers because the Boston field office had convinced headquarters that they were indispensable. It was a critical season in the bureau's ongoing campaign against the Mafia. In the spring of 1982, as officials debated what to do with Whitey and Flemmi, FBI technicians were enhancing the audio tapes from the bugs that would lead to the September 1983 arrests of Jerry Angiulo and the rest of the Boston Mafia leadership. What would come of that case if two of the informants the FBI relied on were charged with murder?

The overreach had claimed a businessman, a bystander, and a bad guy. John Connolly was beginning to worry that the heat might claim them all. Still, he didn't ask Whitey if he had killed Halloran and Donahue. Instead, he said, "You guys are going to get a lot of heat on this."[56] Flemmi, however, had no doubt that Connolly knew that Whitey had done it. Whitey told Connolly that Halloran had mistakenly fingered the wrong man in his dying declaration and that Jimmy Flynn had nothing to do with the killing.[57] Connolly believed he could manage the finger-pointing that had engulfed his office since the murders, but he felt uneasy about all the interest his colleagues were showing in John Callahan. Other FBI agents were determined to question Callahan. He was the link to the Wheeler and Halloran homicides, the only obvious connection between the two.

Connolly told Whitey and Flemmi that Callahan wouldn't stand up. He was a civilian. He wasn't a wiseguy, just a wannabe.[58] Whitey agreed and knew it was time to meet face-to-face with Johnny Martorano and give him one more job. After an elaborate series of phone calls, the meeting was set for the Marriott Hotel at LaGuardia Airport in New York. The choice of hotel was no accident. Martorano knew somebody who worked there and got a reduced rate.

Martorano flew up from Florida, using as his alias the name Richard Aucoin. Whitey and Flemmi drove down to New York. "Your friend is not going to stand up," Whitey said, as soon as they sat down. Whitey did all the talking. He kept repeating that John Connolly had warned him: "We're all going to end up going to jail for the rest of our lives if he doesn't hold up."[59] And he tried to talk Martorano into doing it, building his case logically like a lawyer at a trial. "Whitey told me Halloran had gone to the FBI and told the FBI that I killed Roger Wheeler," Martorano said.[60]

"I killed Halloran to protect you," Whitey said.

"Thanks," Martorano replied. "I appreciate it."

And, now, in Whitey's mind, it was time to reciprocate. But

Martorano resisted. He knew Callahan was many things, but he was not a rat—he told Whitey that Callahan wouldn't give them up. But that's the point, Whitey countered. "Callahan gave you up," Whitey said, "to Halloran."[61]

Martorano was heartsick. Callahan had helped him on the run. Gotten him an apartment, a car, some furniture. They had had a lot of good times together. He was a friend, and Martorano had never killed a friend before.

Whitey closed his argument with one final question.

"Can he do twenty years?" Whitey asked.

Martorano thought about it, and he had to be honest. Callahan was a party animal. He liked the good life. Martorano couldn't imagine Callahan doing hard time. "No," Martorano said, and John Callahan was at that very moment as good as dead.

Whitey said no more bodies in Boston. They were already feeling enough heat. Lure him down to Florida. Kill him. Take his wallet and watch, leave them in Little Havana. It will look like a drug deal gone bad. Have Joe McDonald help you. A week later, Whitey and Flemmi met John Connolly at Connolly's house in Southie. "We talked to Johnny Martorano about Callahan," Whitey said. "We gave him the information and he said he'd take care of it."[62] A few weeks before Callahan was murdered, Connolly would file a 209 informant report based on information that Whitey fed him, suggesting that Callahan was involved in criminal activity with a bunch of Cubans in Miami.[63] They were creating a list of plausible suspects and pushing the direction of an investigation of a murder that hadn't happened yet.

Martorano couldn't find Callahan for weeks. He didn't know that Callahan had spontaneously left for a trip to Ireland. When he got back, he found a stack of messages from Martorano. "Come on down," Martorano told him. "I want to see you. We can hang out."[64]

The plan was to stay at Callahan's condo in Plantation, just outside Fort Lauderdale. Callahan flew in, and Martorano met him at the gate. He even carried his luggage, all the way to his Dodge van in the airport parking garage. As Martorano went to the side door to put the bag in the middle row of seats, Callahan settled into the front passenger seat of the van, a captain's chair. Martorano tossed the bag in the side door of the van, then picked up a .22 that he had hidden under a blanket, put it to the back of Callahan's head, and fired. Martorano pulled Callahan's body down between the two captain's chairs, closed the van door, got in the driver's seat, and drove off.[65]

Joe McDonald, who had kept watch, followed in another car. It was just after 11:00 p.m., and if there was anybody else around, they didn't notice. Martorano had parked the Cadillac that Callahan used when he was in Florida in a garage so they could move the body into the trunk without being seen. But as Martorano and McDonald were moving the body, a noise emanated from Callahan. It sounded like a moan. McDonald asked for Martorano's gun, extended his arm into the trunk, and fired repeatedly into Callahan's head. There was no more moaning. They took his wallet and watch and anything else in his pockets and left them in the men's room of a bar in Little Havana.[66] Then they drove the Cadillac to the airport in Miami and left it in a parking lot. A couple of days later, one of the parking lot attendants noticed a foul odor emanating, and something dripping, from the trunk.

John Callahan was dead but his Swiss bank accounts were still very much alive.

A month after the murder, Whitey and Flemmi sent word for Callahan's friend and business partner, Mike Solimando, to visit them at the Triple O's. Solimando dabbled in real estate and was a part owner of Durgin Park, a famous restaurant in Faneuil Hall Marketplace. He was in charge of Callahan's estate, and Whitey and Flemmi said they had an interest in it. Solimando was escorted to the private room on the second floor. Despite his powerful weightlifter's body, he looked uneasy as he took his seat at one of the round tables.

Whitey pulled up a seat next to him. He held a machine gun and put it on his lap.

"John Callahan owed us money," Whitey said. "His debt is now your debt and we want our money."

How much?

"Six hundred thousand," Whitey said. "And we know it's in those Swiss accounts."

As he was saying this, Whitey pushed the machine gun under the table, into Solimando's crotch. "If we don't get our money, we'll kill you, your partners, your family," Whitey said.

Flemmi just watched and smirked. It was a scam. Callahan didn't owe them anything. But Solimando was in no position to demand proof. Whitey pulled the machine gun from underneath the table and pushed the barrel into Solimando's chiseled chest. "All those muscles aren't going to do you any good now," Whitey sneered.

Solimando agreed to get the money even if he had to fly to Switzerland. Whitey lowered the gun and he was free to go. But Whitey had a parting shot. Just as Solimando got to the door that led downstairs, he called out to him. Solimando stopped and turned. "Don't go to the FBI," Whitey said. "If you go to the FBI, I'll know in five minutes."[67]

Callahan's murder continued to intensify the pressure on Whitey and Flemmi and, by extension, on Connolly and Morris. Connolly closed out Flemmi as an informant seven weeks after Callahan's murder, but only on paper. He didn't tell Flemmi he had been closed, and continued to meet with him. Whitey was kept open, and he was credited with information that, as so often before, came from Flemmi. It was a formality, a diversion. Whitey and Flemmi were still in business and knew that Connolly and Morris were still watching their backs. They reminded Morris how much they appreciated his loyalty. They gave Connolly another case of wine, with an envelope stuffed with a thousand dollars, and, once again, he delivered it to Morris in the garage at the FBI's Boston office. This time, Morris took it without raising an objection.[68]

Gerry Montanari, the FBI agent whose informant had been cut to shreds on the waterfront, kept after Connolly, saying he wanted to talk to Whitey and Flemmi. "Gerry Montanari is trying to make a career out of the jai alai case," Connolly complained to Whitey and Flemmi, without a hint of irony.[69] There was also pressure coming from agents in the FBI's office in Oklahoma City, who were being pushed by Mike Huff, the Tulsa homicide detective. In April 1983, FBI agents in Oklahoma asked for permission to interview Whitey and Flemmi, but Boston refused. The request did, however, prompt Connolly to file a report creating an alibi for Whitey on the days of the Wheeler and Callahan murders.[70]

Still, Huff and the Tulsa PD wouldn't go away. They continued to press for an interview with Whitey and Flemmi. In November 1983, Connolly gave in and arranged for the two to meet with Montanari to answer questions about the murders of Wheeler, Halloran, and Callahan. The whole process was a sham meant to insulate his informants, and the transcript of that November 2, 1983, interview reveals a number of major irregularities and breaches of FBI protocol. For starters, Whitey and Flemmi were interviewed together, a highly unusual procedure that removed any chance of catching them in contradictory statements. They insisted the interview take place at the old Mullens clubhouse in Southie, not at the FBI's offices. And Connolly, like a defense counsel prepping a low-life client, warned them in advance to dress in business suits, because the photos that Montanari would take would be sent to the grand jury in Tulsa investigating Wheeler's murder.

In their report, Montanari and FBI agent Brendan Cleary said Whitey claimed that under normal circumstances he wouldn't submit to such an interview at all, but that he and Flemmi wanted to clear the air and put on record that Halloran's story about their being involved in Wheeler's murder—not to mention allegations that they had killed Halloran, Donahue, and Callahan—was patently untrue. He denied everything: that he and Flemmi had anything to do with any of the murders; that they had anything to do with Halloran, whom Whitey dismissed as a liar, a bully, and a braggart. Whitey told the FBI agents that he and Flemmi would never get involved in a crime outside of the Boston area because they couldn't control the situation. And he said that it would be more their style to simply take somebody's money and then not bother with the crime. The guy they cheated couldn't very well go to the police, Whitey said.

As for their getting a skim from World Jai Alai, Whitey said that was nonsense. He cried poormouth, saying that he and Flemmi had inherited from their Winter Hill partners a $250,000 gambling debt to the Mafia but were only paying the juice, or interest, of $2,500 a week. If they were getting money from World Jai Alai, Whitey said, they would have paid that debt back in full by now.

He also reminded them that there was a long line of people who wanted to kill Halloran, who had habit of robbing people and was completely unreliable, coked up half the time, drunk the other half. And even as he denied being responsible for Michael Donahue's murder, he tried to justify it. He claimed that Donahue was Halloran's getaway driver after Pappas was shot in the Chinese restaurant, waiting for him outside in a van that took him to Donahue's house. That was a lie, spread by Whitey, repeated by others, including Connolly, to muddy Michael Donahue's name, to suggest he wasn't just a bystander who gave a guy he knew from the neighborhood a ride home. Whitey ended the interview by refusing to take a polygraph, saying he didn't trust the results. Once again, he was setting the terms.

Connolly, too, seemed to come out of it clean. His informants were implicated in the murder of four men, one a businessman, one an innocent bystander, the other two potential murder case witnesses who could expose the FBI's arrangement with Whitey and Flemmi. But Whitey's handler was flying high. He had normally received excellent performance evaluations, but in the wake of the murders of Wheeler, Halloran, Donahue, and Callahan, John Connolly's annual evaluation was positively effusive. Not surprisingly, it was written by John Morris. "Connolly's performance in this area substantially exceeds the performance standards of superior and is truly exceptional," Morris wrote in November 1982. "He independently has developed, maintained and operated a corps of extremely high level and productive informants. His direction and their resultant information has brought about results exceeded by none in the Boston Division's Organized Crime Program. . . . His performance has been at the level to which all should aspire to attain but few will realistically reach."

John Connolly, Morris was saying, was the FBI's poster boy—the model agent, the quintessential G-man.

In the end, the plan to take over World Jai Alai had led to three separate, cold-blooded shootings that left four men dead: Roger Wheeler, Brian Halloran, Michael Donahue and John Callahan. Whitey called the hits the Holy Trinity, and he looked back on them with regret.[71]

But he had been right about one thing. Killing Roger Wheeler was a mistake. It led to other mistakes. And it was making it harder and harder for the FBI to justify protecting Whitey. In reaching for some easy money, Whitey had overreached. He had put his empire and himself at risk.

And he knew it.

11

The Wrong Man

When he made his historic deal with John Connolly in 1975, Whitey Bulger set only three conditions. Two had been predictable; one came out of left field. The first was that he would never give up his friends, meaning his closest gang comrades. He said that his brother Bill should be kept entirely out of it. And then, unexpectedly, he insisted to Connolly that he would never give up the IRA.

This came as a surprise, because Connolly had never mentioned the slightest investigative interest in the Irish Republican Army, whose illegal activities in the United States were ostensibly under the FBI's purview. IRA sympathizers in Boston regularly raised money and procured weapons for the group, but that wasn't Connolly's concern. His entire focus was on the Mafia—on information that could help infiltrate and devastate the Italian criminal organization. He had no problem excusing Whitey from responsibility to provide information about the IRA, because it wasn't a priority, and perhaps because Connolly himself was sympathetic to, or at the very least ambivalent about, the IRA.[1]

Whitey was more than sympathetic to the cause; it was a pas-

sion, like his patriotism. From the outbreak of civil unrest in Northern Ireland in 1968, Whitey had taken a keen interest in the conflict
known as the Troubles. Like many others in Southie, he instinctively
sympathized with Irish Catholics in Northern Ireland, seeing them
as an oppressed minority and the IRA as their righteous defenders.
The fact that they were also killers—well, that was the price of war.
"Jimmy got me involved in Ireland," said Kevin Weeks. "He read a
lot of books on it. He understood it. Jimmy considered it noble. It
wasn't doing crime. It was helping the cause."

In South Boston, being Irish was an essential element of identity,
one that conferred a certain standing in the neighborhood. It was
part of the attitude that sustained Southie exceptionalism, that the
Irish were special and this place was theirs. While there were plenty
of Italians and Lithuanians and Polish in the neighborhood, the
Irish ruled the roost. They held almost every elected and appointed
position. Most of the cops and firefighters in Southie were Irish.
The neighborhood's unofficial mascot was a leprechaun, his two
fists balled up, itching for a fight. Its annual rite of ethnic unity was
and is the St. Patrick's Day Parade. "In most South Boston schools,
there was also a special emphasis on the social and cultural heritage
of the Irish race," said the historian Thomas H. O'Connor. "Irish
songs and stories were an integral part of the instructional program;
Irish saints and Irish feast days were usually celebrated with extra
enthusiasm; and at St. Augustine's School romantic scenes from the
Irish countryside were painted on the walls of the auditorium."[2]

Irish rebel songs like "The Rising of the Moon" and "A Nation
Once Again" were also ubiquitous in Southie, not just in its many
barrooms but at virtually any neighborhood celebration. When Bill
Bulger became the state senator for Southie in 1970, he presided over
the annual St. Patrick's Day political roast, at which it was considered de rigueur for politicians, after offering a tired joke and exposing themselves to the emcee's astringent wit, to warble a rebel song.

Beyond the surprise, there was also an unacknowledged irony in
Whitey's declaring the IRA off-limits even as he agreed to become

an informant. There is nothing worse in the Irish consciousness than being a snitch. Informers have been the bane of Irish revolution-aries for centuries, their treachery ruining countless uprisings and rebellions against the British. And in Southie, in particular, there was an unforgiving attitude about snitching. Some said it was worse than being a murderer. Again, an Irish thing. "In Southie, there was nothing worse than being a rat," said Weeks. "Jimmy said that all the time. He never forgot that one of his partners gave him up in those bank robberies."[3] Weeks didn't know, of course, that Whitey had given up his accomplices, too.

It was an ethic inculcated in early childhood. Whitey's brother Bill said that the hostility to informers was writ large in the Old Harbor housing project during his and his older brother's forma-tive years. In his memoir, he recalled a time when one of the neigh-borhood kids broke a streetlight and police were hunting down the offender.

We were told that a recently impounded baseball would not be returned unless we identified the lamp breaker. We were disgusted with the miscreant, since essential equipment was being held hostage because of him. But we loathed informers. It wasn't a conspiratorial thing—our folklore bled with the names of informers who had sold out their brethren to hangmen and worse in the lands of our ancestors.[4]

The truth was that, on the night Whitey signed on as an infor-mant, there was very little he could have given Connolly on the IRA. Up to that point, he had merely donated relatively small amounts of money to the Irish Northern Aid committee, or NORAID, the IRA's main support group in the United States. But once he had the FBI in his pocket, his involvement quickly intensified. It became more than giving cash—it became a hands-on thing. Whitey first sent a small consignment of weapons to the IRA and then prevailed upon a friendly FBI agent to acquire C-4 explosives, according to

Steve Flemmi. Finally, in 1984, Whitey sanctioned and helped organize the biggest-ever shipment of weapons from the United States to the IRA. He considered the mission his crowning achievement, an interlude of honor in his long criminal career. It was an audacious project, but one that was doomed to failure because of that bane of Irish revolutionaries, the informer.

With help from Connolly, Whitey would identify who had given the mission up and set out to kill him. But, as happened during the Southie gang war when he shot Donnie McGonagle thinking it was Paulie McGonagle, Whitey got the wrong man.

Joe Cahill was accustomed to doing business in barrooms, but his haunts were usually in his native West Belfast, not South Boston.

Still, there was a war on, and Joe Cahill would go anywhere to get weapons for the Irish Republican Army. So there he was, in the private room on the second floor of Triple O's, Whitey Bulger's redoubt on West Broadway. Cahill nodded approvingly at the Irish tricolor strung across the bare brick wall. There was a TV propped up on the bar, and Cahill pulled a videocassette out of a shopping bag.

His short stature, thick eyeglasses, and retiring, grandfatherly manner belied a certain ruthlessness that fit in with the men grouped around him at Triple O's. There was Whitey, whose reputation preceded him. There was Pat Nee, the Irish-born Mullen gang survivor who had gone from hunting Whitey to hunting others with him. And there was Joe Murray, Whitey's newest associate, the biggest marijuana trafficker in town.

They were mere racketeers; Joe Cahill was a revolutionary. He was also a legend.

When he was twenty-two, Cahill had been convicted of killing a policeman in Belfast during one of the IRA's short-lived campaigns of violence in the 1940s. Cahill and his three friends were sentenced to death. His friend and co-conspirator, Tom Williams, was hanged. But the Vatican intervened, asking the British government to spare the other three Catholics facing the hangman. The British would come to regret the mercy they showed Joe Cahill, first in sparing him the noose, then in releasing him after just eight years in prison.

Cahill continued to fight in the IRA's sporadic, quixotic uprisings. He resigned from the organization briefly in the 1960s, accusing its leaders of going soft and focusing too much on the far-left ideology that was spreading across Europe. He believed that they weren't concentrating enough on their own immediate struggle. His warnings proved prophetic. When marauding bands of Protestant thugs tore through Catholic neighborhoods in Belfast in 1968, the IRA was impotent, its small, pathetic cache of rusty guns useless at stopping a pogrom. Some took to daubing walls in West Belfast with the taunting slogan "IRA—I Ran Away." Cahill rose from that humiliation, pushed the politicos aside, and reasserted the muscular tradition of physical-force republicanism. He became one of the founders of a new, more aggressive reincarnation of the republican movement's military wing, the Provisional IRA.

In the early 1970s, as the IRA took the fight to the British, Cahill went looking for weapons abroad. In 1973, he was captured off the coast of Ireland on a ship loaded down with five tons of guns and explosives, a gift from the Libyan leader Muammar Gaddafi, who hated the British almost as much as Cahill did. When the judge who heard the case described Cahill as the ringleader of the gunrunning scheme, Cahill stood, bowed gallantly toward the judge and said, "You do me an honor."[5]

Cahill served three years in prison. As soon as he was released, he again began looking abroad for weapons, and it was inevitable that his quest would take him to Boston. In the working-class enclaves of South Boston and Charlestown, it was common to see pro-IRA graffiti painted on the walls. In Southie, a liquor store owner had a huge mural painted on the side of his West Broadway storefront, proclaiming, "Ireland Unfree Will Never Be at Peace." It remains there to this day. A mechanic painted a towering mural over the entrance to his Lower End garage with the words "Óglaigh na hÉireann," which meant nothing to most passersby but which was appreciated by Joe Cahill: It means "Irish volunteers" and is what the IRA calls itself in Gaelic, the Irish language. In other neighborhoods, expressing solidarity with an outlawed group would be considered strange, even scandalous. In Southie, it was good for business.

Cahill noticed. "When they drove me around Southie, it reminded me of West Belfast," he said.[6]

It was common for hats to be passed around the myriad Southie barrooms, collecting for a relief fund for the families of IRA prisoners. Some bars also had permanent jars for donations to NORAID. The debates over where the money went were irrelevant: Even if it didn't go directly to buying weapons—and there was considerable evidence that some of it did just that—it went to prisoners' dependents, allowing the IRA to spend its funds elsewhere.

One of NORAID's leaders, John Hurley, had survived the Charlestown-Somerville gang wars to become a Winter Hill Gang associate, but he spent most of his time raising money, and finding guns, for the IRA. It was Hurley who told Whitey in 1982 where he could corner and murder Brian Halloran, the Winter Hill leg breaker who shopped Whitey and Steve Flemmi to the FBI. And it was Hurley who urged Joe Cahill to meet with Whitey Bulger.[7] Hurley knew that if Boston's Irish criminals were going to coalesce to help the IRA, Whitey had to sign off or it wouldn't happen. Whitey had contributed to NORAID regularly, taking the money from his gang's expense fund, but he styled himself more than just a barstool patriot—he styled himself Irish. He obtained Irish citizenship through his maternal grandmother, Jane O'Brien McCarthy, who was born in Cork City in 1866. Whitey acquired his Irish passport in 1987.[8] Beyond its sentimental value, he knew that the passport would be an asset if he had to go on the run.

But while Whitey always supported the IRA, it was Joe Cahill's visit to the Triple O's that dramatically escalated his involvement. Whitey idolized few people, but Joe Cahill was one.[9] And when Cahill insisted on going to South Boston to meet him, Whitey was flattered. "Jimmy really looked up to Joe Cahill," said Kevin Weeks. "Cahill was a legend."

As a convicted killer and gunrunner, Joe Cahill was barred from entering the United States. But he was not barred from entering Canada, and the Boston gangsters perfected a scam for sneaking him across the border. The IRA was told to send Cahill to Canada during the winter, so that the trips coincided with when the Boston Bruins hockey team was playing the Canadiens in Montreal. IRA sympathizers in Charlestown and Southie then chartered a bus to bring Bruins fans to the games. Cahill usually traveled with three companions, so four Boston hockey fans were induced to stay a few extra days in Canada; Cahill and his traveling party took their place on the bus. Border inspections were perfunctory at the time; as long as the number of heads on the bus heading south was the same as the number that had been counted heading north, the men were waved through the checkpoint. On four different occasions, Joe Cahill was smuggled into the United States this way.[10]

After one such border crossing, Joe Cahill headed for the second floor of Triple O's. Whitey insisted that no alcohol be served; this was business. He took a seat with Pat Nee, Joe Murray, John Hurley, and Kevin Weeks and watched the videocassette that Joe Cahill brought with him from Belfast. It was a documentary, showing British soldiers and members of the Royal Ulster Constabulary firing plastic bullets into the middle of roiling crowds in Northern Ireland. "The movie had pictures of little girls, dead," said Weeks. "They had been shot in the head by plastic bullets." The inflammatory video bordered on propaganda and had exactly the effect Joe Cahill desired.

When the movie ended, Cahill flicked off the power on the TV and stood to face the assembled gangsters. "Lads," he said, folding his hands in front of him, as if he were in prayer, "we need your help."[11] With that, the founder of the Provisional IRA convinced the Irish mob in Boston to act as weapons procurers for the cause. It was a task the gangsters took on enthusiastically, even if their association was one the IRA was loath to admit and determined to keep secret. The British government, in concert with the Irish and American governments, had spent years trying to paint the IRA as nothing more than a criminal gang using the conflict as a cover to engage in ordinary robbery and murder. So cautious was the IRA about preserving its reputation among civilian sympathizers who provided safe houses and looked the other way during IRA operations that Cahill refused to let his operatives employ car thieves to steal the cars the IRA often used to mount attacks, move guns, and carry bombs.[12] He insisted IRA men steal the vehicles themselves, and some of them were utterly useless at it. Better they fail at boosting a car than be seen relying on common criminals, Cahill reasoned.

Yet three thousand miles away, Cahill was content to sit in a room with some of the most notorious criminals in Boston. The IRA's association with Murray, the marijuana and cocaine importer, was even more astonishing. If Murray had sold drugs in Belfast the way he did in Boston, his friends in the IRA would have felt duty-bound to shoot him; they viewed drug dealers and their customers as vulnerable to a squeeze by police because of the stiff sentences they often faced and thus more likely to become informers than other criminals. Whitey shared the IRA's reservations. The only thing he liked about drug dealers was the cash he could extort from them.

He had only recently hooked up with Murray. After learning that Murray had used a warehouse in Southie to store a boatload of marijuana, Whitey arranged a meeting in a park in Charlestown. They met near the Bunker Hill Monument, an iconic structure that looms over the city's northern skyline. The monument commemorates a Revolutionary War battle that the colonists lost but recalled as a victory because they had killed so many British. As they sat beneath the 221-foot white obelisk, Whitey explained the niceties of Boston's geography. By impinging on Southie, Joe Murray had crossed a line and incurred a debt. "You're being fined," Whitey told Murray. Still, he let him off relatively easy, extracting from Murray sixty thousand dollars and a promise to give Whitey a cut of his future transactions in Southie.[13]

The IRA was willing to overlook Murray's drug dealing because Murray routinely did favors for them. He was a generous donor. His seedy Charlestown bar, the Celtic Tavern, was a veritable bed and breakfast for IRA men on the run. It was Murray and the Charlestown crew who had the strongest connection with the IRA. But when Joe Cahill came to Boston, he went to Whitey Bulger's place to make his pitch. He knew where the power center was.

In the early 1980s, Whitey bought a van and Weeks brought it to a garage in Southie where a young mechanic was enlisted to build a hidden compartment—a hide, as they called it—in the van's chassis. In it, Whitey stashed guns and a block of C-4 plastic explosives.[14] Flemmi claimed the explosives were a gift from John Newton, an FBI agent introduced to Whitey by John Connolly.[15] He said Newton, a former Green Beret, had invited him and Whitey to his house in Southie, saying, "I've got something for you." Whitey and Flemmi were excited, according to Flemmi, when Newton gave them a gray wooden case with rope handles loaded with forty pounds of the plastic explosives. Just a couple of pounds of it could take out a truck. Newton told them he had obtained the C-4 while training at Fort Devens, northwest of Boston, according to Flemmi.[16] Newton denies having given the gangsters C-4, saying he did not have access to such explosives. He added that they were tightly controlled and that it would have been impossible to sneak them out of Fort Devens.* Newton never faced criminal charges stemming from Flemmi's allegation.

The van with the weapons was shipped overseas, and the smuggling operation proved successful. Whitey was disappointed, however, when he learned that the IRA had torched the van after

---

*John Newton, in an interview with the authors in September 2012, called Flemmi's claim that he gave Whitey and Flemmi C-4 bizarre and outrageous and said he had never been questioned about it by law enforcement.

retrieving the guns and explosives. "What a waste," Whitey told Weeks. "That hide was a thing of beauty. We could've used it."[17]

The IRA was impressed that Boston gangsters had been able to ship weapons across the Atlantic so easily. But by the end of 1983, the IRA was looking for much more than could be stowed in a van. Joe Murray had the boats to take over a large shipment. He had been using fishing trawlers to move marijuana and cocaine up and down the East Coast for years, amassing a fortune. Murray was all for arming the IRA, though he wasn't as quick to sign on to the audacious idea to send over a large load of weapons on one of his ships. "We convinced Joe he should be a good Irishman, that it would be good for his business," says Nee.[18] For all their influence, the Irish mob in Boston did not have a navy. Murray, on the other hand, had a fleet.

The idea was to use the *Valhalla*, one of the trawlers Murray had been using to smuggle pot, to load it down with weapons and head to sea under the cover of a fishing trip. The American ship would meet the *Marita Ann*, an Irish boat controlled by the IRA, in international waters. The arms on the *Valhalla* would be transferred to the *Marita Ann*, and then both ships would head back to their respective ports, pretending they had just gone fishing.[19]

The IRA liked the idea and sent one of its operatives, John Crawley, to Boston to coordinate the mission. At the time, Crawley was twenty-six, a stocky, muscular man with something of a baby face. He was perfect for the assignment, as he did not hail from a traditional Irish republican family, so he wouldn't be flagged boarding a transatlantic flight. He had not, like so many, been radicalized by beatings at the hands of police or British soldiers on the streets of Belfast and Derry. Rather, he was born in New York and had grown up in Chicago. His parents moved back to their native Ireland when Crawley was fourteen, just as the Troubles were starting. Living in the sleepy Dublin suburbs, Crawley became fascinated with the conflict to the North when it was the lead news story day after day.

In 1975, he moved back to the United States so he could join the US Marines. He served for four years and was trained in explosives and specifically trained to plant bombs in electrical plants behind enemy lines, useful skills for a budding Irish radical. When he returned to Ireland in 1979, Crawley joined the IRA, bringing with him something valuable—his intimate knowledge of weapons and explosives. He also brought something invaluable—American citizenship. Given the sensitivity and size of the proposed gunrunning mission, the IRA's ruling Army Council handpicked Crawley for the task because of his American background.[20]

He wasn't, however, keen on the idea of working with criminals, and he was especially wary of Joe Murray and Whitey Bulger, according to Pat Nee. "Sean," as Nee called Crawley, "didn't like or trust Whitey. He thought Whitey was full of himself. Whitey tried to suggest to Sean that the IRA start firebombing civilian airplanes while they were on the ground, and Sean looked at him like he was crazy. Whitey didn't understand how the IRA worked. The IRA knew that killing civilians hurt their cause. Whitey didn't care. Sean didn't like Joe Murray because Joe was arrogant, but Sean would just shrug and say, 'He's got the money and the boats, so we'll have to deal with him.'"[21]

According to Nee, they raised the one million dollars needed to buy the weapons for the mission by shaking down drug dealers in South Boston and Charlestown. Whitey signed off on the shakedowns, viewing them as almost charitable in nature. "To be honest, once we explained what it was for, most of them were glad to contribute. We didn't have to threaten anybody. I guess they felt like they were doing something useful or honorable," Nee said. "There is such a thing as honor among thieves."

The crew would be unpaid. A trio of Boston-based IRA sympathizers volunteered to serve in the role, even though none of them knew the first thing about boats.[22] Murray prevailed upon Bob Andersen to captain the *Valhalla*. Andersen had sailed ships smuggling Murray's drugs up and down the eastern seaboard for years. Murray also convinced one of the mules who doubled as an engineer on his drug boats to make the trip: John McIntyre.

McIntyre was the son of an Irish American father and a German mother. During World War II, his father served in the army intelligence unit that would later become the Central Intelligence Agency. He grew up in Quincy and enrolled at Northeastern University, hoping to become an engineer. But in 1970, McIntyre stunned his parents by announcing that he would walk away from his draft deferment, dropping out of college to join the army. "He wanted to go to Vietnam because his father was a very good patriot and he idolized his father," his mother later testified.[23] But his army career fizzled quickly and he was soon back in Quincy.

McIntyre got back into Northeastern in 1974 but dropped out after only a month. He drove a cab, then tried his hand at underwater construction and asbestos removal, both hard, dirty jobs that didn't pay well. As much as he struggled on land, McIntyre was gifted once he stepped onto the deck of a boat. He could make any engine work. He was a struggling fisherman, in and out of work with an asbestos crew, when he stumbled into a salvage yard in Chelsea, just north of Boston, looking for parts. Somebody noticed him tinkering with engines and asked if he'd like to make a lot of money. He began hanging out at Heller's, a Chelsea dive that, despite its down-at-heels appearance, was the bank for local bookmakers. In no time at all, John McIntyre was Joe Murray's engineer.

McIntyre started drinking at the Celtic Tavern, Murray's bar, and his mother remembers he suddenly developed an interest in his Irish ancestry. He started talking about how Catholics were being mistreated in Northern Ireland. John McIntyre was, overnight, a starry-eyed Irish patriot. "It came out of nowhere," his mother said.

The captain, Bob Andersen, was sympathetic to the IRA cause, but his involvement was mostly professional. Murray told him he could keep the proceeds of any swordfishing they could manage after transferring the arms shipment on the high seas. Andersen was an experienced skipper, and he and McIntyre knew the limits of the *Valhalla*, which was relatively small for a transatlantic crossing. They hesitated when Murray told them the gunrunning mission was planned for the middle of September—high hurricane season.

Andersen argued that they were pushing their luck already, using an eighty-seven-foot boat to cross the Atlantic, but Murray and Nee were anxious to complete the mission before winter set in. So was Whitey, who, while Nee was doing the bulk of the legwork, was quick to tell everyone he had approved the whole thing. They thought the storm threat would actually enhance their cover: What gunrunner would be crazy enough to sail in the middle of hurricane season?

They had six months to gather the weapons. Crawley was incredulous when Pat Nee explained that they could obtain most of what they needed by buying munitions legally, in parts, through a magazine called *Shotgun News*.

"How can this be legal?" Crawley asked.

"Relax, Sean," Pat Nee told him, putting a reassuring hand on his shoulder. "You're in America."

Nee arranged to have the gun parts mailed to him at the Columbia Yacht Club in South Boston, under his cheeky alias: Patrick Mullen. "Once a Mullen," Nee said, "always a Mullen." Nee didn't clear the alias with Whitey, convinced that he would not see the humor.

Between April and August of 1984, Nee spent more than five hundred thousand dollars of Joe Murray's money on weapons and weapons parts, all of it purchased legally, all of it mailed via UPS, all of it delivered to an unpretentious boat club on the South Boston waterfront. "The easiest thing we bought was the antiaircraft stuff," Nee said. "Just mail order."[24]

The shipment was supplemented by many gangsters, including Whitey, who donated some of their own weapons. Whitey liked the idea that guns he had used in South Boston would be used to kill British soldiers and policemen in South Armagh, an area in Northern Ireland that he admired for its nickname: Bandit Country. "It was like a status symbol to have one of your guns on the *Valhalla*," Nee said. "Guys were lining up to donate guns. Whitey put in more than one."

Whitey even enlisted Stevie Flemmi, who had nothing Irish about him, to help. Flemmi asked his brother Michael, a Boston police officer, how they could acquire bulletproof vests that presumably would be worn by IRA assassins when they set out to murder police officers in Northern Ireland. Michael Flemmi reported his bulletproof vest stolen from his car. It was soon in the hold of the *Valhalla*, waiting to be shipped to the IRA.

As night fell on September 13, 1984, Crawley and Nee led a caravan of six vans to Gloucester Harbor, one of the busiest fishing ports in the United States and just north of Boston. Whitey drove his Malibu to the top of a hill overlooking the harbor. He and Weeks sat there with binoculars, monitoring police frequencies, making sure that the loading of the weapons onto the *Valhalla* went smoothly and without detection. "How great is this?" Whitey murmured, holding the binoculars to his eyes.[25]

His enthusiasm was justified. He and a band of Irish American gangsters had assembled the biggest cache of weapons ever shipped to the IRA. And after just a few hours, the load was secure: ninety-one rifles, eight submachine guns, thirteen shotguns, fifty-one handguns, eleven bulletproof vests, seventy thousand rounds of ammunition, plus an array of hand grenades and rocket heads. Captain Bob Andersen also ordered twenty tons of ice and more than three tons of bait, so that it would appear to anyone who might inquire that the *Valhalla* was off to catch swordfish.

They set sail just after midnight. McIntyre looked over the engine while a crew of hoodlum landlubbers prepared for their first journey on the high seas.

Pat Nee stood on the dock and waved one final time to Crawley, who waved back. From the hill overlooking the harbor, Whitey put down his binoculars and turned the ignition.

"Let's get out of here," he told Weeks.

With hangdog eyes and a lilting accent, Sean O'Callaghan did not fit the stereotype of an IRA assassin.[26] He grew up in a staunchly republican family in Kerry, the most pro-IRA area in the Irish Republic. His father had been an IRA man in the 1940s, jailed without trial, so Sean was considered a legacy. Joining the IRA was expected of him, but he only made the decision after watching televised images of Protestant thugs burning Catholics out of their homes in Belfast in 1969. He was fifteen.

He grew up in Tralee, a sleepy harbor town in Kerry, and when young IRA recruits from the North started showing up there to train in weapons and explosives, O'Callaghan eagerly joined them. He was seventeen when a bomb he was assembling exploded; he wasn't badly hurt, but he was arrested for subversive activity and spent six months in jail. In 1974, he was sent to join an IRA unit in Northern Ireland and took part in an attack on a local army base. A woman serving with the local national guard was killed.

A year later, O'Callaghan was given an assignment. An assassination. There was a member of the Royal Ulster Constabulary's Special Branch, Peter Flanagan, whom the IRA wanted dead. Flanagan was hated not only because he had proved an effective interrogator of IRA members but also because he was Catholic. The IRA went out of its way to murder as many Catholic police officers as possible, to dissuade others from joining the force.

O'Callaghan tracked Flanagan to a pub where he drank while off-duty. Flanagan was reading a newspaper and nursing a pint when he looked up and saw O'Callaghan pointing the gun.

The brazen daylight assassination earned O'Callaghan praise from his superiors. But, at twenty, he had already begun to question what he was doing. He was in an apartment with other IRA men, making tea, when a news program on television reported that a female police officer had just been killed by an IRA bomb. "I hope she's pregnant," one of the IRA men laughed, "and we get two for the price of one."

O'Callaghan, disillusioned by the bloody amorality of it all, returned to Tralee and quietly resigned from the IRA. He moved to London, started an office cleaning business, and got married. But he was haunted by what he had done for the IRA, and by what he considered his naïveté. After spending most of his life convinced it was necessary to kill to bring about a united Ireland, he now had second thoughts. He gradually grew to hate the IRA, believing it indulged in the very acts of sectarianism and barbarism that it condemned in the British forces.

The IRA had trained him in duplicity. He decided to use those skills against his old band, eliminating operatives and frustrating its mission. In 1979, he moved back to Ireland, rejoined the IRA, and secretly offered his services to the Garda Síochána, Ireland's national police force. O'Callaghan contends that there is nothing worse in Ireland than being an informer but that he was willing to become one because he believed that the IRA had no right to take impressionable teenagers and turn them into killers.

O'Callaghan compromised many IRA operations, including one in which he was supposed to blow up the Prince and Princess of Wales, Charles and Diana, and anyone else unfortunate enough to be near the Royal Box at the Dominion Theatre in London for a Duran Duran concert in 1983. His actions resulted in dozens of former comrades going to prison.

And it was O'Callaghan who would eventually, without knowing it, send Whitey Bulger scurrying to find, and kill, an informer—the man he thought had sold out the glorious voyage of the *Valhalla*.

O'Callaghan knew something big was afoot when an aide to a top IRA commander in Belfast showed up in Tralee in the spring of 1984. The emissary from Belfast told O'Callaghan that the IRA needed underground bunkers to hide a huge consignment of weapons from America that would be landing soon in Kerry. O'Callaghan said he would make the arrangements, but privately he was appalled. The idea of Americans importing weapons that would be used to kill Irishmen was anathema to him. "No American has any right to send guns to my country, whether for financial gain or for some spurious political reasons," he later said.[27] He had another reason to foil the plot. His longtime local nemesis in the IRA, Martin Ferris, was planning to be on the *Marita Ann* when it took the weapons from the *Valhalla* in the open sea transfer.

O'Callaghan worried that Ferris suspected he was an informer. Too many missions that had O'Callaghan's fingerprints on them had been compromised. Besides, O'Callaghan didn't like Ferris and considered him a bully. Their extended families were close, but O'Callaghan despised Ferris as one of the IRA's top recruiters, someone who talked young people into throwing their lives away.

When O'Callaghan pressed for more details about the upcoming weapons shipment, Ferris told him to concentrate on his job of securing the bunkers. Everything else was being done on a need-to-know basis, standard IRA procedure. O'Callaghan found another way in. Having learned that a local fishing boat captain and IRA member, Michael Browne, had been recruited to sail his boat, the *Marita Ann*, to collect the weapons from the American ship, O'Callaghan began plying Browne with drinks at a pub and soon knew more about the upcoming mission. O'Callaghan invited Browne to live with him over the summer as the gunrunning mission entered its final planning stages. O'Callaghan only knew that the arms shipment involved American sympathizers; even Browne didn't know they were criminals.

By August, Browne was acting so erratically that O'Callaghan saw an opening to provide himself some cover. He reported Browne's behavior to other IRA men. "There's something wrong with Michael," he said. "It's not just the drink. He's acting odd. We'd better keep an eye on him."

O'Callaghan persuaded Browne to enter a clinic—to get healthy before the big mission. O'Callaghan assured a worried Ferris that Browne would be back in time, and he was. O'Callaghan delivered a fit and chipper Browne to Ferris in early September, weeks before the *Marita Ann* was supposed to rendezvous with the *Valhalla* somewhere near Porcupine Bank, 120 miles off the west coast of Ireland. Ferris was impressed.

A few hours before the *Marita Ann* set sail, Ferris and O'Callaghan met in a Tralee café for what would be the last time.

Ferris suggested that O'Callaghan join him for the historic mission.

O'Callaghan stirred his tea and shook his head.

"I'll see you," he told Ferris, "when you get back."

The *Marita Ann* had barely left port when O'Callaghan called his police handler.

Back aboard the *Valhalla,* nothing was going well. The September seas were hard on the small boat, especially with seven tons of weapons onboard. South of Nova Scotia, on the first day of sailing, *Valhalla* ran into the butt end of a small hurricane, and fifteen-foot seas battered her. It got worse. On the third night out, Andersen spotted a small blip on the radar screen: they were being followed. It was a small blip but a big ship; Andersen assumed it was military, probably Canadian. If it was the Canadian navy, it was keeping its distance—three miles. But it was definitely following *Valhalla*. "Wake up the others," Andersen told Crawley.

While Andersen kept a steady course, the crew moved the weapons up on deck and covered them with a tarp. Andersen told Crawley what he didn't want to hear: If whatever was following them sped up, they'd have to dump their payload into the ocean.

Then Andersen tried an evasive maneuver. He slowed *Valhalla* to a trawl and lit up the ship, to make it appear as if they were any other vessel out swordfishing. Whatever was following them suddenly changed course. The blip disappeared from the radar screen. But the delay would cost them hours.

At the end of the first week, a hurricane that had been in the

Bahamas when *Valhalla* left Massachusetts suddenly caught up to them. A forty-foot wave swamped *Valhalla* and blew out the windows of the pilot house. Broken glass left deep cuts on Andersen's right hand. McIntyre wrapped it with black electrical tape and Andersen kept the bow pointed into the waves.

McIntyre suggested they head to Newfoundland to fix Andersen's hand and the *Valhalla*'s assorted knocks. But Andersen knew that the Canadian authorities would board the ship and that they'd all be arrested. He stayed on course, toward Ireland. McIntyre went down below to repair the soaked generator and restore electricity.

The gangster crewmen were useless. They couldn't drive a boat, and when the seas started rocking they were too sick to do anything. "They wouldn't even get out of their cabins," McIntyre complained.[28]

The storm finally ended, and over the next week *Valhalla* made steady progress over calm seas. On the fourteenth day, Andersen was climbing to the pilot house when he spotted a plane. The only planes he'd seen in the open seas were weather planes, but this didn't look like one of them. It was flying too low. Andersen was convinced it was a military plane, flying at reconnaissance altitude to take photos.

After nightfall, the *Valhalla* was two hundred miles off the coast of Ireland when the radio crackled. "You're two days late!" Martin Ferris barked. Ferris was one of the most senior and most feared leaders of the IRA. But Bob Andersen was in no mood to be lectured by someone who hadn't just crossed the Atlantic, dodging two hurricanes, in an eighty-seven-foot fishing boat. Crawley took the microphone away from a seething Andersen and calmed everyone down. They set the time and coordinates for exchanging the weapons.

The two boats drew alongside each other, but the seas were choppy. The waves were rising to ten feet, and *Valhalla* kept smashing against the *Marita Ann*, damaging the *Marita Ann*'s hull. The ships separated and Andersen suggested ferrying the weapons over by dinghy.

McIntyre volunteered to be the ferryman. They attached the ends of a hundred-foot rope to each of the ships, and McIntyre drew himself across the churning seas, hand over hand. With each trip, another crate of weapons was loaded into the rocking dinghy. On the fourteenth and final trip, Crawley was ferried over to the *Marita Ann* with the last of the guns.

Crawley reached down to shake hands with McIntyre.

"You were brilliant!" the IRA man shouted.

McIntyre gave a thumbs-up and made the final leg, hand over hand, back to the *Valhalla*. It was daybreak.

Andersen pointed *Valhalla* south and sailed away. The *Marita Ann* turned toward the southwest coast of Ireland, where a welcoming party awaited.

With Whitey's blessing, Pat Nee and Joe Murray had flown to Ireland with their wives and had hoped to be on the *Marita Ann* when the weapons were transferred at sea. But the IRA vetoed that plan at the last minute. Nee broke the news as they sat in the lounge of the Shelbourne, the most luxurious hotel in Dublin.

Joe Murray was furious. "I pay for the fuckin' thing," he fumed. "They use my fuckin' boat. They use my fuckin' people. I fly the fuck all the way over here, and now I can't go?"

"Joe," Nee told him, "this is IRA business. This is how they do things. We can't second-guess them on this stuff."

Murray downed his pint, made some excuse about his wife, three months pregnant, being sick, and headed for the airport. He was back in Charlestown before the *Marita Ann* left port.

Nee rented a car and headed to the countryside with his wife and another couple. A few days later, they were driving through Charlestown—the one in County Mayo—when a bulletin came on the radio: A fishing trawler off the southwest coast had been fired on and seized by the Irish navy. A large trove of weapons had been found, and a group of IRA men onboard had been arrested. Nee and his companions headed for a ferry on Ireland's east coast. They sailed to France, fearing that they might be arrested if they went to an Irish airport.

Nee knew this wasn't simply chance: Someone had ratted out the mission.

As Martin Ferris, Mike Browne, John Crawley, and the other IRA men were marched into a courthouse in Dublin, Joe Cahill, the founder of the Provisional IRA, stood nearby watching.[29] The gunrunning mission that had been born that day he stood in a bar in Southie, asking Whitey Bulger and the rest of the Irish mob in Boston to become the IRA's patrons, was a resounding failure. The resulting propaganda, showing the IRA in bed with Boston criminals, could be much more damaging than losing seven tons of weapons.

At about the same time Cahill was standing in the shadows in Dublin, Whitey Bulger, standing in his condo in Quincy, heard the news come on TV about a boat loaded down with weapons being seized off the coast of Kerry. There was a DEA bug planted in the wall of Whitey's condo at the time, and, for a moment, his usual discretion abandoned him. "That's our stuff," Whitey said.[30]

Staring at the TV screen, Whitey Bulger knew someone had given them up. And as *Valhalla* headed back across the Atlantic toward Boston, he was already trying to find out who.

Valhalla docked at Pier 7 in Boston Harbor not long before midnight, Friday, October 12, 1984. Andersen told the crewmen to scatter. He and McIntyre assessed the damage to the boat with furrowed brows. "We've got to fix this," Andersen told McIntyre. "If we go back to Gloucester looking like this, we're done for." But within twenty-four hours, before he could even begin the repairs, McIntyre was under arrest. Not for gunrunning, but for trying to visit his estranged wife. He'd rung the doorbell at her house in Quincy, and when no one answered he'd climbed to the balcony. A neighbor reported a burglary in progress. When the police showed up, ordered him down, and checked his ID, an old warrant for failing to appear in court on a drunken driving charge popped up on the computer. He was arrested but wouldn't go to court before Monday morning. McIntyre had been pushed to the limit after six harrowing weeks cooped up on a boat, dodging hurricanes and forty-foot seas. The prospect of spending the next twenty-four hours in a jail cell sent him to a desperate place. He started babbling about drugs and guns and the IRA and gangsters. The cop who booked him didn't know what McIntyre was talking about, so he called Dick Bergeron, a Quincy detective who was known to know the wiseguys.

Ever since he realized Whitey Bulger had made Quincy his home away from Southie, Bergeron had made the pursuit of him something of an obsession. He had been instrumental in getting the DEA bug into Whitey's condo. Bergeron had been working with a DEA agent, Steve Boeri, trying to nail Bulger for drugs, and when he heard that some fisherman was in the lockup, talking about guys from Southie and Charlestown and the IRA and drug boats, he hustled down to the station and called Boeri.

By the time Boeri showed up at the police station, John McIntyre had already made a big decision. "I'd like to make a deal," John McIntyre told Bergeron and Boeri, who tried to hide their incredulity and delight. "I'd like to get out of here and get those two old warrants off me. And I'd just like to start living a normal life. It's like, it's almost like living with a knife in you. . . . I mean, I didn't start out in life to end up like this. You know?"[31]

"Yeah," Boeri replied. "So you want to cooperate with the government?"

"Yeah," McIntyre said, "if you can get me out of this jam."

The jam was entirely of McIntyre's making. The authorities had nothing on him before he volunteered it. But he was tired of the life that had put him in the company of dangerous men while doing little for his own bank account. He had been the engineer on seven of Murray's drug smuggling voyages and had little to show for it. During the long night of questioning, McIntyre evaded Boeri's questions about the South Boston gang. He never mentioned Whitey's name, and he knew Kevin Weeks only as Kevin. But he knew Pat Nee, saying Nee was the driving force behind the gunrunning mission.

Boeri knew all the players and knew the risks they posed.

"I want to get something straight now," the DEA agent told McIntyre. "You definitely want to disengage yourself from this criminal element that you've been going with?"

"I'd like to be able to sleep at night without having to look over my shoulder," McIntyre replied.

"Do you want to stay in the Boston area?" Boeri asked.

"Yeah."

Boeri knew what Whitey was capable of; he sensed that McIntyre did not.

"There's no way I could talk you into, like, going somewhere else?" Boeri asked.

"No."

Boeri eventually got to the point: "How would you feel about, would you be willing to feed us information about working with these guys?"

"I'd do it," John McIntyre replied, "if it would get me out of this."

The following day, McIntyre was interviewed by FBI agent Roderick Kennedy, the FBI's liaison with the DEA. McIntyre acknowledged that "an individual named Whitey who operates a liquor store in South Boston" was in the drug business with his boss, Joe Murray.[32] Kennedy sat in on additional meetings as Customs agents interviewed McIntyre. Kennedy later insisted that Connolly overheard him and other agents talking about someone on the *Valhalla* cooperating.

Connolly arranged to meet with Whitey to tell him what he knew. His information was not precise. The *Boston Globe* had published a photograph showing Andersen and McIntyre walking off the *Valhalla* for questioning by Customs agents. Flemmi said Connolly told Whitey that one of those two men in the photo was cooperating.[33]

Whitey suspected McIntyre from the beginning. He considered Andersen to have been around and involved with Murray long enough to keep his mouth shut. McIntyre was a wild card.

Besides, Connolly had told them it was Dick Bergeron, a Quincy police detective, who had rolled the informant. Whitey knew Andersen was a North Shore guy; McIntyre lived in Quincy on the South Shore. It had to be McIntyre. "This kid won't stand up," Whitey said, and he was right.

According to Weeks, Whitey went to see Joe Murray and told him he believed McIntyre was talking. Murray was crushed; not only was his drug empire in peril, but he was about to lose the best marine engineer he ever had. He suggested sending McIntyre to South America to stay with his drug contacts there. "We could keep him there until this whole thing blows over," Murray said. "Or we could kill him down there."[34]

Alternatively, Murray suggested, they could coach McIntyre on what to say before a grand jury so that it would be impossible for indictments to spring from his testimony. Whitey just stared at Murray. Whitey wanted to get McIntyre alone so he could interrogate him—torture him, if need be. He needed to know how much DEA and Customs knew; if they knew he was involved in the *Valhalla*; if they knew he was making millions from the drug trade. Whitey was confident that, if he could get McIntyre alone, he could get the truth out of him. But he wanted corroborating evidence to point to as he worked him over. Whitey instructed Pat Nee to approach McIntyre and solicit twenty thousand dollars as McIntyre's investment in a drug shipment that the South Boston gang was putting together.[35] Whitey knew McIntyre was broke; he didn't have that kind of money. But he could obtain the cash from his government handlers if he went running to them to tell them of the proposal from Nee. "If he can come up with twenty grand," Whitey said, "then he's working with Customs or DEA."[36]

Within days, McIntyre came up with the money. Now Whitey needed to get him alone.

Whitey laid out the ruse to Nee: Tell McIntyre they had to drop some beer off at Nee's brother's house in South Boston for a party. Pat Nee picked McIntyre up in Quincy. There were two cases of beer in the backseat of his car. "We're gonna go by my brother's," Nee said. "We need to drop this stuff off."

Nee's brother was away in New Hampshire. Nee parked in front of the house, at 799 East Third Street, and took a case of Miller Lite out of the backseat. He headed toward the front door and called back over his shoulder to McIntyre, "Grab the other case and follow me."

It was noontime on a Friday, a week after Thanksgiving, and John McIntyre thought he was doing Pat Nee a favor when he walked into the house. Then he saw Kevin Weeks and Stevie Flemmi standing in the kitchen. Whitey stepped from behind the refrigerator, holding a MAC-10 machine pistol equipped with a silencer. He pointed the gun at McIntyre's chest. McIntyre put the beer down and stumbled backward, trying to get away. But Weeks sprang forward and grabbed him by the throat with one hand and the back of his hair with the other, lowering him to the ground.

It was eerily quiet, and very crowded in the cramped kitchen.

"Let him up," Whitey said.[37]

Weeks pulled McIntyre to his feet while Flemmi and Whitey put a hand on each of McIntyre's shoulders and pushed him down onto a kitchen chair. Without a word, Flemmi pulled handcuffs, leg shackles, and a long chain from a duffel bag. With practiced precision, he fastened them around McIntyre.

"We need to talk," Whitey said, putting the machine gun on the table. Whitey pulled up a chair and sat right in front of him. McIntyre's eyes drifted unconsciously toward the gun. He appeared resigned to his fate even before Whitey asked a single question, and within thirty seconds, Flemmi recalled, McIntyre confirmed Whitey's suspicions. "I'm sorry," McIntyre said. "I was weak."

McIntyre had done more than talk to the police about the gunrunning mission. He had helped the DEA seize a boatload of

marijuana from which Whitey was supposed to have received a
three-million-dollar cut. That was all Whitey needed to justify killing him. And McIntyre seemed to understand that. But getting
McIntyre to confess was just the beginning. Whitey was looking for
information. And so he tried to reassure McIntyre. "Relax. You're
going to be okay," Whitey told him. "We're going to work something out."

Whitey said they might have to send him down to Joe Murray's
friends in South America for a while until the heat died down. But
it's doubtful even John McIntyre believed that. Whitey's questioning was perfunctory. McIntyre admitted that it was Bergeron and
Steve Boeri who had flipped him. He admitted that Customs had
given him the twenty thousand dollars in cash to pay for his share
of the drug shipment. The trap Whitey had concocted had worked
perfectly.

McIntyre apologized to Nee, insisting that he had not been the
informant who gave up the *Valhalla*. Sounding a bit like Whitey
nearly a decade before in John Connolly's car on Wollaston Beach,
McIntyre said, "I'd never give up the IRA." Whitey believed him
about the IRA, but that was already ancient history as far as he was
concerned. This was personal; did the DEA know enough to take
him down? It was also professional. He'd long wondered if he was
getting a fair cut from Joe Murray's drug importations. McIntyre
could help him figure that out.

It was enormously important for Whitey to find out how much
product Murray was moving, what had been shipped lately, what
was still in the works. Flemmi stayed in the kitchen with Whitey
through an interrogation that lasted six hours. Weeks sat in the living room, watching TV. The voices from the kitchen were never
raised. "We're gonna give you some money, John," Whitey told him.
"We're gonna send you away."

But thirty-two-year-old John McIntyre got no farther than the
bottom of the stairs that led to the basement at 799 East Third
Street. The chains jangled as he walked. In the basement, he was

pushed down into another chair. But there were no more questions. Flemmi stood there and watched as Whitey wrapped a think rope around McIntyre's neck and tightened it.

John McIntyre just went limp. He submitted to his own execution. But the executioner was having trouble. The rope was too thick to dig into McIntyre's windpipe and cut off his air supply. Instead, it made McIntyre gag and throw up.

Whitey stepped away, his brow shiny with sweat, his hands and arms tight from exertion. "This ain't working," he said. He grabbed a gun. It was a .22-caliber rifle cut down, with a pistol grip and a silencer. Whitey waved it so McIntyre could see it.

"Would you like one in the head?" Whitey asked, solicitously.

"Yes," McIntyre replied, sitting up slightly after catching his breath. "Please."

Whitey obliged and fired a shot into the back of McIntyre's head. The bullet exited his chin and McIntyre fell once again.

Flemmi, who typically played coroner to Whitey's executioner, put his head to McIntyre's chest and felt his neck.

"He's still alive," Flemmi said.

So he grabbed McIntyre's slumped head by the hair and held it aloft so Whitey could come around and pump a volley of shots into McIntyre's face.

Flemmi let go and McIntyre's body slumped to the floor.

"Well," Whitey said. "He's dead now."

Flemmi took his pliers out and began removing McIntyre's teeth. Kevin Weeks started digging up the cellar floor. Whitey went upstairs and took a nap.

"Kevin," Flemmi said, as Weeks was digging. "C'mere a second."

Weeks stepped over and Flemmi held forth his pliers, waving them back and forth. A piece of John McIntyre's tongue wagged at the end of the pliers.

"He won't be using this no more," Flemmi said.

Weeks didn't see the humor. He went back to his digging.

After John McIntyre's body was buried, Whitey and Flemmi

went to get something to eat. Whitey was pensive, replaying the interrogation in his head. He told Flemmi that McIntyre had told the truth about one thing: He didn't give up the *Valhalla*. Somebody else did.

On the other side of the Atlantic, that somebody else, Sean O'Callaghan, had briefly prospered with Martin Ferris out of the picture. He had become the IRA's top man in Kerry. His superiors in Belfast ordered him to find out who gave up the gunrunning mission and to arrange the prison escape of Ferris and the other IRA men arrested on the *Marita Ann*.

The IRA commander from Belfast overseeing the gunrunning mission lost his position over the debacle. The IRA, meanwhile, was convinced the mission had been given up by someone in Ireland and began an internal investigation.

O'Callaghan tried politics and was elected as a councilor in Tralee. But he became paranoid, thinking others knew he had given up Ferris. He abruptly moved to England and offered his services to MI-5, the British domestic counterintelligence agency. His mental condition deteriorated. Four years after he gave up the *Valhalla*, he walked into a police station in Kent, England, and told the astonished desk officer that he had killed two people in Northern Ireland.

By the time the authors of this book interviewed him in a prison in Northern Ireland in 1994, O'Callaghan knew that he had unwittingly gotten John McIntyre killed. In 1996, O'Callaghan was released from prison after serving eight years of a life sentence.

He lived under the constant threat of IRA assassination. But he was already dead to his family. His admissions of being an informer bought him new friends in some Tory parlors in London, but he was widely shunned in Ireland. Among the Irish, even those who hated the IRA, O'Callaghan was looked upon as someone to avoid: a tout, an informer, the worst.

O'Callaghan embraced his new identity, writing a memoir called

The Informer. In 1997, just hours before he flew to America for a publicity tour, he learned that his father, Jack, had died earlier in the week. No one in O'Callaghan's family had bothered to tell him. O'Callaghan didn't go to the funeral.

The graveside oration for Jack O'Callaghan was given by Martin Ferris, the IRA leader Sean O'Callaghan had put in prison for ten years. Ferris praised Jack O'Callaghan as a republican hero. The hero's son, an informer, was not mentioned.

A few years earlier, while still in prison, Sean O'Callaghan had marveled at Whitey Bulger's ability to play the game. Whitey, the snitch, had just skipped town for good, tipped off by John Connolly that he was about to be arrested. "I have to give him one thing," Sean O'Callaghan said. "He was better at it than me."

12

Deep in The Haunty

Whitey called it The Haunty, because what took place there was haunting.[1] Pat Nee's brother's house, just 250 feet down the street from Bill Bulger's place in South Boston, was a plain, two-story Cape, with a narrow vestibule that poked out from the front door. It was surrounded by three-deckers, dwarfed by its neighbors, and was often vacant—Nee's brother spent a lot of time out of town. On the first floor, there was a kitchen and a living room; on the second, two bedrooms and a bath. Most important to Whitey, there was an unfinished basement with a room that had a dirt floor. It was 799 East Third Street and it became his secret burial ground.

After the scorching law enforcement heat that followed the Holy Trinity murders, Whitey was convinced he had to start burying his bodies again. He and Steve Flemmi had long had a motto: no corpus delicti. If there was no body, there was usually no case. They had let themselves flout that cautious rule—but no more. "Jimmy changed his M.O. after the Holy Trinity," said Kevin Weeks. "He didn't go after anybody. He lured them to him. So he could dispose of the bodies."[2] For that savage purpose, The Haunty was just right: Matters could be dealt with discreetly there; it offered perfect cover. Flemmi's parents lived next door to Bill Bulger. If anyone in law enforcement wanted to know why they were spending so much time on East Third Street, both Whitey and Flemmi had a perfectly good alibi. They were just visiting family.

As partners, Whitey and Flemmi were moving on in other ways as well. The easy money promised in the World Jai Alai deal had of course not materialized. Whitey wouldn't let Flemmi forget about that debacle, which Flemmi had talked him into. In any case, by the summer of 1983, Whitey had found a new score.

This time the easy money was in the possession of Arthur "Bucky" Barrett, who was destined to become the first permanent guest at The Haunty. They had already taken a run at Barrett, a renowned safecracker who had helped an independent band of thieves get past the security systems at the Depositors Trust in Medford. A break-in and heist at the bank over the Memorial Day weekend in 1980 landed Barrett's group some $1.5 million. It was bold but foolhardy—a lot of the loot taken was owned by Mafia and other organized crime interests, much of it jewels and unreported income held in safe deposit boxes. It wasn't just the cops who were looking for the robbers. The wiseguys were looking for them, too.

And some of the robbers, in fact, were cops. Three of the six burglars who broke into the bank were police officers. They enlisted Barrett to get into the bank and around its security system. Barrett's reputation as a master thief and safecracker was known to both cops and criminals in the Boston area. But he wasn't a tough guy, he never carried a gun. That made him a soft touch for the likes of Whitey Bulger.

John Connolly, as part of his ongoing effort to buff Whitey's credentials as an informant, had tried to give Whitey credit for being the first to identify the Depositors Trust robbers. In a June 25, 1980, report, he noted that Whitey had told him that "the word on the street" was that Barrett had set up the heist and had control over most of the gold and diamonds taken.[3] Connolly conveniently left out of his report that Whitey had instructed him and John Morris to tell Barrett that Whitey was looking for him and wanted a cut, and that he could save himself by joining the Witness Protection Program and giving up all the crooked cops who had helped him rob the bank.[4] This marked a new dimension in the conspiratorial bond between Whitey and the FBI. Now it was the mobster telling agents how to cultivate informants and who to go after. Connolly and Morris dutifully carried out Whitey's plan. But Barrett refused to go along. He believed he had his own insurance policy: Frank Salemme, Flemmi's old partner, who had cast his lot with the Mafia.

Barrett had intended to give a hundred thousand dollars from the bank heist to Whitey, as tribute for Winter Hill, and a hundred thousand dollars to Salemme, for the Mafia, because it was common knowledge he had pulled off the Medford bank job, and it behooved a small-time crook to share proceeds with the criminal powers in town.[5] But for reasons that were never clear, Whitey didn't get his cut, a slight he nursed for three years before moving on Barrett. He wanted his money and he also wanted information on Joe Murray's drug operation, which Barrett was now connected to. Whitey had a lucrative but uneasy deal with Murray; he always had the feeling— even before the *Valhalla* misadventure—that he wasn't really getting his share.

The plan was to lure Barrett to The Haunty; to get him in a place where he would have to give up everything he had. Whitey knew Barrett well enough to know he could not pass up a score involving diamonds, so he had a mutual friend contact him about some stolen gems he might want to buy on the cheap. Barrett liked what he saw and agreed to go to a house in City Point in Southie to see the rest of the haul. The setup man brought Barrett to The Haunty for the viewing, but, once inside, all Barrett saw was Whitey, holding a 9mm machine gun with a silencer. Flemmi was standing by, waiting to handcuff their prisoner. "Bucky Barrett," Whitey announced, "freeze."[6]

Weeks thought he was watching a shakedown. "Jimmy never said anything about killing him," Weeks said. "This was just an extortion." As usual, Weeks went into the adjoining living room to watch television while Whitey and Flemmi chained Barrett to a chair and interrogated him with great patience. Whitey asked for, and Barrett supplied, a detailed outline of Joe Murray's drug business: who was in it, how much he was making, where he was storing his marijuana and cocaine. Once Whitey had exhausted Barrett's knowledge, he demanded Barrett's money. Not some of it. All of it. Barrett called his wife at their house in Quincy, a fifteen-minute drive away, saying he needed to bring some friends by on business. "Turn off the alarm," Barrett said, and then he instructed her to take their sons— one two years old and the other thirteen weeks old—"and go out for a couple of hours."[7]

Within an hour, Whitey and Flemmi were back with the forty-seven thousand dollars Barrett had stashed at home. Whitey then forced Barrett to call everyone he knew who could give him money. His partner at a restaurant in Faneuil Hall Marketplace came up with ten thousand dollars, which was duly collected. Barrett called Murray and pleaded with him, saying he needed money desperately, but Murray was unsympathetic. Convinced he had wrung as much out of Barrett as possible, Whitey decided it was time to kill him. He pulled Flemmi aside and said Barrett wasn't leaving the house alive; that he wouldn't be leaving the house at all. Flemmi led Barrett toward the door that led to the cellar. "Bucky's going downstairs to lie down for a while," Whitey told Weeks.

Barrett had followed Flemmi down a couple of the cellar steps when Whitey aimed his gun at the back of Barrett's head. But he had trouble pulling the trigger, which seemed stuck. There was a momentary pause as Whitey fumbled to put his glasses on. He looked at the gun and saw that the safety was on. He clicked it off and aimed again. Barrett was almost at the bottom of the steps when a quick burst of gunfire went into the back of his head. He fell down the last two steps and came to rest near Flemmi's feet.

Flemmi was furious.

"That coulda gone through him and hit me!" he yelled.[8]

Whitey waved him off and turned to Kevin Weeks.

"I couldn't trust Bucky," Whitey said by way of explanation. "He had to go."

Weeks said nothing.

"Go downstairs and help Stevie," Whitey said. "I'm gonna lie down."

As Weeks dug a grave in the cellar, Flemmi pulled Barrett's teeth and Whitey took a nap on the living room couch. "As soon as Bucky was dead, Jimmy just calmed down," Weeks said. "It was like he took a Valium."[9] Weeks was sickened, especially when he looked at the kitchen table and saw Barrett's open wallet, which showed a photograph of Barrett's young son. But Whitey simply fell asleep. It was a pattern Weeks observed: in the days and hours leading up to a murder, Whitey appeared hyperactive, but in the immediate aftermath of a murder, his body language changed. He appeared relaxed, contented, spent.[10]

The real value in Barrett was not his money but his information on Joe Murray. Whitey, whose defenders credited him with keeping drugs out of Southie, had the leverage now to demand better terms from the city's biggest drug importer. He was to get a cut of everything Murray moved, no matter where it was landed and warehoused. It was the most lucrative shakedown of his career.

A year after Barrett was buried in the dirt floor, John McIntyre was buried next to him. While McIntyre's status as an informant for various law enforcement agencies meant that his disappearance brought more scrutiny than Barrett's had, the heat was more easily deflected than that following the murders of Wheeler, Halloran, Donahue, and Callahan. After all, there was no body. McIntyre was simply gone.

The third and final guest at The Haunty was Deborah Hussey, and she would turn out to be the last person whose murder was blamed on Whitey and Flemmi. The fact that she had been like a stepdaughter to Flemmi did not stand in the way of his molesting her, from her early teens onward, even as he continued to treat her mother as his common-law-wife. Deborah Hussey started using drugs soon after the abuse started. Tom Hussey blamed Flemmi for his daughter's addiction.

It is safe to assume that Tom Hussey is the only man who ever spit in Flemmi's face and lived to tell the tale. "Stevie had just moved in with my wife. I was still drinking at the time, and Stevie walked into this bar on Columbia Road called Lombardi's. I walked right up to him and spit in his face," Tom Hussey said. Flemmi beat him and left him bloodied. Tom Hussey soon left Boston, moved to Florida, joined the plumbers' union, and stopped drinking. Debbie had started acting up in her teens, so he told her to come down to Florida to spend time with him and get away from trouble. The visits helped; away from Flemmi, she seemed her old self for long stretches. But she would always go back to Boston and to Flemmi and the drugs. "She was a smart girl, a beautiful girl," Tom Hussey said. "I got her to come down and live with me when she was about twenty. I got her a job at a hotel in Boca Raton, and the manager said she was the best waitress he ever had. But she couldn't stay off the drugs and she went back to Flemmi."[11] It wasn't just the drugs. Debbie was dancing in a strip club and prostituting herself to buy heroin. Flemmi claimed he was scandalized because she brought black clients back to the family house on Blue Hill Avenue in suburban Milton.[12] It was in that spacious home, around the fall of 1982, that Debbie told her mother Flemmi was the reason she couldn't get off drugs. Debbie was in bed, sick from the narcotics, and Flemmi was slapping her when Marion burst in and demanded to know what was going on.

Debbie blurted out that she had been performing oral sex on Flemmi since she was a teenager.[13]

Marion was floored. Her knees went weak.

"I've been doing it for years," Debbie said.

Flemmi gathered her up and dragged her out of the house. His two sons were downstairs. They couldn't hear this. "I'm not lyin',

Ma!" Debbie cried over her shoulder, as Flemmi bundled her out the door. Debbie, a junkie, had been lying about her life for years, but Marion believed her now. "Get out," Marion told Flemmi the next day. And he did.[14]

Debbie kept getting arrested downtown, usually for prostitution. She was dropping names. Flemmi's name. Whitey's name. Sometimes, too, the name of Flemmi's brother, Michael, the cop. This can't go on, Whitey told Flemmi. As he had with Debra Davis four years earlier, he started pressing Flemmi to deal with Debbie Hussey. It was inevitable that his partner would cave.

On a cold night in January 1985, Whitey picked up Kevin Weeks. "We're gonna meet Stevie," Whitey said.[15] When Whitey parked in front of The Haunty, Weeks felt odd. The only time they went there was to kill someone. For the first time, he wondered: Was it his turn? Whitey soon put Weeks's mind to rest when he explained that someone else would be joining them at The Haunty. "Stevie's out buying her a coat," Whitey said. A half-hour later, Debbie Hussey walked into the house; Flemmi had lured her there by saying he was thinking of buying the house for her. Kevin Weeks was in the upstairs bathroom when he heard a thud. He says he walked downstairs and came upon Whitey, lying on his back in the living room, his legs wrapped around Debbie Hussey's waist, his hands wrapped around her neck. As Whitey choked the life out of her, Flemmi stood there. Whitey denies that he was the killer, but the accounts of Flemmi and Weeks closely agree.*[16]

Flemmi put his ear to Debbie's chest and apparently heard something, because he put a rope around her neck and tightened it, using a stick as a lever. When it was over, the trio assumed their usual roles: Weeks started digging, Flemmi started pulling Debbie's teeth, and Whitey lay down to take his nap.[17] Later that night, after Debbie had been buried, Whitey was driving around Southie. He

---

*Steve Flemmi pleaded guilty in 2003 to participating in ten murders, including those of Davis and Hussey, and was sentenced to life in prison.

was his typical self after a murder: relaxed, relieved. Another threat averted. "What was that all about?" Kevin Weeks asked. "I don't know," Whitey replied, "maybe Stevie was fucking her and she was going to tell." Actually, he went on, it was more than that. Debbie was a junkie. "She was bringing niggers back to the house and fucking them," Whitey said. "It couldn't go on."[18]

A few months after Debbie Hussey's murder, Whitey and Weeks were driving through City Point when Pat Nee waved them down in front of The Haunty. Nee leaned into the window and said, "My brother's selling the house." This was not good news. What if the person who bought the house decided to renovate the cellar? Whitey turned to Nee in anger. "Why can't you control your brother?" he asked. "It's his house," Nee said, shrugging. "What am I going to do?"

Whitey took his time deciding what to do. They considered pouring cement over the dirt floor. They talked about buying the house outright, but that seemed extravagant. Whitey's solution was cheaper and, in his mind at least, more practical. "We're gonna have to move the bodies," he told Weeks. Flemmi was in favor. Weeks dreaded the idea, knowing that much of the work would fall to him. But first he and Whitey drove around town looking for a new burial spot. Whitey picked it out, a wooded area across from Florian Hall, the Boston firefighters function hall nearby in Neponset, a section of Dorchester. The trees and brush provided natural cover. The hum of traffic from the nearby Southeast Expressway would drown out the noise of the digging.

On a crisp October night in 1985, Whitey set up surveillance, and Weeks and Flemmi started digging. They filled ten large duffel bags with dirt—they would need it to cover the bodies—then put the bags in the eight-foot-wide hole and covered it lightly with topsoil. Whitey put a twenty-dollar bill under a rock on top of the pre-dug grave. "If that's gone when we come back," Whitey said, "we're outta here."[19] Two days later, on Halloween, they went to The Haunty to dig up the bodies of Bucky Barrett, John McIntyre, and

Debbie Hussey. Weeks, Nee, and Flemmi arrived in the pre-dawn darkness.[20] They were dressed for work, with painters' masks and gloves. Whitey left them to do the dirty work, sleeping late into the day, as usual. As he slept, Whitey missed scenes right out of a horror movie. Barrett's body was so brittle and dry that when Weeks lifted it the head detached from the torso. Removing the decomposed bodies of McIntyre and Hussey was even more grotesque. The masks did only so much to minimize the stench. The corpses were put in body bags Flemmi had obtained from a local funeral director.

At nightfall, Whitey showed up with a wood-paneled Ford station wagon he called the Hearse. He parked it in the driveway next to the bulkhead that led down to the cellar. They were loading the second body in the back of the station wagon when an old man walked past the driveway. Weeks and Flemmi froze, but Whitey told them to relax. "He didn't see anything," Whitey said. "Besides, it's Halloween."[21]

It took less than ten minutes to drive the five miles from City Point to the new gravesite. They took turns burying the bodies and keeping watch. Weeks was the lookout, lying on his stomach, holding a machine gun, when a young man emerged from a Halloween party across the street at Florian Hall. The man got into his car but apparently needed to relieve himself, so he drove just across the street and got out of his car. The car stopped twenty feet from where Whitey, Flemmi, and Weeks were hidden by trees and brush. Weeks sized up the driver and figured he was just emptying a beer-filled bladder. He was right, and the young man drove off. But Whitey was mad. Weeks had made a mistake by letting the guy get too close. "You shoulda shot him," Whitey said. Weeks disagreed but didn't say so. He couldn't get the smell of the bodies out of his nose, or his head, for days.

Closing down The Haunty marked, in retrospect, a turning point in Whitey's history. It would prove the end of the most violent phase of his criminal reign. Extortions continued at a brisk pace, but threatening to kill people, rather than actually killing people, became the new business model. And to make it really pay, he expanded his extortion enterprise. Ordinary businesspeople became targets, too, and Stephen and Julie Rakes were the first test of the new approach.

Rakes and his wife had bought an old gas station across the street from the Old Colony project and converted it to a liquor store. Stephen Rakes's prices were lower than those at other nearby liquor stores, and as soon as he opened up, he and his wife began receiving threatening phone calls. A guy kept calling saying that there was a bomb in the store. Rakes wondered if he should go to the cops. His sister, Mary O'Malley, went to Whitey instead. She approached Whitey and Kevin Weeks at Triple O's and asked them to find the guy who was making the phone calls. They canvassed the neighborhood, talking to the owners of other liquor stores. No one knew who was doing it.[22]

Then one day Whitey and Weeks were driving through Andrew Square when an old bookie they knew waved them down to talk. Out of the blue, the bookie, who owned his own liquor store in Andrew Square, told them he had been calling in bomb threats to Stephen Rakes's store, trying to snuff out a competitor. "You can't do that anymore," Whitey told him. "That guy's father is a friend of Kevin's."[23] Weeks and Whitey went to see Rakes and tell him he had nothing to worry about; that his business was secure. But not long after, Mary O'Malley was back at Triple O's. This time, she said her brother wanted to sell the store. The idea intrigued Whitey: a legitimate cash business would be a good investment, a way to wash their dirty money. Besides, he had been looking for a new place to serve as a headquarters, where he and Flemmi and Weeks could meet regularly without drawing notice. The liquor store and the adjoining convenience store, Rotary Variety, would do the trick.

A few days later, Whitey and Weeks showed up at the store. Rakes seemed reluctant to talk in front of his wife. Swing by my house, he suggested. There, they agreed on a price: one hundred thousand dollars. "Then he [Rakes] reneged," Weeks said. "He wanted more money. It was just a shakedown. And you don't shake down Jimmy Bulger." Stephen Rakes tells a different version of the story, not nearly as benign as the one offered by Weeks. Rakes said he never wanted to sell the store. Instead, Whitey and Flemmi showed up at his house one night with Weeks, an old friend of the family. "You've got a problem," Whitey announced as soon as they sat down at the kitchen table. "We were hired to kill you." As if to underscore the point, Flemmi pulled a .38 from his coat and slapped it down on the table. Rakes's eyes fixated on the shiny steel of the revolver. Whitey said that there were people who didn't like Rakes undercutting their prices.

"I've got a better deal," Whitey told him. "We're going to buy the store."

"It's not for sale," Rakes replied.

Whitey realized that Rakes hadn't heard what he was really saying. "I'll fucking kill you," Whitey explained. "You don't know how lucky you are."

At that point, Rakes's one-year-old daughter, Meredith, wandered into the kitchen. Flemmi reached down and picked her up and put her on his lap. The little girl reached for the gun and spun it around, like a toy. Flemmi tousled her hair and smirked at Rakes, who sat mortified. "You wouldn't want your daughter to grow up without a father, would you?" Flemmi asked. Whitey was smirking, too. He clicked his switchblade, letting the blade flash open and then recoil. He did it over and over, letting Rakes think it over. "Here," Whitey said, tossing a brown paper bag stuffed with sixty-seven thousand dollars. "Now we own the liquor store."[24] He had soon renamed it the South Boston Liquor Mart.

Julie Rakes, stunned by the menacing takeover and incredulous that her children had effectively been used as pawns, called her uncle Joe Lundbohm, a Boston police detective, and told him what had happened. Lundbohm called John Connolly. Who else would he call? Connolly was from Southie. He worked the wiseguys. Lundbohm didn't know that Connolly was Whitey's handler. They arranged to meet for coffee, and Connolly seemed to know exactly how to make this go away. "Would they wear a wire? Would Stephen wear a wire?" Connolly asked Lundbohm.

"They'd be afraid to," Lundbohm said.

"There isn't a helluva a lot we can do," Connolly replied.[25]

The day after Lundbohm met with Connolly, Whitey paid Rakes another visit.

"Tell Lundbohm to back off," Whitey hissed.

Rakes knew then that Whitey had a direct pipeline to the FBI.

The investigation, such as it was, went away. So did Steve Rakes. To Florida, to get away from it all. By then stories were going around Southie that Whitey had murdered Rakes, and Whitey was still very sensitive about his reputation in the Town. Usually, such rumors were good for business, stoking his reputation as a killer. But the Rakes family was big and well known in Southie, and Whitey didn't want people thinking he'd killed some guy to take over his liquor store. So they had Rakes's sister give them his number in Florida, and Weeks told Rakes he had to get back to Southie to dispel the rumors. Rakes said he'd be back in a couple of weeks. Whitey took the phone and growled, "Get back now!"

It was an odd sight. In the middle of winter, Stephen Rakes stood in front of the liquor store he used to own with the new own-ers, Whitey Bulger and Kevin Weeks, talking for an hour. Then they went up to Perkins Square and stood at Southie's busiest intersec-tion, so everybody could see them with the guy they had suppos-edly killed.[26]

As 1986 came to a close, Weeks realized that almost two years had passed since Whitey had killed anyone. It was the longest he had gone without a hit since Weeks had started working for him full-time six years earlier. Between 1981 and the murder of Deb-

bie Hussey in early 1985, Whitey had been involved in the murders of eight people: Roger Wheeler, Debra Davis, Brian Halloran,
Michael Donahue, John Callahan, Bucky Barrett, John McIntyre,
and Deborah Hussey. It wasn't just Whitey; Stevie stopped killing
people, too. The murder of Debbie Hussey shook him like nothing
before. Flemmi used to be even more likely than Whitey to suggest
killing as a solution to a problem; now he, like Whitey, was content
to threaten people.[27]

But even with The Haunty shut down, and his approach to his
business changed, Whitey's life remained a complicated straddle of
his criminal and domestic realms. There was a gang to manage, with
operations in loansharking, extortion, and drugs; he had to sustain
his bond with the FBI by supplying a regular flow of tips; and he
was also still keeping two households. Early evenings with Teresa
Stanley, late nights with Cathy Greig. Stanley was still in the dark
about Greig, and Whitey wanted to keep it that way. That trick
alone could test a man's stamina.

If weeknights meant dinner at Stanley's, Sunday afternoons
meant dinner at Mary Flemmi's house.[28] Whitey, accompanied by
Stanley, would always arrive impeccably dressed, showering Mary
Flemmi with small gifts. Mary did the cooking, so Stanley could
relax with a drink. She made sure not to drink more than a couple of
glasses of wine, because Whitey frowned on it.[29]

Adjacent to the Flemmis' house was a screened-in structure.
When it was first built, in the late 1980s, Stanley and her girlfriend
Terry stayed after dinner one night to clean it and decorate it for a
party. They vacuumed up the sawdust, arranged the couch and chairs,
lined up the barstools by a counter. They put flower arrangements
around the room. Stanley and Terry drank wine as they worked, and
the hours flew by. The two women had finished sometime around
3:00 a.m. when Whitey stormed in. He was in a rage. He had come
by the house around midnight and had seen the lights out. He had
driven to Stanley's home, and when he couldn't find her there, he'd
driven all around South Boston looking for her. Now it was late, and

Stanley must have appeared tipsy, because Whitey made a remark about her drinking and then suddenly grabbed her by the throat and shoved her forcefully. She flailed in his grasp, knocking over tables, sending the flower arrangements crashing to the floor. "Leave her alone!" Terry screamed.

Whitey ignored her. He kept pushing Stanley violently into the furniture, leaving her with a black eye and bruises. "It was a bizarre, horrible night," said Stanley, realizing for the first time just how volatile Whitey's temper was. The party was canceled. Whitey ordered Stanley to stay away from Terry; Stanley didn't see her friend for another eight years "because I didn't want trouble," she said.

Whitey's first and only attack on Stanley was a sign of the increasing strain he was under, or perhaps of his diminished capacity as he aged to deal with the strain that had always been there. In the late 1980s, when he was in his late fifties, he began to have disturbing nightmares. He'd had night terrors after the LSD experiments he had volunteered for in Atlanta, but the nightmares rivaled those. Now he asked Weeks to accompany him to a psychiatrist's office in Watertown, just outside Boston. Weeks believed Whitey was sincere on one level; that he needed professional help. He also thought that he was working an angle—putting on record, with a doctor, what the LSD testing had done to him. If he ever found himself in court, he wanted a piece of paper saying that the federal government had used him as a human guinea pig and that he still suffered the consequences decades later. "The doctor was a Harvard professor," Weeks said. "After the fourth visit, the doctor said he couldn't see Jimmy anymore. He was scared to death over what Jimmy was saying. Jimmy described these dreams of blood and gore. It was dark stuff, and it freaked the doctor out. The doctor referred Jimmy to somebody else, but Jimmy never followed up on it. I think he decided that no doctor could really help him."

Although he had entered the LSD testing program willingly, Whitey held on to it as a grievance. He obsessed over the government's duplicity in not informing him and other participants that the testing was part of a secret CIA mind-control experiment. His grievance only grew after he read the 1979 book *The Search for the Manchurian Candidate*, by John Marks, which lays out in great detail how Whitey and others were duped. The experience and the haunting memories left him with a lifelong mistrust of the medical profession and of modern medicine in general. "I have been sick and injured many times these years but treated myself with over-the-counter medicine," he wrote, in papers seized from Stanley's house and made public by the FBI after he had left town. "I developed or tried to develop a belief that the body cures itself with over-the-counter medicine. I can't bring myself to trust medical people." In those same papers, Whitey acknowledged that he had sought out a psychiatrist because of his nightmares. He was referring to the doctor in Watertown. "I did go to a doctor, a psychiatrist who has studied LSD and the long-term effects. I paid for his services and paid for batteries of brain wave tests—brain wave scans and was told by this doctor he felt I definitely have been brain damaged (physically) by LSD."

Whitey also had occasional bouts of arrhythmia, and in the late 1980s he had regular appointments with a cardiologist at Massachusetts General Hospital. He began taking Atenolol to prevent chest pain and lower his blood pressure. When the doctor advised him to reduce the stress in his life, Whitey had a solution. "He dropped two of his girlfriends and stuck with just Teresa and Cathy," Weeks said. "Jimmy said women brought on more stress than other criminals."

Weeks was convinced that Whitey's determination to simplify his life included the conscious effort to stop murdering people.[30] "Part of it was, we didn't need to kill anyone anymore," Weeks said. "But a big part was Jimmy just trying to do what the doctors were telling him, and what his own body was telling him. He had to take a step back."

Stanley had come to accept that part of being Whitey's companion meant biting her tongue. It meant suffering his lectures and badgering. But after Whitey started seeing the psychiatrist and after he began taking seriously his doctors' admonitions to reduce stress and lower his blood pressure, Stanley noticed a change, too. He stopped arguing over every little thing. Living with Whitey Bulger got easier. "He wasn't as angry," she said. "He wasn't as tough or tense. He'd say he didn't want to argue. Whereas before his temper would get the better of him. I remember him saying the doctor said there was something wrong with his heart. Nothing bad. He was told he had to simplify his life or, they told him, you're going to have a heart attack or a stroke."

As the 1980s rolled on, Whitey continued to rely on extortion as a reliable source of cash, knowing that even when things got messy, as they did with Rakes, John Connolly and the FBI could make it all go away. Connolly, who had continued to use Flemmi as an informant after going through the motions of closing him in 1982, won approval to reopen him in 1986. Whitey and Flemmi, as ever, felt invincible. "Someone hired me to kill you," Whitey told Ray Slinger, a Southie real estate agent he had summoned to Triple O's in 1987. It wasn't what Slinger expected to hear. A decade after the school busing debacle, Southie had become the hottest real estate market in Boston. Yuppies were flooding in, buying condominiums in newly converted three-deckers. Whitey had previously gone to Slinger's office asking for advice on how to catch the real estate wave. Slinger thought the meeting at Triple O's was about property; instead, Whitey had a proposition. Slinger could pay him to kill the guy who wanted Slinger dead or pay him to scare the guy. Slinger opted for the scare option and asked if one or two thousand dollars would cover it. "My boots cost more than that," Whitey told him.[31] He set the price at fifty thousand dollars.

Slinger, terrified and confused, called his friend Jimmy Kelly, a city councilor. Kelly had been on the fringes of the Mullens gang but had made a respectable career in politics on the strength of his pugnacious leadership during the anti-busing movement in the 1970s.

Slinger told Kelly what had happened and asked Kelly to intervene with Whitey. Kelly called Slinger back soon after and said, "Everything should be okay." It wasn't. Slinger was summoned to the second floor of Triple O's again. He was so scared that he borrowed a gun from a friend—a futile gesture, given that Slinger didn't know the first thing about firearms. Whitey's minions, the two Kevins, Weeks and O'Neil, the Triple O's owner, took it off him as soon as he arrived. They patted him down to see if he was wearing a wire, and, having ascertained that he wasn't, they started beating him. They sat him down in a chair. Whitey sauntered over and took out his own gun. He poked the top of Slinger's head with the barrel of the gun and explained that if he shot Slinger at that angle, the bullet would travel straight down his spine, with the added benefit of spilling little, if any, blood. Whitey turned to the two Kevins. "Get me a body bag," he said.[32]

A terrified Slinger agreed to pay Whitey fifty thousand dollars. But he couldn't keep up with the weekly payments, and he knew what that would mean, so he called the FBI. Unannounced, agents John Newton and Rod Kennedy arrived at Slinger's real estate office. Newton was one of John Connolly's best friends on the job and had developed a friendly camaraderie with Whitey and Flemmi. He let Connolly use his South Boston home to meet with the two informants, who often arrived with steak bones for Newton's two golden retrievers. Newton and Kennedy managed to sit through the interview with Ray Slinger and not file any reports. Newton said that Kennedy, the lead agent on the investigation, took notes during the interview, and that he thought that Kennedy had filed a report.[33] But Kennedy testified years later that he didn't remember the interview.[34] Again, the FBI made the potential case against Whitey go away. Slinger was the sort of person—a snitch putting him at risk—whom Whitey would almost automatically have killed in the past. But now he saw no need. Why risk it when the FBI was so willing to protect him? With carte blanche from the bureau, Whitey continued to summon people like Ray Slinger to Triple O's, using his standard line: "I'll let you buy your life." He used it over and over again, amassing a war chest that would one day finance his years on the run.

Whitey's problem was never with the FBI which had no intention of going after him. It was a group of honest local cops, state police officers, and Drug Enforcement Administration and IRS agents who had tried for years to make a case against him. The honest cops didn't just hate him; they hated the FBI. The bureau's protection of Whitey had made him a higher-priority target for others in law enforcement. But Whitey had skirted many efforts to bring him down. His unnatural luck had bred paranoia among other agencies, who knew that Whitey had others looking after him. They believed his protectors included his brother, now senate president William Bulger.

The target on Whitey's back grew considerably larger in 1986 when a presidential commission on organized crime identified him as a bank robber, drug trafficker, and murderer. Not long after it was published, Whitey objected to one of the commission's findings while attending a wedding. "I'm no drug trafficker," he insisted.[35] But the presidential commission did more than challenge the myth of Whitey's anti-drugs policy. It put his name in the public domain, inviting media and even public scrutiny like never before. A pair of South Boston community activists, Dan and Nancy Yotts, began to question the way the neighborhood was run. They specifically challenged the power of the Bulger brothers. Dan Yotts spoke openly about Bill Bulger controlling the legitimate aspects of South Boston life, especially through patronage jobs, and about Whitey Bulger controlling the underworld.[36] Such public criticism in Southie was unprecedented, but the Yottses spoke for a growing constituency disgusted by the increasing use of drugs in the neighborhood and its attendant crime, and tired of the myths about Whitey's role. "I had blind loyalty once," Nancy

Yotts, a former anti-busing leader, said. "But I saw it was ridiculous. You're supposed to walk the way they walk, talk the way they talk, and think the way they think."

Not long after Dan and Nancy Yotts were quoted in the local newspapers criticizing the power structure in Southie, their home was pelted with eggs. Then the tires on their car were slashed. When the anonymous threatening phone calls wouldn't stop, they moved out of Southie late in 1987.[37]

But a precedent of truth telling had been set. Besides his mention in the presidential report, Whitey's name featured prominently in the long trial of Jerry Angiulo and the Mafia leadership. Angiulo and other Mafiosi boasted about their relationship with Whitey and about how dangerous he was. Long a menace only whispered about, Whitey was suddenly a public figure. He and Flemmi knew that with two successive waves of Mafia prosecutions out of the way, they were now the main event. Not only had Jerry Angiulo and his brothers been carted off to prison, the Mafia leaders who replaced them were arrested, too, along with their underlings. Whitey and Flemmi were in everyone's crosshairs, including the *Boston Globe*'s.

In 1988, the *Globe* set out to unearth and tell one of the great unwritten stories of Boston, a story about the intersection of politics and the underworld: the rise and reign of the Bulger brothers, Bill and Whitey, the state's most powerful politician and the gangster who dominated the South Boston rackets. The story had been out there for years, but the news media had adopted Southie's wary deference, leaving Whitey out of Billy's world. It didn't seem fair to tar a politician for being the brother of a mobster. But there were many people in Boston who believed that the brothers benefited from each other's domination of their chosen fields.

Bill Bulger cooperated with the *Globe* reporters on the newspaper's investigative unit, the Spotlight Team. Bill saw the story as almost a biography of his family and how he had risen to become the longest-serving senate president in Massachusetts. But Connolly's antenna went up early. A month before the *Globe*'s four-part series was published, Connolly sent a memo to Special Agent in Charge James Ahearn, warning that the captioned source BS 1544-TE—Whitey—might be identified. "Over the past several weeks writer has been made aware that the *Boston Globe* intends to write a Spotlight Series of articles and captioned source will be prominently mentioned with the possibility that writer's name may also be linked to captioned source," Connolly wrote. "The SAC [special agent in charge] is aware of some of the past associations that have been made, however, this could be different."[38]

Connolly speculated that the *Globe* had him and Whitey under surveillance and said he planned to stay away from his informants for a while. His memo, however, made no mention of the FBI's extensive efforts to prevent the *Globe* from revealing the bureau's secret relationship with Whitey. Two months before the series was published, FBI agent Tom Daly called the Spotlight office at the *Globe*. A secretary passed the call on to Kevin Cullen, then a member of the investigative team. Daly was agitated. He said he had gotten a phone call from Tony Ciulla, the star witness in the 1979 horse race–fixing case that had resulted in charges against the entire Winter Hill Gang leadership except Whitey and Flemmi. Ciulla had gotten a letter from someone at the *Globe*, asking about the case. Cullen told Daly that his *Globe* colleague Dick Lehr had sent the letter. "I'm a little annoyed you didn't call me," Daly said. He didn't like the newspaper going behind his back to talk to his informant. "Ciulla will not talk to you, first off. I know Billy Bulger's been interviewed by the *Globe*. Ciulla told me, 'Give them a message. Be very careful about what they say about Whitey. Whitey is a dangerous guy. You don't want to piss him off.'"

Daly said he was only telling Cullen this because he was a friend. But Cullen barely knew Daly and certainly didn't consider him a friend; and Daly's tone was not friendly. "Whitey Bulger," Daly said, "is the type of guy, if you write the truth he has no problem with that. But if you embarrass him or his family, or write something untrue then, and this is what Ciulla said, 'The guy would never live with that. He wouldn't think nothing of clipping you.' Especially you Kevin. I mean it in all sincerity. I'm not trying to be dramatic. He's extremely dangerous. I know you live over there in South Boston."

Daly's warning was both menacing and mendacious. He claimed that the warning was coming from Ciulla, but he was adding details—such as Cullen's living in Southie—that Ciulla didn't know. So was the warning coming from a criminal or the FBI—or both? And was there a difference? Cullen and the other reporters and editors huddled. They all believed that the FBI's motive was to get the *Globe* to back off the story.

The idea that Whitey would go after a reporter did have some precedent. In the late 1960s, Whitey occasionally stopped by the Boston Press Club, a local watering hole frequented by the press, and argued with reporters about their stories. But he had avoided the media during the years of his brother's political rise. Then, in 1980, a bookmaker who worked for Whitey, Louis Litif, was found dead in the trunk of his Lincoln Continental. There were rumors all over Southie that Whitey had killed him. Paul Corsetti, a reporter for the *Boston Herald American*, had been hearing snippets of the story and was looking for a scoop when Whitey caught wind of it. The way Whitey heard it, Corsetti was looking into a story that would link Whitey to a recent visit to South Boston by Irish Republican Army operatives looking for weapons. Worse, as far as Whitey was concerned, was that Corsetti was trying to throw Whitey's brother Bill into the mix.[39]

Corsetti was something of a barfly, and on Saturday nights he was usually found in the Dockside, a popular bar in Faneuil Hall Marketplace. By 1:00 a.m., the crowd had thinned, and a man Corsetti didn't recognize walked up to him.

"You Paul Corsetti?" the man asked.

"Yeah."

"You know who I am?"

"No," Corsetti replied.

"I'm Whitey Bulger, motherfucker, and I fuckin' kill people for a living."[40]

Whitey let that sink in a moment and leaned in toward Corsetti.

"I understand you're going to do a story on my brother. I heard you're trying to tie me and my brother together."

"There's nothing there," Corsetti told him.

Whitey ignored him and proceeded to list where Corsetti lived, his wife's name, where she worked, his daughter's name, where she went to school.

"If I wanted to do you," Whitey sneered, "you'd be easy."

Whitey gave Corsetti one last look of sheer contempt and walked away. Corsetti was shaken. Not only did he tell the police, he went to the Mafia. "Larry Baione owed me a favor," Corsetti said of the consigliere of Boston's Mafia. "I kept his name out of the paper on some story." Baione told him Whitey couldn't be intimidated out of anything by the Mafia. "The best I can do for you is have someone talk to him after the story comes out—then you can figure out how sore he is," Baione told Corsetti.

After the story appeared, giving vague details about Litif being murdered because he had angered certain elements in the South Boston underworld, Baione called Corsetti. "No problem," he told the relieved reporter. Left out of the story was a relevant detail, something Corsetti couldn't have known at the time: Louie Litif was John Connolly's informant, too. So one of Connolly's informants was suspected of murdering another. And, as was Connolly's pattern, he filed a report that distracted attention from the true killer, suggesting that Litif's murder was done in gangland fashion but naming no suspects. The source of the report was Whitey Bulger.[41]

The account of Corsetti's brush with Whitey didn't appear in print, but it spread through the ranks of journalists in Boston. The menace that Whitey projected helped explain why he was so seldom the subject of serious journalistic inquiry. Many people were simply afraid of him.

In September 1988, the *Globe* published its series, which included the bombshell that Whitey and John Connolly had a special relationship that had led other law enforcement agencies to conclude that the FBI was protecting Whitey. As a precaution, Cullen and his wife moved out of their South Boston condominium temporarily and stayed at a hotel in Cambridge. They moved back after an informant told the state police that the only thing Whitey was upset about in the series was a section that described him beating up a wino outside Teresa Stanley's house. Whitey thought it made him look like a bully. "That was no wino," Whitey told the informant.[42]

The truth was that Whitey was more than a little unhappy when he read the *Globe* stories, not because the paper was wrong on some sordid detail or other but because it was right about the most important thing, his gravest secret: his work for the FBI. That could get a man killed, even a man like him. And Whitey knew who had let the secret about him out. "That was that fuckin' Morris," Whitey told Connolly.[43]

He was right. John Morris, as he would later admit, had been one of the *Globe*'s sources, confirming the longstanding suspicion that Whitey was an FBI informant. Gerard O'Neill, the editor of the *Globe*'s Spotlight Team, had persuaded Morris to provide the confirmation. It was essential to getting the story in the paper. Morris claimed he wanted to force the FBI to drop Whitey and Flemmi, that they had become too dangerous, too emboldened.[44] Whitey believed Morris was trying to get him killed. But he was also confident that his criminal associates would see the *Globe* story not so much as being about him but, rather, as an attempt to throw mud on his brother Bill.

That's how John Martorano saw it from Florida, where he had been for almost a decade after he fled the horse race–fixing indictment. That's how the Mafia saw it, too, according to Anthony Cardinale, a prominent defense lawyer who represented Mafiosi in both Boston and New York. Cardinale said he talked about the report with two of his clients, Jerry Angiulo and John Gotti, the boss of the Gambino crime family in New York. "They didn't believe it," Cardinale said. "They didn't believe that the FBI would get into bed with someone as vicious as Whitey Bulger."[45]

The FBI didn't think anyone would believe it, either. The bureau kept Bulger and Flemmi as informants for another two years. Connolly, meanwhile, used his media contacts to dismiss the *Globe*'s story as fantasy, the disgruntled conjecture of state police and DEA agents who had to blame someone for their failed investigations. Ahearn, the FBI agent in charge of the Boston office, demanded that the *Globe* retract the story but got nowhere. A year later, as Ahearn prepared to leave Boston, his agents prepared for the annual office Christmas party. The door prizes were bottles of liquor purchased in South Boston, at Whitey's liquor store. When the DEA and the Boston police raided the liquor store in 1990, they found a receipt for $205 and a piece of paper showing that an FBI agent who bought the door prizes for the Christmas party had come with a reference that was noted alongside the transaction: "Dick Baker— friend of John Connolly."[46]

The records were seized by the Boston police and the DEA as part of an investigation that resulted in the August 1990 arrest of fifty-one people who sold cocaine in Southie. They were part of a ring that paid Whitey tribute to operate. As one of the dealers told an undercover agent, if you wanted to deal drugs in Southie, you had to pay Whitey "or you end up dead."[47] Whitey's defenders, including his brother Bill and John Connolly, were quick to trash the drug case, pointing out the absence of any charges against Whitey. But the only reason Whitey wasn't the fifty-second person indicted in the Southie drug ring was that federal prosecutors had turned a key witness over to the FBI instead of the DEA. The man, a mortgage broker named Tim Connolly, was one of the many Whitey had threatened in the name of extorting cash. Summoned to Rotary Variety, next to the South Boston Liquor Mart, in the summer of 1989, the broker was led to a storage room, where Whitey said, "I'll let you buy your life." Then Whitey pulled a knife from the sheath on his calf and began stabbing boxes to punctuate his demands for fifty thousand dollars. The broker went to the US Attorney's office, offering up Whitey, but prosecutors decided not to turn him over to the DEA—even though the broker was connected to the big drug case—but to the FBI. In the bureau's hands, no surprise, the case would languish for years.[48]

John Connolly had given Whitey and Flemmi so much over the years that they wanted to give him something in return. Something more valuable than money. Something more personal than the diamond ring they'd sprung for when he got engaged.[49] And so they gave him Sonny Mercurio.

Mercurio, a Mafia soldier, had approached Whitey and Flemmi back in 1986, after Jerry Angiulo and his brothers had been convicted and carted off to prison. Whitey and Flemmi had been extorting rent from bookies who had been operating on their own as the Mafia lay rudderless after the Angiulo arrests in 1983. Now, three years later, Mercurio told them the Mafia was back in business. Vinnie Ferrara, an ambitious Mafioso who was trying to replace the Angiulos, had assembled a new crew, and they were rounding up the bookies to explain the new arrangement. In particular, Mercurio told Whitey and Flemmi to stay away from a pair of elderly Jewish bookies, Mo Weinstein and Doc Sagansky. They belonged to the Mafia.

Whitey and Flemmi learned that the Mafia was using Mercurio's sandwich shop in the Prudential Center downtown as a meeting spot, rounding up bookies like Weinstein and Sagansky.[50] After Whitey and Flemmi reported all this to Connolly, the FBI was able to plant a bug in the sandwich shop and start building a case against the fledgling Mafia leadership. It was a feather in Connolly's cap and a boon for Whitey and Flemmi. But Whitey went a step further. He told Connolly that Mercurio was disgruntled, vulnerable, ripe for the picking: He would make a great informant.

Connolly took a run at Mercurio and found that Whitey was right. Not only did Mercurio become Connolly's informant, he provided him with the biggest coup of his career. With his help, the FBI was able to plant bugs inside a house in Medford where four men were inducted into the Mafia in 1989. Twenty-one Mafiosi were arrested on the strength of the tape recordings, but the induction ceremony's significance went far beyond the arrests. It became the foundation for every Mafia prosecution in the United States that followed. It was hard for defense lawyers to argue that La Cosa Nostra didn't exist when the tapes of the induction ceremony captured men swearing fealty to This Thing of Ours, promising to commit murder, pricking their trigger fingers, burning pictures of saints, and pledging themselves to *omertà*, the Mafia code of silence.

US Attorney General Dick Thornburgh and FBI director William S. Sessions flew up from Washington for the press conference announcing the induction ceremony indictments. It was the ultimate humiliation of the Mafia and the ultimate vindication of John Connolly's ability to develop informants. Later, Sessions sent Connolly an effusive letter, enclosing praise for his talent in cultivating informants and a fifteen-hundred-dollar bonus.[51] Connolly was now more than a valued agent; he was a role model. And his crowning achievement had been delivered to him by Whitey and Flemmi.

The induction ceremony even gave Connolly the working title for the memoir he planned to start writing after his December 1990 retirement. As he pulled the door shut on the house where the ceremony was recorded, a Mafioso remarked, "Only the fucking ghost knows what really took place over here today, by God." So Connolly was going to call his book *Only the Ghost Knows*.[52] He planned to model his account on the 1988 book written by his old friend Joe Pistone, an FBI agent whose ability to infiltrate a Mafia family in New York became the basis for the film *Donnie Brasco*, starring Johnny Depp and Al Pacino. When Pistone came to Boston for dinner in the mid-1980s, Connolly arranged for Whitey and Flemmi to join them—Connolly wanted to show them off.

Having reached the summit of his career, it was a perfect time for Connolly to retire in glory, to take a job with a plush office as director of security at Boston Edison, a local utility company. His retirement party was a must-attend event, held in the upstairs function room of Joe Tecce's restaurant in the North End. It was filled with cops and politicians and those who ran charities in Southie. Whitey didn't show—that would have been a little much—but Bill Bulger was a featured speaker. He stood at the lectern and, after making a few jokes, turned serious. He quoted one of his favorite philosophers, Seneca: "Loyalty is the holiest good in the human heart."

"John Connolly is the personification of loyalty," Bill Bulger said, "not only to his old friends and not only to the job that he holds but also to the highest principles. He's never forgotten them."[53]

When Connolly retired from the FBI, on December 3, 1990, so did Whitey and Flemmi. They couldn't trust anyone the way they could trust Connolly; and besides, they were looking forward to retirement, too. Flemmi had invested more than one million dollars in property in the Back Bay and some Boston suburbs.[54] Having used murder and mayhem to build his fortune, he intended to tap the easy riches of Boston's booming property market. Whitey, meanwhile, had stashed money all over the country, and in Dublin, London, and Montreal. He was thinking ahead and was ready for whatever would come next, but he wasn't ready for this: Just six months after he was closed as an informant for the FBI, he hit the lottery. He and three other men, including Kevin Weeks, came forward to claim their share of a $14.3 million winning ticket in the Massachusetts Lottery. No one could believe it was on the level, but Whitey's share gave him a legitimate source of income for the first time since he'd worked construction following his release from prison in the 1960s. Years later, the feds would say it was a scam, based on informants' claims that Whitey had paid seven hundred thousand dollars to the winning ticketholder—the brother of a close associate—in exchange for a one-sixth share. But Weeks insisted that Whitey had a legitimate stake in the winnings and concocted the payoff story to appease Flemmi, who was furious he didn't get a share. Whitey told Flemmi that he was pretending to receive lottery proceeds to make it appear that he had legitimate income but was secretly returning the money to the real winner.[55] Either way, thanks to the lottery, as Whitey began looking for a place to retire, he had eighty thousand dollars a year in after-tax income to spend. He could travel more freely, making contingency plans in case the retirement of his FBI handler stirred up old investigations. He had no guarantees that an FBI office that didn't include John Connolly was willing to cover his back. As was often the case, Whitey was prescient in his fears.

Even after the *Globe* outed Whitey as an informant, even after the arrest of the fifty-one cocaine dealers bruised his carefully cultivated image as a benevolent gangster who kept drugs out of Southie, even after Connolly retired, neither Whitey nor Connolly was worried. They felt they could control the narrative in Southie and beyond. Bulger loyalists, many owing their jobs to Bill Bulger, clung to the fraying myth that Whitey made their streets safer. And Whitey was busy reinventing himself as a patriotic philanthropist. He had pumped money into the Korean War memorial on Castle Island, which includes the name of his sister's husband and nineteen others from Southie who were killed in the war. He and Flemmi donated five thousand dollars for a stone bench at the Korean War statute in the Charlestown Navy Yard where his father once worked.[56] And when Flemmi invited him to attend the fiftieth anniversary celebration of the US Airborne Division in Washington in July 1990, Whitey jumped at the chance. He listened intently as General William Westmoreland, the Vietnam War commander, extolled America's paratroopers. Whitey had spent the last twenty-five years studiously avoiding being photographed in public, but at the reunion he proudly posed next to a Medal of Honor recipient in a ballroom at the Mayflower Hotel as cameras snapped away.[57] At veterans' posts in Southie, tales of Whitey's generosity in the cause were swapped like war stories.

They were shaping up as golden years for three conspirators. But even as they sought to reinvent themselves in their post-FBI careers, Whitey, Flemmi, and Connolly had two problems. The first was that Chico Krantz wasn't from Southie. The second was that Tom Foley wasn't with the FBI.

Burton "Chico" Krantz was the biggest bookie around. Tom Foley was a Massachusetts State Police sergeant. In the fall of 1990, Foley set his sights on Krantz, and it would be the beginning of the end of Whitey's charmed life. Tall, prematurely gray, and with the military bearing typical of the state police, Foley had grown up in Worcester, a city in central Massachusetts where the politics were as parochial as Southie's. Beginning in 1984, he'd worked on a task force with the FBI targeting Mafia-connected loansharks. Foley was monitoring conversations at a listening post when John Connolly, still at the time a star in the bureau, approached him with an outstretched hand. "You're Dan Foley's nephew, aren't you?" Connolly said.

Foley's uncle was the senate majority leader, Bill Bulger's right-hand man, and Foley smiled and nodded as Connolly proceeded to sing the praises of Bill Bulger.[58] Foley could tell right away that Connolly was an operator, but he couldn't help liking him. Foley had risen through the ranks of the state police, acquiring along the way a suspicion of the FBI's relationship with Whitey Bulger. Working on task forces with the FBI only intensified his skepticism. After he helped the FBI indict a state trooper who was deemed too close to a bookie, Foley watched with incredulity as the FBI let an office secretary who had leaked information to a mobster quietly resign. The double standard irked him.[59]

In 1990, Foley was put in charge of the Special Services Section of the state police, which focused on organized crime. They worked regularly with the FBI, but it was, as ever, an uneasy alliance. As soon as he took over, Foley had one thing in mind: targeting Whitey Bulger and Steve Flemmi. And he knew exactly how to do it. "We're going to go after the bookies," Foley told Ed Quinn, supervisor of the FBI's organized crime squad, one afternoon as they were sitting around, plotting strategy. As the case agent in the FBI's biggest case ever in Boston, the takedown of the Jerry Angiulo regime, Quinn should have appreciated the strategy. It was information from disgruntled bookies—not the gossip of Steve Flemmi and Whitey Bulger—that showed the FBI the way to get the bugs into the Mafia's headquarters in the North End. Instead, Quinn turned up his nose. "That's a waste of time," he said.[60] Foley ignored him. There was little point in trying to persuade an FBI man that the Staties had a better idea of how to take down gangsters. Like many state cops, Foley couldn't understand why Whitey and Flemmi had been given a pass, even as the FBI was still pursuing pathetic mob wannabes trying to fill the power vacuum left by successive Mafia prosecutions.

He decided that the only way to get Whitey and Flemmi was to freeze the FBI out discreetly. He assembled a team of state troopers to round up the bookies. The idea was not just to arrest them but to seize their money, creating an incentive to cooperate. It was common knowledge that Whitey and Flemmi had taken advantage of the troubles befalling the Mafia by shaking down bookies for tribute. "If we get enough of them, and take their money, some of them are going to talk," Foley reasoned.[61]

And if Chico Krantz talked, Whitey and Flemmi were history. Foley knew Chico was paying Whitey and Flemmi protection money, because Chico had been picked up on a state police bug planted inside a seedy bar in Chelsea called Heller's, complaining about it. Heller's was the bookie bank, where bookies went to cash their checks from gambling proceeds. Chico was there to wash his money, and he started bitching and moaning to Mike London, the banker to the bookies. London sat in a teller's booth, behind thick, bulletproof glass, and commiserated. He knew just how dirty this business was. And how lucrative.[62] London didn't raise an eyebrow when the bookies signed the checks with obviously made-up names:

Arnold Palmer, Marvin Hagler, Bill Russell. He took 1 to 2 percent of every transaction, and London was washing up to fifty million dollars a year. His bar was in Chelsea, one of the poorest cities in Massachusetts. His house was in Weston, the richest.[63]

Chico was tired of paying Whitey rent for nothing. London told Chico he was wasting his time with Whitey and Flemmi, who just took your money and didn't help chase down debts. He urged Chico to walk away from them and join up with Vinnie Ferrara, the ambitious Mafioso who was trying to replace the Angiulo regime. "Vinnie will work for you," London told Chico. "This guy here will go to bat for you."[64]

The feds had used electronic surveillance gathered in the mid-1980s to indict Mikey London and Vinnie Ferrara in 1990. But they let the bookies skate, because bookies were considered small fish: You threw them back. But the conversations gleaned from the bookie's bank at Heller's and then at Sonny Mercurio's sandwich shop, where Ferrara was trying to reinvent the Mafia, was manna for Foley and his team: They learned that Chico was an unsatisfied customer. Chico hated Whitey and Flemmi. In the right circumstances, Chico might talk.

The Staties needed a break, and it came in the hulking form of Vinnie "Fat Vinnie" Roberto. It was hard for Fat Vinnie to lose a tail, and one day in February 1991 state troopers followed him all the way to Chico Krantz's front door in Chestnut Hill, one of the most exclusive suburbs in the Boston area. Vinnie delivered a huge bag of cash. Chico had his money. Foley's team had their probable cause for a search warrant. During a search of Chico's house, the police found a safe deposit box key. They traced it to a bank in a neighboring suburb. It was opened in the presence of a startled bank manager, who exclaimed, "There's more cash here than we have in the entire bank."[65]

There was one million dollars in that box, and another million in another box. Chico was in Florida when the Staties grabbed his money. He flew back and arranged to meet with Foley. Chico showed up without his lawyer. He wanted to make a deal, and he wanted his money back. He complained about the police tactics, saying that there had always been an unwritten rule that they didn't raid bookie's houses. "Yeah, well," Foley replied, "it's a new ball game."[66]

Foley explained that if Chico was willing to talk, they might be able to work something out. Chico flew back to Florida, and Foley sensed an opening. He called one of his mentors, Pat Greaney, a state trooper who had worked organized crime for years. Foley and Greaney followed Chico to Florida and spent several days trying to convince him to become a confidential informant. Greaney put Chico at ease, telling stories about old bookies. Foley kept the pressure on, reminding Chico that Whitey and Flemmi were taking his money and giving him nothing in return. The more Greaney and Foley talked, the more Chico realized how much he hated and resented Whitey and Flemmi. He had grown up in Dorchester, in the days when Jewish kids like him were often the targets of Irish and Italian kids like them. Chico made something of himself and went to college. The idea of people like Whitey and Flemmi taking his money was especially galling.

Chico had first met Whitey in the 1970s, when Whitey was muscle for the Winter Hill Gang. Whitey went right up to Chico on the street, demanding $86,000 that Chico owed a bookie who was paying rent to Winter Hill. "Pay up," Whitey told him, "or I'll kill you." Then, in 1979, after the FBI allowed Whitey and Flemmi to escape the horse race–fixing indictment that scattered the rest of Winter Hill, Whitey and Flemmi began rounding up all the bookies. They went back at Chico, saying he had to pay them rent. It started at $750 a month, but within five years it was $3,000. When Chico complained that another bookie owed him money, Whitey arranged a meeting at a restaurant in Cambridge. The dispute was resolved, and Whitey turned to Chico and demanded a $5,000 mediation fee on top of the rent. "What am I paying these guys for?" Chico asked.[67]

But what really bothered Chico was the way Whitey treated bookies. Sitting in a hotel that straddled the Massachusetts Turnpike in Newton, not far from his house, Chico told Greaney and Foley how Whitey had summoned a bookie Chico was friendly with for a sit-down. Whitey accused the bookie of cheating him. He poured bleach on the bookie's arm, burning him. The bookie screamed, and Whitey smiled and said, "Do you think I'm fuckin' around?"[68] With every story, Chico's resentment flourished. Still, every time Foley suggested he testify and put Whitey and Flemmi away, he got scared. "They'd kill me," he said. "They'd kill my family."

Foley got a second search warrant, and they hit Chico's house again. This time, they had enough evidence, between bookmaking records and cash and surveillance, to put Chico away. They also had evidence implicating Chico's wife, Jacqui, in money laundering: She was depositing cash for him. Foley called Chico and said they needed to talk. It was urgent. Late on a Saturday night, Chico met Foley and Greaney in the parking lot of a strip mall in West Roxbury, near Chico's house in suburban Chestnut Hill. Chico got in and sat in the passenger seat next to Foley, who put the car in drive and headed out of the parking lot. Greaney was in the back with a bag of muffins and three coffees. He handed Chico a cup of coffee. Foley handed Chico a draft indictment.

"Chico," Tom Foley said. "Jacqui's going to be indicted."

Chico leafed through the papers. It didn't tell him anything he didn't already know. Jacqui had been moving his money.

"Chico," Foley said, "your options are pretty limited. You're going to be a cooperating witness, or Jacqui's going to jail."

Chico stared out the window.

"Chico," Pat Greaney said from the backseat, "do you think Whitey and Stevie give a shit about you? They'd cut you up in little pieces and throw you in the river."[69]

Chico knew they were right. It was time to play ball.

They drove him back to his car at the strip mall. Chico got out and looked around the parking lot. He started walking toward his car but turned back as if he'd forgotten something. Pat Greaney rolled down the window and Chico leaned in.

"Hey," Chico Krantz said. "Are you gonna eat that last muffin?"

Greaney handed Chico Krantz a blueberry muffin. For a man about to risk his life and turn the tables on Whitey Bulger, it was the least he could do.[70]

PART THREE
THE RUN

13

A Head Start

John Morris: What do you think these guys really want from us?
John Connolly: I think all they want is a head start.[1]

Teresa Stanley was home alone when a woman called her South
Boston house late one night in the fall of 1994, looking for
Whitey. "He's not here," Stanley said. "I think we have to talk," said
the caller, identifying herself as Cathy Greig and making a vague
reference to her involvement with Whitey. "Something bad is going
on."[2] The name meant nothing to Stanley, but she suddenly felt anxious. Women didn't call her house looking for Whitey, and now a
stranger was on the phone. Stanley had heard rumors about Whitey's womanizing, but he had convinced her she was his only lover.
She didn't know about the son he had fathered and lost. She didn't
know much about what Whitey did when he wasn't with her. Stanley was speechless when Greig asked if she could pick Stanley up at
the home she shared with her twenty-something daughter and take
her someplace private to talk.

Minutes later, Greig pulled up outside Stanley's house in a green
Ford Explorer, and Stanley climbed in. It was an awkward moment,
the first time the two women Whitey had so carefully kept apart
for decades met. Stanley's heart was pounding, but she willed her-

self to stay calm and dignified. At fifty-three, she was still a beautiful woman, shapely, with platinum blonde hair and clear blue eyes. Greig, ten years younger, had also kept up the looks that had drawn Whitey to her. They drove in silence during the six-mile trip to Greig's home in the Squantum section of Quincy, a narrow peninsula where modest homes are crammed together on postage-stamp lots. Whitey had bought Greig the four-bedroom split-level ranch with a white picket fence, just as he had bought Stanley her house in Southie. Greig led Stanley into the living room, where she took a seat, nervously lit a cigarette, and listened in silence as Greig revealed that she had been having an affair with Whitey for nearly twenty years, that she loved him and had been devoted to him and that he supported her—even though she had known all along about Stanley. She knew about Whitey's many other women, too, she said, and they had often fought about it. She was tired of living a double life and wanted Whitey to choose between her and Stanley. She was ready to break off the relationship once and for all, and telling Stanley about their long, secret affair was the best way she could think of to make him mad enough to finally let her go.

Stanley listened intently as Greig talked for twenty minutes, struggling to maintain her composure, and then said softly, "Thanks for telling me." Inside, however, she was thunderstruck. She hadn't known about Greig. She hadn't known about the other women Greig mentioned. She felt like a fool. Thirty years together and she didn't know?[3] The two women were still sitting, stewing in awkward discomfort, when a highly agitated Whitey showed up with Kevin Weeks in tow, banging on the door until Greig let him in. Both Stanley and Greig had witnessed this before—Whitey breathing heavily, battling his temper. These were dangerous signs. Whitey was under tremendous pressure already—a grand jury had been hearing testimony from Chico Krantz, the embittered bookie, among others. Whitey had been hearing rumors that a multicount extortion indictment was being prepared. Now his personal life was imploding, too. Someone who had seen the two women drive off together had called him. Even before he got to Greig's house, Whitey knew what was going on.

"Let's go," he snapped at Stanley.

"No!" Stanley screamed. She had always been meek and deferential around him. No more. "She told me everything," Stanley said. "You've been living with her. . . . This is it!"[4] Whitey started swearing and screaming at Greig as he grabbed Stanley by the arm, trying to force her to leave. Greig was yelling back, over and over. "I'm tired of being the second fiddle. You're going to have to choose."

Finally, Whitey succumbed to his rage. "He grabbed Cathy by the neck, whipped her down to the floor, and started choking her," Weeks recalled. "He lost it. He had both hands on her neck squeezing her. I thought he was going to kill her."[5] Almost ten years before, Weeks had stood by when he had come upon Whitey strangling Deborah Hussey in The Haunty on East Third Street. This time he reacted, as much to save Whitey as to save Greig. Relying on his old skills as a bouncer at Triple O's, Weeks tugged hard on his boss's arm, dragging him away from Greig and toward the door. Greig struggled to her feet, trying to regain her breath and her composure.

Weeks turned to Stanley and said, "Let's go, Teresa. There's going to be trouble here."[6] Whitey again demanded that Stanley follow him, and this time she complied. In the car, the argument continued as they drove back to Southie. Whitey acknowledged that he had had a long affair with Greig, but he insisted that he had already ended it. "It's over between us, and she's just doing this because I left her for you," he told Stanley.[7] Stanley wasn't buying it. She lit a cigarette, defying Whitey's smoking ban. He didn't say anything. "You're a liar!" Stanley shrieked, staring straight ahead. "You're a liar!" Stanley knew that Greig was telling the truth, and she was devastated. She never saw her again, and she never felt the same about Whitey. She couldn't get over his betrayal, which quietly continued. A few days after the blowup, Whitey was back at Greig's door, and Cathy wouldn't or couldn't turn him away.

Whitey decided that, in the name of peace, Stanley needed,

or deserved, more attention. He took her on a whirlwind tour of
Europe, making stops in Dublin, London, Venice, and Rome. But it
wasn't just a vacation. Whitey suspected that the grand jury targeting
him was wrapping up its investigation. It was time to finalize prepa-
rations for a life on the run. While they were staying at Le Méridien
Piccadilly, a five-star hotel in the heart of London's West End, he
accessed a safe deposit box he had opened at a nearby Barclay's bank
two years earlier using his name and Stanley's. In the box he left fifty
thousand dollars in US and foreign currency and his Irish passport.

They had only been home a week or two when, a few days before
Christmas, US Attorney Donald K. Stern alerted FBI officials that
his office was poised to indict Whitey and Flemmi. He wanted to
know if what had long been suspected was true. Was Whitey an FBI
informant? It would take eighteen days for the FBI to respond, and
the grudging answer was that, yes, he was. And so was Flemmi.[8] But
it only took hours for Whitey's former FBI handler, John Connolly,
to find out what was up and give Whitey the head start he had long
ago promised. Dressed in an impeccably tailored suit, he stepped
into Whitey's South Boston liquor store and stamped his feet. It
was December 23, and the wind was gusting off the nearby water
at up to fifty miles per hour.[9] Connolly had been inside the liquor
store before, looking for Whitey. But this was different. He looked
around, then walked to the counter where Weeks waited; Weeks
betrayed neither surprise nor warmth.

"Is the other guy around?" Connolly asked.[10]

Weeks shook his head.

"What about Stevie?"

Again, Weeks shook his head.

"Listen," Connolly said, anxiety bleeding through his usual
cocky front. "I've got to tell you something. It's really important."

Weeks led him to a walk-in cooler where they kept the beer. The
cooling fans would drown out any possible listening device. "They're

gonna indict Jimmy and Stevie and Frankie Salemme," Connolly said. "It's imminent. They're trying to put them together over the holidays and grab all three of them at once. There's only four people in the FBI who know this. One of them is Dennis O'Callaghan, and he told me." O'Callaghan was the No. 2 man in the FBI office in Boston, and a close friend of Connolly's.[11]

Connolly made Weeks repeat back to him what he had just said. "It's really important you remember this," Connolly said. "You've got to tell Jimmy and Stevie." As soon as Connolly left, Weeks beeped Whitey, who was just heading out with Stanley for some last-minute Christmas shopping. He was still being very solicitous of her. Whitey pulled his car in front of the liquor store and Weeks climbed into the backseat. Weeks didn't dare say anything in the car. It wasn't Stanley so much as a bug he was worried about. It took them about fifteen minutes to get to Copley Square in the midafternoon traffic. Stanley wanted to go to Neiman Marcus. "Go ahead," Whitey told her. "I'll catch up." Stanley went to window-shop, and Weeks and Whitey walked to the back of the parked car.

"Zip came by," Weeks said. He repeated what Connolly had told him.

"Did you tell Stevie yet?"

"No," Weeks said. "Not yet."

Whitey said nothing for a while, then he turned and whistled sharply.

"Hey," he yelled at Stanley. "Let's go." There would be no last-minute shopping.

"You gotta get a hold of Stevie and let him know," Whitey said. "I'll call him, too."

Whitey took Stanley aside and said he had a surprise: they were going to go on a cross-country trip for Christmas. She didn't ask why.[12]

They said little in the car on the way back to Southie. Whitey dropped Weeks off at the store at 4:30 p.m. Flemmi came in about an hour later. Weeks repeated the warning, but Flemmi was blasé.

"My guy is right on top of everything," he said, referring to Richard Schneiderhan, the corrupt state cop who had been feeding him information for years. "He knows what's going on."

"Only four people know about this," Weeks said. "Maybe your guy isn't one of them."

"My guy knows," Flemmi replied. "I've got time."[13]

A few days after Christmas, Flemmi came strolling into the convenience store next to the liquor store Whitey used as a base. Weeks was flabbergasted.

"What are you still doing around?"

"My guy's on top of it," Flemmi replied. "He'll let me know."

"What are you still doing here? Jimmy's already gone."

Weeks couldn't understand Flemmi's attitude.

"Leave for a couple weeks," Weeks said. "If nothing goes down, you can come back. If they're looking for you, you get a head start."[14]

But Flemmi never got his head start.

Stanley wasn't happy about missing Christmas with her kids and grandkids, but Whitey had to get out of town fast, and he had promised her a good time. They spent Christmas Eve in New York and New Year's Eve in New Orleans—staying at Le Richelieu, a small boutique hotel in the French Quarter, under their actual names. Next, they drove to Clearwater, Florida, where Whitey picked up cash and some phony identification he had stashed in a safe deposit box years earlier. He had long thought Clearwater might be the place for him to retire. In early 1993, he was jogging on the beach on Sand Key, a barrier island off Clearwater, when he spotted a condominium complex called Bayside Gardens II. He asked a woman who lived there if there were any condos for sale. She pointed him to Unit 216, overlooking the bay. He sent the woman flowers and champagne after closing on the condo—Whitey's idea of a finder's fee.[15] Then he set to work remaking the unit to his own taste, ripping up the carpet and replacing it with sleek tile. But he would never get a chance to enjoy the improvements. He had bought the condo under his real name. He knew now the feds would be onto it soon enough.

He was ready to take on his new identity as soon as he had to but didn't want to jump the gun on such a huge, disruptive, and perhaps permanent change in his life. He checked back home every day, and there was still no word of an indictment; maybe it was a false alarm. "Let's go home," he told Stanley a few days after New Year's. But at almost exactly the moment Whitey was turning his car north from Florida, the FBI, the state police, and the DEA were finalizing their arrest plan. Tom Foley and his state police team and DEA agent Dan Doherty were still wary of including the FBI in the arrests, but they had no choice on this one. It was a federal charge of extortion—squeezing money from a bookie—and the FBI had been part of the investigation. Whitey hadn't been seen for days, but a team was assigned to find him at either Stanley's house in Southie or Greig's in Quincy. Even if Stanley had been oblivious for years, Whitey's juggling act with the two women had long been known to the law.

Flemmi was spotted first. On the evening of January 5, he walked out of Schooner's, a new restaurant his son was about to open in Boston's Financial District. Flemmi had his new Chinese girlfriend with him, and they were just getting into her white Honda Accord when the officers made their move. Doherty, the DEA agent, and state troopers Tom Duffy and John Tutungian had orders to act immediately if Flemmi went mobile. The troopers used their car to box in the Honda. Flemmi ducked down in his seat; he thought he was going to be hit. Doherty pulled open the door, pressed the barrel of his gun to Flemmi's temple, and screamed, "Put your hands where I can see them, Stevie!"[16]

Doherty took a hunting knife and some Mace from Flemmi's pocket. Flemmi's girlfriend was breathing hard, almost hyperventilating. Flemmi said that she was afraid of them because she had been a protester at Tiananmen Square. "She doesn't like cops," he said. They let her go and brought Flemmi to the FBI's office in Boston to be held in a cell overnight until the courthouse opened in the morning. Flemmi exuded confidence as he sat in a fingerprinting room with two state troopers and an FBI agent. "I am not worried about this," he said, suggesting the case hinged on the word of a bookie. Duffy, the state cop, shot back, "Do you think this is a one-person case? We have about fifty witnesses lined up against you now and more coming in every day." But Duffy was puzzled when the FBI agent, Charlie Gianturco, sidled up to the gangster and said, "This thing of ours, it's not like it used to be. There's no more respect." The exchange gave the state police officer an uneasy feeling. "It was like he was saying, 'Don't expect this asshole to treat you with the respect you deserve,'" Duffy said.[17]

Still, there was no sign of Whitey. An FBI agent had knocked on the wrong door on Silver Street, but even when they found the right one, the house was empty.[18] At that moment, Whitey and Stanley were somewhere on Interstate 95, heading north. Tom Foley and state police detective lieutenant Pat Greaney drove out to Cathy Greig's house in Quincy to see if Whitey was there. Greig walked into the driveway even before they got near the door. Her arms were folded.

"You got a warrant?" she asked.

"We just want to talk," Foley told her.

"Get the fuck off my property," she said.

"We just want to ask you some questions," Foley said.

"Go fuck yourselves," Greig replied.

She started yelling, so Foley turned back to the car. Greaney shook his head. "You don't know how to talk to women," he whispered to Foley. "Watch this."

Greaney had only taken a few steps toward the house when Cathy Greig lit into him. "What are you? Stupid?" she barked. "I told you to get off my property." A sheepish Greaney got back in the car and Foley suppressed a smile.[19]

Weeks, meanwhile, was playing cards in the L Street Tavern in Southie, sitting in the booth next to the jukebox, when Steve Flemmi's brother Michael, the Boston cop, walked in and motioned him outside. "They just pinched Stevie," Michael Flemmi said. Weeks shook his head. "I told him to take off two weeks ago," Weeks said. After Michael Flemmi left, Weeks noticed cars driven by men in suits circling the block.[20] He slipped out the back door of the bar, jumped in a friend's car, and raced away, not knowing there was no arrest warrant for him because investigators had yet to gather enough evidence to charge him.

Whitey and Stanley were somewhere in Connecticut when the news of Flemmi's arrest came over the radio. Whitey immediately turned around and headed south for Manhattan, where they checked into a hotel.

Frank Salemme had also managed to slip away after learning of Flemmi's arrest, but he had done no contingency planning. His flight path seemed haphazard. He went to Florida, not exactly an unheard-of destination among wiseguys, and was captured seven months later in West Palm Beach, living in a six-hundred-dollar-a-month town house five miles west of the walled mansions of Donald Trump, Jimmy Buffett, and Rod Stewart.

Whitey was much better prepared. As soon as he turned his car south, he became someone else: Thomas F. Baxter, of Selden, New York, a town on Long Island. He had acquired the alias even before the real Thomas F. Baxter, who lived in a suburb north of Boston, died in January 1979. Whitey obtained a Massachusetts license with his own photograph and Baxter's name, birth date, and Social Security number and renewed it every four years. In 1990, he also obtained a New York driver's license as Baxter, then renewed it in 1994, using the Long Island address of Weeks's cousins. His trump card was fifteen years old before he had to pull it.

Even as the state police were preparing to fan out and arrest Whitey and Flemmi, Tom Foley let two of his best investigators leave for Florida: There was a chance they had found John Martorano. Foley decided to expend the much-needed manpower because he hoped to press the Winter Hill hit man to turn against Whitey, his old partner. Like Bulger, Martorano had been a source of bitter friction between the FBI and the state police, with the Staties determined to find him, while the bureau showed little interest. Martorano had not only extorted bookies with Whitey but had been with him on several murders. If they found Martorano, they might be able to squeeze him, to get him to pin the killings on Whitey.

Steve Johnson, a state police detective, had an idea of where to find him. Johnson had been tracking another fugitive, a bookmaker and loanshark close to Martorano. Culling through a long list of calls to and from the bookmaker's cell phone, one number kept jumping out at him. Johnson traced the cell phone's billing information to an address in Boca Raton. "I think it might be Johnny Martorano," Johnson told Foley.

It was more hunch than anything, but Foley thought Johnson was onto something and authorized him to fly to Florida along with Trooper Michael Scanlan. They drove their rental car out to the address in Boca and had been sitting on the house for only a couple of hours when Martorano walked outside. He hadn't bothered to change his appearance at all. The FBI had been "looking" for John Martorano for sixteen years. The Massachusetts State Police found him in less than a day.

Foley told Ed Quinn, the FBI supervisor, of Johnson and Scanlan's success. Quinn was stunned. This was shaping up as a major embarrassment for the FBI. The bureau had to have a piece of the arrest if only to save face. Johnson and Scanlan were told to hold off until an FBI agent could fly down from Boston with a new arrest warrant. Johnson's worst fears were confirmed when the agent bearing the new warrant turned out to be Mike Buckley—a friend of John Connolly's, part of the organized crime squad that had protected Whitey for years. Johnson told Buckley they had been following Martorano for three days and that he was worried that Martorano would recognize their rental car. He asked the agent to rent a different one, but Buckley just shook his head. "I'm just here to keep an eye on you guys," he told them.[21]

Martorano had taken his nine-year-old son and a playmate out for a treat at an ice cream parlor and was outside the store with the boys when Steve Johnson called his name. Martorano didn't resist—he wasn't about to make a scene in front of the kids. Then, with Martorano on his way to the county jail, Johnson, Scanlan, and Buckley drove back to the gangster's house. Scanlan interviewed neighbors. Johnson sifted through the trash. Buckley sat in the car doing nothing.

Johnson found some burnt papers in the trash outside and was trying to piece them together when Martorano's girlfriend, sopping wet from the shower, burst from the house wearing just a towel. She started grappling with Johnson. "You have no right to go through our stuff!" she yelled, flailing at Johnson, who towered over her. Johnson held her back with one hand and held the burnt papers with the other, trying to explain the legal concept of abandoned property and his right to examine it. Buckley watched the scuffle from the car and didn't move a muscle. A few hours later, Johnson and Scanlan flew back to Boston. Buckley remained behind to help with the press release, which unsurprisingly gave the FBI equal billing in the arrest of John Martorano.[22]

A few days after a warrant was issued for Whitey Bulger's arrest, an FBI agent was turned away from the State House office of Senate President Bill Bulger.[23] He left his card and phone number with the receptionist. Shortly afterward, on January 9, 1995, Bill Bulger called the agent, John E. Gamel, at the FBI. It was a brief conversation. He said he didn't know where his brother was, didn't want to talk about him, and wasn't interested in answering any questions. "Well," Gamel said, "if you hear from him, please advise him to give me a call and we'll work out an arrangement for surrender."

The senate president told Gamel what he wanted to hear: that he'd consider the request. But Bill Bulger's loyalty to his brother trumped any obligation he might have felt to either the FBI or the public good in general. He had no intention of calling John Gamel back. He did, however, have every intention of talking to his brother. A couple of weeks after Whitey had fled, Weeks told Bill that Whitey wanted to talk to him. By then, Whitey and Flemmi had been indicted on federal racketeering and extortion charges for teaming up with the Mafia to shake down bookies. Assuming his own phones were tapped, Bill arranged for Whitey to call him at the Quincy home of Eddie Phillips, a friend who worked at the State House and had served as his driver for years.[24] He arrived at Phillips's home just as the Phillips family was sitting down for dinner. The house was bustling. Bill Bulger waited alone in a room for his fugitive brother to call.

They didn't talk long. "He told me that he's doing fine, that he'll be okay," Bill Bulger later told a grand jury investigating Whitey's disappearance. "I told him I cared about him deeply, and I still do. And that I just hoped that it would have a good ending." But Bill Bulger did not convey Gamel's request to his brother. He wasn't going to help talk Whitey into surrendering. Bill said he gave his brother legal advice but did not suggest he turn himself in "because I don't think it would be in his interest to do so. . . . I do have an honest loyalty to my brother, and I care about him. It's my hope that I'm never helpful to anyone against him."[25]

Whitey did, in fact, briefly consider turning himself in. He had Weeks reach out to John Connolly to discuss the possibility. Weeks told Connolly, "Somebody wants to talk to you." He told Connolly to go to the office of a mutual friend, Franny Joyce, who, like Connolly, was a Bill Bulger protégé. Connolly's and Joyce's offices were near each other in the Prudential Center, where the retired agent was working for the Boston Edison power company, and where Joyce, with Bill Bulger's patronage, had been ensconced as the head of the Massachusetts Convention Center Authority.[26] When the phone rang, Connolly said he picked it up, thinking it would be Flemmi, calling from jail. Instead, it was Whitey, and he was furious.

Whitey was hot because the indictment against him and Flemmi was all about the gambling business the FBI had authorized them to conduct as long as they fed the bureau information about the Mafia. Whitey was right on this point, and he had every reason to be livid. As he listened to Whitey rant, Connolly suddenly grew worried about his own safety and that of his wife and three sons. He knew what Whitey was capable of, especially if he thought someone had betrayed him. "Jimmy," Connolly said, "you know I did not do this."[27]

Connolly promised he would testify in court that Whitey and Flemmi had been authorized, if not encouraged, to engage in gambling and loansharking activity to enhance their cover with the mobsters they were ratting on. Whitey believed that his deal with the FBI protected him from the charges he faced, and he was prepared to turn himself in, but only if he had a guarantee that he and Flemmi would be released on bail to await trial. After his Alcatraz years, he had resolved never to go to prison again. "I don't think that's possible," Connolly replied. "It would depend what your lawyer could do for you."

Whitey thought for a moment. "Who should I get?" he asked.

They agreed to talk again, a week later, and when Whitey called back, Connolly gave him the names of three lawyers. Two of them had been prosecutors. He could hear Whitey writing the names down.

"Good luck," Whitey told his former handler.

"Good luck to you," Connolly replied.[28]

They haven't spoken to each other since.

Whitey made other phone calls during those first months on the run, trying to find out what was happening. The case against him soon expanded to include new charges that he had extorted money from drug dealers. No call was more personal than the one he made to John Morris at the FBI in Quantico, Virginia. Morris, a month shy of his fifty-first birthday, was nearing the end of his FBI career. Despite having been censured for leaking information to the *Boston Globe* for its 1988 series on the Bulgers, he had been promoted to director of training at the academy. It was a soft landing given his former position and the nature of his transgression. But things were taking an ominous turn. Someone kept leaving messages. "Tell him Mr. White called," the man told the secretary. "Tell him I'll call back."[29] Finally, Mr. White got through, and Morris knew who it was even before the first threat crackled down the line. "John," Whitey began, "I figured it out. You were the one who tried to get me killed with the story 'Whitey Bulger is a paid FBI informant.'"

"I'm sorry," Morris replied. "I made a mistake."[30]

"You were my paid FBI informant, you motherfucker," Whitey snarled. "If I had known it then I'd have blown your fucking head off. You were my informant. I bought information. I didn't give information or sell it."[31] He added, "You took money from me, and if I go to jail, you're going to go to jail."[32]

Whitey gave him an ultimatum. Call his contacts at the *Boston Globe* and get the story describing Whitey as an informant retracted. Tell them it was just a ploy to discredit Whitey and his brother. Tell them it was all untrue. Morris said that wasn't in his power, but Whitey ordered him to use his "Machiavellian mind" to remedy the situation.[33]

At that moment, Whitey heard a thud and the phone went dead. Morris had collapsed and was rushed to a hospital. He was revived on the operating table. "He had a heart attack!" Whitey boasted, recalling the exchange years later.[34]

In a letter to an old friend from his prison days, Whitey was insistent that he wasn't an informant, and that he felt smeared by Morris and the *Globe*. "[T]he guy in the FBI I protected by my silence . . . was the person who told the press to get me killed—what a plot! Alfred Hitchcock couldn't have thought that up!"[35]

When Weeks told Connolly about Whitey's threatening phone call to Morris and Morris's terrified reaction, Connolly started chuckling. "He died twice on the table," Connolly told Weeks. "It must have been some phone call."[36]

As they turned around on I-95 in Connecticut and headed back to Manhattan on the night of Steve Flemmi's arrest, Whitey tried to reassure Teresa Stanley that they were just on an extended vacation. But after a month on the road, she had had enough. She was homesick and also still miffed over Whitey's affair with Greig. She had felt flattered, at Christmas, that Whitey had chosen her to accompany him, but now it was February, and a life in hotels and motels and who knew where else was not appealing. "I want to go home," Stanley said. Whitey didn't seem surprised. He didn't fight with her or browbeat her as he usually did to get his way. Instead he called Weeks and told him he wanted Greig to join him on the run.

Stanley knew nothing of the arrangement as she stepped out of the black sedan that still had a new-car smell. She was standing in the parking lot of a Chili's, less than a mile from her daughter's house in a suburb south of Boston. Their farewell, the ending of what was essentially a thirty-year common-law marriage, was anticlimactic. "See ya," Whitey said. "See ya," Stanley replied.[37]

Whitey was soon back on the highway, navigating the twenty-minute drive to a scruffy stretch of sand in Dorchester known locally, without irony, as Malibu Beach. It was about halfway between the South Boston Liquor Mart and the hidden graves. Whitey would wait for Cathy there; Greig was now Whitey's No. 1 woman.

Everything had been choreographed. It was almost as if they were eloping. Weeks pulled up just as Greig was descending the stairs that ran down from Thomas Park in Southie. It was 7:30 p.m., cold and dark, and Greig was right on time. Her twin sister, Margaret, had dropped her off and had given Greig her own driver's license. Greig had already entrusted to Margaret the only things she cared about as much as Whitey: her two French poodles, Nikki and Gigi. If Greig thought she was heading out for a long time, she hadn't packed for it. She had a small weekend bag slung over her shoulder. She told her sister she'd only be gone for a few months.[38]

Weeks drove around for an hour before he picked up Greig to make sure he wasn't being tailed. He repeated the routine before driving over to Malibu Beach. Weeks and Greig were walking toward the prearranged meeting spot on the Savin Hill side of the beach when Whitey appeared out of the shadows. He looked like a cowboy: a Stetson hat, black leather jacket, jeans, and cowboy boots. Greig almost ran to him, throwing herself into his arms. They held the embrace. Weeks stood to the side awkwardly. "It was like something out of *Casablanca*," Weeks recalled.[39]

Greig was glowing as they walked to Whitey's Mercury Grand Marquis. He had chosen her; when it came down to it, he had chosen her. And he had married her. Not in real life, but in the lives they were about to assume. They weren't Whitey Bulger and Cathy Greig anymore. They were Tom and Helen Baxter, from Selden, New York. They had just retired and were off on a cross-country adventure.

When you follow Route 1 in Louisiana through the bayous to its southernmost tip, you cross a long drawbridge to a small resort island called Grand Isle. Grand Isle calls itself the Cajun Bahamas and the Sportsman's Paradise. Louisiana's only inhabited barrier island boasts sandy beaches, saltwater marshes, and tracts of oak-hackberry forests where thousands of migratory birds stop for a brief respite during their annual north-south journeys. Modest vacation homes and rental cottages built on pilings above the flood line dot the flat coastline. Most of Grand Isle's thirteen hundred year-round residents earn their living shrimping or working on offshore oil rigs. Its population swells to more than six thousand in the summer. It is a place to come if you want to fish, lured by the promise of some 280 species, to swim, bird-watch, or just watch the sun sink over the Gulf of Mexico. Or, in Whitey's case, if you want to disappear. Most of the houses were built for vacationers and in the off-season were vacant. There were only a couple of small supermarkets, and two restaurants still open, on the quiet day when Whitey and Greig—calling themselves Tom and Helen Baxter—arrived, during the off-season, in early 1995. There wasn't even a bank on the island. But that was fine by Whitey. He had his own bank in a pouch slung around his waist: rolls of hundred-dollar bills that he peeled off whenever he needed to buy something. Greig went to the hair salon run by the police chief's daughter to have her hair cut and colored. She brought her own hair coloring, alternating between L'Oreal Light Ash Blonde and the extra light platinum blonde.

Whitey fell in love with the place and the people, the peace and quiet. He and Greig thought about living there permanently.[40] But their first visit was brief; they left for a cross-country tour that took them from Long Island to Wyoming. They went back in the fall of 1995, staying a few days at the modest wood-shingled Wateredge Beach Resort on Route 1.

They were out for a drive one day not long after arriving back in town when they came across a brush fire on the island and saw a woman standing outside her house watching it. The woman had two black Labrador retrievers with her, so Whitey grabbed a bag of dog biscuits that Greig kept in the trunk just for such occasions. "Those are some beautiful dogs you've got there," he said, feeding the dogs as Greig knelt down and patted them.[41] Penny Gautreaux, a twenty-nine-year-old meter reader for the town, smiled at the two strangers. She liked dog lovers, so she liked them. Whitey said that they were looking for a place to rent, and Penny pointed them toward a beachfront duplex called It's Our Dream. It was a modest cottage on stilts overlooking the Gulf, a bargain at four hundred dollars a month. They stayed for two months.

One day soon after they took up residence in the duplex, Whitey stopped by the Gautreaux house as Penny was cooking for her husband, Glenn, and their four kids. The smell of Cajun spices hung pungent in the air. "Do you have enough for us?" Whitey asked amiably. And, as abruptly as that, Penny and Glenn Gautreaux had new best friends: Tom and Helen Baxter. Tom told them he'd made his money in the real estate business and was retired. Helen was a dog groomer but had put that aside to travel with her husband. The Baxters had a knack for neighborly relations and never showed up empty-handed. They would arrive laden down with groceries, and they ate with the Gautreauxs every night for weeks on end. Whitey raved about Penny Gautreaux's fried potatoes, and, at his insistence, Penny taught Greig how to make them. Whitey and Greig would leave the island for weeks and even months at a time, but they'd always come back to Grand Isle and they'd always come back to the Gautreauxs.

Whitey cherished this nightly ritual of a sit-down dinner. The Gautreaux household replaced the one he had had to leave behind at Stanley's home in Southie. As in Southie, he took charge of the table as if it were his own, insisting that the meal be a formal occasion, with everyone, adults and children, gathered round. Everyone heeded what Whitey, the autocrat of the dinner table, had to say. He chided Penny when she grabbed a plate and sat on the sofa, watching TV. He lectured the Gautreaux kids the same way he had lectured Stanley's kids on the importance of doing homework, of eating well, of staying in shape. Once, Penny started crying when Whitey was stern with her kids, but she swiftly forgave him. He was just trying to get through to them, his strictness just a sign of how much he cared.[42]

Whitey, in particular, was all over Glenn, telling him he needed to be more ambitious, more energetic. He bought him tools so he could start his own carpentry business. "Get off your lazy butt," Whitey told Glenn. "You've got beautiful kids. You need to make something out of your life."[43] Penny marveled at how her husband would jump when Whitey told him to.

And Whitey was as generous with gifts as he was free with advice. Over the months, he replaced all of the Gautreauxs' kitchen appliances. He bought them a stove, a refrigerator, and a freezer, and he paid for a fence around their property to keep the dogs from straying. When two of the Gautreaux children came home from school with a note saying they needed glasses, Whitey and Greig took them to an optometrist at the closest Walmart and paid for it. He peeled off hundred-dollar bills from his wad and bought the kids clothes, toys, and books. He bought eighteen-year-old Glenn Jr. a hunting knife that was considerably bigger than the pearl-handled switchblade Whitey always carried.

The kids couldn't have known it, but their company was good cover. Whitey and Greig did their own errands and shopping at the Walmart in the middle of Cajun country with what appeared to be their grandchildren—hardly the profile of a pair of fugitives from Boston. Once, however, Whitey's mask slipped. When the checkout line at the Walmart moved too slowly for his liking, he made a scene. "Do you know how much money I spend in here?" he boomed. He stormed out of the store. Greig followed with the kids, calming him down in the parking lot.[44]

The children started calling them Uncle Tom and Aunt Helen, and as fond as they seemed of the kids, there was one place where Uncle Tom drew a line. Whenever Penny or Glenn tried to take a photograph, Whitey said no. Greig thought it was harmless and was about to pose with the kids one day when Whitey put his foot down. "No pictures," he growled. The Gautreauxs shrugged, chalking it up to Tom's sometimes quirky personality—quirky and sometimes, as in the Walmart checkout line, alarmingly hot-tempered. One night, Whitey treated the Gautreauxs to dinner at Anthony's, an upscale restaurant on the mainland. The hostess led them to a table, and Whitey turned and said, "It's too noisy." He pointed to a table in the corner.

"Oh, sir, I'm sorry," the hostess said brightly, "but you have to sit here."

Whitey glared at her. "No I don't," he said.

Whitey insisted on the table in the corner, and he got it.[45]

Except for the occasional outburst, he was compelling company, and oddly thoughtful. He had a soft side and wasn't afraid to show it. Once, when one in a litter of new black Lab puppies got ill, the Gautreauxs brought it to a veterinarian. The puppy was in great pain, and the vet recommended that they put the dog down. When the Gautreauxs told Whitey, he was adamant that the dog should not be given a lethal injection. He insisted that shooting the dog was more humane because it would suffer less. But he couldn't watch. When Glenn Gautreaux leveled his gun at the back of the puppy's head, Whitey turned away. As the shot echoed across the water, Whitey Bulger wept.[46]

Whitey and Greig eventually left the island but returned in the spring of 1996. Things had changed at the Gautreaux house in their absence. Glenn's in-laws from his previous marriage, Thomas "Black" Rudolph and his wife, Mary, had moved in. Whitey seemed to resent the imposition more than the Gautreauxs; the newcomers upset the domestic routine he had spent months carefully cultivating. He didn't like that Black Rudolph saw no reason to defer to him. "He had this attitude like he was the boss," Black Rudolph said of Whitey. Whitey liked to point out his relative sophistication to Black, who, in Whitey's view, was just a country bumpkin. Whitey bragged about traveling the world, saying that he had made enough money to retire early and that he was in better shape than men half his age.

That last one got to Black Rudolph. "I'm in better shape than you," said Black, who, at sixty-two, was four years younger than Whitey. Black got up from the dinner table, dropped to the floor, and performed three one-handed push-ups. "I'll do a one-hand for every two-hand you can do," Black said. Whitey declined the challenge. "I'm a lot older than you," he said. Black Rudolph slapped his driver's license on the table. "Let's see yours," he said. Whitey waved him off.

In July 1996, Tom and Helen Baxter left Grand Isle and never came back. They said they were headed to San Diego. It was a lie. The truth was that their cover had been blown, and by someone very close to Whitey. They made a hasty escape, heading for Chicago.[47]

The local police chief, Roscoe Besson Jr., found out later that the man he knew as Tom Baxter had a bounty of two hundred fifty thousand dollars on his head. He recalled one morning that he'd been directing traffic outside the island's elementary school when Whitey stood at the curb, waiting to cross. "I stopped the traffic and let two hundred fifty thousand dollars get across the street," the chief said.[48]

Whitey hadn't forgotten about Teresa Stanley. During one of his pre-arranged phone calls with Weeks, he asked about her. Weeks told him she had taken up with Alan Thistle, a dubious character from Southie whose criminal record dated back to his teen years and who had, in recent years, been making like Whitey: informing for the FBI. In May of 1996, Whitey bought five twenty-dollar calling cards in a country store in Okemah, Oklahoma. He used one of them to call a friend of an elderly aunt of Stanley's. "Tell her to stay away from that piece of shit Thistle," Whitey hissed.[49]

Whitey didn't like Thistle, and if he had only known the half of it, it is unlikely Alan Thistle would have been alive to romance Teresa Stanley after Whitey took off. Thistle worked initially as an informant for two Boston police detectives, Frank Dewan and Jimmy Carr, who had been trying to take Whitey down. Then, in the early 1990s, he became an informant for John Gamel, the FBI agent who was part of the squad investigating Whitey. One of Thistle's greatest accomplishments was helping the FBI plant a bug inside one of Whitey's hangouts, the Rotary Variety Store in South Boston. One morning he'd duped the woman who opened the store for Whitey at dawn each day by flattening a tire on her car and offering to take it to a nearby shop to get it fixed. She gave him her set of keys—which included the one to the store—and FBI agents quickly made a duplicate while Thistle had the tire repaired. Agents, who had been unable to bypass the store's elaborate alarm system, were able to open the door with their own key in 1994 and install a bug.

But Whitey always assumed his hangouts were bugged and acted accordingly; the bugs only picked up idle chatter.

Thistle met Stanley at a friend's house in February 1996 while both were working as banquet waiters at the Boston Convention Center. They started dating and fell "crazy in love."[50] He moved in with Stanley, started driving the white Grand Marquis that Whitey had bought for her, and worked out in the gym Whitey had built in her home. Thistle insisted he would have made a move on Stanley even if she hadn't been Whitey's girlfriend, but he also secretly hoped that she would lead him to Whitey and that they could share the reward for his capture. Gamel wrote Stanley a letter a year after Whitey had fled, telling her that her life was in danger because she knew too much. She showed the letter to Thistle, who persuaded her to talk to the FBI. He called his old handler, and a meeting was arranged for April 29, 1996.

But even Thistle wasn't prepared for what Stanley told the FBI agents who brought them to a room at the Sheraton in downtown Boston for a debriefing. "Do you know what name he might be using?" one of the agents asked. "Yeah," Stanley replied, "Thomas Baxter."

During the series of meetings that followed, she revealed Whitey's early hideouts on Long Island, New York, and the location of safe deposit boxes where he had stashed money and documents. Stanley and Thistle accompanied FBI agents to Selden, New York, where she showed them the dealership where Whitey had bought a car, the motel with a glass-enclosed pool where he swam, the gym where he worked out, and the house where Whitey had stayed with cousins of Kevin Weeks. A black Grand Marquis belonging to Whitey was parked in a garage near the house.

"Let's feel the hood and see if it's warm," Thistle said excitedly.[51] Instead, the agents sent Thistle and Stanley home, saying they needed to set up surveillance; they'd let them know when they got him. "We thought, 'This is it,'" said Thistle, who returned to South Boston with Stanley, waiting for word of Whitey's arrest. Days and then weeks went by and nothing happened. Stanley was growing increasingly anxious and regretted what she had done. She was angry after learning that Whitey had picked up Greig after dropping her off, but she did not want to be the one whose tip led to his capture.

Still, she wasn't about to take relationship advice from her old, two-timing lover. Not only did she ignore Whitey's long-distance order to break up with Thistle, but she resented it. Weeks decided to pay her a visit and try to reason with her. "This guy is a bum," Weeks told her. "He's an informant. Everything you tell him, he's telling the cops. He's just pumping you for information."[52] Weeks spent almost three hours in her living room, trying to get Stanley to promise to stay away from Thistle. Finally, he slapped his thighs and got up to leave.

"Well," Stanley sighed. "It's too late anyways."

Weeks stopped dead in his tracks.

"What do you mean, too late?"

Stanley got up, and Weeks followed her into the kitchen. She lit a cigarette and held it her hand, which shook. She did not want Thistle to take the blame for what she had done. She went to her purse and handed Weeks a business card. It was FBI agent John Gamel's. "I told him everything," Stanley said. "Thomas Baxter. Selden, New York. Everything."[53]

Weeks knew he had to tell Whitey. But he had no way to reach him; all he could do was wait for him to call, and more than a week passed before he did. Whitey wasn't panicked when Weeks told him the extent of Stanley's betrayal. "At least I know," he said. He knew he could never return to Selden; that he had to ditch his Baxter alias and the two black Mercury Marquis he had registered in New York under that name. One of the cars—the one the FBI was watching— was still on Long Island. He and Greig climbed into the other one in Grand Isle and drove to Chicago. They left the car in a parking lot and later made arrangements for Weeks's cousin to drive it back to New York.

As he scrambled to get new identities, Whitey called Weeks

with a plan. He needed his brother Jack to be brought in to help. He instructed Weeks to get a phony mustache, put it on Jack, and take some photos that Whitey could use to create new identification. Though Whitey was nine years older than Jack, the two strongly resembled each other. They had the same broad forehead and similar features. Before they hung up, Weeks asked Whitey if he wanted him to kill Alan Thistle. Whitey thought about it for a moment. "Nah," he said. "Going out with Thistle is Teresa's punishment."⁵⁴

As the clerk magistrate of Boston Juvenile Court, Jack Bulger was a sworn officer of the court. But he didn't hesitate to break the law to help his fugitive brother. He paid the monthly rental fee for a safe deposit box Whitey kept at a bank in Clearwater, Florida, and had spoken to him twice during prearranged telephone calls. Twice he lied when he was subpoenaed to testify before federal grand juries, insisting he hadn't spoken to his fugitive brother and didn't know where he hid his money. "He sounded good," Jack Bulger told Weeks after speaking briefly to Whitey late one night on the phone at a physical therapy clinic in Southie. It was no surprise that Jack Bulger agreed to help his brother obtain bogus identification. When Weeks showed up at his South Boston home with a fake mustache, he glued it over his lip and struck a serious pose as Weeks snapped several photographs.⁵⁵ And whereas Whitey was willing to let Stanley off the hook for cooperating with the FBI, Jack was less forgiving. Later, when he bumped into her while strolling around Castle Island in South Boston, he snarled, "I wish you were dead. Look at what you've done, all the trouble you caused."⁵⁶

Weeks enlisted a well-known local forger to craft a bogus driver's license, using Jack Bulger's photograph and the name and Social Security number of a Massachusetts man, Mark Shapeton. Then Weeks drove to Chicago with a girlfriend in a rental car. Whitey and Greig were waiting for them at the Water Tower, one of Chicago's most famous landmarks, located on the Magnificent Mile. Whitey frowned when he looked at the new ID. The photo was all wrong. Whitey's mustache was pencil-thin. Jack's was big and bushy. It looked like he had a caterpillar over his lip.[57] They went to a department store and bought a blue bed sheet, then went to Whitey's motel room and took some new photos of Whitey in front of the blue backdrop—the same color used on Massachusetts driver's licenses. Whitey ordered Weeks to take the photos back to Boston and have the forger come up with some new names and make him a handful of Massachusetts driver's licenses.

Whitey seemed outwardly calm, but inside he was agitated and preoccupied with securing new IDs. That night, the two couples strolled to a Japanese restaurant for dinner. Three young men outside made some remarks about Greig and Weeks's girlfriend. "What are you looking at, you motherfuckers," Whitey shouted. He pulled the switchblade from the sheath on his calf. Weeks pulled a knife, too. The three men ran off. It wasn't exactly a show of discretion for a man on the run, but Whitey could never completely control himself. Then, almost as quickly as his rage surfaced, it was gone. They walked into the restaurant, and Whitey seemed his old self again. He was even philosophical. "Every day out there is another day I beat them," he told Weeks. "Every good meal is a meal they can't take away from me."[58]

Tom and Helen Baxter never left Chicago. As they walked into Union Station on July 23, 1996, past crisp limestone walls, through the Great Hall, Whitey and Greig became Mark and Carol Shapeton. They boarded an Amtrak train bound for Penn Station in New York. They spent the next seven weeks moving from one New York City hotel to another—looking, to all they encountered, like a couple of tourists, and waiting for Weeks to arrive with more fake identification.

Back in Boston, the FBI's relationship with Whitey had created a rift within law enforcement, resulting in two competing fugitive investigations. The FBI's Boston office fueled the perception that it didn't really want to catch Whitey by putting the manhunt in the hands of its organized crime squad—John Connolly's old unit, which had protected Whitey for so many years. The state police–DEA team that had built the extortion case against Whitey suspected that FBI agents were leaking information to Connolly and sabotaging efforts to capture Whitey. When an informant told Tom Foley's group of investigators about Whitey's efforts to get new identities, they made a calculated decision not to share the news with the FBI.

The informant said Weeks had enlisted him to get fake driver's licenses for Whitey. The informant's job was to come up with a few more names of people with no criminal histories. Then he got his associate, a local counterfeiter, to make the fake identities.[59] Foley dispatched state police sergeant Steve Johnson to the state Bureau of Vital Statistics, where he combed through records and came up with a handful of names of recently deceased people with unexpired licenses.[60] The informant delivered those names to the counterfeiter, who created the bogus IDs that were handed over to Weeks. Whitey would get his IDs, but the state police could trace the new names.

The state police–DEA team stepped up surveillance of Weeks, determined not to lose him when he went to deliver the new IDs to Whitey. The plan went awry when Weeks concluded that it was too risky for him to meet Whitey again.[61] He noticed helicopters and planes hovering overhead when he left his house. He had already found a tracking device on his car and knew he was being followed by the FBI, the DEA, and the state police. Whitey wasn't happy about the plan, but Weeks told him he was afraid he would lead investigators to him if he tried to deliver the identities in person. He gave the package to Peter Lee, a longtime friend from South Boston who was not part of Whitey's organization and drew no attention from law enforcement.[62] Lee took an Amtrak train to Manhattan and met Whitey and Greig outside the New York Public Library at Fifth Avenue and Forty-second Street. They headed to a nearby Irish pub for lunch, and Lee handed Whitey the package. But even as he was trying to restore his cover, Whitey again drew unnecessary attention to himself. The waitress who was serving them casually tucked her bra strap under her blouse after it slipped off her shoulder. Whitey, always phobic about germs, flew into a rage, ranting that she was serving his food with the same tainted hand.[63]

After they left the pub, Whitey asked Greig to wait for him while he took a walk with Lee. The two men had only walked a short distance when Whitey suddenly pushed Lee down a subway stairway that was no longer in use, following close behind him. At six foot three, Lee towered over Whitey, but he was gripped by fear as he stood alone with him in a darkened hallway. He was convinced Whitey was going to kill him, and perhaps he was. But suddenly a door opened and several transit police officers appeared. "What are you doing here?" one of them asked. "Screw."[64] Lee scrambled to the top of the stairs. "That's it, I'm outta here," he shouted. As Lee ran off, Whitey just stood on the sidewalk.

Foley assigned a trooper to check law enforcement databases every day, hoping Whitey would get caught using one of his new identities. But Whitey didn't slip up and the trail went cold.

He and Greig had taken a train back to Chicago after Labor Day, still posing as Mark and Carol Shapeton. A couple of months later, Weeks managed to rendezvous with Whitey in New York City for what would be their last meeting. Whitey was relaxed and even stopped a police officer to ask for directions. "The best place to get lost is a big city," he told Weeks as they walked away from the unsuspecting cop.[65] "People are just walking around thinking about their own problems. You don't stand out there."

They had a last supper, and then, as they walked toward Penn Station, Whitey turned serious, repeating something he had said to Weeks months before in Chicago: "If anything ever comes down, put it on me."[66] They paused at one of the entrances to Penn Station. "I'll be in touch," Whitey said.

But he never called again. Weeks wasn't surprised. He sensed that Whitey knew that Steve Flemmi was growing antsy in jail. As Whitey was living it up on the run, his criminal sidekick was cooped up in a small cell. He'd always said Flemmi couldn't do time, and he knew Flemmi had only one card to play. He was right. A few months after Whitey disappeared down the stairs into Penn Station, Flemmi decided to tell his story and to offer his defense: How could he and Whitey be guilty of the crimes the federal government had charged them with? They had committed those crimes with the permission of the FBI.

14

Where's Whitey?

The hum of hair dryers and the clatter of conversations in both English and Vietnamese washed over Cathy Greig when she opened the door at Fountain Hair & Nails one day in January 2000. Sandwiched between a dry cleaner and a barbershop in a small strip mall, the salon was right off a main road in Fountain Valley, California, a sprawling suburban community in Orange County not far from Disneyland. It is one of those places, one of many in that part of California, where everything seems pleasant enough but nothing sticks in memory and nobody stands out, which made it a perfect place for Greig and the gruff-looking, elderly man behind the wheel to stop. Smiling politely, Greig said she didn't have an appointment and asked if anyone was available to color her hair quickly. She was pressed for time, she said, her husband waiting impatiently in the car. She held up a package of blonde dye she had purchased herself. The salon was filled with customers, but the owner, Kim, smiled and steered Greig toward an empty chair. Did her husband want to wait inside? No, thanks, said Greig, and the man stayed in the car, facing the shop's large plate glass windows, keeping Greig in sight the whole time. She made little conversation, paid cash—sixteen dollars for the coloring, plus tip—then slid into the passenger seat and they were gone.

Nothing about the visit seemed remarkable to Kim, the salon owner, until some FBI agents showed up a couple of weeks later flashing Wanted posters of Whitey Bulger and Cathy Greig. They had been tipped by a regular customer who watched *America's Most Wanted* and recognized the fugitive couple. The customer had been in the salon when Greig had had her hair colored and had noticed the elderly man waiting and watching.[1] The FBI had been fruitlessly searching for Bulger for five years, and there had been no reliable sightings of late. Surely this was the big break they had been hoping for, a clear sign that Whitey had adopted Southern California as his hiding place.

But nothing about Whitey and the FBI was ever as it should be. After quietly investigating the lead for a few months, the FBI's Los Angeles office went public, announcing that Whitey and Greig had been spotted at the salon and might still be in Southern California. But the FBI's Boston office, in charge of the search, was less impressed with the tip and immediately downplayed its significance. It issued a press release saying an individual "resembling" Greig had been spotted, and that there was "no confirmed sighting of Bulger."[2] It was the sort of bureaucratic bobble and turf-conscious bickering that had typified the search thus far, and had contributed to the image of the bureau, or at least its Boston branch, as either remarkably inept in its search for Whitey or insincere in its desire to catch him. For the FBI, Whitey Bulger the fugitive was Public Embarrassment Number One. Despite spending millions of dollars and thousands of man-hours on the search, with agents running down look-alike sightings all over the world, the bureau had come up empty time and again.

Those who believed the FBI failure was no accident had plenty of reason for their suspicions. After Whitey disappeared just before Christmas in 1994, having been tipped to the pending indictment by John Connolly, the FBI assigned control of the search for him to Connolly's old unit, the organized crime squad. With many options at hand, the least defensible was chosen. Worse than that, the agent eventually put in charge of the hunt was none other than Charlie Gianturco, a man whose family felt personally indebted to Whitey after he'd been credited with saving the life of Gianturco's brother, Nick, during an undercover operation. It was a disastrous start, indicating to all involved that the FBI's effort would be a farce, and, at least during Whitey's first two years on the run, a farce it seemed to be. Whitey slipped back into Boston at least a couple of times during that stretch, once to drop off Teresa Stanley and pick up Cathy Greig. But neither Greig nor Kevin Weeks, who drove her to the rendezvous with Whitey, was under surveillance at that time. FBI agents waited more than a year to approach Stanley. And when they finally did and she agreed to cooperate, they were slow to follow up on the leads she provided. Agents performed a cursory check of a calling card found in a car Whitey had abandoned in New York, mistakenly believing he had made only one call instead of dozens. Agents didn't interview Connolly until two years after Whitey had vanished. And then, when they did finally sit down with the retired agent in his office at Boston's Prudential Center, he was completely unhelpful and spoke fondly of Whitey. He recalled Whitey's having bought him the ice cream cone when he was a boy—an anecdote he told the agents he planned to include in the first chapter of his autobiography. He insisted that former supervisor John Morris had promised Whitey and Flemmi protection from prosecution because they were such "good informants." As the agents stood up to leave, Connolly made it clear where his loyalties lay. "I hope he's never caught," he said.[3]

He very nearly got his wish, as the litany of FBI missteps continued. The agency waited two years before it offered a reward—two hundred fifty thousand dollars—for information leading to Whitey's arrest, and more than four before adding him to its Ten Most Wanted list in 1999, a designation that provided more resources for the manhunt and committed all of the bureau's field offices to treat tips about Whitey as a top priority. But by then, the trail had been cold for years. The best chances to catch Whitey had been early in his run, especially after his initial alias had been compromised by Teresa Stanley. They were squandered as the FBI tried to keep the search to itself—and was glacially slow to act on leads.

Indeed, it seems possible that the FBI would never have ramped up the search for Whitey had it not been for relentless focus on the case by a man little known to the public but something of a legend in the law, Mark Wolf. The federal judge assigned to hear the racketeering case brought against Whitey, Steve Flemmi, Frank Salemme, John Martorano, and another mobster, Bobby DeLuca. Wolf was in many ways the perfect person for the job. He was a former federal prosecutor but, even more significantly, a protégé of former US Attorney General Edward Levi, who had made his name as a crusader against government corruption in the 1970s. Wolf had grown up just outside Boston, very much a child of the region. His father was the accountant for Red Auerbach, the legendary Boston Celtics coach. As a boy, Wolf accompanied his father for business-and-pleasure sessions with Auerbach, which usually included copious amounts of Chinese food, hilarious stories, and blunt wisdom. He learned from Auerbach and his father an uncompromising, no-nonsense approach that followed him to the bench. After graduating from Harvard Law School in 1971, he signed on as a deputy to Levi, who had been appointed by President Gerald Ford with the mission to restore credibility and transparency to the Justice Department after the lawless excesses of Watergate. One of Wolf's tasks as a thirty-year-old Justice Department lawyer was to revise, in 1976, the guidelines for proper handling of informants by federal agents. It was an unintentionally prophetic assignment. Twenty years later, Wolf found himself hearing a case in which agents broke just about every rule he'd crafted.

The idea that Whitey was an informant had been floated since 1988, when the *Boston Globe* first reported it. Anthony Cardinale, an aggressive criminal defense lawyer who represented Mafia boss

Frank Salemme, had long demanded to know whether Whitey or anyone else charged in the case was an informant. The FBI and the Justice Department had steadfastly refused to answer. Now Wolf forced their hand. He ordered the FBI to publicly and unambiguously answer the question. And of course the answer was yes.

As Wolf vowed to get to the bottom of Whitey and Flemmi's relationship with the FBI, the FBI's insistence on keeping control of the Whitey manhunt was criticized as a conflict of interest. But the bureau, which traditionally tracks its own fugitives, refused to relinquish the search to the US Marshals, whose specialty is tracking wanted criminals. Only after two fruitless years of going it alone did the bureau finally, in August 1997, assign a three-member task force—comprised of an FBI agent, a Boston police detective, and a state correctional officer—to track Whitey full-time.

Months later, Wolf initiated what became perhaps the most extraordinary, and consequential, evidentiary hearing in Boston history, lasting almost a year and featuring a parade of nearly fifty witnesses. Many of them were John Connolly's fellow agents and supervisors. None offered testimony as devastating as that of John Morris, whose career had prospered and then spectacularly collapsed because of his association with Connolly and Whitey. Even though Morris was Connolly's boss, he had managed to negotiate an immunity deal for himself with the Justice Department: If he gave up Connolly, he'd stay out of prison. During eight days of riveting testimony, Morris exposed the FBI architecture that supported Whitey's world. He showed how the national prioritization of Mafia hunting led the FBI in Boston to make deals with criminals who killed as freely as the Mafia and in some cases had killed people for the Mafia. Morris came across as pathetic, a careerist and philanderer who used Connolly and Whitey to pump up his personnel file and used Whitey's bribes to fly his mistress in for a tryst. But while the other FBI agents who took the stand denied or deflected the accusations of wrongdoing, Morris's testimony emerged as the most compelling and the most damning.

Sitting day after day in the witness box, he had the manner of a meek and unassuming accountant, his demeanor utterly at odds with what he was saying. He acknowledged, to a packed courtroom, that he feared he'd gotten two men killed by telling Connolly that Brian Halloran was shopping their informants. As Morris spoke, spectators looked at each other knowingly, as if they knew this was a moment of history, that something long hidden was finally being exposed. The defendants—Flemmi, Salemme, DeLuca, and John Martorano—sat in the jury box. Flemmi shifted uncomfortably as Morris explained how FBI agents had shared leisurely meals with Whitey and him. Martorano glared. Law enforcement officers whose attempts to snare Whitey and Flemmi had been compromised over the years sat in the gallery, their heads nodding almost imperceptibly: Everything they had suspected, and even more, was true. During a break in the proceedings, Morris sat alone on a bench outside the courtroom. FBI agents stared at him from a distance. He was alone, a pariah, and, though he was serving the cause of justice with his testimony, by no measure a hero.

As Wolf peeled away at the layers of the FBI's relationship with Whitey and Flemmi, Connolly, seeing the disaster headed his way, quietly launched a counterattack, a campaign of dirty tricks that he hoped would persuade Wolf to dismiss the racketeering case. He leaked internal FBI informant reports and information to Flemmi's lawyer that could be used to discredit several FBI agents who had denied in their testimony before Wolf that the two informants had been promised immunity.[4] In an attempt to portray Morris as an unreliable drunk, Connolly gave Flemmi an FBI tape of conversations that had been bugged years earlier at the Mafia's Boston headquarters. Then Flemmi falsely testified before Wolf that Morris played the tape for Whitey and Flemmi during one of their secret meetings and got so drunk he left it with the two informants.[5] Connolly was determined to smear anyone in law enforcement who contributed to the case against Whitey and Flemmi. He got a supply of Boston Police Department letterhead and sent an anonymous letter to Judge Wolf, falsely accusing Boston Police Sergeant Detective Frank Dewan of planting evidence against Whitey and Flemmi. He wrote a second anonymous letter bashing Dewan to the Boston Police Department on *Boston Globe* stationery.[6] Dewan had spent much of his career trying to put Whitey in prison and was instrumental in helping the DEA build a case against the fifty-one people in the cocaine distribution ring that the DEA busted in 1990. He had a reputation as an honest cop who could not be bribed.[7] Connolly's machinations were not only futile, they would boomerang. He had not taken the measure of the man he was trying to sway, Mark Wolf.

When the judge released a scathing 661-page opus outlining his findings in September 1999, it was obvious that Whitey and Flemmi had been given a free pass by the FBI to pursue their criminal trade with impunity. Wolf painted a portrait of an FBI obsessed with keeping secret its history of accommodating, placating, and protecting Whitey and Flemmi. He rejected Flemmi's claim that the two gangsters had been given true legal immunity in exchange for their information, but he accepted wholeheartedly that they had killed people while under the FBI's protection. The judge cut to the chase: The FBI had not just enabled the Bulger-Flemmi partnership; the FBI had created it; in the name of taking down La Cosa Nostra, the bureau was willing to allow the two to do almost anything. "The FBI made Bulger and Flemmi, who were previously acquainted but not close, a perfect match," Wolf wrote. "In Boston, Flemmi and Bulger uniquely shared an antipathy for [La Cosa Nostra], a desire to profit criminally from its destruction and, most notably, the promised protection of the FBI."[8]

His findings forced the Justice Department to launch a criminal investigation of FBI corruption, but Wolf made it clear that Connolly was not the only culpable party at the bureau. "I also do not view this case as a problem of what the government has at times referred to as a few 'bad apples,'" said Wolf. He was convinced that more than a dozen FBI officials in Boston and Washington had engaged in misconduct to protect Whitey and Flemmi.[9]

By forcing the FBI to admit that Whitey and Flemmi were informants, Wolf had started an avalanche. One by one, Whitey's henchmen turned on him. For months, John Martorano sat grim-faced beside Flemmi in the jury box as a parade of witnesses came before Wolf and exposed the cozy relationship between Whitey and Flemmi and the FBI. Martorano felt like a fool. He had murdered people for Whitey and Flemmi, and all the while they were giving up information on their friends, including him. Midway through Wolf's hearings, Martorano decided he had heard enough and agreed to cooperate. He drove a hard bargain; he knew he had a lot to offer, especially on the murders. Prosecutors and investigators, desperate for such testimony, felt obligated to give him an exceptionally good deal: twelve years for twenty murders. The families of Martorano's victims were outraged, but prosecutors defended such leniency, saying it led to solving the murders and, more importantly, put them in a position to charge Whitey and Flemmi with many of them. "If we didn't go forward with this agreement, there would always be the lingering suspicion that part of the reason for not going forward with this agreement was to protect the FBI," said US Attorney Donald K. Stern.[10]

And Martorano's testimony did not disappoint. In one particularly arresting moment, he explained in a chilling, matter-of-fact manner why and how he had shot Roger Wheeler between the eyes in the parking lot of the Tulsa country club. After hearing the testimony, even Wheeler's son David ruefully accepted the sentencing deal as perverse but necessary. "I think it's a sad state of affairs where we have to turn to mob hit men to find the truth about our FBI," David Wheeler said.[11]

Two months after Wolf's findings were issued, Kevin Weeks was indicted for racketeering. That was not good news for either Whitey or John Connolly. Ever since Whitey had taken off, Weeks had been meeting with Connolly regularly. They often had dinner at the Top of the Hub, the restaurant on the fifty-second floor of the Prudential Tower that offers sweeping views of the city and beyond. Weeks had grown deeply disillusioned when he'd found out that Whitey and Flemmi were informants. He was also afraid. Because he was so close to both men, he feared others would assume he was an informant, too. He started carrying two guns at all times.[12] He visited Flemmi in jail and complained that they had put a bull's-eye on his back. Flemmi was dismissive, saying that no one would think Weeks was an informant. At one of their Top of the Hub dinners, Connolly was equally dismissive, telling Weeks to wait until the whole story came out. "They were giving up everybody," Weeks said. "No," Connolly replied, "they weren't."[13]

Connolly tried to convince him it was all part of a brilliant plan to take out the Mafia, that Whitey and Flemmi had saved their own lives by helping the FBI prosecute their principal criminal rivals. But as he leafed through the FBI reports that Connolly handed him, Weeks could see that Whitey and Flemmi had given information on others, including old friends from the Winter Hill Gang. Connolly told him that Flemmi had given him 90 percent of the information, and that he had given Whitey credit for some of it to buff his reputation within the bureau. But Weeks wasn't buying the story. He had packaged some of the cash that Connolly had taken from Whitey and Flemmi, and he knew there was a corrupt nexus among them.[14]

Weeks, forty-three and the father of two teenaged boys, was in custody only a few weeks when he agreed to cooperate. For all their years together, and for all the admiration with which he had long regarded him, Kevin Weeks felt he owed Whitey nothing now. He owed Flemmi nothing. He owed Connolly nothing.[15] He admitted being an accessory to five murders and would serve five years in prison. If John Martorano gave police detailed accounts of murders, Kevin Weeks gave them the graves, the hidden places that exposed simultaneously the remains of Whitey's victims and the depths of his conspiracy with the FBI.

It had been fifteen years, and the trees and brush that had provided such good cover as they reinterred the bodies from The

Haunty were gone, but Weeks led the state police and DEA team right to the spot. It was a bone-chilling January night and snow was falling as a backhoe began digging up the frozen ground while traffic on the Southeast Expressway hummed above. A half-hour later, the heavy metal bucket dredged up human bones. The digging continued by hand, as workers painstakingly sifted the soil. They worked through the night, with heaters and tents shielding them from the howling wind as they gathered the remains of John McIntyre, Bucky Barrett, and Deborah Hussey.[16]

Judge Wolf's hearings prompted two separate investigations. Prosecutors Fred Wyshak and Brian Kelly, who had brought the state police and DEA cases to fruition, began building murder cases against Whitey and Flemmi. The FBI, meanwhile, fielded a task force under a special prosecutor, John Durham, to build cases against Connolly and, presumably, the other FBI agents and supervisors who Wolf found had engaged in misconduct. Again, there was little confidence among other law enforcement agencies that the FBI would aggressively ferret out corruption within its ranks. And as the clock on the statute of limitations ticked down, it appeared Durham's team would in fact strike out. Then they got some unexpected help from an unlikely source: the Mafia leader Frank Salemme.

It wasn't exactly an altruistic gesture, given that it had been the young, ambitious John Connolly who arrested him in 1972 as he walked down a Manhattan street, landing him in prison for fifteen years. And even though Salemme had been able to briefly avoid arrest after Connolly's tip-off allowed him and Whitey to skip town, the Mafia leader felt no obligation to keep quiet now—*omertà* didn't apply to corrupt FBI agents. He testified that Connolly had promised he would be included in the head-start tip-off. That was enough to get Connolly indicted. Revenge was only one factor in the Mafia boss's highly unusual decision to testify for the government. Salemme was trying to get his eleven-year sentence for racketeering reduced, and he was facing an additional eighteen months in jail if he refused to testify. "I wasn't going to do 18 hours for any-body," Salemme said, "never mind 18 months."[17]

Connolly's use of Whitey as an informant in the FBI's war against the Angiulos had been, in effect, the Irish mob's master-stroke against La Cosa Nostra. Salemme's role in getting Connolly indicted was the Mafia's revenge: The agent who brought down the Mafia was in turn brought down by the Mafia. Three days before Christmas, 1999, FBI agents knocked on the door at Connolly's stately home in Lynnfield, an affluent suburb north of Boston. Arresting him so close to the holiday was not an attempt to humili-ate him so much as a matter of beating the clock: The statute of limitations for tipping Whitey off so he could flee, two days before Christmas in 1994, was due to expire the next day.

Connolly was ashen, sick with the flu. The agents who arrested him did not share his view that certain defendants should be shown certain courtesies: They handcuffed him. When he walked into the courtroom, his hair, normally perfectly coiffed, looked unkempt. Instead of his usual tailored suit, he was wearing a sweat suit. Every-thing had changed, except for Connolly's pride. He was unbowed. "This investigation should have been dubbed, if it wasn't already, Operation Scapegoat," Connolly's lawyer said after he was released on bail to await trial.[18] Connolly got a call from Bill Bulger offer-ing support. "I was just expressing an interest in his situation," Bill Bulger told a grand jury later, "and just giving him a call to tell him that I still have confidence in him."[19]

As Connolly awaited trial, the digging resumed, this time at Tenean Beach in Dorchester. They found the remains of Paul McGonagle, the old Mullens gang leader. Months later, they found what was left of Tommy King along the shore of the Neponset River across Dorchester Bay in Quincy, about a hundred yards from the condo complex where Whitey had lived with Greig in the 1980s. The final dig was for Debra Davis. Her gravesite was near King's, just across Dorchester Bay from the waterfront campus of the Uni-versity of Massachusetts. When the digging began, the university president, Bill Bulger, was preparing to host a presidential debate between George W. Bush and Vice President Al Gore. With the national spotlight about to fall on the university stage, generators hummed all night across the bay, fueling the spotlights that state police had set up at the dig. It looked like they would never find her when they came up empty after nearly two weeks. The search was suspended just days before the candidates and the national media swarm hit town. Then investigators, armed with new information, resumed the dig a couple of weeks later and finally found Debra Davis's body.

In September 2000, Whitey was charged with nineteen murders in a sweeping new federal racketeering indictment; Flemmi was charged with participating in ten of them. Months later, state murder indictments carrying the death penalty were brought against Whitey, Flemmi, and John Martorano in Tulsa and Miami for the killings of Roger Wheeler and John Callahan. The small band of state police and DEA investigators, working with prosecutors Wyshak and Kelly, had found the bodies and cut controversial deals to build a staggering case against the two informants who had almost gotten away with murder. The idea propagated by Whitey's apologists that he was simply the biggest bookie and loanshark in Southie was officially dashed. All that was left was to find him and hold him to account.

John Connolly's fall from grace was swift and stunning. A jury sitting in Boston found the testimony of Connolly's corrupt supervisor John Morris and Whitey's grave digger Kevin Weeks more credible than all the awards and honors the FBI had bestowed on Connolly, who never took the stand. As the verdict was read, he stood next to his wife, Liz, nineteen years his junior and a young FBI secretary when she began dating him. He was convicted of racketeering, obstruction of justice, and lying to an FBI agent. His only solace was that the jury had acquitted him of the most serious charges: leaking information that led Whitey and Flemmi to kill potential witnesses against them. Connolly was allowed to remain free until his sentencing, and a few hours after his conviction he sat down with his three sons, a twelve-year-old and eleven-year-old twins, to explain the verdict. He called it the worst night of his life.[20]

More than two hundred people wrote letters to Judge Joseph Tauro asking him to show mercy to Connolly. Some of them, like Joe Pistone of *Donnie Brasco* fame, and William Friedkin, the Hollywood director, were famous.[21] Most, however, were ordinary people who extolled Connolly's generosity and kindness. The mother of a man who had been beaten to death at an ice rink during an argument over a youth hockey game explained how Connolly had become almost a surrogate father to the dead man's boys; Connolly drove them to their hockey games and laced up their skates.[22] Other letters noted how Connolly, who had suffered from skin cancer, regularly donated blood and platelets, and how he raised money for charities in Southie and beyond.[23] Tauro was not much moved; he sentenced Connolly to ten years in prison. Connolly was stunned. He barely had enough time to hand his wedding ring to his wife before he was hustled off to prison, still insisting on his innocence. "I'm guilty of bad judgment, maybe, but I never intended to commit a crime," Connolly said after the verdict.[24] He had lost everything except his own illusions.

Sitting in solitary confinement at the maximum security prison in Walpole, south of Boston, Steve Flemmi felt he was out of options. He was sixty-nine years old, he was doing hard time, and his once-taut body was withering. He had been locked up for almost nine years. His friends had turned against him. His former FBI handler was in prison. And Whitey was off somewhere, flying in the wind. Flemmi finally swallowed his pride and caved. In October 2003, he pled guilty to ten murders and agreed to testify for the government. For that, he was spared the death penalty. He spilled details of the long years of FBI corruption, including evidence that soon had Connolly facing a murder charge in Miami for helping to get

John Callahan killed. Flemmi's words also led to charges against retired FBI agent Paul Rico in Oklahoma for plotting with Whitey, Flemmi, and John Martorano to kill Roger Wheeler. Rico, unrepentant to the end, would die a few months later while awaiting trial. He was seventy-eight.

Even as Connolly awaited his murder trial, questions lingered about the other agents who received money and gifts from Whitey. What about the supervisors, in Boston and Washington, who had looked past Whitey and Flemmi's crimes and rewarded Connolly with commendations and raises? Only Connolly had been called to account. John Durham, the special prosecutor, acknowledged those questions and promised to answer them with a final, full report. It was never produced, and no one in the FBI besides John Connolly ever faced charges for protecting Whitey Bulger.

While the world he had created imploded, one sensational revelation at a time, Whitey was nowhere to be found. As the new millennium dawned, he was in his seventies and looked like any other balding grandfather with fair skin and blue eyes. The FBI had seized his assets—his condo in Clearwater, Florida, his lottery winnings, his various bank accounts and safe deposit boxes—hoping to cut off his money supply. But they had no idea how much money he had stashed all over the country and the world. There had been sightings in many places, most of them bogus, but in November 2000 the focus was squarely on California as the FBI quadrupled its reward for his capture, from two hundred fifty thousand dollars to one million dollars. It made the announcement with great fanfare at press conferences in Boston, San Diego, and Los Angeles—saying it now believed the sighting of Whitey and Greig at the beauty salon in Fountain Valley earlier in the year was credible. There was another reported sighting of Whitey around the same time in Venice Beach, California, where he had vacationed with Teresa Stanley before his years on the run.[25] The FBI circulated

Wanted posters of Whitey and Greig along the Mexican border, speculating, quite correctly, that he might follow the well-worn path into Tijuana for cheap, readily available prescription drugs.

They were finally closing in and also trying, it seemed, to close the yawning gap of trust between them and other law enforcement agencies. At the same time that it quadrupled the reward money, the FBI announced that it was teaming up with the state police and the DEA to find Whitey. It was a symbolic truce, aimed at ending decades of bad blood and mistrust engendered by the FBI's association with Whitey. The move more than doubled the number of investigators assigned full-time to tracking him, from three to eight.[26] State police Major Thomas Foley, Sergeant Thomas Duffy, Sergeant Stephen Johnson, and DEA agent Dan Doherty—the same investigators who had been busy debriefing John Martorano and Kevin Weeks and digging up bodies—cautiously agreed to join a task force that included two FBI agents, a Boston police detective, and a correctional officer. The enlarged team was moved out of the FBI's Boston headquarters to spacious new quarters inside a building that houses the Coast Guard offices and overlooks Boston Harbor. It was neutral ground for the agencies that had clashed over the Whitey investigation, as well as a private and secure place to store sensitive files and interview people. Finally, it looked like tips would be shared, resources pooled, and grudges buried. But the best of intentions quickly collapsed in the face of old enmities and FBI high-handedness. Just before the new help was scheduled to arrive, the bureau, incredibly, slapped Foley, Duffy, and Johnson with subpoenas demanding their cell phone and work phone records. They were told they were targets of a Justice Department investigation into media leaks about the Whitey investigation, but they saw it as a poorly disguised attempt by the FBI to discover who their sources of information were. Stung, they refused to work with the FBI. It was an absurd situation that destroyed any chance of reconciliation or merging of the two manhunts. Several other state troopers and a DEA agent would later be added to the FBI-led task force, but it remained a strained partnership. Whitey was, as ever, the beneficiary of the divisions and the disarray.

He also indirectly benefited, at least initially, from the September 11, 2001, attacks on the United States by Al Qaeda. Two of the planes used in the 9/11 attacks had taken off from Boston's Logan International Airport, and every agent in the FBI's Boston office was assigned to the terrorism investigation. A couple of weeks later, the Bulger Task Force was the first team to go back to its regular duties, chasing what turned out to be another Whitey look-alike in South America. But the FBI, as an institution, was suddenly preoccupied with terrorism. While technically Whitey's status as a Top Ten fugitive meant he was a top priority, the post-9/11 reality meant that, outside the task force, he was not.

The FBI fielded some two thousand leads on Whitey in 2001— more than during any year since he had fled.[27] Many came from overseas. A balding, elderly man in Barcelona bore such a striking resemblance to Whitey that he could only be ruled out through fingerprints. It turned out he was a priest. Agents pursued another Whitey look-alike on a wild chase through the streets of Rio de Janeiro only to discover that he was a Portuguese national wanted for money laundering. In 2002, a British businessman called the FBI with the most promising tip since Greig had had her hair colored in the Fountain Valley salon. He said he had spotted Whitey Bulger strolling alone down a busy street near Piccadilly Circus in London. "He was freshly tanned," said the man, insisting he immediately recognized Whitey as the US tourist he had befriended in 1994 while working out at a health club inside Le Meridien Piccadilly hotel in London.[28] During that earlier visit, the man said, he had sat at the hotel bar with Whitey, eating a sandwich and drinking a beer as the elderly American talked about his life—including his stint at Alcatraz.[29] The Bulger Task Force was convinced the tip was credible because Stanley had previously told agents that she had stayed at Le Meridien Piccadilly with Whitey during their whirlwind trip through Europe months before he became a fugitive.[30] Stanley had also revealed years earlier that Whitey had a safe deposit box at a London bank, but the FBI had been unable to find it even after dispatching an agent overseas. The Whitey sighting brought new intensity to the search, and inspectors from New Scotland Yard located the safe deposit box. They also made the startling discovery that when Whitey opened the box in 1992, he listed his brother Bill, then the Massachusetts senate president, as the contact person on bank records.[31] When the London bank relocated its offices to another building while Whitey was on the run, a bank official called Bill Bulger's South Boston home to report that the box was being moved. The unidentified person who took the 1997 call advised the bank that James Bulger could not be located. Later, Bill Bulger told a congressional committee that neither he nor anyone in his family recalled getting the call. The safe deposit box contained fifty thousand dollars in assorted currency. The FBI located more safe deposit boxes belonging to Whitey in London, Dublin, and Montreal and launched a media campaign overseas, trying to elevate his profile in Europe. The task force appeared on the BBC show *Crimewatch UK* to appeal for the public's help, but after pursuing fewer than a third of the one hundred leads viewers called in after the show, the Boston investigators returned home. Whitey had taken a backseat because British authorities who had been working with the Bulger Task Force were diverted to more urgent cases: apartment raids of suspected terrorists, homemade bombs in a flat near Gatwick Airport, and a scare involving the deadly poison ricin.[32] And for all the promise of the original tip from the British businessman, the trail there was ice cold. Whitey had not returned to London since he'd gone on the run. In fact, he later confessed that, after that European swing with Stanley, he only left the country for his brief forays into Mexico to buy cheap prescription drugs.

The devastation Whitey had left behind in his hometown wasn't limited to his criminal conspirators and his corrupted friends in law enforcement but enveloped those closest to him. His family and friends took the heat for his absence. Loyalty came at a cost, especially to Whitey's brothers. Not long after Whitey took off, federal grand juries were convened to force those who knew him best to cooperate in the probe. The Bulger Task Force traced calling cards to Whitey and Greig and identified dozens of homes and businesses they had called in the Boston area in the summer of 1996, when the gangster was scrambling to obtain new identities. The two people closest to Greig—her twin sister, Margaret McCusker, and her loyal friend Kathleen McDonough—were convicted of lying about phone calls they received from Greig. They were sentenced to six months of house arrest, followed by probation, and each fined two thousand dollars.[33] McCusker, who had been reluctantly caring for Greig's beloved French poodles, Nikki and Gigi, realized her sister wasn't coming back anytime soon. Being stuck in the house with the dogs steeled her resolve: She had them euthanized.[34] The FBI then cleverly announced on *America's Most Wanted* that the dogs had been put down, hoping it might trigger some slip-up by Greig. It almost worked. One of McCusker's neighbors received a frantic call from Greig in early 1999, pleading, "What happened to my dogs?" The frightened neighbor hung up without responding.[35]

The Bulger Task Force also put pen registers, or traces, on the telephones of Whitey's brothers, Bill and Jack, which allowed all numbers dialed from their South Boston homes to be tracked. But Flemmi's corrupt state police friend Dick Schneiderhan sent a message through Weeks alerting the Bulgers to the scrutiny.[36] What the government couldn't accomplish on its own, Whitey did unwittingly, by using phone cards to call his brothers, which put them in compromising positions. For someone who seemed so sophisticated at eluding surveillance, electronic and otherwise, Whitey's not knowing that the phone cards could be traced seems uncharacteristically naïve. But he admitted his ignorance, as well as his regret that so many got in legal trouble because of his calls home.[37] "I put the heat on people" by phoning Boston, Whitey acknowledged. "My brother Jack was trapped." The same thing happened to Greig's sister and her friend, who were indicted, leading Whitey to stop calling friends and family.[38]

Bill Bulger paid an especially heavy price for his devotion to his older brother, both in reputation and position. He was well into a new phase of his career, having stepped down as president of the state senate at the beginning of 1996 to assume the presidency of the University of Massachusetts, when he was summoned before the federal grand jury looking into Whitey's disappearance. He admitted during the secret proceeding that he had spoken to his brother while he was on the run, and that he felt no obligation to help in his capture. Bill Bulger, his wife, and their children had been repeatedly questioned over the years about Whitey's whereabouts, and they had always insisted that they knew nothing. His new testimony, revealed in 2003 in the pages of the *Boston Globe*, triggered a political firestorm. The Massachusetts attorney general accused him of putting his fugitive brother's interests over those of the state's higher education system and called for his resignation. Bulger refused to step down. "Changing the course of my brother's life is something I tried to effectuate for many years—that I was not successful is a matter of great personal pain," he said. "I have done everything one could possibly do to influence the course of another person's life."[39]

But it was his appearance in Washington before the House Committee on Government Reform, which was investigating the FBI's relationship with Whitey, Flemmi, and other informants, that sealed Bill Bulger's fate, ending his public life. He was humiliated and, at one point, unusually for him, speechless. When first called before the committee in December 2002, he refused to testify, citing his Fifth Amendment right against self-incrimination. He looked like he was hiding something, but he wasn't about to give it up. The committee granted him immunity, and six months later Bill Bulger sat in front of his wife, Mary, and five of their nine children, staring at a table of congressmen. It was an inquisition that lasted for five hours. Always so comfortable, even cocksure, in public, Bulger looked anything but. He was evasive, sometimes annoyed. Some of the congressmen were equally irked that Bulger, a man of self-conscious learning who could recite long passages of the classics from memory, kept saying he didn't remember. One of them wondered aloud why Bulger needed immunity to say he didn't remember anything. Congressman Stephen Lynch of South Boston, who, before coming to Washington, had held Bulger's former state senate seat, might have been expected to be gentle with Bulger, but he was not. When Lynch asked Bulger if he had ever accepted money from Whitey or his criminal associates, Mary Bulger and two of her sons looked at each other in horror and then shook their heads in disgust. Bill Bulger merely said, "No." When another congressman asked if he wanted his fugitive brother to give himself up, the normally loquacious Bulger sat for several moments, unable to speak. He opened and closed his mouth several times, but nothing came out. The hearing was televised live, and back in Boston people waited for what seemed an eternity for Bill Bulger to answer a simple question.

"Do I want him to?" Bill Bulger repeated, before adding, "I hope he does what is the right thing." But the right thing for him, he insisted, did not include aiding in the capture of his brother. That answer gave Bulger's political enemies what they finally needed. Massachusetts governor Mitt Romney accused him of giving purposely evasive answers and pushed for his resignation as university president. Bill Bulger still had powerful supporters—including US senator Edward M. Kennedy, who, in the years since their testy dealings during the school desegregation imbroglio, had grown to be a friend—but he nevertheless resigned in August 2003. He consoled himself by leaving with a state pension of about two hundred thousand dollars a year. The following month, on Whitey's seventy-fourth birthday, September 3, 2003, Jack Bulger was sentenced to six months in prison and six months of house arrest for lying to two grand juries and thwarting efforts to catch his brother. He was stripped of his pension as the clerk magistrate of Boston Juvenile

Court. Loyalty to Whitey had cost him his freedom and his income, and it cost Bill Bulger his job and, in the eyes of many, his good name. It was an outsize price to pay for a principle—family above all, including the law.

Bill Bulger's forced retirement from the public arena signaled an end to an extraordinary political career and to his extraordinary patronage network. Many friends, relatives, and constituents had landed in government jobs over four decades because of Bill Bulger. There were bus drivers and train operators who owed their job to him. The running joke was that MBTA, the acronym for the Massachusetts Bay Transportation Authority, stood for Mr. Bulger's Transit Authority. But the benign view of political patronage, not to mention the iron-fisted approach he brought to leadership, left with him.

Whitey's abrupt exit, meanwhile, had altered the underworld landscape, especially in Southie. An East Broadway tavern owner recalls that a fringe player in Whitey's organization showed up at his newly opened bar shortly after Whitey fled, demanding payment for protection. The tavern owner, an Irish immigrant, told the would-be extortionist to get lost.[40] Whitey was gone, as was the specter of his power. The Mafia, wrecked by the long series of prosecutions, was a shell by the 1990s. At the dawn of a new millennium, a few dozen Mafiosi struggled to make a living off sports gambling, while the Irish mob had disappeared entirely.[41] New ethnic groups, from Dominicans to Cape Verdeans, occupied the lower rungs that the Irish and Italians had clung to a century before. They changed the texture of the city, and their gangs became the major focus of law enforcement.

The ethnic neighborhoods that had been home to the most prominent of the city's organized crime groups—the Irish in Southie and Charlestown, the Italians in the North End—were gentrified throughout the 1980s and especially the 1990s. Young professionals took over the North End apartments that had been homes to successive generations of immigrants. In Charlestown, the native-

born Townies took to calling the new arrivals in their neighborhood "Toonies," an irreverent reference to the natives' penchant for
stealing high-end stereos from the BMWs and Saabs that suddenly
flooded the narrow, hilly streets.

Southie was the last of those ethnic neighborhoods to be truly
gentrified. Throughout the 1990s, its signature three-deckers were
converted into condominiums. By 1999, condos accounted for 66
percent of all residential sales in Southie, triple the citywide average.[42] Many of those condos were bought by people who didn't grow
up in Southie and replaced apartments occupied by those who did.
Along Broadway, the dark, dingy taverns where bookies sat at the
bar all day and night were replaced by bright, airy bar-restaurants
with exposed brick walls and French doors that showcased the
young, trendy crowd. Even Triple O's, Whitey's old hangout, was
transformed into an upscale bar; the images of the Seven Dwarfs on
the walls were painted over. If people wanted to gamble, they did so
legally. The bookies were gone, replaced by state lottery machines.

But it wasn't just Southie that was changing. The city of Boston, with a population of 589,000, became majority minority in the
1990s, with nonwhites outnumbering whites for the first time. In
that decade, nearly 50,000 whites left the city, replaced by an equal
number of immigrants.[43] More minorities moved into Southie, especially after the housing projects, including the one in which Whitey
had grown up, were integrated beginning in the late 1980s. Southie
was 98 percent white in 1970; by 2000 it was 84 percent white, and
by 2010 it was 79 percent white.[44] The Southie that Whitey had left
behind looked very different ten years after he'd fled.

It was a glum affair, the tenth anniversary of Whitey's life on the
run in December 2004, marked by the FBI with a press conference detailing the efforts of investigators, showcasing belongings
of Whitey they had seized, and pledging their continuing com-
mitment to find him. They showed off the silver skull ring Whitey

had worn, the coin collection, knives, and Irish passport that were seized from his girlfriends' homes and safe deposit boxes around the world. They had the travel books, Alcatraz memorabilia, and a journal he had left behind, but the actual news of the day was considerably less impressive: The last credible sighting of Whitey, the agents conceded, was in London in 2002. Task force maps and charts detailed a log of Whitey's travels during his first couple of years on the run, before the trail went cold. In the past year alone, they had pursued leads on five continents—in Australia, Singapore, Thailand, South Africa, Mexico, and Canada—and in nearly every state. Agents visited an Irish pub in Cambodia and resort towns in Uruguay. They had launched Internet and billboard campaigns. At the US Attorney's insistence, the state police and the DEA abandoned their own manhunt and assigned investigators to the FBI-led task force. FBI agents were rotated in from around the country for stints on the task force. But the all-points frenzy of the pursuit did little to dampen the perception that the FBI wasn't really looking very hard. "All of us on the task force believed that we could catch this guy and we would catch this guy," said William Chase, who oversaw the task force as assistant special agent in charge of the FBI's Boston office from 1998 to 2003. In fact, he said that the FBI believed it was imperative that Whitey be caught—to restore public confidence in the bureau. "If we caught him, that would lift some of the suspicion the office was under."

Task force investigators complained that they were in a no-win situation: They were criticized for chasing tips to popular resort destinations—more a golf vacation than a fugitive hunt, some charged—yet there was the constant fear that if they didn't follow every lead they could miss the real one.

Some leads, however, were, unaccountably, not pursued. In 2008, a Las Vegas man called *America's Most Wanted* saying he had spotted Whitey on the Santa Monica Pier talking about Boston with a young passerby who was wearing a Celtics shirt. The man's tip, name, and number were passed along to the FBI, but he never got a call.[45] That same year, off-duty Santa Monica police sergeant Gary Steiner overheard a man trying to sell a gun with an obliterated serial number at a gun shop in Newhall, California. When the store clerk said the weapon was illegal and urged him to turn it over to police, the man said he was afraid to do that because it belonged to a relative who had once been Whitey Bulger's bodyguard. Steiner called the sheriff's office and held the man until a deputy arrived and seized the gun, and then he alerted the FBI. But he said that the FBI never pursued the tip; nor did the sheriff's department.[46] Another off-duty officer also complained that the FBI failed to aggressively investigate his tip after he reported seeing Whitey at the premiere of *The Departed* in San Diego in 2006.[47] The movie was set in Boston, and Jack Nicholson portrayed a character modeled loosely on Whitey. The officer trailed the elderly man from the theater but lost him when he boarded a trolley. By contrast, the reaction was electric when a DEA agent on vacation in the Sicilian resort of Taormina shot a video in April 2007 of a couple he suspected was Whitey and Greig. He did not confront the couple and instead returned home and turned the video over to agents from the Bulger Task Force, who jumped on a plane and combed hotels, marinas, bars, and ferries in Sicily, to no avail. The FBI posted the video on its website and publicized the hunt for Whitey on television in Europe. After FBI agents appeared on a German crime-watch show, a viewer identified the couple strolling through Taormina as his parents, a German couple.

On September 3, 2008, as Whitey celebrated his seventy-ninth birthday a free man, the FBI increased the reward for information leading to his capture from one to two million dollars—the largest the bureau had ever offered for a domestic fugitive.[48] After thirteen years of hunting him, they had no clue where he was, no idea at all that Whitey was living stateside in quiet comfort, hiding in plain view.

Two months later, sixty-eight-year-old John Connolly shuffled into a Miami courthouse, shackled, handcuffed, and wearing a red prison jumpsuit. It was a routine he had followed for the eight weeks that his trial for the murder of John Callahan had dragged on. His old friend Franny Joyce, Bill Bulger's former senate aide, stood outside the courtroom and handed the court officers a hanger with a fresh change of clothes. Minutes later Connolly emerged through a side door and walked to the defendant's table. His finely tailored Armani suits were gone, replaced by a modest dark suit coat and tan pants. His jet-black hair had reverted to prison gray. His complexion was pallid, the product of more than three years in solitary confinement awaiting trial. When the jurors walked in to deliver their verdict, Connolly searched their faces, but they kept their eyes averted, and he had been in enough courtrooms to know what that meant. "Guilty of murder in the second degree," Judge Stanford Blake said.

John Connolly stared straight ahead, knowing that the judge's words meant he could die in prison. A jury in Miami was willing to accept what a jury in Boston would not: that he had helped Whitey kill a prospective witness. The key difference was that this time Flemmi was part of the prosecution, blandly describing Connolly as a virtual member of their gang. Whitey and Flemmi had given Connolly $235,000 over the years, he testified, and the agent had to know he had, in effect, given them a license to kill. "When you give us information on one person and they got killed, when you give us information on a second person and they get killed, when you give us information on a third person and they got killed," said Flemmi, before pausing, "I mean, he's an FBI agent. He's not stupid." After the jury and judge left the room following the verdict, Connolly stood with his brother, a retired DEA agent, his sister, a retired Boston schoolteacher, and Franny Joyce. "I'm gonna fight on," he told them. "What can I do?"[49]

A few hours after Connolly was convicted, Fred Wyshak, the prosecutor, DEA agent Dan Doherty, and state police lieutenant Steve Johnson sat at a patio table on a sidewalk outside a faux Irish bar on South Beach, nursing beers. It was supposed to be a celebration, but the mood was subdued. Connolly was finished. But nothing had happened to the other FBI agents and supervisors who had winked and nodded and patted him on the back, and who had taken gifts from Whitey. The statute of limitations had run out on all of them. Worst of all, Whitey was still out there. "He's probably in a place just like this," Steve Johnson said, gazing toward the darkened beach across Ocean Drive.[50]

As usual, Steve Johnson was right.

15

St. Monica's West

In the fall of 1996, after nearly two hectic years on the road, Whitey and Cathy Greig were looking to settle down. They had zigzagged the country by car and train, with long stops in Louisiana and short visits to Texas, Arizona, and Wyoming, among other states. The weather in Southern California had drawn Whitey before, and now he was looking to stay. Indeed, as Whitey and Greig strolled along Palisades Park in Santa Monica, a hip, affluent beachfront city surrounded on three sides by Los Angeles, they thought they had found the perfect place. All they needed was the perfect cover.

The park stretches for blocks along a sandstone bluff overlooking the Pacific Ocean, offering panoramic views of rolling surf, sandy beach, sunsets, and the glittering Santa Monica Pier. Its breathtaking vistas, walking paths, rose garden, and shuffleboard courts, shaded by towering palm trees, make it a popular destination for visitors and locals. Amid the moneyed tourists and the modest strollers, the homeless and the alcoholic, the mentally ill and the drug-addled also meandered, asking for change, talking to themselves, passing time. Most people averted their eyes, trying not to draw the attention of the scruffiest characters on the walkway above the crashing waves.

Not Whitey Bulger. He was trying to meet the people everyone else was trying to avoid. He had a business proposition to discuss.

Charlie Gaska was homeless and suffering from severe mental health problems when Whitey approached him. At first, Gaska wanted nothing to do with him and waved him off. But Whitey was persistent, saying he could make it worth his while; all Gaska had to do was let him use his Social Security number. Whitey wore Gaska down and, not long after he pocketed the other man's identification, he and Greig were standing in the manager's office at the Princess Eugenia apartment complex on Third Street, just a couple of blocks from Palisades Park.[1] Whitey peeled off hundred-dollar bills to put a deposit down on Apartment 303, a two-bedroom with a balcony. They filled out a few forms, signing their new names: Charles and Carol Gasko. Whitey had changed one letter in Gaska's name, a variation so subtle it would not arouse suspicion.

As a boy, Whitey had ignored his mother's entreaties to spend his free time at St. Monica's, the church just down the street from the family home on Southie's Logan Way. Jean Bulger was convinced that her rambunctious son would settle down if he would, like his brother Bill, let Father Dwyer, the parish priest at St. Monica's, work his magic. There was some irony, then, in the fact that Whitey thought he'd found safe haven in the California city named for Monica, the patron saint of difficult children. The city had everything he wanted: the sun, the ocean, and the anonymity of living in a vibrant place that attracts transients and vacationers. Their distinct Boston accents drew little attention. Being from somewhere else meant little here. The assumption was you had come for the same reasons as everybody else.

Whitey and Greig hadn't believed their luck when they'd first spotted the "apartment for rent" sign posted outside the Princess Eugenia complex, a modest white three-story building at 1012 Third Street. It was a nice place, reasonably priced, and, best of all, rent-controlled. There were twenty-seven units in all, with balconies framed with green wrought iron, affording a view of palm trees and the elegant Mediterranean hotel across the street. The vacant apartment was just two blocks from the beach and a short walk to one of America's most famous landmarks, the Santa Monica Pier. The only drawback, in Greig's eyes, was that the Princess Eugenia did not allow pets. She had been infatuated with animals and had even groomed dogs as a hobby, but she would have to adapt.

Tenant screening was nonexistent at the Princess Eugenia. The Gaskos were not required to sign a lease, show a driver's license, submit to a credit check, or provide references.[2] Santa Monica required no income verification for rent-controlled apartments. Not only did Whitey and Greig face little scrutiny, but they were assured that their rent would increase only slightly every year—staying well below market rates. They said that they didn't own a car and had no need for a reserved parking space in the basement of the complex. But they said that they would store some of their belongings in a storage space in the garage. They moved into Apartment 303 in late 1996,[3] with rent starting at just $837 a month for their two-bedroom, two-bath unit.[4] The complex, once home mostly to art scholars at the J. Paul Getty Museum, now drew a mix of retirees and young professionals. Whitey's apartment came furnished with the modest, functional pieces the Getty had supplied for the student tenants, who had then left them behind.

It was no coincidence that the fugitive couple had surfaced on Third Street. Four years earlier, Whitey's niece Mary, one of Bill's daughters, had lived in a small apartment building at 2805 Third Street, just two miles from the Princess Eugenia. Greig let slip to a neighbor that "she had a niece in Santa Monica," said Birgitta Farinelli, a Swedish immigrant who was one of the property managers at the Princess Eugenia. "That's why they came over."[5] Bill's daughter had moved back to South Boston by the time Whitey moved to Santa Monica. Whitey had also visited Santa Monica when he and Teresa Stanley traveled to Venice Beach in 1994, as he scouted places to retire.[6]

Santa Monica is a place where some people go to reinvent themselves, and that's exactly what Whitey and Greig set out to do. They became known as just another pair of amiable retirees who loved animals and were known for stopping to pet dogs and cats during their daily walks through the neighborhood. Fox's *America's Most Wanted* would devote sixteen segments to the worldwide hunt for Whitey, all in vain, for he had morphed into the grandfatherly Charlie Gasko and nobody recognized him—not even some of his neighbors who had relocated from Boston and knew Whitey Bulger by name and repute. "We were looking for a gangster and that was part of the problem," said Charles "Chip" Fleming, a retired Boston police detective who spent six years assigned to the FBI-led task force that worked full-time trying to track Whitey. "He wasn't a gangster anymore." He was, in fact, mostly a shut-in, someone who spent an inordinate amount of time watching television. He had his favorite shows, including the one that aired all those episodes dedicated to snaring him: He watched *America's Most Wanted* religiously. He was also a fan of *Brotherhood*, a drama series about two brothers—one a gangster, the other a politician—that was inspired by Whitey and Bill Bulger. Whitey had reservations about the character based on him. "Violent guy!" he remarked to a friend.[7]

Charlie and Carol were model tenants. They were fastidious and quiet, and they treated neighbors with almost excessive kindness. They paid the rent early and always in cash, but the property managers never questioned it because some other tenants did the same. Every month, about a week before the rent was due, Greig would walk across the street to the property manager's office at the Embassy Hotel Apartments, an elegant old hotel owned by the same landlord. Birgitta Farinelli would take the white envelope stuffed with crisp hundred-bills from Greig and joke, "Carol, did you rob the bank again?"[8] The two would laugh. Greig usually fibbed that she withdrew the money from the bank while running errands. The cash proved too tempting for one former property manager, who pocketed Whitey and Greig's rent payment a couple of times.[9] The theft was exposed, but instead of switching to checks, the Gaskos insisted on leaving their monthly cash payment with the trustworthy Farinelli, who was the same age as Greig. Greig often brought a small gift for her: a box of chocolates, a scarf, blueberries. The two women chatted about the best place to get a haircut or manicure or to shop for a good bargain. "I can't tell you how incredibly nice these people were," Farinelli said. "They were very low-maintenance. These people never complained."

But if the Gaskos acquired a reputation for being thoughtful neighbors and pleasant company, they were also intensely private. They told some neighbors that they were from Chicago and others, who recognized their accents, that they were originally from Boston. They said that they came for the warm weather and didn't have any friends or family in the area—a plausible explanation for why nobody ever came to visit. When Whitey and Greig moved into the Princess Eugenia, all of the apartments had a house phone, which was an extension line connected to the main hotel across the street. Tenants were billed for calls made, but Whitey and Greig never used their phone. One day, Farinelli knocked on their door and told them that the old system was being disconnected and that tenants needed to get their own phones. "Oh, we don't need a phone. Charlie doesn't want any phones in here," Greig said, as Whitey stood by her side. "We don't have any family or friends to call. No one is going to call us."[10] Farinelli laughed, thinking it was a joke. A few days later Greig dropped by to give her the number of her new cell phone. Buying it fulfilled an obligation to their landlord without the need for a listed phone number.

Whitey was wary, consumed with avoiding capture and expert at spotting a tail. The formerly clean-shaven gangster, now in his late sixties, sported a white beard and mustache. When he ventured outside, he wore large, old-fashioned eyeglasses and a fisherman-type canvas hat with the brim pulled low over his face. Greig, in her mid-forties, seemed more interested in appearing attractive than she did in disguising herself. Whitey seemed partial to blondes, so Greig, who had been lightening her naturally dark blonde hair for years, continued the ritual of buying her own dye and having a hairdresser color her hair, even though the FBI had publicized her habit of doing so. She remained particular about her appearance, never leaving the apartment without make-up, lightly and expertly applied. She ironed their clothes, even their blue jeans. The couple dressed casually but impeccably, generally both in jeans or light-colored slacks and white long-sleeved shirts layered over a t-shirt. Greig often wore all white—a white blouse, white pants, white sun hat.

But if Whitey had methodically abandoned everything connecting him with his old life, there was one thing he refused to give up: his stockpile of weapons. He had collected some thirty shotguns, rifles, pistols, and revolvers, taking advantage of lax gun laws in Nevada to buy some of them at a gun show in Las Vegas while on the run.[11] The firepower was enough to arm a small platoon and more than he would ever need if cornered, but guns had always fascinated him, and he felt more comfortable with an arsenal at hand. He considered his stockpiling of weapons a hobby. "It's recommended to have a hobby after one retires," he told a friend half-jokingly.[12]

He cut several holes in the walls of the apartment, including the walls of the bathroom next to his bedroom, a hallway, and the wet bar. He stuffed the guns, ammunition, and knives inside some and stacked neatly piled wads of cash totaling hundreds of thousands of dollars in others. He covered the gaping holes with mirrors and pictures. Whitey worried about his stash when minor earthquakes struck. All he could do was ride out the tremors and hope that the mirrors wouldn't shatter.[13] For day-to-day expenses, he kept a cash drawer in the kitchen, with neatly stacked rows of bills in denominations ranging from $1 to $100.

Mindful that he might not have time to reach his weapons and money if someone burst into his apartment unexpectedly, he kept a loaded handgun and a stack of crisp bills on a shelf next to his bed. He slept alone in the master bedroom, which had its own bathroom with a shower stall. The bedroom windows were covered with opaque plastic held in place with duct tape, over which hung black curtains. Whitey tucked several loaded guns behind books on a bookshelf. Greig slept in the guest bedroom, which was as bright as Whitey's room was dark. A white curtain over the single window allowed the sunshine to pour into the room.

Whitey maintained his fitness regimen by working out on exercise equipment inside the apartment. He had a martial arts dummy, shaped like a man's torso, and when he wasn't using it for sparring, he tossed a fedora on it and placed it in front of the window overlooking the street. It created the illusion from the street that someone was home, peering out.[14]

The balcony of the couple's third-floor apartment overlooked palm tree–lined Third Street. Unlike other tenants who sometimes relaxed on their balconies, Whitey and Greig barely used theirs. They had no patio furniture. Greig sometimes ventured onto the balcony to put seed in a bird feeder or to dust the wrought iron railings. For Whitey it served more as a lookout post. At night, he often stood there with binoculars, canvassing the neighborhood for any sign that he was being watched.[15] Sometimes he'd peer into the windows of the hotel across the street. "I told the maids to be careful when they were cleaning because the little old man across the street was spying on them," said Enrique Sanchez, the building's longtime maintenance supervisor.[16]

Using her Carol Gasko alias, Greig subscribed to the *Los Angeles Times* and got Whitey a subscription to *Soldier of Fortune* magazine, which is geared to those interested in weapons and military tactics. An avid reader, Whitey had a collection of several hundred books, many about military history, war, and organized crime. Among the volumes were *Escape from Alcatraz*, *One Bullet Away*, *Turn Around and Run Like Hell*, *The Master of Disguise*, and *American Mafia*. Some, like *Secrets of a Back-Alley ID Man*, offered practical advice for the fugitive gangster on topics such as how to forge identification documents.

Whitey used his newly acquired skills to create business cards for Greig under various fictional names. When his former underworld associates back in Boston published books, detailing their exploits with Whitey, he added them to his collection, though he considered them distorted accounts written only to make money.[17] He was especially angry after reading *Street Soldier*, by Ed MacKenzie, a Southie con man whose wildly embellished tale portrayed him as one of Whitey's enforcers. Whitey maintained that he had only had two conversations with MacKenzie, one after he ordered him to return Hummel statues MacKenzie had stolen from an old woman's house. MacKenzie's version of that story has him robbing a gangster's house.[18]

Aside from the unusually well-stocked library of books about the Boston underworld, there were few clues in the apartment to the true identity of the couple who lived there. It was, in most respects, a deeply ordinary place, though a visitor might find it odd how little the couple had done to make it their own. Mirrors and framed prints of works by famous artists decorated the walls, but they were the same ones there when the fugitives moved in.[19] There were no pictures of the two of them or of any friends or relatives. Instead, the animal lovers kept photos of dogs and cats, including Nikki and Gigi, the two French poodles Greig had left behind with her sister in Southie. In his bedroom, Whitey tacked up a map of the world on the wall and propped a framed print of the American flag on top of a bookshelf, emblazoned with the words "God Bless America." A decorative pillow in his bedroom read, "Give a man an inch and he thinks he's a ruler." The apartment décor was similarly austere, with wall-to-wall gray carpet in most of the rooms, an oversized blue chair in the living room, and a green couch. Only a few people who lived or worked in the building were ever invited inside the apartment, and those visits were brief and rare. On one occasion Farinelli visited, she said, "Oh my goodness, it's so dark in here."[20] "He kind of likes to rest and have the television on," said Greig, gesturing toward Whitey, who appeared to be dozing in the blue chair in the middle of the afternoon. Whitey typically stayed up into the early morning hours watching TV and rarely ventured out during the day. Greig covered for him by telling neighbors that her husband had emphysema and only went out mornings and evenings, when there was less smog. "Charlie's sleeping. He can't breathe," Greig would say sweetly if anyone dropped by asking for him. "Don't bother him."[21]

Mostly, Whitey and Greig's life centered on the mundane, and the distribution of labor between them was decidedly old-school. Greig kept a weekly planner, listing doctors' appointments, department store sales, and when it was time to change the sheets on their beds. She kept the apartment spotless and did all of the household chores. Whitey accompanied her to the basement laundry room, standing protectively by her side as she moved their clothes from the washer to the dryer, then helping her carry the laundry upstairs. When Enrique Sanchez, the maintenance supervisor, walked into the laundry room one day, Greig couldn't resist a dig at Whitey's old-fashioned views on the division of domestic labor. "Enrique, why don't you teach him how to do laundry?" Greig joked. "I don't want to learn how to do that," Whitey shot back. "That's why I have you."[22]

Greig ran all the couple's errands, and she paid their utility bills with money orders. They lived off the cash Whitey had hidden in the walls of their apartment. Knowing it might have to last for many years, they were frugal.[23] Greig shopped for bargains at the 99 Cents store and T.J. Maxx. She used coupons and bought household items like mouthwash and detergent in bulk. She made some purchases through mail catalogues, including the Vermont Country Store, which sells flannel nightgowns and New England jellies. She bought castile soap by the case from a Kentucky company and ordered Whitey's $103 New Balance sneakers from Road Runner Sports. Twice a week, she shopped at the farmers' market at the Third Street Promenade, pulling a metal cart down the street filled with her purchases and munching on dried apricots and nectarines she bought at one of the stands. Whitey had made millions in his years as a mobster, but now they lived on a fixed income like most other retirees. This was doubtless a matter of strategy—flamboyant spending would only attract curiosity—but also a by-product of Greig's simple tastes. The fugitives even joined the American Association of Retired Persons, through which they received the AARP magazine and, more importantly, senior discounts.

Occasionally, however, they did splurge, dining at Michael's, a high-end restaurant two blocks from their apartment. They always asked to be seated at Table 23, nestled in a quiet corner of the restaurant's outdoor courtyard, with trees and bushes behind it.[24] Besides being intimate, the table afforded a view of the whole courtyard, allowing Whitey to keep an eye on everything. They always paid in cash and left a 20 percent tip—just enough to seem considerate, not so much as to stand out. The month Whitey turned eighty—September 2009—he and Greig ate well at Michael's, enjoying a foie gras appetizer, lobster out of the shell, a ten-ounce dry-aged New York strip steak with pommes frites, and Grey Goose cocktails and Patz & Hall chardonnay.[25]

Initially, Whitey and Greig kept such an extraordinarily low profile that neighbors sometimes wouldn't see them for days or even weeks. But as the years went by and the fugitives became more comfortable, they settled into a familiar routine and became more visible. They took long walks together twice a day, around 6:30 a.m. and before sunset. They canvassed the neighborhood, strolling to Santa Monica pier, Palisades Park, or past the upscale shops on Montana Avenue, where it was not unusual to spot celebrities. At Palisades Park, they had a favorite bench, a peaceful spot where they sat with their backs to the ocean, overlooking the Rose Garden.[26] Often they headed to the Third Street Promenade, wandering the outdoor mall's designer clothing stores, high-end gift shops, gourmet restaurants, and top-shelf bars. Street performers danced and sang; fortune-tellers enticed passersby. Whitey and Greig liked to sit on the benches, people watching. They seemed unconcerned about surveillance cameras or that they had made their home just four miles from the Los Angeles office of the FBI. They were hiding in plain sight, and it was working.

Some neighbors considered the Gaskos a "darling" retired couple; the two were sometimes seen holding hands during their daily walks. But a few women who knew them said that they rarely showed affection, and that Charlie seemed controlling and unappreciative of his wife. "I never thought he treated her so well," said Barbara Gluck, a photographer who lived down the hall from the Gaskos and knew them for more than ten years. "I thought she was a very kind person. . . . She was young and she looked very pretty. He was old and grizzled. I kept thinking to myself, 'What are they doing together?'" But for Greig the Santa Monica years were more like a dream, long-deferred, now come true. After years of having to share Whitey with Teresa Stanley, she relished her role as sole caretaker. She was devoted to him, according to neighbors, almost to an extreme. Janus Goodwin, a minister who lived three doors down from the Gaskos, said that when she talked to her in the hallway, Greig would frequently end their conversations abruptly to rush back to Whitey "like he was God."[27] Greig would often smile broadly and say in an exaggerated voice: "Someone needs me. I'm needed!"

If Cathy Greig handled most of the household chores, Whitey took charge of a key task: making sure they didn't get caught. He was obsessed with always having a stock of working aliases in hand. He had had to scramble after Teresa Stanley told the FBI about the Tom Baxter alias in 1996, and he wasn't going to get caught short again. Once in Santa Monica, he and Greig began assembling an array of phony names and IDs. Their daily walks had a utilitarian purpose beyond exercise and neighborly appearances. They trolled Venice Beach and the oceanfront walk in Santa Monica, where the homeless gathered. They bought driver's licenses, Social Security numbers, and other identification documents from at least a half-dozen alcoholics, drug addicts, and mentally ill people who willingly sold them for cash. They reserved the Gasko name for people they met in their Santa Monica neighborhood but used other aliases when visiting doctors and dentists or when making trips across town or even out of state—a strategy aimed at preventing anyone from tracking them to their apartment.

One day they were walking in Palisades Park, just a few blocks from their apartment, when Whitey noticed a man sitting alone on a bench who looked perfect for a proposition he had in mind.[28] James William Lawlor, as he introduced himself, was well dressed, but Whitey sensed vulnerability. Most important, Lawlor looked an awful lot like Whitey: the same white beard, the same balding head, the same ruddy complexion. Whitey sat down and struck up a conversation. Lawlor confided that he was originally from the Lower East Side of Manhattan, that he had lost his wife, and that he had no contact with his family. He didn't have to say he drank too much. Whitey knew that look well, and he saw it in his face.

He gave Lawlor some money, and he also gave him attention, which Lawlor seemed to appreciate just as much. The two men had some things in common. They both liked to read, and both were veterans. And they talked easily about their shared Irish heritage. Whitey especially admired the tattoo on Lawlor's right arm: "US Army Irish."[29] After several meetings and much talk, Whitey convinced Lawlor that he was an illegal immigrant from Canada and needed a driver's license to stay in the country and work. He paid Lawlor a thousand dollars for his California driver's license, Social Security number, and birth certificate.[30] He then opened a bank account in Lawlor's name and used it to make small purchases. When Whitey needed to drive, pick up a prescription, dip into a bank account, or register a car, he often went as James Lawlor.[31] There were some crucial differences between the two of them. Whitey was seven years older, but his clean living, and Lawlor's rough life, narrowed the gap. At 5 foot 4, Lawlor was five inches shorter than Whitey and considerably heavier. And his eyes were hazel. Whitey addressed these discrepancies in 2003 by getting the California Department of Motor Vehicles to issue James Lawlor a senior citizen's identification card by mail. It listed Lawlor's height as four inches taller than he actually was, put his weight at only 170 pounds, and gave him blue eyes.[32] In exchange for taking his new friend's identity, Whitey gave Lawlor another twenty-five hundred dollars and paid the rent on Lawlor's one-room apartment at the West End Hotel, a hostel on Sawtelle Boulevard in Los Angeles.

If Whitey exploited Lawlor's vulnerability, as he surely did, he also seemed to have had some real affection for him. He maintained regular contact, paying Lawlor's rent for ten years.[33] He also tried to get him to quit drinking, but Lawlor was lonely and insisted he could not. He had never gotten over the death of his ex-wife and kept her ashes in an urn in his room. On August 3, 2007, the seventy-year-old went to the front office to pay his rent with cash Whitey had given him. He mentioned that he was tired and planned to go to bed. Five days later, tenants noticed a foul odor emanating from his room. The motel manager found Lawlor dead on the floor. The Los Angeles coroner listed the cause of death as heart disease. No one claimed the body. His remains were buried at Riverside National Cemetery, about sixty miles east of Los Angeles. The urn was buried with him. After not hearing from Lawlor for some time, Whitey had Greig call the motel to check on him. Whitey was shaken by the news about his friend but continued to use his name.[34]

Whitey's attentiveness to Lawlor was, for him, an uncommon show of concern. He and Greig did not stay in touch with the other vulnerable people whose identities they bought, and they bought many. They were sitting on a bench in Palisades Park one day when Sidney Joe Terry walked by them. He was ten years younger than Whitey and, at 6 foot 1, considerably taller. But the two men resembled each other, and Whitey was desperate for more IDs. Terry, who had been abusing heroin and other drugs for years, looked desperate for money. Whitey made small talk with him and then made his pitch: two hundred dollars for his Nevada driver's license.[35] Terry was elated. He quickly made the exchange and offered to throw in his Social Security card and a Sam's Club membership card for another fifty dollars.

A woman with a history of mental illness was pulling a broken suitcase along Venice Beach when Whitey and Greig—a couple she would remember as having nice white teeth—came to her rescue. They took her to a nearby store and bought her a new suitcase that cost forty dollars. They told her that they were from Canada and were looking for identification documents they could use to stay in the United States. The woman handed over her Social Security card and another piece of identification in exchange for two hundred dollars.[36]

Workable ID was essential for one of the couple's occasional errands, the two-and-a-half-hour trip from Santa Monica to Mexico, where Whitey could buy medicine for his heart condition without a prescription.[37] He would drive to the border with Greig, park in one of the massive lots on the US side, and walk into Tijuana. He had several driver's licenses, including Lawlor's and Terry's, and used them one after another to pass through security; none of the people he was pretending to be passed border control so frequently as to attract notice. In Tijuana, he was able to purchase Atenolol, the drug he had been taking for years for chest pain and high blood pressure. Wanted posters for Whitey and Greig were circulated in English and Spanish at the Mexican border because there was speculation by the FBI—accurate, it turned out—that he traveled there to buy medicine. But no one ever spotted them; the border at Tijuana sees such steady traffic that the level of scrutiny for US citizens is low.

They were, however, likely on one of their Tijuana excursions when they stopped at the hair salon in Fountain Valley and Greig was recognized. After the FBI publicized the sighting, she stopped coloring her hair, reverting to gray. The couple saw no need to uproot themselves, however. Whitey, now facing nineteen murder charges and exposed as a longtime FBI informant, had no intention of reclaiming his old life—and, besides, he no longer bore much resemblance to the face on the FBI's Most Wanted posters. He and Greig may also have taken comfort in the fact that, after the 9/11 attacks, the FBI made terrorism—not aging fugitives—its top priority.

Not long after the beauty salon incident, the FBI became distracted by a series of Whitey sightings overseas. Still, Whitey and Greig never left the United States, except for their occasional day trips into Mexico. Soon after 9/11, they even stopped those, for fear of tightened border security.

All the same, after years of keeping people at arm's length, Whitey and Greig seemed to yearn for social contact. They set aside caution to take a trip to Las Vegas, where Whitey played the slots and won more than he lost. They had a close call when Whitey thought that he had spotted one of John Connolly's old friends, Joe Pistone, the retired FBI agent who became a legend by infiltrating the Mafia while working undercover as Donnie Brasco.[38] Nobody recognized Whitey and Greig, however, and they returned to Santa Monica feeling even more confident that nobody would. They had been living at the Princess Eugenia for about ten years when they began initiating more conversations, especially with newer, younger tenants. Greig also widened her circle by signing up for evening courses at a local high school, taking classes in everything from how to operate a computer to how to repair a toilet.[39] The couple began cultivating friendships with neighbors but remained selective, gravitating toward people who were too busy or polite to ask personal questions. Often they were notably generous with those they came to like. They bought a neighbor with lung disease a four-hundred-dollar air purifier. They gave Enrique Sanchez, the maintenance supervisor, some tools. They passed out flashlights to women in the neighborhood so they could walk home more safely at night.

Greig would sort through magazines and junk mail left on the floor in the lobby of the Princess Eugenia and deliver it outside the doors of other tenants' apartments. She fetched the newspaper for Catalina Schlank, an elderly woman who lived on the first floor, and occasionally tucked a mango or an orange into the plastic newspaper bag. When Schlank offered a copy of her house keys to Greig in case of an emergency, Greig declined after checking with Whitey, saying, "My husband doesn't want to be responsible."[40] They occasionally invited Janus Goodwin into their apartment. Goodwin eyed a couch so shabby that even the Salvation Army would have rejected it.[41] "They seemed very lonely," Goodwin said. "I think they were starving for company." The three would talk for up to an hour about movies, art, the weather, and local events, but Goodwin was never invited to sit down or offered anything to eat or drink. "It was almost like they were out of practice," Goodwin said of the couple's social skills.

Whitey grew obsessed with following local crime news. He regularly placed the free Santa Monica newspaper at the doorsteps of the tenants he befriended and cautioned them to read the police blotter on Fridays. When a homeless man began loitering on the front steps of the apartment building, he told him to leave or he would call police.[42] "We thought he was a paranoid guy telling us to watch out, be careful of crime," said a middle-aged man in the building. "We didn't know he had experience."[43] Whitey seemed especially drawn to some of the young people at the Princess Eugenia. Their busy lives interested him, and their safety became his concern. When a young single woman moved in, Whitey and Greig took her under their wing and Whitey offered self-defense advice.[44] He urged her to let him install locks on her apartment windows and warned her to put patio furniture on her first-floor balcony so "if anyone hopped your balcony you could hear them with the furniture and plants there." He cautioned her to walk on the side of Wilshire Boulevard that was better lit when heading home from the gym at night and advised her to hold her key in a way that would allow her to fend off an attacker. One night, the woman heard a knock and opened her door to find Whitey and Greig standing there. "You have to protect yourself," Whitey told the woman, handing her a large can of Mace. "Just flip it open and spray it in his face." Later, when she admitted she didn't carry it because it was too bulky, he produced a smaller can that fit in the palm of her hand. "He was very protective of me," she said.

Whitey and Greig rarely talked of their past, and when they did, not surprisingly, what they shared was largely invented. He claimed he was a military veteran who had fought in Korea. Hints of the real man sometimes filtered through. He confided to Enrique Sanchez that he carried a knife and that he used to have a violent streak. "I used to like weapons and I used to fight," Whitey told him. "I just thought that was because he was in the military," Sanchez said later.[45]

Joshua Bond, a tall, young Mississippian, was hired as a property manager at the Princess Eugenia in 2007 and moved into the apartment next door to the Gaskos. He had graduated from Boston University two years earlier and had a Boston decal on the back of his car. Despite having lived in Boston for four years, Bond had never heard of the legendary Whitey Bulger. Whitey, in any case, seemed unconcerned about the Boston connection. Bond, who played in a country band, stayed up late playing music as Whitey listened through the walls. Whitey started calling Bond "Tex," and one day he appeared at Bond's door. "I've heard you play," Whitey told him. Whitey handed him a box and urged him to open it. It was an expensive black Stetson cowboy hat. Whitey said he no longer wore it and thought that his young neighbor might like it. He showed up at Bond's door offering him a half-full bottle of Grand Marnier, saying a nephew and his wife hadn't finished it during a recent visit—a rare reference to family or house guests. Bond appreciated the gestures, though sometimes Whitey's attention seemed over-the-top. Whitey complained when Bond and his friends smoked cigarettes on the adjacent balcony. When Bond had friends over, Whitey sometimes eavesdropped and recounted their conversations to Bond, word for word, the next day.[46]

Bond grew especially uncomfortable after he noticed that the gifts Whitey kept giving him were often aimed at improving his personal appearance. Whitey gave him a brake light for his bike, an inducement to ride more. A curling bar to build his biceps. A squeezer to build his forearms. A crunch machine to work on his abdomen. A trimmer and a comb for his beard. "He told me I needed to take care of my beard better," Bond said.[47] It got a little creepy. Bond comforted himself by thinking that Charlie and Carol were "such a nice old couple,"[48] and then, once again, Charlie would veer over the line. One time, Bond failed to acknowledge a small gift left hanging on his doorknob in a plastic bag. "You didn't write me a thank-you note," an indignant Whitey complained when he confronted Bond a few days later.[49] Chastened, Bond went home and scribbled a gracious message on a piece of notebook paper: "I'm sorry. I couldn't ask for better neighbors. You guys feel like family." Whitey and Greig responded by presenting Bond with a box of stationery, and Whitey told him, "That was the sweetest thing we've ever gotten." Beyond that one sharp rebuke, Bond never saw evidence of Whitey's temper, infamous in Boston, all but invisible in Santa Monica. But he did get a sense of how jumpy Whitey was when he startled him once by approaching from behind on a bicycle. "Jesus fucking Christ!" Whitey screamed. "What the fuck, Josh. Don't sneak up on me like that." Whitey then quickly regained his composure, and Bond never gave it another thought, knowing how concerned the old man was about crime.

Just as in Grand Isle, Whitey and Greig charmed their Santa Monica neighbors with their demonstrative love of animals. During their daily strolls, they stopped just about anyone walking a dog, chatting amiably as they stroked the animal. "I love bull terriers," Whitey gushed the first time he spotted his neighbor Denise Walsh walking toward him on Third Street, led by her muscular white terrier with its distinctive egg-shaped head. Whitey played with the dog, confiding that as a boy he'd had a bull terrier that had lived to be twelve. "They're the sweetest dogs ever," said Whitey, complaining that the powerful breed had an undeserved bad reputation.

Greig in particular had a deep empathy for pets in pain or otherwise neglected. She was always rescuing cats that tumbled from balconies in the apartment complexes around their neighborhood and then making calls and knocking on doors to reunite them with their owners. When she spotted a fluffy white cat roaming the neighborhood with a tight pink harness partially imbedded in its fur, she brought the animal to a veterinarian and paid for its removal and for follow-up treatment. Then she put an ad in the local paper, appealing to "CAT LOVERS" to give the animal a home.[50] After an elderly man in the neighborhood died, his striped cat, Tiger, began hanging around the Princess Eugenia. "We would see her searching in the bushes for the cat," said a neighbor.[51] "The cat would not go near anybody else." At least twice a day, around 6:00 a.m. and again in the evening, Greig crouched on the sidewalk in front of her apartment building with tin cans of food or plastic bags filled with tuna and fed the abandoned tabby as Whitey, who also had a soft spot for strays, stood by protectively.[52] Whitey and Greig brought Tiger to the veterinarian by taxi when he was sick and kept a framed picture of the cat on the wall of their apartment. Their devotion caught the attention of many, but especially Anna Bjornsdottir, a former actress and beauty queen, who lived in the neighborhood for months at a time and sometimes stopped to chat with the Gaskos as they fed the tabby.[53]

"Isn't she nice?" Bjornsdottir said of Greig to a neighbor. The two women, whose faces had become well-known for very different reasons, bonded over the cat, becoming friends. Bjornsdottir had competed as Miss Iceland in the 1974 Miss Universe pageant, where she was voted Miss Congeniality by her fellow contestants. By 1980, she and her Icelandic rock musician husband had relocated to California and were living the glamorous life in Los Angeles. A profile of the couple in *People* magazine described her as "one of the world's most beautiful and successful models"; she had earned more than two thousand dollars a day for appearing in commercials for Vidal Sassoon and Noxzema—she was one of the blondes in the iconic "Take It Off" commercials. Shortening her name to Anna Bjorn, she had landed feature roles in several movies, among them *The Sword and the Sorcerer*, and guest-starred on television shows, including *Remington Steele* and *Fantasy Island*. She eventually divorced her husband, and over the years settled into a quiet life in Iceland, away from the spotlight, working as a graphic designer and yoga instructor. She married Halldor Gudmundsson, an Icelandic businessman, with whom she published a book about the exploits of Mosa, a cat they adopted after it survived weeks being lost in the mountains.

Sometime around 2000, the couple began staying in Santa Monica for several months each year, initially at the Embassy Hotel across the street from Whitey and Greig's apartment complex, then in another apartment a few blocks away. Bjornsdottir often walked by the Princess Eugenia and was impressed by how kind Greig was to Tiger. She was less impressed with Whitey, who launched into a tirade and berated her when she voiced admiration for the nation's first African American president, Barack Obama.[54] Whitey grew openly hostile one day when she suggested that Tiger was so ill that the most humane thing to do was to euthanize the cat. When Tiger died, Greig was heartbroken, and the cat's demise seemed to increase her concern for Whitey, who had recently turned eighty and was beginning to show his age. Greig fretted over her arthritis and Whitey's prostate and worried about paying their medical bills.[55] She subscribed to health magazines like *Prevention*, shopped for healthy foods, and put herself and Whitey on a reduced-sodium diet aimed at lowering their blood pressure.[56] He was not a very good patient. A dentist in Marina del Rey who treated him later noted in his file that he was "a high fear patient and hated needles."[57] Whitey joked that he was a "dental chicken from Chicago."[58]

Whitey's aversion to doctors was so strong, in fact, that he worried he might lose his temper with one them and get himself in trouble. But Greig helped him control himself, often playing goodwill ambassador while accompanying her cranky old boyfriend to dentist and doctor visits.[59] A doctor who treated Whitey (under the name Lawlor) at a Los Angeles clinic complained that he "had a temper and would push the nurses around."[60] Whitey complained about arthritis, but when the doctor suggested he get a cortisone shot, he bristled, admitting he was scared of needles. Greig calmed him down and smoothed things over with the medical staff. He introduced her as his wife. When asked why he traveled all the way to the Los Angeles clinic since there were many closer to his Santa Monica home, Whitey told the doctor, "You run a clean place. I like to come to you."

Greig, increasingly, tried not to leave Whitey alone for too long and told neighbors he was ailing, though he always appeared fit and alert during his daily walks. Every few weeks, Greig got her hair cut at the same salon on Wilshire Boulevard, The Haircutters, stopping on the way to pick up medication for Whitey at the pharmacy and groceries at Whole Foods supermarket. She confided to her hairdresser that her husband had a problem with his prostate and that she was concerned about his health. "She was very worried," Wendy Farnetti, her hairstylist, said.[61] The Carol Gasko that had her hair cut and lightened every two or three weeks had changed considerably over the years. She didn't color her hair. It was as if she were consciously changing her appearance.

Greig and Farnetti chatted easily during the haircuts. One day the talk turned to men. Farnetti mentioned an ex-boyfriend who was trying to talk her into joining him in Texas. "You're going to probably not like it," Greig told her, "because it's probably hot and, you know, you like California. And besides, I'd lose my hairdresser." Farnetti nodded. She knew that going back to her boyfriend would be a mistake. "I have the worst taste in men," Farnetti said. "I'm a bum magnet. If there's a bum in the room, I'll attract them by magnetic force." Greig laughed. "I really love the bad boys," she told Farnetti. "My husband was a really bad boy when I married him, but he's a lot more mellow now."[62]

Whitey's hard edge was on display, however, when he dipped into the books written about him by former associates. Some had dubbed him "King Rat," scorning his role as an informant. Some of the accounts cast him alternatively as a homosexual or as a sexual deviant who liked to have his way with teenage girls.[63] It infuriated Whitey that people were making money off his life, his story. He seethed when John Martorano, the hit man–turned–government witness who served just twelve years in prison for killing twenty people, appeared on CBS's *60 Minutes* in 2008 and gave a chilling account of his criminal exploits with Whitey. Martorano talked nonchalantly about the people he'd murdered, insisting he killed out of loyalty to Whitey and other members of the Winter Hill Gang. He also styled himself a noble warrior and lashed Whitey as a scoundrel who had betrayed his friends. "I'll go along with a lot of things, but not no Judas, not no informant," said Martorano, adding that he would kill Whitey if given the chance. After watching the broadcast in the quiet refuge of Apartment 303, Whitey sat down and began writing his own memoirs.[64] In his small, neat handwriting, he began: "I've been driven to this by the lies of JM and seeing his insane interview on 60 Minutes was the last straw." Calling Martorano's version of events "20 minutes of lies," Whitey wrote that it "pushed me to write this true account." He only got about a hundred pages into his manuscript. The anger that had inspired him to begin seemed to dissipate. He found he now had trouble staying mad, something new for him. It was a gradual but unmistakable change. The emotions that John Martorano inspired were from his old life. His new life was a much better place. Whitey had evolved while on the run. "Became a real citizen and became a different person," he told a friend, "experienced emotions, feelings that I'd shut down for years."[65]

After so many years in Santa Monica, he saw himself, in fact, not so much as a criminal in hiding as a man in love. Greig's loyalty, proven over so many years, meant more to him than anything. He was not a man prone to regret, but regretted not meeting Greig right after he got out of prison in 1965. If he had, he felt he could have left his criminal life behind. "By the time we met it was too late," he said. "I was in too deep, had done too much to even consider an honest way of life."[66] Whitey Bulger had not gone soft as much as he had gone native. He was a man of Southern California now, and he had never been happier.

16

Uncontrolled Wickedness

Tommy Donahue was standing in the outfield in Wainwright Park in Dorchester, bored. His baseball glove, too big for his hand, hung limp by his side. He was eight years old, and hardly anyone hit the ball to the outfield in the minors in Little League. He turned and looked at the fence on the third-base side where his father used to stand. But Michael Donahue wasn't there. "It kind of hit me, like a punch in the stomach, during that baseball game," Tommy Donahue later recalled. "This realization." The father who had been at all of his games, who consoled him when he struck out and praised him when he got a hit, was gone for good. At the end of the inning, Tommy Donahue ran in from the outfield with his head down so his teammates couldn't see the tears. He sat at the end of the bench and turned away.

There was a similar realization, that Michael Donahue was really gone, among the neighbors on Roseland Street in St. Mark's Parish when the Fourth of July came and went without fanfare two months after his murder in 1982. For years, Michael Donahue had organized the neighborhood Independence Day block party. He rolled barbecue grills onto the sidewalk. He set up games for the kids. He handed out ice-cold beers to his neighbors. He had a friend in Chinatown who supplied him with fireworks, and Roseland Street lit up with sparklers and bottle rockets as night fell. One Fourth of July, Michael handed a Roman candle to someone wearing a Roman collar: the parish priest. The priest was figuring out how to light the thing as a Boston Police cruiser inched down Roseland Street. The cop slowed down, looked at the priest, then shook his head as the priest tried to explain how he came to be holding some illegal fireworks. The kids howled with laughter.

Roseland Street was a stable place. Many of the neighborhood kids, including the three Donahue boys, went to St. Mark's School, the same red brick Catholic elementary school Whitey Bulger had attended in the 1930s. You could walk to everything. The kids walked to school, the mothers walked to Maria's Market on Dorchester Avenue, the men walked up to the Peabody Tavern after work. And Michael Donahue was the pope of St. Mark's, the glue on Roseland Street; when he was murdered, things just seemed to come loose. The block parties stopped. Families moved away. The neighborhood changed. Even the Donahues moved away. Patricia Donahue lost the house. She took her three boys to a suburb south of Boston, thinking the change of scenery might help. But it didn't. Over the years, whenever Michael Jr. or Shawn or Tommy bumped into childhood friends, their father's death inevitably came up in the conversation, and the consensus was that the fond memories of their childhoods ended when Whitey Bulger murdered Michael Donahue on the waterfront. "Whitey didn't just kill my father," Tommy Donahue said. "He killed a neighborhood."

While Whitey was reinventing himself as a retiree in sunny Santa Monica, the families of his victims in Boston struggled with the dark legacy he had left behind. Many of them had no idea why their loved ones had died. Some had no bodies to mourn; they had just disappeared. Others, including the Donahues, had buried their father but had no idea Whitey was the culprit. Still, in their despair, they mustered the moral force that helped bring Whitey down.

In the years after Michael Donahue died on the South Boston waterfront next to Brian Halloran, Pat Donahue made it her cause to try to find out who killed her husband and why. The FBI and the police had told her that a gangster named Jimmy Flynn had shot her husband while gunning for Halloran. They told her that Michael Donahue was killed only because he happened that day to be driving Halloran home. So when Flynn was arrested two and a half years later and charged in the killings, Pat Donahue thought it was the end of the story.

She had no way of knowing that the police were innocently mistaken and that the FBI was feeding her lies.

Pat Donahue sat through the trial of Jimmy Flynn and was crushed when he walked free. He had multiple alibis placing him at home, eating dinner, fifteen miles from the murder scene. Brian Halloran's dying declaration that Jimmy Flynn had shot him wasn't enough for the jury that acquitted him in 1986. "We just thought a guilty guy got off, that there was nothing more we could do," Pat Donahue said. "The FBI kept saying it was him, it was him. And I believed them. I had no reason not to. So it was over."[1]

Judge Mark Wolf's September 1999 ruling, and the revelatory evidentiary hearings that led up to it, upended the Donahues' world and that of many other families whose loved ones had died at Whitey Bulger's hands or on his orders. Judge Wolf found evidence that John Connolly had told Whitey and Flemmi that Brian Halloran had implicated them in the murder of World Jai Alai president Roger Wheeler. Wolf found that the tip may have provoked Whitey and Flemmi to kill Halloran—and Donahue, the innocent bystander. "We had never heard Bulger's name mentioned in connection with Michael's murder," Pat Donahue said. "Judge Wolf changed everything."

So did John Martorano and Kevin Weeks. Martorano's decision to become a witness in 1998 convinced Weeks he should do the same the following year. Martorano and Weeks gave the state police–DEA team that built the case against Whitey the evidence they needed to bring murder charges—the story, the motives, and the long-hidden bodies. The police, in turn, gave some answers to families that had been in the dark for fifteen to twenty-five years.

Bill St. Croix, Steve Flemmi's thirty-nine-year-old son, was recovering from treatment for cancer of the thymus at the Weymouth condominium of his mother, Marion Hussey, in January 2000 when DEA agent Dan Doherty and Massachusetts State Police detective Steve Johnson knocked on the door. "We think we found Debbie," Dan Doherty said. They had to do a lot of testing before they would know for sure, and the testing would take time. St. Croix had always looked up to his big sister, who had now been missing for fifteen years. Flemmi had been telling St. Croix's mother all those years that she had run away and that he was trying to track her down. St. Croix didn't wait for the testing. He knew a quicker way to identify the remains that had been pulled from the grave beside the expressway. He and his uncle, Mike Flemmi, a Boston police officer, drove down to the jail in Plymouth where his father was being held.

"Is that Debbie in the ground?" St. Croix remembers asking.

"Yes," Steve Flemmi said softly.

"Did you kill her?"

"Yes," Flemmi said, "but I can explain."

"There is no explanation you can give me," St. Croix said.

Mike Flemmi took his brother's side: Debbie was a junkie; she had been prostituting herself to black men in her mother's house, and something had to be done. St. Croix stood up and slapped his uncle. Then he turned to his father.

"Was Bulger there?"

"Yup," Flemmi said. Later, Weeks recounted on the witness stand how Whitey choked the life out of Deborah Hussey as he and Flemmi watched. Then Flemmi made sure she was dead. Whitey would later dispute this account, putting Flemmi's hands, not his own, on Debbie's throat. But there is no question, according to both

Flemmi and Weeks, that Whitey was present, approved of the killing, and shared in the blame for Hussey's brutal end.

St. Croix felt sick to his stomach. He was haunted by the image
of his sister gasping for air. He had always seen his father as a man
of honor, even though he knew he was a gangster. Growing up, he
had no idea his father had molested his sister as a teenager. He knew
his father had killed people, but he presumed those people were
other gangsters who would have killed his father if they had had the
chance. Now he couldn't look at him. "To be able to kill my sister
and then go home and have relations with my mother, [to be] able
to put his arm around my mother knowing how he killed my sister,
I would say that's a classic sociopath," St. Croix said. "Or maybe not
even classic. Maybe it's something new."[2]

The recovery of Deborah Hussey's remains did more than change
Bill St. Croix's view of his father; it galvanized him to act. He told
investigators about his father's jailhouse confession and about a plot
Flemmi had hatched to escape from prison. He led them to a cache
of seventy machine guns and sawed-off shotguns and pistols that
Whitey and Flemmi shared. Michael Flemmi was later convicted of
helping his brother hide the guns.

The disclosures at Judge Wolf's hearing and then at John Connolly's trial led the families of thirteen people killed by Whitey and
Flemmi during their years as informants to file civil suits against
the United States. In cases brought between 2001 and 2003 seeking
more than $1.3 billion in compensation,[3] they argued that the FBI
was responsible for the deaths because the bureau had protected
Whitey and Flemmi from prosecution and in some cases agents
had leaked information that led directly to the slayings. The law is
stacked against those seeking financial compensation for official
wrongdoing by a federal agency, especially, as in this case, wrongdoing that occurred many years ago. Eight of the suits were ultimately dismissed because they were deemed to have been filed too

late. Under federal law, the families were required to make claims against the government within two years of when they knew—or a reasonable person should have known—that FBI misconduct was involved. The key question for the courts was: At what point should the families have known?

The families and their advocates believed that simple decency would lead the government to be generous in its interpretation, given the grievous loss of life, Connolly's blatant corruption, and the long, dismal history of official malfeasance. Instead, Justice Department lawyers from Washington stubbornly fended off most of the suits by arguing that any "reasonable person" should have known by 1997 or early 1998 that the FBI was implicated in the slayings—even though the FBI was still staunchly denying it at that time, and even though some of the victims were still buried in secret graves. The government insisted that the families should have known better—even though two separate investigations into the murders and FBI corruption were still under way, and Judge Wolf was still hearing evidence. At the very least, the families should have paid more attention to media accounts about the FBI's corrupt relationship with Whitey and Flemmi, the government lawyers said, instead of relying on the FBI's insistence that it had done nothing wrong. They pointed to anguished statements the victims' relatives made to the press as the scandal was unfolding in court as proof that they knew the FBI was liable and that the families had waited too long to file suit. It was a strategy that shifted responsibility from the guilty to the departed and those who mourned them. It shook the public's confidence in the justice system, but it worked: A federal appeals court sided with the government, handing down decisions between 2004 and 2011 that barred six of the families from ever taking their suits to trial and overturned awards that two other families had won at trial.

From the earliest stages of the investigation, the FBI had blocked efforts by Tulsa police to solve the murder of businessman Roger Wheeler, withholding evidence that its informants, Whitey and Flemmi, had been identified as suspects. An FBI agent once even suggested to Wheeler's son Lawrence that his mother might have been involved in the slaying.[4] The Wheeler family's $860 million civil suit was the first to be dismissed because it was filed too late. "There's a lot that we should have known that we didn't know," Lawrence Wheeler said. "But here I am supposed to have known that the FBI was covering things up."

The Justice Department was unapologetic about pursuing a legal strategy supported by case law as opposed to one grounded in commonsense principles of right and wrong. They weren't being cruel; they were being good lawyers. "This is a sympathetic case, I realize that," Deputy Assistant Attorney General Jeffrey S. Bucholtz told an appeals court in Boston, referring to the claim brought by the Wheeler family. But Bucholtz insisted that the Justice Department should not have to apologize for arguing that the families of Whitey's victims had waited too long to file suit. "No one here was lulled into not filing the suit."[5]

Those families whose cases weren't thrown out on statute of limitations grounds were forced to listen as the Justice Department reversed its legal arguments in the civil proceedings. The DOJ had used Flemmi, Martorano, and Weeks as star witnesses to prosecute John Connolly. Now Justice Department lawyers defending the FBI declared those same witnesses devoid of credibility. In the criminal proceedings, their testimony was hailed as evidence; in the civil proceedings, government lawyers argued that their testimony should be disregarded as hearsay. The government went on to argue that Connolly and Morris were corrupt agents acting outside the scope of their duties when they leaked information to Whitey and Flemmi. How, then, could the FBI be held to account for their misdeeds? "He's a traitor to the FBI," Justice Department lawyer Thomas M. Bondy said of Connolly to the appeals court in Boston. "This guy crossed to the other side. He was a criminal who had a day job as an FBI agent."[6]

It was all well within the parameters of accepted legal practice, but the government lawyers appeared unaware of or indifferent to public perception. Donald K. Stern, the US Attorney in Boston at the time, turned over responsibility for the civil suits to Justice Department lawyers in Washington. He reasoned that, with prosecutors on his staff working with the families of Whitey's victims on the criminal case, it would be awkward for them to argue against the families in civil cases. "My expectation at the time was the Justice Department would recognize and acknowledge the misdeeds of the FBI and try to come to some sort of resolution instead of fighting those suits tooth and nail," Stern said. "I sort of assumed it would be a friendlier resolution."

But something got lost in translation between Boston and Washington. "The outcome ended up turning on legal doctrine, which probably had less to do with ultimate fairness and more to do with individualized facts," Stern said. "The resolution did suffer from the fact that lawyers handling it probably had no gut instinct or feeling about the impact of those lawsuits on the history of Boston, and how law enforcement has been viewed."[7] The Justice Department focused on preserving the legal precedent that makes it difficult to sue the government, and defending the image of the FBI. It insisted that whatever took place was the result of a rogue agent, not a rogue agency. The FBI, one government lawyer insisted, was and will always be "the nation's premier law enforcement agency."[8]

Stern said that the government should have acknowledged that its handling of Whitey and Flemmi had gone horrendously wrong. "The government should have accepted responsibility for what happened, the corruption in law enforcement. Instead they ended up handling and trying the cases in a way that fed into the perception that there's more of the same." He further added, "You had the appearance of once again the FBI being protected. I don't think it was the intent, but that's how it played out."

The Justice Department had been offered an honorable way out of the mess. In 2002, federal judge Reginald Lindsay suggested that the government create a victims' compensation fund to settle the suits. "I'd like to see all these cases settled," Lindsay told Justice Department lawyers during a hearing on the suit filed by Michael Donahue's family. Lindsay offered as examples the funds created to pay the victims of the September 11 attacks and the victims of sexual abuse by priests in the Archdiocese of Boston. The judge's idea drew widespread political support. William Delahunt, a congressman whom Whitey Bulger had once smeared, with John Connolly's connivance, in various informant reports, was among those who approved of the idea of the Justice Department's settling all of the cases—which sought damages ranging from $15 million to $860 million—and compensating the victims. Delahunt said that the DOJ was "denigrating the American justice system" by arguing in a criminal court that John Connolly and the FBI got people killed, and then arguing in civil court that the FBI was blameless. But despite Lindsay's push, the Justice Department would not negotiate with lawyers for the families. They insisted on fighting it out in court for fear of allowing the Boston cases to set a precedent, leaving the government open to all sorts of claims for compensation.

Only seven cases ever made it to trial; the Donahues' was one of them. Lindsay ruled that the FBI was responsible for Michael Donahue's murder and urged Justice Department lawyers to settle with his family. But at each turn, the government refused and insisted on litigating the case. Michael Donahue stood out—with Debra Davis, Roger Wheeler, and Deborah Hussey—as being a sympathetic victim. He was killed only because he gave Brian Halloran a ride home. He had never posed a threat to Whitey. He was a victim of other people's circumstances.[9] But his family was repeatedly dragged through a process that more than one federal judge decried as unnecessary. In its determination not to weaken the case law that favored the government, the Justice Department made no distinctions among victims. Rather than settle with the Donahues, the government spent millions on ten years of litigation, flying Justice Department lawyers up from Washington and putting them up at four-star hotels in Boston for weeks on end. The government even refused to stipulate certain obvious facts, such as the autopsy findings. "I got the impression that they wanted us to listen to how my father died, in all its gory detail, again and again, so we'd just throw our hands up and say, 'We don't want to do this,'" Tommy Donahue said.

The low point for the Donahues came during a hearing in 2008, when a Justice Department lawyer suggested that Pat Donahue had moved her three sons to a Boston suburb out of racial animus—that she was fearful of blacks who were moving into their Dorchester neighborhood as the city's ethnic geography evolved. Pat Donahue was shocked by the accusation. She turned instinctively toward Judge Lindsay, who was black and had grown up in the Jim Crow South.

"They were trying to paint me as a racist in front of Judge Lindsay and I was almost speechless," Pat Donahue said later. "I'm not prejudiced. I moved the boys from Roseland Street to start over, because their father had been murdered." The Donahue boys, in the gallery watching their mother on the witness stand, struggled to control themselves. It was true that the Donahues had moved out of the neighborhood as it was becoming more integrated, but race wasn't the reason. With Michael dead, Pat Donahue couldn't afford the house anymore. It was equally true that the Donahues had in more recent years moved back into a section of Dorchester where they were one of the few white families on the block. They occupied all three floors of a three-decker, and many of their neighbors and friends were black and Asian. One of Tommy's teammates on his darts team at the local pub was black and lived in the neighborhood. Given the racial history of the city, accusing a white, working-class Irish Catholic family in Boston of being racist was incendiary. The Donahues were embarrassed that they had to defend themselves. "They don't know a thing about us, and they played the race card in front of Judge Lindsay," Tommy Donahue said. "I don't know how much lower you can get."

In an open rebuke of his own Justice Department colleagues,

prosecutor Fred Wyshak sat in back of the Donahues in the court-room to show them support. He was joined by DEA agent Dan Doherty and Massachusetts State Police detective Steve Johnson. They were part of the team that defied the FBI to bring criminal charges against, and expose the FBI's protection of, Whitey and Flemmi. After the Justice Department tried to portray the Dona-hues as racists, Wyshak, Doherty, and Johnson approached Pat Donahue and told her that they were embarrassed by the govern-ment's tactics. After his mother testified, Tommy Donahue took the stand. He broke down in tears explaining what it was like to grow up without a father, and what his father's murder had done to his family. A Justice Department lawyer asked him how much his father had earned as a truck driver before he died. "I have no idea," Tommy Donahue said. "I was an eight-year-old boy."

In 2006, the family of John McIntyre, murdered by Whitey in 1984 after the failed *Valhalla* gunrunning mission Whitey had helped organize, was the first of the victims to get its case to trial. Judge Lindsay had initially thrown out the McIntyre claim, saying it was filed too late. But after an appeals court overturned his ruling, he heard the case.

Lindsay was visibly upset by some of the Justice Department tactics. John McIntyre's mother, Emily, was German-born. She had married a US intelligence officer and had come to the United States in 1954. Seventy-seven years old in June 2006, she seemed beaten down even before she sat down in the witness box. Her son's disap-pearance haunted her; the authorities had told her nothing. In the absence of any real information, a lawyer looking to write a book fed her a wild conspiracy theory: that John McIntyre had been killed by British intelligence agents in a bid to protect a mole inside the IRA. She was willing to believe it because the government had never bothered to tell Emily McIntyre the truth—that her son had been tortured and killed by Whitey Bulger. The pain was still vivid for her;

it might have been an appropriate time to apologize or at least offer a kind word. Justice Department lawyer Bridget Bailey Lipscomb at first appeared to recognize the sensitivities involved. Earlier testimony had centered on how, after Whitey shot John McIntyre in the head, Flemmi removed McIntyre's tongue. "I know it's been a tough week for you, reliving some bad memories," Lipscomb began. "I need to ask you some difficult questions, and I hope you understand that."

But no one understood where Lipscomb was going when she asked Emily McIntyre if her son had liked to read books about Adolf Hitler, a comment evidently on his German heritage. Judge Lindsay was appalled by the question and told Emily McIntyre she didn't have to answer it. Under Lindsay's orders, Lipscomb stayed away from that baffling and insulting line of inquiry. Instead she asked Emily McIntyre how much time she had spent with her son and whether schizophrenia ran in the family—questions aimed at Emily McIntyre's effort to collect damages for the loss of her son's companionship and his potential future earnings. McIntyre turned on the lawyer, speaking for many victims. "You should have questioned how my son was tortured," she said, shaking with emotion and rage. Lipscomb said that she was only doing her job. "No," Emily McIntyre corrected her. "Your job is justice." Emily McIntyre took a deep breath before delivering her withering assessment. "Your type of justice," she told the government lawyer, "destroyed my life."[10]

McIntyre's trial marked the first time that Steve Flemmi had testified publicly since he had pled guilty to ten murders. Taking the stand just a few days before his seventy-second birthday, he looked deceptively meek, with his graying dark hair—a boy's regular cut— and slight build. In a soft, casual voice, he recounted how he and Whitey murdered not only McIntyre but many others. He said they killed McIntyre because John Connolly had warned them he was cooperating with the law. He described Connolly as someone who "treated me like an equal" and estimated that he and Whitey had paid their handler about $250,000 between 1975 and 1990. He said they also gave cash payoffs ranging from $2,500 to $5,000 to five other agents during the 1980s. Lindsay awarded $3.1 million to John McIntyre's mother and brother, rejecting the government's contention that Connolly was a rogue agent. The judge found that Connolly's superiors "up the chain of command" approved of using Whitey and Flemmi as informants, even knowing that they were suspected of murders, drug trafficking, and other crimes.

The judge chastised the government lawyers for withholding evidence in a bid to get the case dismissed.[11] Lipscomb repeatedly argued that the McIntyre suit should be dismissed because there was no evidence that John Connolly did anything to cause McIntyre's death. But on the eve of the civil trial, at Fred Wyshak's insistence, she gave the trial judge a report showing that Flemmi had told investigators in 2003 that he and Whitey killed McIntyre because Connolly warned them he was cooperating against them. Wyshak, the prosecutor who helped build the murder case against Whitey and Flemmi, was incredulous that his counterparts in the civil branch of the Justice Department took the position that they weren't required to turn over the document. A magistrate judge found that the government's civil lawyers withheld evidence while acting in bad faith and were obligated to pay the McIntyre family's legal costs. The Justice Department finally agreed in late 2011 to pay McIntyre's mother an additional $700,000 in legal fees, but only if the court would vacate the rulings finding that the government had acted in bad faith. Justice Lindsay died before he could issue a final ruling on legal fees, but Judge William Young, who adopted the case, refused to go along with the Justice Department's caveat. He denounced the Justice Department for suppressing the truth. "I will not be part of it," Young told a Justice Department attorney.[12] "This is duplicity pure and simple." The government dropped its appeal and paid the McIntyre family. The money helped but could not erase the image Emily McIntyre carried in her head of her dead and mutilated son.[13]

Judge Lindsay had also found overwhelming evidence that the

government was liable for the killings of Donahue and Halloran. He held a bench trial on the agonizing question of how much the two men's lives were worth. Lindsay's death came before the final enumeration of damages. Those cases were also taken over by Judge Young, and in 2009, he awarded the Donahues $6.3 million and Halloran's widow $2 million. Young acknowledged that Halloran was a criminal, but he said he was murdered while trying to turn in the FBI informant who killed him. "It is next to inconceivable that our government, through negligence, inattention, self-interested hubris, and outright corruption, could cause, as Judge Lindsay has already found, the truly horrific murder of two of our citizens," Young said from the bench.

Young gave the Donahues more than money; he gave the family their good name back. "This was a happy, vibrant family," Young said, as Pat Donahue sat ten yards away, nodding. "Its social relationships were measured not by money but by faith, by mutual support, by the sharing of life together in the finest family tradition." Michael Donahue was "an extraordinary caregiver in every sense of the word. . . . Here there is overwhelming evidence of a family destroyed. That's unfair to them. They weren't destroyed. They went on. They made a life. The sons have grown up to honorable manhood. But the loss of the father, this father, in those circumstances, is, in this court's eyes, and I so find, compelling."

A few hours after Judge Young spoke, the Donahues walked through Cedar Grove Cemetery. It was May, springtime in Boston. They walked to the grave and Tommy Donahue looked down. "It's over, Dad," he said. "It's over."[14]

But it wasn't. The Justice Department had sixty days to file an appeal, and on the fifty-fifth day it did. Again the argument was that the Donahues had waited too long to bring their suit. Two district court judges had rejected the government's argument, but two judges on the First Circuit Court of Appeals agreed and threw out the award to the Donahues. Judges Bruce Selya and Jeffrey Howard said that they sided with the government "without endorsing the FBI's conduct, which we regard as reprehensible." They said information about the FBI getting Michael Donahue killed had been discussed at the Wolf hearings. They suggested that the Donahues should have read the newspaper accounts a little more closely. "Whether the plaintiffs knew the information is not the issue," Selya and Howard wrote. "Statutes of limitations are designed to operate mechanically. They aspire to bring a sense of finality to events that occurred in the distant past and to afford defendants the comfort of knowing that stale claims cannot be pursued."[15]

But in a ringing dissent, the third jurist on the appeals court panel, Judge Juan Torruella, said that the FBI and the Justice Department deserved no comfort. The family, Torruella argued, couldn't be expected to know, or even believe, the information that was emerging at Wolf's hearings. Their government had lied to them for years. Every time Pat Donahue asked the FBI for information on her husband's murder, she was stonewalled. "Not content with mere stonewalling, at one point FBI agents accused her of having an affair, which the agents suggested was the cause of the murder," Torruella wrote in his minority opinion. Summoning the moral indignation that his colleagues lacked, Torruella refused to go along with "such an unjust outcome which rewards official uncontrolled wickedness."[16]

For the Donahues, then, there was no damage award but there was some consolation in Torruella's words. Finally someone had pronounced, from the bench, the truth that was so obvious to them. Someone had spoken up for them.

What comfort they found was swiftly overtaken by their dismay at the decisions in the cases that followed. Debra Davis and Deborah Hussey, the government argued, had brought on their deaths by taking up with the likes of Flemmi. He was an evil man; they should have known that. Marion Hussey, Deborah's mother, had enjoyed the good life for many years as Flemmi's girlfriend, living large off

his "blood money." What business had she now making a claim on
the government for monetary damages when the life she'd chosen
led inexorably to her daughter's death? "That's all blood money
coming to her from Flemmi from his life of crime, and she comes in
here, says it's not my fault . . . she washed his clothes after he cut the
teeth out of all these people," Justice Department attorney Lawrence Eiser said during the civil trial.

In fact, Marion Hussey did not have a good life with Flemmi.[17]
She lived in fear of him, and the death of her daughter left her shat-
tered. Deborah Hussey was only a toddler when her mother hooked
up with Flemmi, who raised the child as his own. He started having
sex with Deborah when she was in her early teens. Deborah Hussey
wasn't Flemmi's girlfriend, as the government lawyer argued; she was
his victim. The Justice Department lawyer said she had been killed
because she had become a nuisance to him. But he left out what was
most salient: Deborah Hussey knew that Whitey and Flemmi were
informants. She wasn't a nuisance; she was a threat.

Separately, the government argued that Whitey and Flemmi
killed Debra Davis because she had decided to leave Flemmi for
another man, again leaving out a small detail: Debra Davis was
killed, by Flemmi's own admission, because she knew that Flemmi
and Whitey were FBI informants. Olga Davis, Debra's mother, died
during the seven years it took for her suit to make it to trial, but the
sons representing her estate pressed on. Justice Department lawyer
Lawrence Eiser suggested during the trial that Olga Davis, a mother
of ten, shouldn't collect damages for the loss of Debra's companionship because "she had many other children who were providing her
support and society."[18] Several mothers seated in the spectator section of the courtroom gasped.

In the end, the same appeals court that threw out the Donahues'
award upheld awards of $350,000 to Hussey's mother and $1.3 million to the estate of Davis's mother. The irony was that many lawyers thought that the Hussey and Davis families had had the highest
legal hurdles to clear. But once they survived the statute of limita-

tions challenge, they were able to prevail. Their success suggested that the other families would have prevailed if only their cases had been heard. Ultimately, the government paid about $13 million for the wrongful deaths of five people.

The outcomes left the Donahues disillusioned and embittered. Taking account of the dead, taking the measure of an era of uncontrolled wickedness and assigning a price to it, had, in the end, proved beyond the power of the courts. And really, Tommy Donahue said, a simple apology might have sufficed. "Forget the money," he said. "Our own government—the FBI, the Justice Department—has never said to my mother, to me and my brothers, 'We're sorry.' They talk about how arrogant Whitey Bulger was, how arrogant John Connolly was, how arrogant John Morris was? What could be more arrogant than the FBI and the Justice Department never having the decency to apologize to my family?"[19]

17

Captured: The Man Without a Country

Whitey Bulger couldn't sleep. He had always stayed up late, but he stayed up even later in Santa Monica. He had placed a full-size mattress on a futon frame in the living room, and he wore headphones while watching TV so he wouldn't disturb Cathy Greig. The screen was his constant companion.

And so he was almost certainly tuned in a little after 8:30 p.m. Pacific time, on May 1, 2011, when President Barack Obama appeared on the TV screen. "Good evening," the president began, "Tonight I can report to the American people and to the world that the United States has conducted an operation that killed Osama bin Laden, the leader of Al Qaeda, and a terrorist who's responsible for the murders of thousands of innocent men, women, and children." A couple of blocks away from Whitey's apartment, on the Third Street Promenade, people spilled out of Barney's Beanery and other bars and restaurants. If Whitey had been standing on his balcony, he would have been able to hear the "USA! USA!" chants floating up from the Promenade.[1]

But if the news of bin Laden's death led to spontaneous celebrations in Santa Monica and across the country, it had a different effect on Whitey: With bin Laden off the FBI's Most Wanted list, he was arguably now the bureau's most notorious target. The caution that had defined the last sixteen years—indeed, his entire criminal career—suddenly morphed into paranoia. Whitey and bin Laden had, despite their wildly different circumstances, been living similarly barren existences, stuck mostly indoors, shunning visitors, determined to stay out of sight. Bin Laden never left his compound in Abbottabad, Pakistan; Whitey confined his excursions to daily walks, early in the morning and at dusk. After bin Laden was killed, the walks ended. More than ever, being Most Wanted meant being invisible and doing almost nothing. He became even more of a recluse. He stopped circling items in the police blotter published in the local paper and leaving tear sheets for neighbors. He stopped pestering the young woman in the building whose personal safety had so concerned him. He stopped cornering Josh Bond, the young property manager, for the sort of idle conversation that used to drive Whitey crazy when he was a young prisoner in an eight-man cell in Atlanta.

Greig now had to come up with new excuses for his absence. For years, she'd told curious neighbors that Charlie had been a heavy smoker and had emphysema. In fact, Whitey never smoked. Throughout their years in Santa Monica, his health problems—some real, some invented—had been convenient cover for the rarity of his forays outside the apartment and his sometimes cranky behavior. Now she leaned on it even more. Barbara Gluck, a photographer who lived down the hall, remembered chatting with Greig in the hallway one day when Whitey came up behind Greig, his arms folded, his brow knitted. "Stop talking to her," he barked. "Let's go." Whitey was walking away when Greig smiled, slightly embarrassed, and told Gluck, "He's got dementia."[2] She also began ascribing Whitey's odd behavior to early Alzheimer's disease. The descriptions of his illnesses were all over the map. After bin Laden was killed, Greig told neighbors they hadn't seen Charlie because he was sick. He had been hospitalized. It was emphysema. It was his prostate. It was Alzheimer's. It was a pulmonary blockage. Neighbors accepted the litany of woes that are the standard ailments of old age. Some did their best to help. Catalina Schlank, eighty-eight, sent Whitey several Sudoku puzzles, thinking it would keep his mind sharp. Greig sent Schlank a thank-you note, adding, "Charlie is too overwhelmed."[3]

Whitey's heightened paranoia forced Greig to alter her routine. He didn't want her leaving him alone. Greig skipped her usual haircut appointment, failing to show up for more than a month. When she finally did, her hairdresser, Wendy Farnetti, was shocked at her disheveled appearance. "She came in and she looked really distraught, really nervous, really like something was wrong," Farnetti said. "And her hair was a mess. It was long, and it looked like she had been pulling on her hair or cutting her own hair." Greig sat in the salon chair and Farnetti looked at her crestfallen face in the mirror. "What's wrong?" Farnetti asked. "You don't know," Greig replied. "You just don't even know." She didn't elaborate, and Farnetti didn't pry.[4]

Neighbors noticed that a handwritten sign appeared on the door to the Gaskos' apartment, asking people not to knock. Whitey's fears ebbed as the weeks passed and no one came for him. But he had been right to be nervous. In Boston, the task force that was hunting him had been reinvigorated with new strategic thinking, a shift that started a year before bin Laden's death, when the FBI pleaded for help from the US Marshals. There was still a widespread view, particularly among law enforcement agencies outside the FBI, that the bureau had never tried very hard to find Whitey. He was, after all, their nightmare; arresting him would only return the spotlight to the worst case of corruption in the bureau's history, dredging to the surface decades of grievous mistakes. John Connolly was on the record about his hope that Whitey would never be caught. There were other former agents who shared that view.

But there was a countervailing view, and in May 2010 it emanated from the courthouse on the South Boston waterfront named after Congressman Joseph Moakley, the Bulger family's old neighbor in the Old Harbor project. Noreen Gleason, the assistant special agent in charge of the FBI in Boston, and Rich Teahan, the agent who had been supervising the Bulger Task Force since 2006, sat down in a conference room with David Taylor and Jon Murray from the US Marshals Service. The FBI's critics had always found it curious that the bureau had refused to turn the manhunt over to the marshals, the nation's leading fugitive hunters. If the FBI really wanted to find Whitey, the thinking went, the marshals would have led the search. There had been, to be fair, previous overtures, but the FBI brass wouldn't concede the leadership role. Now, after more than fifteen fruitless years, the FBI agreed that it was time to turn to them. "This is about Whitey Bulger," Gleason said, cutting to the chase. "We can't catch him. We need your help."[5] It was a humbling thing for an FBI agent to say, but it was also a turning point in the hunt for Bulger. "Why don't you just turn it over to us?" Taylor suggested. Gleason replied that the FBI was looking to improve the task force, not abandon it. "Look," she said, "this is one of the biggest black eyes in the FBI's history, and we want to be there when he's apprehended."

Taylor, the chief deputy marshal in Boston, once belonged to the large fraternity of FBI skeptics in local law enforcement, but he believed that the bureau's attitude had changed over the years, and he sensed in Gleason and Teahan a real sincerity. They owed nothing to John Connolly and the other retired FBI agents who had protected Whitey; in fact, Connolly's machinations had inflicted great harm on the bureau and, by extension, all who worked for it. "This crew wanted him caught," Taylor said. "They had nothing vested in not having him caught. It was a very cordial and informative meeting. There was no animosity." There was, instead, a promise to ask US Marshal John Gibbons for permission to add a deputy marshal to the FBI task force. Taylor knew that Gibbons, appointed to the job five months earlier after serving thirty years with the Massachusetts State Police, would be all for it. Gibbons was willing to work with anyone, and he was willing to let all the suspicion, all the bad blood, all the resentment go.

Murray, the assistant chief US Marshal, said he had the perfect guy for the job: Neil Sullivan. Sullivan was thirty-nine, with fifteen years of experience hunting fugitives as a deputy marshal. He had grown up in Massachusetts, on Cape Cod, and had come to work in the Boston office in February 2010 after ten years in the Albany office. Sullivan knew how to track people who didn't want to be found, but, more important, in Murray's and Taylor's eyes, he knew how to get along with anybody. In a business where egos, both individual and institutional, clashed frequently, Sullivan's easygoing nature was as crucial as his highly regarded investigative skills. "This is a win-win," Taylor told Murray, after the two FBI agents had left the conference room. "If it takes us sixteen years to find his bones, we will have done better than the bureau. But I think we'll catch him in a year. He's catchable. He's no rocket scientist."

The marshals' headquarters in Washington was not thrilled about devoting resources to a manhunt they weren't in charge of. But the top brass deferred to Gibbons, who cleared the way for Sullivan to join the hunt—although bureaucratic hurdles would delay the deputy marshal's arrival for four months. When Sullivan finally joined the task force's office in September 2010, it wasn't exactly bustling. In fact, the task force had never been smaller. An air of futility hung about the place. It had been relocated from private offices near the courthouse to the FBI's Boston office. FBI agent Phil Torsney and an FBI analyst were the only ones working the case full-time. Another FBI agent was off on National Guard duty. A state police investigator was out on medical leave. Teahan, who had been exclusively supervising the task force, was now supervising the FBI's gang task force as well. "After we exhausted the leads over many years, the investigation became more about luck than investigative skill," said Jonathan Mitchell, a former federal prosecutor who oversaw the task force for seven years. "It evolved from a real effort to track leads in the traditional sense to just a matter of continuing to fuel some of the publicity and act on the leads generated by the publicity. That didn't require as many agents."[6]

Sullivan brought a jolt of energy to the team. He hit it off immediately with Torsney, a new arrival in the Boston office who had almost thirty years' experience hunting fugitives for the FBI. Torsney joined the task force in August 2010 but was familiar with the Bulger case because he had been part of an FBI team that had reviewed the manhunt files years earlier to make sure the task force hadn't missed anything. He was also a long-distance runner who brought a slow and steady outlook to his investigations. Shortly before he transferred from Cleveland to Boston, Torsney had been involved in a three-year hunt for a doctor from Cleveland who murdered his wife with cyanide. The doctor was finally caught after being detained at an airport in Cyprus. Torsney considered that long manhunt a once-in-a-lifetime case,[7] a notion that now seemed quaint; Whitey had been missing five times longer than the doctor and was wanted for nineteen homicides. Sullivan and Torsney brought no baggage to the search. If there was a whiff of burnout clinging to the task force, they chose not to smell it.

Sullivan flew to FBI headquarters in Washington to comb through the Whitey files, sixteen years of dead ends and false sightings. As he went through the record, he studied the extensive profile of the fugitive that had emerged over the years. When Sullivan got back from Washington, he and Torsney compared notes. Besides getting along at a personal level, the two men shared a similar view of what needed to be done and where their focus should be. They were convinced that Whitey was still alive; there was longevity in his family tree, and he had been health-conscious. They were also convinced that he was still in the United States; for all of Whitey's overseas travel, he knew, they believed, that an American stuck out in foreign countries. And they were confident that he would be in a warm climate, near the water; he had regularly traveled to Florida, Mexico, and California during his pre-fugitive days, and he almost always vacationed by the sea. Wherever Whitey went, he enjoyed walking by the ocean. By the spring of 2011, Sullivan and Torsney were also sure that the best way to get to Whitey was through Cathy

Greig. She was younger and more distinctive-looking than her companion on the run, more likely to be out and about and not nearly as hard-wired to caution.

It wouldn't be the first time the task force had tried to get to Whitey through Greig. Several months before Sullivan and Torsney arrived, the FBI had taken an ad out in a monthly newsletter for plastic surgeons because Greig had had breast implants, a face-lift, liposuction, and eyelid surgery long before she became a fugitive. The ad noted that Greig might be looking to replace the breast implants she had since in 1982. As a former dental hygienist, Greig was also obsessive and punctual about having her teeth cleaned. The FBI put an ad with photos of Whitey and Greig in the American Dental Association's newsletter. Sullivan and Torsney were determined to get a much wider audience, and they wanted to broadcast the best photographs they had of Greig. With Teahan's blessing, and fifty thousand dollars in hand, the FBI commissioned a thirty-second ad and bought three hundred fifty time slots in fourteen different television markets across the United States during daytime TV shows. The time slots were during commercial breaks for shows like *The View*, *Ellen Degeneres*, and *Live with Regis and Kelly*, whose audiences were overwhelmingly female. The premise was that a woman would be most likely to recognize Greig from a supermarket or a hair salon or somewhere else. "We're looking for people sitting in a hospital waiting for an appointment with a doctor where there are three or four [TV] monitors on the wall, and they are watching these shows," said Teahan. "Or people who are in a beauty salon or barber shop. We're trying to cast a wider net. Instead of focusing on an eighty-one-year-old man, people can focus on a sixty-year-old woman."[8] But for all the money spent on those ads, it was free TV, a news report on the FBI's latest strategy to find Whitey, that provided the breakthrough. As Whitey would later lament, "A cat got me captured."[9]

Anna Bjornsdottir recognized Cathy Greig's face as soon as it flashed on the screen. Bjornsdottir was sitting in her apartment in Reykjavík, in her native Iceland, watching a CNN report on the

FBI's new TV ads. She knew immediately it was Carol, the nice woman in Santa Monica who had taken care of Tiger, the orphan cat. On June 21, shortly after 8:00 p.m. Pacific time, she called the FBI's Los Angeles office from Reykjavík, leaving a message on an answering machine that she recognized the fugitives as Carol and Charlie Gasko in Santa Monica. Bjornsdottir's tip, one of two hundred generated in the first two days of the ad campaign, was forwarded to the Bulger Task Force office in Boston. The next morning, Sullivan arrived for work and was going through the previous night's tips. He saw a summary of Bjornsdottir's message and was curious. "How'd she sound?" Sullivan asked the young FBI analyst who had listened to the voicemail. The analyst said that she had sounded genuine and had used the phrase "100 percent" to describe how sure she was about her identification of Carol and Charlie Gasko.

Sullivan was intrigued that the tip mentioned Santa Monica. That fit with what he and Torsney considered Whitey's profile and his likely choice of a place to lay low. But when Sullivan called the phone number left on the voicemail, the call did not go through. The analyst had had trouble with the woman's accent—mistakenly believing that she had said that the Gaskos lived on Surge Street instead of Third Street—and her voice had trailed off at the phone number. But she had also left an email address. Sullivan sent Bjornsdottir an email, and when she replied, she included her phone number. As Sullivan talked to her, he felt a surge of adrenaline: She was ticking all the boxes. Carol was nice; Charlie was nasty. He was a couple inches taller than her. They loved animals, especially dogs. They said they were from New York. Sullivan went through every data base he could think of, looking for evidence that a couple named Carol and Charlie Gasko existed. He found nothing. That convinced him that whoever the Gaskos were, they were doing everything in their power not to be traceable. "You've got to call LA," Sullivan said, standing in front of Teahan's desk.

Even before Rich Teahan called the FBI office in Los Angeles, asking them to send some field agents to Santa Monica to check

Anna Bjornsdottir's tip, Whitey had a bad feeling. The public service announcements didn't appear in the Los Angeles market that included Santa Monica, in large part because of the expense. But Whitey saw a news report about it, perhaps the same CNN report that Bjornsdottir watched. He knew the news wasn't good. He later bragged about predicting his own capture, recounting that after watching the new FBI spot, he told Greig, "This is it."[10] From now on, they shouldn't leave the apartment at all. His paranoia after bin Laden's death now seemed like prescience. Whitey's long run was almost over, and he seemed to know it.

Josh Bond knocked off a little early on the afternoon of June 22. Late nights had caught up to him; he was asleep on his couch when the phone rang at about 3:30 p.m. It was someone in the office, saying that the FBI was there and needed to talk to Bond about a tenant. "Put him on," Bond said.

"This is Special Agent Scott Garriola of the FBI."

"Can we take care of this tomorrow?" Bond remembers saying.

"No," Garriola replied. "We've got to take care of this now."

When Bond got to his office in the hotel across the street from the Princess Eugenia, Garriola and another agent showed him a series of photographs. Bond recognized the subjects as Charlie and Carol Gasko and told Garriola that the couple were in Apartment 303.

"How sure are you?" Garriola asked.

"One hundred percent," Bond replied, adding that they were his next-door neighbors.[11]

Garriola turned to the other agent. This was not the answer they were expecting. What they had thought was a routine assignment, checking out a tip, ramped up quickly. They called in more agents. Bond gave Garriola a key to Apartment 303 and another agent went to a room in the Embassy Hotel that was directly across the street from the Princess Eugenia. The agent saw Whitey appear briefly on the balcony. Garriola asked Bond to go to Whitey's apartment and knock on the door. "No way," Bond replied. He had just learned that Charlie, the grandfatherly neighbor who had given him a cowboy hat and a beard trimmer and countless other gifts, was really a gangster wanted for many murders. He had been happy to chat with Charlie Gasko, for all his eccentricities, but he'd be damned if he was going to confront Whitey Bulger.

Garriola came up with a ruse. He took a pair of bolt cutters and snapped off the lock on Whitey's storage locker in the garage, then instructed Bond to call the apartment and let them know that their locker had been broken into. Bond called the cell phone number Greig had listed, but there was no answer. The agent stationed across the street communicated with Garriola—there were two people in the apartment, he said, a man and a woman. Garriola asked Bond again to knock on the door and bring the couple down to the storage lockers, but Bond wouldn't do it. As Bond and Garriola haggled over how to get Whitey out of the apartment, Bond's phone rang. "Josh, it's Carol," Cathy Greig said. "Did you just call?"

Bond told her that their storage locker had been broken into, and he offered to meet them to inspect the damage or to call the police for them. Greig suggested that it would be best if her husband met Josh at the storage locker. Whitey grumbled, but he went down. It was about 5:45 p.m., and he was walking toward the locker in the garage when FBI agents and Los Angeles police officers rushed up and surrounded him. They pointed guns at him. He had none to point back.

"Get down on your knees!" one of them yelled.

Whitey refused.

"We will shoot!" one of the cops shouted.

"Go ahead!" Whitey shouted back.

Whitey's biggest concern, he later said, was that there were oil stains on the garage floor where he was standing. He didn't want to ruin his pants. "I'm moving two steps to my right into clean space, then I'll kneel down," Whitey told the phalanx of cops surrounding him.

"Don't or we'll shoot!"

"I thought they would," Whitey later recalled. He took one step. "I could feel the coming lead." He took a second step.[12]

The cops and agents held their fire, moved in, and handcuffed him.

Janus Goodwin, the minister who lived a few doors down from Whitey and Greig, was walking through the garage on her way to the laundry room when she saw Whitey standing with a group of men, some of them in police uniforms. She saw that her neighbor was handcuffed and overheard some of the heated exchange; she was mortified. She assumed that Charlie Gasko had done something weird or threatening because of his deteriorating mental state, and she went to his defense. "You know, sir," Goodwin said, approaching the men keeping watch over Whitey. "This man has Alzheimer's." One of the agents looked at her and said, "Ma'am, when you see so many FBI [agents], you should know something serious is going on."

Whitey kept his eyes down. To Goodwin, he suddenly looked old and defeated.[13] An agent held a cell phone up to Whitey's mouth. "Stay in the apartment," Whitey told Greig. "I've been arrested." When Goodwin went back upstairs, she saw Greig talking to a few FBI agents. She looked calm, even relieved. Whitey's demeanor changed quickly, too. By the time Josh Bond walked over from the hotel to the garage, ten minutes after the arrest, Whitey was hand-cuffed but relaxed, chatting with the cops and FBI agents. "He looked like he was joking around with them," Bond said.[14] And he was. Greig stared at the friend and neighbor who had set the trap for them. "Hi, Josh," she said. When Bond didn't answer, she said it again.

Garriola's insistence that Whitey be lured out of the apartment was vindicated as soon as agents began searching the apartment. There was a handgun resting on a shelf of the bookcase in Whitey's bedroom. From a hole in one of the walls, agents removed thirty shotguns, rifles, and pistols. From another hole, they took $822,198 in cash. When Garriola told Whitey that they had found the guns, his immediate concern was to cover for Greig. "All the guns are in my bedroom," he said. "Catherine never goes in my bedroom. Catherine has never held a gun in her hands." As the freshly caught couple were being hauled off to jail, Garriola told Whitey that they had found about a hundred pages of a handwritten manuscript. "Shit," Whitey said, grimacing, "you found it? Did I name names?" Whitey turned to Greig. "Cathy," he said, "did I name names?" "I don't think so," she replied.[15]

The partnership of FBI agent Phil Torsney and Deputy US Marshal Neil Sullivan had swiftly borne fruit. It was a victory that flowed from the FBI's grudging acceptance that it needed more help, and from pure luck: Anna Bjornsdottir had been watching CNN as Whitey and Greig's photos flashed across the television screen.

Tommy Donahue was sound asleep on the top floor of his family's three-decker in Dorchester when the phone rang. It was his girlfriend's fourteen-year-old son, Joey. "Bagga," Joey said, calling Donahue by his family nickname, "they caught Whitey Bulger."

It was one o'clock in the morning, and Tommy was still half-asleep. His first reaction was to ask Joey why he was up so late. Then it hit him. "They finally caught the bastard," Tommy said. He walked down to the second floor and woke up his mother and his brother Shawn. Patricia Donahue shook the sleep out of her head and sat up in bed and gave Tommy a "this better be good" look.

"California?" Pat Donahue said. "He was in California?"

Tommy walked down to the first floor and told his brother Michael and Michael's wife. The lights were now on, on all three floors, and no one would go back to bed. Then Tommy picked up the phone and called David Wheeler in Oklahoma. The Wheelers, a wealthy family from the heartland, and the Donahues, a working-class clan from Boston, couldn't be more different. But they shared something: a husband and father and breadwinner taken from them by Whitey Bulger. And now Whitey would have to answer for it.

"David," Tommy Donahue began, "you're not going to believe this."[16]

As they drove to Los Angeles, Whitey couldn't resist chatting up his captors. It had always been his habit to joke with the cops—when he was tailgating trucks in his teens, when he was robbing banks in his twenties, when he was driving around with gangsters in his forties, when the DEA put a bug in his car in his fifties. He believed he had an innate ability to charm the law. Whitey kept up his joking patter during his brief initial appearance in a Los Angeles courtroom. He mocked reporters who were watching the proceedings and leaned toward Greig, whispering in her ear and laughing. Greig didn't share his sense of whimsy. Torsney, Sullivan, and Teahan had flown out to LA early that morning and got right back on the plane with Whitey that night for the long flight back to Boston. They were surprised when Whitey traded wisecracks with them. They were new to this, but it was old hat for Whitey: They were the good good guys, he was the bad good guy. By his logic, they were all good guys.

Whitey was boastful. No one was more devoted to his legend than he. He bragged that he had slipped back into Boston "armed to the teeth" after he had gone on the run, to settle some unfinished business. He went to Vegas and won some money. He went to Mexico and bought cheap prescription drugs. He had money stashed all over the country. The underlying message was vintage Whitey: While you dopes were looking for me in London and God knows where else, I went where I wanted, when I wanted. Whitey viewed himself as the smartest guy in the room.

Even as he congratulated his captors for finding him, he lectured them on their tactical mistakes: They should have focused on Cathy Greig a long time ago, he said. She was the weak link, the one out in public most of the time. Whitey was proud of his ability to stay a step ahead of the law, explaining in detail how he had assumed Charlie Gaska's identity and changed one letter in the name to create a new person. He freely admitted that he bought driver's licenses and other ID from vulnerable people and created phony IDs for himself and Greig.[17] He also spent part of the flight making excuses for two people: Greig and John Connolly. Cathy didn't know anything about the guns in the apartment, Whitey insisted. John Connolly didn't belong in jail, he said, but John Morris sure did.[18]

It was the moment most of his victims had given up hope of ever seeing: Whitey Bulger, his hands and feet bound in chains, shuffling into Courtroom 10 in the Moakley federal courthouse on the South Boston waterfront. The room was packed with more than a hundred people, but Whitey almost immediately made eye contact with his brother Bill in the second row on the right side and mouthed a hello. Bill, sitting between two of his sons, nodded his acknowledgment. Whitey didn't miss a beat when the judge asked him if he could afford a lawyer. "Well," Whitey replied, "I could if you'd give me my money back." Pat Donahue sat in the back of the courtroom with her three sons and shook her head. "He's worried about his assets?" she whispered. "He should be worried about his ass."

Whitey flashed a wry smile at his brother and nephews as the marshals put the chains on him and he shuffled out the way he'd come in. As the gallery filtered out of the courtroom, the four men who had been with the case the longest—state police lieutenant Steve Johnson, DEA agent Dan Doherty, and the prosecutors Fred Wyshak and Brian Kelly—came over to say hello to the Donahues. There were hugs and handshakes and backslaps. "People talk about justice," Tommy Donahue said, watching the last of the spectators leave. "I think the only justice we'll see is what we just saw. Whitey's in chains. He's going to die in prison. He can bitch and moan and scream and yell and he'll still die in prison. And he'll die a rat. Because that's what he is. A rat."[19]

Even as the FBI took bows for capturing Whitey Bulger, it felt compelled to release a statement denying speculation that Whitey's arrest was a staged event. "Any claim that the FBI knew about Mr. Bulger's whereabouts prior to the FBI's publicity efforts this week are completely unfounded," Special Agent in Charge Richard DesLauriers said. "When we learned of his location, he was arrested promptly."

Whitey was sent to the Plymouth County Correctional Facility, not far from where he had once dispatched a man to protest school desegregation by trying to blow up Plymouth Rock. Deputy marshals put Whitey and Greig in the same black SUV for the drive to their respective jails. They rode mostly in silence, and when they got to Plymouth, Whitey stared sadly at Greig and said good-bye as he was led away. It was the last time they were together. For the first time in almost fifty years he was known by an inmate number again. He was Prisoner 57950, assigned to Cell 108 on Unit G. He wasn't impressed. "Wish I was back on Alcatraz," he lamented.[20]

Even as he approached his eighty-second birthday, Whitey was treated as a high-security risk. A guard sat outside his cell twenty-four hours a day. Whitey was amused that three shifts of guards rotated to the chair; he was shocked one day when he opened his eyes and saw that the guard on that particular shift was a woman. The cell door had just a small pane of glass. His food, almost always cold, was passed through a slot. A camera in the cell watched his movements. For twenty-three of every twenty-four hours, he was inside his 8 x 12 foot cell. He exercised in his cell every day, doing 155 push-ups in six sets, pacing back and forth. He got fresh air for an hour, walking as briskly as he could in a small open area surrounded by concrete walls, under the gaze of a prison guard holding a German shepherd on a leash. If he wanted a shower, he had to take it during his hour of fresh air. Three times a week, he was allowed to shave and was given a change of bright orange prison garb. He slept on a 4½-inch-thick mattress with a rubberized cover. The mattress lay on a ledge mounted to the wall. Attached to the opposite wall were a stainless steel toilet and sink, and a narrow desk and stainless steel seat.

For the first few months, he complained that he was strip-searched and had his cell torn apart a minimum of five times a day. The routine was maddening. "I know what Pavlov's dog felt like," he told a friend. He referred derisively to the guards who carried out the searches as the Just Following Orders Squad. The only upside was that, with the lights kept on twenty-four hours a day, the number and severity of his nightmares that were a legacy of his LSD testing in the 1950s seemed to abate.

He complained that the security precautions assigned to him were more onerous than those of Richard Reid, the confessed Al Qaeda "shoe bomber" who was held in Plymouth after trying to blow up a plane in 2001. He compared himself to Robert Stroud, the infamous Birdman of Alcatraz, who spent sixteen years in isolation on The Rock. With characteristic self-aggrandizement, he saw his predicament in literary terms. "I feel like Philip Nolan in 'Man Without a Country,'" Whitey wrote. "Isolated—no human contact." Nolan, the protagonist in Edward Everett Hale's short story, is a US Army officer who renounces his citizenship during his trial for treason and is sentenced to spend the rest of his life at sea. Whitey saw his exile in the Plymouth jail in similarly epic terms, the punishment of a man who knew too much about his government's dark side.

He railed against the CIA using him as a guinea pig. He railed against the FBI using him and discarding him. His upcoming trial was framed in literary terms. "Want to refute lies and try to get my name cleared," he wrote. "That's my Gordian Knot." He was especially determined to prove that he did not kill the women he was charged with murdering, Debra Davis and Deborah Hussey. He called his trial The Big Show and The Big Circus. Despite occasional bouts of defiance, he was coldly realistic. "Chances are I'll die in this cell."

Whitey became a magnet for letter writers, the vast majority of them strangers, some of them strange. Eight women wrote asking if he was their father. He found the letters sad and wrote back, telling them that he was not. Still, he was wary of including his signature. He boasted that people were selling his autograph online for hundreds of dollars, though there is no evidence of it. Whitey seemed proud of his infamy. He claimed that an Alcatraz historian had written to him saying that the tourists who flocked to The Rock asked more about "Whitey B." than Al Capone or other legendary inmates. Whitey's use of his nickname is telling. Throughout his criminal career, he had angrily corrected or threatened anyone who dared call him Whitey to his face; he now embraced the moniker as part of his legend.

For someone who spent most of his life using violence or the threat of it to relieve people of their money, Whitey was genuinely miffed at the prospect of so many people trying to make money off his story. He ignored a letter from NBC's Matt Lauer asking for an interview. He did the same when ABC came calling. He was furious that some of his former associates got paid to write nonfiction books he considered fiction. Presumably he was equally aggrieved that tipster Anna Bjornsdottir was paid two million dollars for the information that led to his and Greig's arrest.[21]

Even as he faced the prospect of dying in prison, Whitey was preoccupied with his reputation, especially among those who knew him as Charlie Gasko. He wrote to friends and neighbors in Santa Monica, insisting he was not the monster he was being portrayed as, complaining about his treatment, professing his love for the woman everyone knew as Carol, wishing they were back at the Princess Eugenia, strolling the Third Street Promenade at dusk. His love for Greig was a recurring theme in all his letters. Locked up again, forty-six years after he walked out of federal prison vowing he would never go back, Whitey grew introspective, even sentimental. "Funny but the happiest years were the 16 years on the lam," he wrote. "Quiet life, no crime, like a 16 year honeymoon. . . . Memories keep me sane."[22]

Whitey's prison correspondence revealed someone whose inner tone, as captured in his prose, had shifted, from the hard-edged staccato of the career criminal to something more like a soft romantic. He described his plight in noble, selfless terms. He spoke in a voice that suggested he had come to see himself in the same benign light that Greig had seen him in throughout their years together. He would do anything to repay the loyalty she had shown him. And as she sat in a jail in Rhode Island, he longed for her.

Whitey claimed that he was willing to plead guilty to all of the charges against him, even if it meant facing execution, in Florida, for John Callahan's murder, or in Oklahoma, for Roger Wheeler's, in exchange for Greig's release. But he said that the government refused to make a deal with him: "[I] never loved anyone like I do her and offered my life (execution) if they would free her. But no they want me to suffer."

He believed that Greig deserved praise more than prison. "She did what all the cops, prisons and courts couldn't," he wrote. "Got me to live crime free 16 years—for this they should give her a medal."

Their sixteen years on the run had, he said, been transformative. Always a light drinker, he became a teetotaler. He had been able to experience the normal emotions he had shut down to survive and thrive as a criminal. Greig grew secure as Whitey's one and only love. Hiding didn't weigh them down; it gave them a new perspective and a desire not to waste any of their remaining days and hours together in argument. It pained him that he wasn't allowed to write to her as they awaited trial, but he vowed to figure out a way for them to correspond, even if it meant seeking permission to get married. The return to jail, however, "brought me back to hate and shutdown—nightmares, increased hallucinations, claustrophobia. They call it security, I call it torture . . . designed to break me down."

Even as he pined for Greig, he made peace with Teresa Stanley, who had cooperated with law enforcement while he was on the run. Stanley wrote him a conciliatory letter in jail, also noting that her son Billy had died. Billy Stanley had struggled for much of his life with drugs. Whitey told her that all was forgiven. "I did make things better for her but we fought and I had too many women in my life," Whitey wrote to a friend. "Goes with the Fast Life."

Another of his correspondents was Jerry Champion, an Alcatraz historian who has written books about the prison. He wrote Whitey shortly after his arrest, looking for information about his and other inmates' experiences on The Rock. Initially, Whitey wrote back enthusiastically, but he ended their correspondence abruptly after learning from a friend that Champion worked as a prison guard in Florida. He was put off by Champion's opining on the greatness of America and its prison system. "I'm well aware how great America is," Whitey replied tartly. He touted his own military service, noting that he was honorably discharged and that he had always been a big supporter of the military and of veterans' causes.[23]

Whitey was delighted when he got a letter out of the blue, in March 2012, from Richard Sunday, who had done time with him in Atlanta and Alcatraz. He had always been fond of Sunday. Whitey believed him when Sunday insisted that he had been railroaded on a rape charge when he was a nineteen-year-old army soldier fighting in Korea, the charge that ultimately landed him in Alcatraz. Whitey had called Sunday a few times while he was on the run but had lost contact with him when Sunday moved from Virginia to Pennsylvania. Whitey confessed to being a computer illiterate and said that he had asked a relative to do a computer search for Sunday. They'd found nothing, and Whitey had come to the conclusion that Sunday, like just about everyone else he knew from Alcatraz, was dead. Now, back in touch with his old friend, Whitey wanted to straighten some things out. "No. 1," he wrote, "I never killed any women." And, he insisted, he wasn't an informant. "Sunday believe me," he wrote. "As a kid took many a beating in the police stations trying to make me talk . . . never did . . . never gave in—never even thought of it."

He decided he would try to be Sunday's patron. If Whitey couldn't capitalize on selling his story, he'd get Sunday to sell his. His old comrade had fallen on hard times, and Whitey was determined to use his infamy to help an old prison buddy. He claimed that Mark Wahlberg wanted to do a movie about him and that he could maybe persuade Wahlberg to put Sunday's life story on the silver screen. He advised Sunday to hold on to the letters Whitey was sending him and eventually sell them. "Later I'll write about my crime days etc. to spice up the value of the letter!"

Whitey had been a fan of Sunday's prison poetry. He had kept a poem Sunday wrote about Billy the Kid for years, tucked inside his

Bible. But he told Sunday that poetry didn't sell; stories about crime and prison life did. In letter after letter, he sent elaborate instructions to Sunday on how to find a ghostwriter, how to use his friendship with Whitey to market his literary pitch, how to shake down TV networks for the maximum amount of money for an interview. He was relentless, offering to write the foreword if he lived long enough to do so.[24]

Even as federal prosecutors rejected his offers to plead guilty in exchange for leniency for Cathy Greig, Whitey had still expected her to serve little time and to be able to leave jail and rejoin his family. "They all love her and she takes my place there," he said. He badly misjudged the government's attitude. Prosecutors weren't giving an inch, and Greig threw in the towel. She agreed to plead guilty to helping Whitey evade capture. What was the point in denying it? Through a long series of court hearings, Greig appeared dour. She smiled only at her twin sister Margaret, who dutifully attended each session. She declined each opportunity to make a statement in court, letting her lawyer, Kevin Reddington, do the talking. Reddington insisted that if Greig had to do it all over again, she would. "She's in love with the guy," he said. "If she could be with the guy right now, she'd be with him."

Through it all, Greig's hard façade cracked only once. When she offered to plead guilty, a judge led her through a series of questions, asking her at one point if she had ever received psychiatric care. Greig started crying, and it took her more than a minute to compose herself. "Once," she said. "It was after a suicide in my family." She didn't elaborate, but she was talking about her brother, David, who in 1984, at the age of twenty-six, put the barrel of a blue Smith & Wesson .38 special against his right temple and pulled the trigger. David Greig had been using drugs for years. Cathy Greig never cried for Whitey's victims, but she cried for her brother, twenty-eight years after she found him in his bedroom in the family house in Southie, the gun still in his right hand. Whitey had been with her for nine years at that point and told her he'd take care of her; and, in his way, he did.

On the day Greig was sentenced, Tim Connors stood up in court to give a victim impact statement. He was a baby when his father, Eddie Connors, was gunned down by Whitey and Flemmi. Thirty-seven years had gone by. Tim Connors spoke to Greig, but she wouldn't look at him. He reminded her of the tears she had shed when she pleaded guilty. "If I had a sister like you," Connors said, "I would have killed myself, too." Greig gasped, covered her mouth with her hands, and sobbed.

As cruel as Connors's words were, Paul McGonagle's words cut even deeper, because he was not a stranger but family; Greig had once been married to McGonagle's uncle Bobby. As a boy, McGonagle considered Greig more than his favorite aunt. She was his friend. She took him on vacation, bought him gifts, and showered him with attention. When McGonagle was fourteen, his father, Paulie, disappeared. He spent the next twenty-seven years carrying his father's photograph around with him, fantasizing that he'd bump into him one day and recognize him. But there was no recognizing the skeletal remains that were pulled from Paulie McGonagle's grave on Tenean Beach in 2000. Greig had left Bobby McGonagle for Whitey Bulger, the man who shot Bobby's brothers Paulie and Donnie.

Paul McGonagle left Southie long before he knew what happened to his father. He moved out of state, built a career, and raised a family. But he had come back to see the last hour in court of the woman who had once whispered in his ear that he was her favorite nephew; the woman who loved and harbored and took care of the man who killed his father. "Catherine Greig," he said, "has shown herself to have a knowing and willful disregard for the law but also a callous disregard to me and my family."

Judge Douglas Woodlock sentenced Greig to eight years—six months for each year she spent on the run with Whitey, a period the judge called "sixteen years of extended banality." He ordered her to pay a $150,000 fine. The sentence was harsh: She got three more years than Kevin Weeks, who watched Whitey murder people and buried the bodies, and only a few years less than John Martorano, who admitting to killing twenty people. But she said nothing, smiled wanly at her sister, and left the courtroom wearing the same mask of detached stoicism she had donned for all her public appearances. Whitey was rattled by Greig's sentence and outraged by the government's attempt to seize the homes of Greig and her sister. Margaret's house in Southie had been in the family for more than a century. "The government is relentless and heartless," Whitey wrote, without a trace of irony.

Greig's long sentence led Whitey to reevaluate his own plans. It gave him a new will to live, at least until she got out of prison. "Felt if she was free I'd hang on for couple of years and by then it's over—need the rest. But now it's hang in there for Catherine's sake."[25]

Greig's sentencing also seemed to shift the tone and phrasing of Whitey's jail correspondence. The romantic themes turned more cynical, the focus more on times and places and people lost. The wistful voice toughened again. The government, Whitey fumed, had ruined his woman, ruined his family, and, by busing Southie kids out of their schools and allowing outsiders into the projects, ruined his old neighborhood. Whitey had only seen fleeting glances of the new, glitzy Southie when he was whisked by armored SUV to the courthouse. But from the air, when a Coast Guard helicopter flew him up from Plymouth for a court appearance, the outlines of Southie didn't look that different. The projects he grew up in looked much as he remembered. The brick building at 41 Logan Way had hardly changed since that day in 1938 when James and Jean Bulger moved their kids into the three-bedroom apartment on the third floor. "Patriotism was part of the neighborhood," he wrote. "Sadly it's changing. Rich people moving in, Moslems, illegals. Obama's aunt for one." Whitey saw nothing encouraging about the new Boston. The yuppies were bad enough. "In 16 years I've been gone it's all over for the traditions etc. Progress! Not for the best." His tone had veered markedly toward self-pity and bitterness, and he confided to one friend that he was depressed. But every once in a while, the old, defiant, vindictive Whitey would surface, suggesting no regrets. "I had a good life and I lived!" he wrote. "And Fuck Society and its Court System! I'll laugh when I exit this world."

He had also always vowed never to return to prison, and this was why. The hours without human contact were relentless, their toll inexorable. His freedom was gone, his woman was gone, his town was gone, his power was gone. All he had left was his mind, and he wondered how long he'd have that. Left alone so long, in a place where the lights never went off, Whitey found himself asking big questions, the kind that preoccupied the philosophers his little brother Bill had always been so fond of quoting. In the cell that was coming to feel like his tomb, Whitey Bulger asked, "How long does memory last?"[26]

Afterword

In the months leading up to his trial, Whitey Bulger sat in his cell on a round, stainless steel seat, loose-leaf sheets spread on a shelf that served as his desk, taking stock of his life. His memoirs were contained in the assorted and sundry letters he sent his correspondents. His words wandered into the margins, arrows and numbers directing his readers to the train of his thoughts. His mind raced ahead and then looped back; he added postscripts on smaller scraps of paper. Sometimes the postscripts were longer than the letters. He was running out of time to say what he wanted to say.

The lines in Whitey's missives during that period ranged from the sentimental ("A good woman is Heavenly") to rebellious ("I'll welcome the warmth of Hell if there is a Hell"). But even as he scribbled furiously, the letters were only a prelude, his cell the green room, as he prepared for the biggest performance of his life. His final act.

In the summer of 2012, Whitey's lawyer J. W. Carney Jr. made a big production of announcing that Whitey's defense would star the gangster himself. "The jurors will hear directly from our client," Carney said. "James Bulger will testify. He will present evidence corroborated by others that he received immunity. He is going to tell the truth, if the judge permits him to. And we will show that James Bulger is indeed telling the truth."

Carney's words came as little surprise. It was what just about everyone expected Whitey to do. Who could imagine that the once-dominant figure in Boston's underworld, the man who saw himself as smarter than anyone else in any room, who prided himself above all on being a criminal with an honor code—however strange and selective—would sit quietly while others made his case?

But as his trial played out over two summer months in Courtroom 11 of the John Joseph Moakley US Courthouse, Whitey looked small sitting at the defense table. While defendants in high-profile cases ordinarily don suit and tie to make an impression on jurors, Whitey tried to impress the jury by dressing down. Day after day, he wore jeans, a simple shirt, and white high-top sneakers. He looked like an old man, a man of little consequence. No doubt this was his intention.

As the proceedings unfolded, that meek first impression would be belied by occasional outbursts—Whitey could not suppress his dark temperament and old hatreds—and by the increasingly obvious fact that he was directing his own defense. The longest-awaited and most remarkable courtroom clash in local memory would be, at Whitey's behest, two trials taking place simultaneously. One had prosecutors spelling out in excruciating detail Whitey's sordid crimes, molding a mountain of evidence before the eight men and four women who would judge him. In the other, Whitey's lawyers put the FBI and the Justice Department on trial, presenting less a defense of the man than of his self-image: They argued that Whitey was not an informant, that he paid the FBI for information but gave them nothing in return, that he was a killer, yes, but not, as he was cast by the feds, a killer of innocents or of women.

In the end, both sides got something. Whitey was convicted on thirty-one of thirty-two counts in a sweeping racketeering indictment. But the government looked bad, too, and it went well beyond the venal corruption of John Connolly taking payoffs and Connolly's boss John Morris taking cases of wine from Whitey. The leniency shown to the parade of admitted killers, drug dealers, and thugs who testified against Whitey left everyone in the courtroom, especially the jurors, feeling like they needed a shower. They saw the criminals who testified as evil, scary, and untrustworthy. They saw the government as plainly implicated. They saw evidence never displayed in public before, some of it grisly beyond imagining: victims' skeletons; the Claddagh rings, platform shoes, and remnants of clothes the victims had worn; skulls with bullet holes and missing teeth. The jurors may have wanted to avert their eyes, but they didn't. And, in the end, they saw the truth about Whitey Bulger's criminal career.

If the trial didn't change any minds, it was an exercise in shattering myths about Whitey. First to go was Whitey's uncorroborated claim that, in exchange for his cooperation, he had received a license to kill from prosecutor Jeremiah O'Sullivan. This fantasy never even got before a jury. Appearing before Congress, O'Sullivan denied giving Whitey immunity; he has since died. Whitey had no paperwork to back his claim, and despite Carney's talk about corroboration, all he had was Whitey's word. More likely his imagination. Two judges ruled separately that Whitey's immunity defense could not be raised at trial.

But then from Whitey's side came a surprising and surprisingly successful counterpunch, one that only underscored the government's image problem. Whitey and his lawyers argued that the judge assigned to hear the case, Richard Stearns, should be recused because, as a former high-ranking prosecutor in the US Attorney's Office in Boston, he had a conflict of interest in hearing the case. Stearns refused to step down, even though he counted FBI director Robert Mueller among his close friends. An appeals court agreed with the defense and ordered Stearns to step aside.

It turned out to be a Pyrrhic victory for the defense. Stearns was replaced by Denise Casper, one of the newest judges on the federal bench in Boston. And so, every day, Whitey, a deep-seated bigot and misogynist, looked up to see a black woman presiding over his trial. Casper may not have been a seasoned veteran, but from the first gavel on the first day, she remained poised and professional; her sharp intellect and resolute demeanor alerted both the defense lawyers and the prosecutors that she would not be pushed around.

When the trial got started, Whitey's defense made an unexpected, dramatic concession: They admitted that Bulger had made millions off the drug trade. This was no revelation, at least not to those who had tracked Whitey's career, but it was still shocking to hear coming from Carney's mouth. Whitey and his apologists, including his brother Bill, had for decades recycled the old canard that Whitey kept drugs out of Southie. Carney was playing an angle: Whitey was prepared to admit he was a gangster, a drug dealer, even a killer, in order to defend the two points he cared most about—that he wasn't an FBI informant and that he did not kill women. Whitey had outlined this strategy in his letters to Richard Sunday the year before, and he was determined to stick to it.

The sense of shock gave way to guffaws when Carney went on to proclaim that Whitey couldn't be an informant because he was Irish. The Irish, Carney intoned virtuously, consider being an informer the gravest of cultural crimes. He insisted that Whitey merely paid the FBI for information and told them nothing. Journalists watching the proceedings in the overflow courtroom on closed circuit TV could barely contain their laughter.

If the defense wielded the element of surprise, opening day belonged to prosecutor Brian Kelly, who brought the courtroom to complete silence as he read the names of the nineteen murder victims, showing their photographs on a video screen. "And that, ladies and gentlemen," Kelly said as the photos faded to black, "is what this case is about. A defendant, James Bulger, who was part of a criminal gang which extorted people, paid off cops, earned a fortune dealing drugs, laundered money, possessed all sorts of guns, and murdered people, nineteen people."

For the first few days of his trial, Whitey was a study in understatement both in dress and demeanor. But there were times when his obvious relish for his own ill repute leaked through. The trial was a series of short scenes, with dialogue, from his days on top, and some he clearly enjoyed watching. A few days into the testimony, he smiled watching Dickie O'Brien, a bookie he used to shake down, climb with difficulty onto the witness stand. Eighty-four, a year older than Whitey, O'Brien had grown up in Quincy, and his father was a bookie, so he was a bookie.

The Mafia in Boston was more than willing to take O'Brien's betting action and promised, as he put it, that if "there was a problem they would straighten it out." Meaning if anybody gave O'Brien trouble, the Mafia would kill them. When his new Mafia patrons were jailed on murder charges, O'Brien was suddenly independent—until Whitey Bulger moved in.

When the two first met, in the 1970s, O'Brien testified, Whitey told him, "You're by yourself. You should be with us."

"I was with the North End," O'Brien replied.

"Forget the North End," Whitey told him. "You're with us."

It wasn't negotiable.

One of Dickie's bookies got too ambitious and Whitey made it brutally clear that he couldn't go into business on his own.

"Did you know we have a business besides bookmaking?" Whitey told the plucky young bookie.

"Oh, yeah," the guy asked. "What's that?"

"Killing assholes like you," Whitey replied.

At the defense table, Whitey's shoulders were shaking as he chuckled uncontrollably at his own old lines.

———

To borrow a phrase from Carly Simon, Johnny Martorano, Whitey's favored hit man, walked into the courtroom like he was walking onto a yacht. He looked good, if a little heavy, in a fine suit. Whitey glanced at him wanly. He knew how much his old comrade knew. In the days ahead, the jurors would look closely at Martorano and find him, and the deal prosecutors gave him in exchange for his testimony, repulsive. He served only twelve years in prison for twenty murders.

The last time they were together, during Ronald Reagan's first term, Whitey had talked Martorano into killing his friend John Callahan. Now Whitey tried to ignore him. He wouldn't want Martorano to think he was getting to him as the hit man began reciting a list of the eleven people he said they had killed together.

Martorano knew the history cold, but his flaws as a witness quickly showed through. He had to acknowledge under questioning that he sometimes shot the wrong people. There was the time he went to kill a guy named Herbert Smith who had given Steve Flemmi a beating. In the middle of a blizzard, Martorano climbed into Smith's car and shot him and also killed two others in the car, nineteen-year-old Elizabeth Dickson and seventeen-year-old Douglas Barrett. When he realized he'd killed two innocent kids, Martorano said, "I wanted to shoot myself." Martorano named his youngest son, James Stephen, after Whitey and Flemmi, men he described as "my partners in crime, my best friends, my children's godfathers." Jurors were even shown a photograph of Whitey smiling in a suit as he cradled Martorano's son in his arms.

Whitey's attorney Hank Brennan didn't waste words in his cross-examination. "Mr. Martorano," he said, "you are a mass murderer, aren't you?" Martorano didn't rise to the bait. "You don't like the term 'hit man,' do you, Mr. Martorano?" Brennan asked.

"I," Martorano sniffed, "wouldn't accept money to kill somebody."

He apparently wasn't counting the fifty thousand dollars John Callahan gave him for taking out Roger Wheeler in Oklahoma.

Brennan zeroed in on the two teenagers who had been in the car with Herbert Smith. "You don't want to admit you killed the young woman, do you?" Brennan asked. "They were full-grown and had hoods on," Martorano replied. "I still feel bad."

Brennan made Martorano look like a fool as the hit man recounted stabbing to death a man named John "Touch" Banno. Martorano said he had killed Banno because Banno had embarrassed him when he was out with his date at the old Sugar Shack nightclub. Martorano said Banno came at him in an alley with a knife so he took the knife away and stabbed him with it. Martorano said he shoved Banno into his car so he could take him to the hospital. But on the way to the hospital, Banno started mouthing off again, so Martorano stabbed him a couple more times and killed him. Brennan noted that the autopsy report indicated that Touch Banno was stabbed some twenty times. Martorano disputed that. "I say two, three, four. Maybe a couple more. I don't know," Martorano said. "Because he wouldn't shut up."

Martorano insisted he wasn't a liar. But Brennan noted that Martorano smiled at his good friend John Callahan when he picked him up at the airport in Fort Lauderdale just minutes before he shot him. Wasn't he misleading his friend about what he was about to do? "I think anybody who has to kill somebody has to lie," Martorano explained. "I just wanted to get him in the car."

The debriefing and deconstruction of Martorano would continue for four days as he shared story after story from his days at Whitey's side.

In 1973, Diane Sussman was twenty-three years old, just out of college, a Californian living in the Brighton section of Boston, working at one of the city's great teaching hospitals. She began dating a Boston guy named Louie Lapiana. When the Bruins were in town, Lapiana worked the bar at Mothers, across from Boston Garden at North Station, with his buddy Mike Milano. One night, Sussman dropped by to hang out. She was moving back to California and had just been out on the town at a going-away party with her Boston friends. Lapiana didn't have a car, so Milano offered Lapiana and Sussman a ride home when the bar closed. "Michael had his new car out front," she recalled in her testimony. "It was a Mercedes. He was very proud of it. I had the honor of sitting in the front seat."

It was a beautiful car, but unfortunately it looked just like the car driven by "Indian Al" Notarangeli, who had been marked for death by the Winter Hill Gang. As the three friends drove off, they had no idea they were being trailed by a car full of killers. The death car pulled alongside them at a light and everything exploded. Diane Sussman's Californian instincts kicked in. "Like when you hear an earthquake," she said. "I ducked." The hit car roared off, as did a backup car that Whitey Bulger was driving. Diane Sussman got out of the Mercedes and called to Milano. She looked at him and knew he was dead. She moved to the back seat and asked Lapiana if he was all right. He mouthed a no. His eyes were glazed. He could barely move. She leaned on the horn, blaring for help. She took off her jacket and realized she had been shot. When the cops came, she fought with them because they wouldn't let her get in the ambulance with Lapiana. The cops knew it was a hit and were worried that someone would try to finish her off. They escorted her to the hospital, where she stayed for two days, recovering from her own injury. Then she went to see Lapiana. He was paralyzed from the neck down. After returning to California, she would call Lapiana at the hospital and the nurses would hold the phone up to his ear so he could hear her warm voice. "Louie couldn't answer but the nurses told me he was smiling," she said.

Diane Sussman is now Diane Sussman de Tennen. Forty years later the pain she'd felt that day was evident as she sat in the witness stand. Twenty-four hours before she took the stand, her spot had been occupied by Martorano, the man who murdered her friend, paralyzed her boyfriend, and shot her in the arm. She sat just feet away from Whitey Bulger, who Martorano insisted was part of the hit team that night. Struggling to maintain her composure, she explained in halting tones how the shooting changed her relationship with Lapiana. No longer a couple, they remained lifelong friends. "I was married and my children were not Louie's but part of my life was Louie," she said. Lapiana moved out to the West Coast to be near her. De Tennen learned how to care for him and how to operate his wheelchair. She brought her kids to see him. And when Lapiana died, twenty-eight years after he was shot, a little part of Diane de Tennen died, too.

When her testimony was over, Diane Sussman de Tennen dried her eyes, left the witness box, and walked past Whitey Bulger. Though some of the jurors were in tears, Whitey just doodled on his legal pad, betraying no emotion.

For two weeks, Whitey Bulger had played it cool. When prosecutor Brian Kelly described him as a vile gangster who murdered hoodlums and innocent women alike, Whitey stared straight ahead. But Whitey's infamous temper welled up as he listened to the testimony of John Morris, the corrupt FBI supervisor who twenty-five years earlier gave Whitey up as an informant. In 1988, Morris provided the final, authoritative confirmation for the *Boston Globe* Spotlight Team that Whitey had avoided prison because he was helping the FBI. Morris had insisted he did so because he had been compromised by Whitey and Flemmi, showered with fine wine and short money. Morris figured that if the *Globe* outed Whitey, the FBI would be forced to close him out as an informant and get him off the street. Whitey believed that Morris, with his leak to the *Globe*, was trying to get him murdered by other gangsters, and to this day he remains murderously hostile to him. "You're a fuckin' liar!" Whitey hissed at Morris, several feet away from him in the witness box. Some people in the courtroom heard him. Some, including Judge Denise Casper, did not. But Kelly, the prosecutor, filled her in as soon as the jury left for a recess.

"Mr. Bulger has got a Sixth Amendment right to confront his accusers, but he doesn't have the right to sit at the defense table and say to the witness, 'You're an f'n liar' when the witness testifies," Kelly said, struggling to control his anger. "Now, I know he spent his whole life trying to intimidate people, including fifteen-year-old boys in South Boston, but he should not be doing that here in federal court."

The fifteen-year-old boy Kelly referred to, now fifty-three, had given previous testimony. When Paul McGonagle was fourteen years old, Whitey murdered his father, Paulie McGonagle, and buried his body under the sand at Tenean Beach in Dorchester. For years Paul McGonagle carried around a photo of his father, hoping he'd bump into him and recognize him. He lives with the pain that his favorite aunt, Cathy Greig, sheltered his father's murderer. A year after he murdered Paulie McGonagle, Whitey Bulger rolled up on young Paul in his blue Chevy, his blue eyes hidden behind aviator sunglasses. Whitey told the boy he had taken care of the guys who had taken care of his father. It was an act of extreme cynicism, self-serving and cruel. When Paul McGonagle finished telling his story, several jurors turned to Whitey and stared, as if they were trying to fathom who could do such a thing.

John Morris was just about the last person Pat Donahue expected to apologize, but he turned out to be the first. Not long after he said the words, Pat Donahue was sitting at a table in the cafeteria of the federal courthouse, mixing granola into yogurt. "It's a little late, wouldn't you say?" she said.

Michael Donahue, her husband, the father of her three boys, was murdered in 1982, just a few hundred yards down Northern Avenue from the courthouse. He was murdered because Morris told his subordinate and Whitey's handler John Connolly that a hoodlum named Brian Halloran was shopping information about Whitey. Connolly told Whitey, and Whitey and another man raked

Donahue's car with gunfire as he gave Halloran, a friend from the neighborhood, a ride home. John Morris sat in the witness box and turned to Pat Donahue and her boys—Michael Jr., Shawn, and Tom—and spoke of his remorse. "Not a day goes by that I don't pray that God gives you blessing and comfort for the pain," Morris said. "I do want to express my sincere apology for things I did and I didn't do. I do not ask for forgiveness. That's too much. But I do acknowledge it publicly."

Well-worn tears attended Morris's sorrow. As she stirred her yogurt, Pat Donahue didn't doubt his sincerity. "Oh, I think he's sincere," she said. "But I sincerely believe he is mostly sorry that he got caught. The apology is an afterthought. I think he feels guilty. Living with that guilt is his punishment."

Tommy Donahue was standing in back of his mother, nursing a Red Bull during the morning recess. "Look at my hands," he said. "Look how red they still are. I had to twist my hands listening to Morris. I wanted to scream, 'Apology not accepted!' But I knew they'd throw me out of the courtroom. So I just bit my tongue. And twisted my hands."

It was under the questioning of defense attorney Hank Brennan that Morris made his apology. Their strategy aimed to show that Whitey was more sympathetic to the feelings of his victims than the government was. A perverse pattern was emerging. The *defense* was asking the questions the victims' families wanted asked. As much as he appreciated the gesture, Michael Donahue Jr. reminded his mother and brothers that the defense was trying to get Whitey off.

"Let's not forget that," he said, sitting next to his mother. "It's all well and good what the defense did, but they are defending a guy who murdered my father."

The first time Billy Shea had a substantive conversation with Whitey Bulger, he had just gotten out of prison and they were standing on a street corner in Southie. Whitey patted him on the shoulder and handed him an envelope that contained five hundred dollars. Their last real conversation took place at the bottom of some cellar stairs in the projects with Billy Shea convinced Whitey wanted to kill him.

When Billy Shea sat down to testify against Whitey, it was the first time the two former business partners had seen one another in more than a quarter century. They smiled and Billy cracked some jokes. He even got Whitey to laugh. Billy Shea was nine years younger than Whitey, part of a gang of Southie hoods called the Fifth Street Crew. They had a fearsome reputation. Shea did time for armed robbery, but when he got out of prison in 1977, he hooked up with Whitey, who was looking to appease the Fifth Street Crew. Whitey approached Shea, a freshly minted ex-con, and said, "I heard some good things about you." Meaning Shea could take a pinch, do his time, and keep his mouth shut. "He gave me an envelope," Shea recalled, "and said, 'Welcome home.'" When Shea opened the envelope and counted out the cash, he figured it was a peace offering.

Whitey did more than give Shea some cash. He teamed him up with one of his guys to put loanshark money on the street. Soon his portfolio would expand. Shea asked Whitey for permission to open a card room, where high rollers could play poker without the fear of getting robbed. Shea noticed scores of marijuana dealers walking around Southie with big wads of cash. "I went to Jim and said I could round them up and put them in line," Shea explained. Whitey had noticed the same thing. "But he didn't want to get his image involved in drugs," Shea said.

Still, it was too much money to ignore, so Billy Shea would be Whitey's front man in the drug trade. Shea robbed the dealers, who went to Whitey and explained their predicament. Whitey would straighten everything out and then those dealers belonged to him.

The money from grass was chump change compared to the margins in their cocaine business. Whitey went from getting four

thousand dollars a week to ten thousand dollars. Shea told prosecutor Brian Kelly that he, Whitey's front man, was clearing a hundred
thousand dollars a week. Immediately Shea realized he had said too
much. He looked right at Whitey and made a sheepish admission. "I
know Jim's looking at me, 'You son of a bitch, you made that kind of
money and that's all my end was?'" Whitey chuckled at that. Asked
to identify Whitey, Billy Shea pointed to him and said, "He's the
young fella there."

Whitey laughed again.

Billy Shea liked Whitey. But when Shea wanted to retire, Whitey
said no. And when Shea insisted, Whitey was livid.

Whitey came to his house and Shea, alarmed, put a gun in his
waist and pulled his shirt down. He got into a car with Whitey, Steve
Flemmi, and Kevin Weeks. They drove to a deserted part of the D
Street projects. Whitey ordered him down some cellar stairs and
Shea raced in front to be able to put his back to the wall and see
over Whitey's shoulder. "I was looking at his hands," Shea said. "I
think he took me down there to frighten me or whack me." Shea
was prepared to shoot Whitey, knowing he would die at the hands
of Flemmi and Weeks if he did.

Whitey did most of the talking, reminiscing about their long
partnership. "He mentioned trust," Shea said. Shea reminded
Whitey he took a pinch in 1983 and kept his mouth shut.

It was like a light switch.

"The tension went out of his face," Shea recalled.

It was over.

So was Billy Shea's testimony.

Whitey's lawyer Jay Carney didn't even bother to cross-examine
him.

He did, however, sharply question another of Whitey's drug
dealers, Paul "Polecat" Moore. Prodded by Carney, Moore shared
that Whitey was opposed to angel dust and heroin, and that he drew
the line at selling any drugs to children.

Watching from the gallery, the daughter of one of the men

Whitey was accused of killing, Francis "Buddy" Leonard, shook her head ruefully at what passed for a sense of honor in Whitey's world.

"He didn't sell drugs to children," Connie Leonard said, "but he killed their daddies."

They used to spend every day together. Except Sundays. Whitey Bulger took Sundays off. He was traditional like that. Whitey and Kevin Weeks walked around Castle Island side by side, talking life, talking business, talking trash. Then they'd do crime. Shake down drug dealers. Put guns to people's heads or some other body part. When they did the occasional murder, Weeks got dirty because he was Whitey's gravedigger. Whitey groomed Weeks like the boxer he was, bringing him along slowly. They were mentor and protégé.

And so when Kevin Weeks walked into the courtroom, Whitey couldn't help himself. He had been pretending that he couldn't be bothered to notice most of those testifying against him. But he turned around and craned his neck to watch Weeks approach the witness stand, looking at him for the first time in seventeen years. Whitey would have noticed that Weeks had dyed his hair a darker shade than his natural color. Now fifty-seven, Weeks was twenty-six years Whitey's junior and still seemed youthful in an ineffable way. Ray Liotta could play him in the movie.

Whitey tried not to betray too much interest in what Weeks had to say, which was to implicate Whitey in every crime imaginable, from extortion to murder.

Before Kevin Weeks took the stand, there had been almost a genteel atmosphere in Courtroom 11, a kind of court-ordered comity despite the sordid nature of the testimony. That all changed when Weeks interrupted his droning account to express how upset he was when he learned that Whitey and Stevie Flemmi had been FBI informants. This provoked an exchange.

"You suck," Whitey said.

"Fuck you," Weeks retorted.

"Fuck you, too," Whitey said. Suddenly, the Southie courtroom sounded like a Southie locker room.

"What do you want to do?" said Weeks, jumping to his feet so fast he banged his knee on the witness box. He asked his former mentor if he wanted a piece of him. They sounded like fourteen-year-olds facing off in the courtyard of the Old Harbor project. "Hey, hey!" the judge shouted. "Mr. Bulger, let your attorneys speak for you."

Mr. Bulger's attorneys did just that, as Carney tried to get under Weeks's skin and reveal a little of his thuggish self. It wasn't hard. First, Weeks threatened to meet Carney outside the courthouse and beat him up. Then Carney got Weeks to admit he was a pathological liar. "I lied," Weeks said, shrugging. "I've been lying my whole life. I'm a criminal."

Still, Weeks insisted he was telling the truth now. He was growing impatient with Carney's cross-examination, in which Carney purposely patronized him, suggesting he was a professional witness who had cut himself a sweet deal, serving just five years in prison despite being involved in five murders.

"You won against the system," Carney said.

"What did I win?" Weeks shot back. "What did I win?"

"You won five years," Carney suggested.

"Five people are dead," Weeks replied. "Five people are dead."

"Does that bother you at all?"

"Yeah," Weeks said, "it bothers me."

"How does it bother you?" Carney asked, pushing his buttons.

"Because we killed people that were rats, and I had the two biggest rats right next to me," Weeks responded.

About a half hour after testimony wrapped up, Jay Carney was on the sidewalk outside the courtroom, beaming as much as a defense lawyer with an impossible case can. He'd had a good day, he figured. He got Weeks to lose his cool, threaten him, admit to being an inveterate liar, and talk like a thug. Onlookers saw it as a hollow victory. The jurors now knew what a thug Weeks was, but they also knew who had tapped him as his sidekick and who had shaped him as a criminal: Whitey Bulger.

The Bulger trial coincided with another historic gathering in the waterfront courthouse. One day, Whitey and Dzhokhar Tsarnaev, the accused Boston Marathon bomber, were in the same courthouse at the same time. Tommy Donahue remarked on the odd symmetry of the day. "The two biggest scumbags in recent Boston history are in the courthouse at the same time," he said. "Whitey and that little terrorist. Actually, come to think of it, Whitey was a terrorist, too."

In the hours before Tsarnaev's arraignment, Coast Guard gunboats cruised the inner harbor, sharing the water with commuter ferries and tourist boats. The last time there'd been a show of force like that had been two years before, when Whitey was arraigned at the same courthouse. Whitey terrorized people to accumulate wealth and power. Just why Dzhokhar Tsarnaev and his brother allegedly placed two backpacks with bombs on a crowded Boylston Street sidewalk on Patriots' Day, killing 3 people and injuring 264 others, is anybody's guess. If not for the remarkable work of the police, firefighters, paramedics, and assorted civilians, not to mention the extraordinary skills of the doctors, nurses, and others at the city's hospitals, Tsarnaev might well have been facing as many murder charges as Whitey.

Outside the courthouse, the bank of cameras waiting for Dzhokhar Tsarnaev was five times larger than that of the regular gang attending the Whitey trial. If Whitey knew someone else was stealing the spotlight, it must have driven him crazy.

Before Pat Donahue took the witness stand, there was yet another drug pusher up there talking about how Whitey Bulger had shaken him down. It was getting almost monotonous, the endless river of gritty particulars. Pat Donahue was different. She had raised her three sons alone after Whitey and a second man murdered her husband. Prosecutor Brian Kelly's questioning of Pat Donahue was basic, to the point. Whitey's lawyer Jay Carney bent over backwards to be solicitous to Pat Donahue because doing so served his purpose, keeping the focus away from his client and on the FBI and DOJ corruption. Carney mentioned how little the Justice Department seemed to have done to expose the identity of the second gunman. Carney asked her if she believed the second gunman was Pat Nee, a longtime Whitey henchman.

"Yes," Pat Donahue replied.

When Carney asked her how much interest she had seen the government show in going after Pat Nee, Kelly objected, and Judge Denise Casper sustained the objection. Still, Pat Donahue managed to sum up her family's frustration quite well. "I don't understand why all these people involved in my husband's death are still walking around," she said.

But it was Kelly who got the final dig.

"You are aware that the man who did that shooting is sitting right here, James Bulger?" Kelly asked her.

"Yes," she replied.

The focus remained on Whitey's victims when Steve Davis took the stand. He recalled how his sister Debbie disappeared in 1981, and said that he had always suspected that her boyfriend, Steve Flemmi, Whitey's partner in crime, was responsible. Flemmi kept coming to the Davis house and telling Olga Davis, Debbie's mother, that he was looking for her daughter. Flemmi had helped bury Debbie near the Neponset River Bridge. "Did you ever see your sister again?" prosecutor Zachary Hafer asked. "No," Steve Davis replied. "Not until yesterday." He meant the photos of her remains that had been put on a video screen the day before.

Carney asked Steve Davis if he wanted to say anything else about his sister.

"She was a beautiful young woman," Steve Davis said. "She had no enemies. Except for two."

———

As it was retold in court, Whitey's life story played out like a movie script, with plot twists so bizarre they would be considered implausible by most screenwriters. So it was fitting that Whitey Bulger's trial would see another such twist: the murder of a man he'd taken advantage of years ago, a man chafing to bear witness against him.

One morning deep into the trial, Steve Davis was so concerned that he hadn't heard back from his friend Steve Rakes that he stopped by Rakes's house in Quincy before he headed into the courthouse. Stippo, as Rakes was known, was not there. He was dead, found dumped by the side of a road in Lincoln, a tony Boston suburb. The news of Rakes's death shook the other victims. They had become something of a family, joined by their mutual hatred of Whitey Bulger and the FBI that enabled him.

Pat Donahue shook her head. "I can't believe he's dead," she said. "Steve was such a nice man. We all know each other. We all sit with each other. We all support each other. And now this."

On the day he disappeared, Steve Rakes had been talking about how he was looking forward to testifying—to telling the jury how, twenty-nine years ago, Whitey Bulger and Steve Flemmi and Kevin Weeks forced him to sell his liquor store at gunpoint. "I can't wait," Steve Rakes had said.

He especially wanted to rebut the testimony of Weeks, who had insisted that Rakes was lying about how the takeover of the liquor store at the Old Colony rotary had gone down.

The day before he died, Steve Rakes found out that the government was not going to call him as a witness. Most likely the prosecutors made the clinical assessment that calling someone who would challenge the testimony of their star witness, Kevin Weeks, was not in their interest. Whatever the reason, they were denying Steve Rakes something he had looked forward to for almost thirty years. "He was upset," Steve Davis said. "He had been, like all of us, waiting for the day to point the finger at Whitey and tell the jury what Whitey had done to his family."

The timing of the death fueled all sorts of conspiracy theories, but within weeks the police had charged a shady businessman with lacing Rakes's iced coffee with poison. Whitey, Weeks, and the usual suspects hadn't had anything to do with it. It was just about money.

The reunion of Whitey Bulger and Steve Flemmi was in many ways the climax of the trial. It started as a staring match the day after Stippo Rakes's body was found and ended four days later, with a hail of obscenities in between.

Whitey and Flemmi hadn't seen each other in eighteen years. Flemmi, 79, sat in the witness box, glaring at Whitey, who glared back. On direct examination, Flemmi immediately attacked Whitey's claim that he wasn't an informant. He said that Whitey had done all the talking when the two informants, Whitey and Stevie, had met with Connolly. Flemmi was only on the stand for about fifteen minutes before the judge called it a day. As the jury filed out, Whitey and Stevie glared at each other again. Stevie mouthed curses at Whitey. Whitey mouthed them back. They looked like a pair of ill-tempered children.

When Flemmi got back on the witness stand the next day, he showcased an impressive memory, rattling off details about murders from the 1960s, dispassionately recalling shooting men in the head the way other men of his generation might remember Ted Williams hitting a home run at Fenway Park. Whitey, seated nearby, seemed bored by the rendition. Even when Flemmi started talking about how Whitey had not only convinced him to kill his longtime girlfriend Debbie Davis in 1981 but had strangled her himself, Whitey kept his head down.

Whitey thought Davis knew too much about their criminal partnership and dealings with John Connolly. He wanted her dead. Flemmi testified that he resisted but eventually caved.

"My mother bought a house in South Boston," Flemmi said. "He said, 'Bring her there.'" Flemmi didn't say and federal prosecutor Fred Wyshak didn't ask, but that house was right next door to the home of Bill Bulger, Whitey's politician brother. It was an odd omission by the prosecutors, because they had at other times in the trial seemed to take delight in introducing Bill Bulger's name into testimony, knowing it drove Whitey crazy to discuss his family in public.

"She walked in the entrance there and he grabbed her by the neck," Flemmi testified. "I couldn't do it. He knew it. He told me, 'I'll take care of it.'" Flemmi claims he stood there helplessly as Whitey choked the life out of Davis, dragging her toward the basement steps and into the basement, where they had laid out a tarp to remove her teeth. When Davis was dead, Whitey went upstairs and took a nap on the floor because there was no furniture in the house.

Wyshak asked Flemmi if shirking the dirty work was typical of Whitey. "That's what he does," Flemmi said. Same thing when they were burying Davis. Stevie dug the hole. You mean, Wyshak said, Whitey kills people and lets everybody else do the work? Whitey's lawyers objected. But the jury had heard it anyway. That was all Wyshak wanted.

Whitey's lawyer Hank Brennan had a field day with Steve Flemmi on cross-examination. When Brennan observed that Flemmi had had a sexual relationship with Deborah Hussey, the daughter of Flemmi's longtime live-in girlfriend, Flemmi objected, saying that there had been no intercourse. It was just oral sex. And it was consensual, Flemmi said with a straight face. When Brennan pointed out that what Flemmi did to Debbie amounted to sexual abuse, Flemmi shook his head. "I never inflicted any abuse on her," he said. Flemmi only reluctantly acknowledged that Debbie Hussey had called him "Daddy."

"Didn't Debbie sit on your knee and you read stories to her?" Brennan asked.

Flemmi scoffed at the idea. "I didn't even do that with my own children," he replied indignantly, pointing out that Debbie Hussey wasn't his biological child.

———

The myth that Whitey never killed women exploded with Flemmi's and Weeks's testimony. The myth that Whitey Bulger only killed other criminals died with Michael Donahue, an innocent man, on the waterfront. The myth that Whitey would go out in a blaze of glory died in 2011 on the oil-stained floor of a garage in Santa Monica, where Whitey spent fifteen years hiding in plain view.

Scott Garriola, the FBI agent who pointed his gun at Whitey on that unremarkable early summer afternoon, and the prosecution's last witness, testified that Whitey ignored his demands to kneel down in the garage of the Princess Eugenia apartment complex.

"He swore at us," Garriola testified.

Whitey's defiance was not an attempt at suicide-by-cop.

"He told us he wouldn't get down because there was grease on the ground," Garriola said.

Once cuffed, Whitey quickly dropped the charade that he was Charlie Gasko, the name he'd taken on. He told Garriola where the guns and money were stashed in the walls. And he became the gentleman gangster again, telling Garriola he was being cooperative in the hopes that the feds would show Cathy Greig some leniency. At the mention of Cathy's name during Garriola's testimony, Whitey's face brightened. He looked wistful, no doubt recalling what he considered the happiest years of his life. He looked forlornly at the photos of their old apartment in Santa Monica as they flashed on the video screen on the defense table.

Before Whitey signed the documents consenting to the search of his apartment, he stopped and said, "First time I've signed this name in a long time." He also insisted to Garriola that, despite his arsenal, he had no intention of starting a final firefight. He said he didn't want a stray bullet to hit anybody.

If the first trial about Whitey's crimes ended with Garriola's testimony, the second trial—for his reputation—began in earnest after the prosecution rested. In their defense of the mobster, Jay Carney and Hank Brennan assumed the mantle of prosecutors. Their interest in defending their client appeared secondary to indicting the FBI and the Justice Department. It was obvious that Whitey himself was the author of this strategy.

The first defense witness was retired FBI supervisor Bob Fitzpatrick, called ostensibly to bolster Whitey's claim that he wasn't an informant.

Being an FBI informant is not a crime, and it was not part of the indictment. But Whitey was obsessed with refuting his informant status. Under questioning by Brennan, Fitzpatrick initially seemed to help. He described meeting Whitey in 1981 and said that Whitey told him he wasn't an informant, that he didn't take money, and that he wouldn't testify against anyone. Fitzpatrick recommended closing him out, saying he was an informant in name only. It was just what Whitey and his lawyers wanted to hear.

On cross-examination, prosecutor Brian Kelly stood and fired: "It's fair to say that you're a man who likes to make up stories?" It was a devastating opening, and Fitzpatrick never recovered. Kelly quickly established that Fitzpatrick was fond of embellishment, exaggerating his roles in various high-profile cases.

If Fitzpatrick turned out to be a disaster for the defense, the photos that the defense submitted to the court would have been an even bigger problem had they been submitted to the jury. Whitey's lawyers had intended for the images to show him as an ordinary man who loved people and animals. In one, he sat with Monsignor Fred Ryan. Perhaps this was meant to highlight that respectable folks, especially clergy, saw the good in him. But Ryan, as it happened, was one of the worst sexual predators in the history of the Archdiocese of Boston. Whitey's lawyers only learned of the miscue when Pat Donahue clued them in.

"Hey, that priest in the photo with Whitey is a pedophile," Pat Donahue told Jay Carney after testimony wrapped for the day.

Jay Carney's eyes widened. "Oh, no," he said.

Whitey had told everybody that he'd get up on the witness stand and take on all comers. He wrote long, wounded letters from jail, complaining about the FBI's duplicity, boasting about how he would reveal the government's lies. In the end, he chose not to testify. An old friend from the Alcatraz years to whom Whitey had addressed many of those letters found the silence telling. "It proves he was a rat," said Richard Sunday. "He couldn't face the questions they would throw at him . . . and he folded."

When Judge Denise Casper asked Bulger if he had made the decision not to testify voluntarily, Whitey explained his silence. "I feel that I've been choked off from having an opportunity to give an adequate defense." Whitey said he had saved prosecutor Jeremiah O'Sullivan from being murdered by the Mafia and that O'Sullivan, in gratitude, had "promised to give me immunity."

Whitey had no documents, no witnesses, to back up this claim. O'Sullivan was conveniently dead. But Whitey felt horribly aggrieved. "I didn't get a fair trial," Whitey told the judge just before his defense rested, "and this is a sham, and do what youse want with me. That's it. That's my final word."

He made one last attempt to defend the image that had meant so much to him for so long. After his client decided not to testify, Carney announced that Whitey wanted to donate to the Donahue and Halloran families the $822,000 seized by the FBI from his apartment in Santa Monica.

The prosecutors rolled their eyes. They believed Whitey chose not to testify because he did not want to submit himself to their cross-examination. He would have been presented with court documents from 1956 that showed how, early in his career, he was already playing the role of informant, implicating two of his accomplices in bank robberies to get leniency for himself and his girlfriend. He would have been asked about his family, especially his interactions with his brothers Bill and Jack, in the years when he was murdering people just down the street from their homes, and while he was on the run. Prosecutors were prepared to play taped conversations Whitey had had with Bill during jailhouse visits. The government by law has to share evidence with the defense, so Whitey knew all this when he opted not to testify. He wasn't going to do that to his little brother.

As in their opening statements, the lawyers offered wildly divergent narratives in their closings. Whitey sat at the defendant's table, pushing a pen around a legal pad as prosecutor Fred Wyshak talked for almost three and a half hours, pointing to what was now a mountain of evidence.

Whitey's lawyer Hank Brennan took his turn, also pointing his finger at the bad guy. But it wasn't Whitey. It was the government that had enabled him and then had the gall to sit in judgment of him. Brennan did not mention the specific crimes Whitey was charged with, concentrating instead on the FBI that had protected him. Nothing Brennan said was untrue, and it was impossible for the victims' families in the gallery not to root for him as he ticked off the FBI's atrocious behavior in enlisting, protecting, and tipping off Whitey and then halfheartedly hunting for him when he first went on the run.

There was, however, a disconnect between the defense's almost gleeful recounting of FBI and Justice Department corruption and the truth. What they were describing was merely the cover-up. What they omitted were the crimes themselves and the fact that Whitey was the man behind them.

The prosecution gets to speak last in criminal trials, and that gave Wyshak a second shot. He was much stronger in his rebuttal. He appeared genuinely offended by what Brennan and Carney had said. His voice was louder, edgier, at times cracking with emotion. What bothered him most was the nerve of Whitey and his lawyers. It offended him that they acted as if they cared deeply about the sorrows of the Donahue family.

Wyshak saw nothing but hypocrisy at the heart of Whitey's

empty gesture to offer up the $822,000, which had already been seized by the government. For many years it had been Wyshak, prosecutor Brian Kelly, and State Police Lt. Steve Johnson and DEA agent Dan Doherty who had sat behind the Donahues in court, showing them support, defying their Justice Department colleagues who fought the family's lawsuit seeking damages from the government.

"The defense wants to hold themselves up as sympathetic to the Donahues," Wyshak told jurors. "Don't buy it."

In the end, the jury didn't. It took five days of highly contentious, door-slamming deliberations, but they ultimately convicted Whitey of thirty-one counts in the sweeping indictment and found that he committed twenty-two underlying racketeering acts: drug dealing, extortion, murder, the works.

Whitey stood poker-faced as he learned his fate, showing not a hint of emotion even as the court clerk, Lisa Hourihan, read "not proved" to the first seven charges of murder. Just as quickly, Hourihan began saying "proved" over and over again. Whitey was found to have participated in eleven of the nineteen murders he was accused of as part of a racketeering count. The jury's reasoning was obvious: Any murder in which John Martorano was the sole accuser was a murder "not proved," meaning jurors unanimously agreed that prosecutors had failed to present enough evidence to establish beyond a reasonable doubt that Whitey had participated in those slayings. Family members reacted with bitterness and disbelief to the announcement that the jury could not confirm that Whitey had had a hand in the slaying of the man they'd lost, the father, husband, or son. "Are you kidding me?" gasped the daughter of Buddy Leonard, one of the dead, before running out of the courtroom.

Still, jurors only needed to find that prosecutors had proven that Whitey had participated in two acts to find him guilty of the overarching racketeering count, and in a resounding victory for the prosecutors, they found that he had participated in twenty-two—including eleven of the slayings. The jury found Whitey not guilty of only one of the thirty-two counts, the extortion of bookie Kevin Hayes.

In the cases of Paulie McGonagle, buried in the sands of Tenean Beach, Eddie Connors, slaughtered in a phone booth, Tommy King, buried in the banks of the Neponset River, Richie Castucci, shot in the head as Whitey watched him count money, Roger Wheeler, the Oklahoma businessman gunned down in the parking lot of his country club, Brian Halloran, the potential witness against Whitey, Michael Donahue, the innocent truck driver, John Callahan, the architect of the Wheeler hit, Bucky Barrett, the safe cracker, John McIntyre, the idealistic IRA sympathizer, and Debbie Hussey, the tortured soul abused by the man who was like her own stepfather, Steve Flemmi, the jury found that the prosecution had proven its case.

Whitey could find some satisfaction, in his determined, delusional way, in the fact that the jury reached "no finding" on the murder of Debbie Davis. Jurors said they were divided, with a slight majority in favor of conviction, but in the end it was only Steve Flemmi's direct testimony they had to go on, and they wouldn't believe anything Flemmi said if it wasn't corroborated by someone else.

"At least they didn't say not guilty, or even not proven," said Steve Davis, Debbie's brother, choking back emotion. "I know he was there. I know Whitey was part of my sister's murder. That's all that matters."

Jurors found that prosecutors had failed to prove that Whitey had participated in the slayings of Michael Milano, Al Plummer, William O'Brien, James "Spike" O'Toole, Al Notarangeli, James Sousa, and Francis "Buddy" Leonard.

Whitey gave a thumbs-up to his brother Jackie and two of his nieces, Bill Bulger's daughters, as he was led away. Bill hadn't shown up at the trial. Not once.

———

After the verdict, as the marshals drove Whitey up Northern Avenue for just about the last time—besides his sentencing in November 2013—it may have occurred to Whitey that he never got to set foot on the shiny new Southie waterfront that had been transformed during his sixteen years on the run. And that he never would.

In 1982, when Whitey murdered Brian Halloran and Michael Donahue just a few hundred yards from the courthouse, the waterfront was a derelict section of the city. The stench from the fish processing plants in the Lower End wafted toward it on windy days. There were only a few decent restaurants—Anthony's Pier 4, Jimmy's Harborside, the Daily Catch—and the bars were gin mills that catered to fishermen. Today, the waterfront glistens with new money. Office and apartment buildings go up every year. Gleaming restaurants open every month. Tourists spill from the hotels. While Whitey hid in open view in Santa Monica, the waterfront was rebranded as the Seaport.

Louis, the most exclusive men's clothing store in Boston, where Whitey bought some of his suits, left the classically fashionable Back Bay for the upstart, posh Seaport. The neighborhood even landed a museum, the Institute of Contemporary Art (ICA), with its folding ribbon design and a cantilever hanging boldly above the water's edge. Anthony's was once the city's most profitable and politically connected restaurant, where Whitey's politician brother Bill held "times"—a quaint, provincial term for fund-raisers. But the restaurant's clientele died off or moved to the new, trendy places just down the street. Sitting in the shadow of the ICA's aggressive modernity, Anthony's seemed as old-fashioned as its popovers; it closed in the middle of Whitey's trial.

Further down Northern Avenue, every new restaurant seemed to be doing a booming business. The young people who pay as much as three thousand dollars a month for a nearby two-bedroom apartment think nothing of dropping twelve dollars on a martini.

Gin mills like the Pier, where Halloran and Donahue had their last drink, are long gone, as are the fishermen.

This was the new waterfront that Whitey saw for the first time in June 2011, when he returned for his arraignment after his arrest in California. Back in the 1970s, Whitey was so sure he was going to be assassinated in the Southie gang war that he went out and bought a fancy suit and hung it in his girlfriend's closet. He wanted to look good in his open casket. In a letter he wrote from jail, he wondered whatever happened to that suit. Up until recent years, it probably would have still fit with just a few alterations.

As much as he didn't recognize the waterfront that greeted his return to town, Whitey wouldn't recognize Broadway, east or west. Twenty-somethings holding Starbucks lattes wait for the bus across from the sushi joint that used to be Triple O's. From the Lower End to City Point, the dark, dingy pubs where Whitey's bookies sat half-hidden in the corner, like drowsy dogs, have given way to bright, airy bars with French doors where the point is to be seen. They burst with the young, few of them Southie natives. At Lincoln, across from the West Broadway parking lot where Whitey read the newspaper, patrons wait on the sidewalk for a table. Stylish young women jog around Castle Island, where Whitey walked daily with Kevin Weeks. The liquor store that gave Whitey a legitimate stream of income is now run by a gregarious Vietnamese guy.

The transformation of Whitey's Southie from blue-collar town to playground for new blood and new money is not the only thing that has changed in a city where he will forever be remembered as its most notorious criminal. For two months, as Whitey sat and watched an absurd cast of killers and drug dealers and bookies point at him, all of them, the accused and the accusers, appeared to be visitors from another planet, another time and place. None of them belonged in a city and a neighborhood where Whitey once ruled. Southie moved on. Boston moved on. Whitey just moved away.

The young people who flirt with each other at Whiskey Priest, a new bar located at the spot where Whitey leveled his rifle at Michael

Donahue and Brian Halloran, don't even know who Whitey Bulger is. And they don't care. He is not part of their Southie, their Boston, their world. Whitey is a ghost. He's not even dead yet, but he's a ghost.

Whitey scribbled at the defense table, as he scribbled in his cell in Plymouth. It is said he is back to writing his memoirs. He is still determined to write his own history, to tell his story in a forum where no one asks him uncomfortable questions about his many crimes and cruelties.

In one of his letters, Whitey compared himself to Philip Nolan, the protagonist in the Edward Everett Hale story "The Man Without a Country." Philip Nolan is a noble if flawed character who feels unjustly persecuted by his government.

But Whitey isn't Philip Nolan. He's Gypo Nolan, the protagonist from the great Liam O'Flaherty novel *The Informer*. Gypo Nolan sold out his friends and brought great shame on his family because he was a tout. He was an informer.

And so, the world now knows for certain, was Whitey Bulger.

Notes

Prologue

1 Whitey Bulger, letter to Richard Sunday, March 23, 2012.
2 Whitey Bulger, letter to Richard Sunday, April 2, 2012.
3 Whitey Bulger, letter to Richard Sunday, April 11, 2012.
4 Ibid.

Chapter 1. The Lessons of Logan Way

1 Jim Sullivan, *South Boston* (Charleston, SC: Arcadia Publishing, 2007), 79.
2 United States Circuit Court, Boston, naturalization record of James J. Bulger Sr., and the 1990 US Federal Census Record, the National Archives at Boston, Waltham, Massachusetts, vol. 442, 123.
3 "Charlestown Boy Injured," *Boston Daily Globe*, June 25, 1899.
4 William M. Bulger, *While the Music Lasts: My Life in Politics* (Boston: Houghton Mifflin, 1996), 20. While he has given the *Boston Globe,* and the authors, interviews in the past, William M. Bulger refused to be interviewed specifically for this book. His 1996 memoir therefore is one of the few available sources on the Bulgers' early family life.
5 Ibid., 22
6 Ibid., 32.
7 Thomas H. O'Connor, *South Boston, My Home Town: The History of an Ethnic Neighborhood* (Boston: Quinlan Press, 1988), 192.
8 William Bulger, interview with the *Boston Globe* Spotlight Team, 1988.

9 O'Connor, *South Boston, My Home Town*, 190.

10 William McGonagle (Boston Housing Authority administrator), interview with the authors, February 2012.

11 George Pryor, interview with the *Boston Globe* Spotlight Team, 1988.

12 "Oral History Interview of Robert F. Moakley and Thomas J. Moakley," Moakley Archive and Institute, Suffolk University, April 29, 2003, 6.

13 Ibid., 10.

14 Ibid., 8.

15 Bulger, *While the Music Lasts*, 1–2.

16 Patrick J. Loftus, *That Old Gang of Mine: A History of South Boston* (South Boston: TOGM-P.J.L., 1991), xxi.

17 Bulger, *While the Music Lasts*, 3.

18 Loftus, *That Old Gang of Mine*, 504.

19 Robert Moakley, interview with the *Boston Globe* Spotlight Team, 1988.

20 Will McDonough, interview with the authors, January 1995.

21 Bulger, *While the Music Lasts*, 22.

22 Ibid., 2.

23 William Bulger, interview with the *Boston Globe* Spotlight Team, 1988.

24 Jack Beatty, *The Rascal King: The Life and Times of James Michael Curley, 1874–1958* (Reading, Mass.: Addison-Wesley, 1992), 136.

25 William Bulger, interview with the *Boston Globe* Spotlight Team, 1988.

26 O'Connor, *South Boston, My Home Town*, 191.

27 Ibid., 193.

28 William Bulger, interview with the *Boston Globe* Spotlight Team, 1988.

29 "Oral History Interview of Robert F. Moakley and Thomas J. Moakley," 4.

30 United States District Court, Boston, Presentencing Report for James J. Bulger Jr., 1956.

31 Ibid.

32 Lindsey Cyr, interview with the authors, October 2012.

33 Bulger, *While the Music Lasts*, 31.

34 Ibid., 29.

35 Ibid., 31.

36 Joe Quirk, interview with the *Boston Globe* Spotlight Team, 1988.

37 Sally Dame, interview with the *Boston Globe* Spotlight Team, 1988.

38 Robert Moakley, interview with the *Boston Globe* Spotlight Team, 1988.

39 Sally Dame, interview with the *Boston Globe* Spotlight Team, 1988.

40 Ann McCarthy, interview with the *Boston Globe* Spotlight Team, 1988.

41 Bulger, *While the Music Lasts*, 32.

42 Ibid., 31.

43 William Bulger, interview with the *Boston Globe* Spotlight Team, 1988.

44 Dick Lehr and Shelley Murphy, "Agent, Mobster Forge a Pact on Old Southie Ties," *Boston Globe*, July 19, 1998, Part 1 of the *Boston Globe* Spotlight report in 1998 by Gerard O'Neill, Dick Lehr, Shelley Murphy, and Mitchell Zuckoff. All of the John Connolly interviews were with Murphy, one of the authors of this book.

45 Lehr and Murphy, "Agent, Mobster."

46 William Bulger, interview with the *Boston Globe* Spotlight Team, 1988.

47 John Connolly, interview with the authors, November 1985.

Chapter 2. Stick-up Man

1 Whitey Bulger, letter to Richard Sunday, March 23, 2012.

2 Bulger, *While the Music Lasts*, 30.

3 Ibid., 33.

4 Report by the Classification Committee, US Penitentiary, Atlanta, February 4, 1959.

5 Charles Clifford (lawyer from Charlestown who represented bank robbers for many years), interview with the authors, October 2010.

6 George Pryor, interview with the *Boston Globe* Spotlight Team, 1988.

7 William McGonagle, interview with the authors, February 2012.

8 Kevin Weeks, interview with the authors, January 2012.

9 Annual Review, United States Penitentiary, Atlanta, 1956.

10 *Pawtucket Evening Times*, May 17, 1955.

11 *Providence Journal*, "Grim Trio Cows 19 in Branch of Industrial National," May 18, 1955.

12 Presentencing Report for James J. Bulger Jr., 1956.

13 *Hammond Times*, November 24, 1955.

14 Teletype from Miami Police Department to Boston Police Department, December 2, 1955.

15 Federal Bureau of Investigation report made by Special Agent Herbert F. Briick, July 13, 1956.

16 Ibid.

17 Whitey Bulger, letter to Richard Sunday, June 30, 2012.

18 Presentencing Report for James J. Bulger Jr., 1956.

19 "South Boston Man Gets 20 Years for 3 Holdups," *Boston Globe*, June 21, 1956.

20 Betsy Drinan (niece of Father Drinan), interview with the authors, June 2012. The Drinans were not related to the family of the same name who lived in the same Logan Way building as the Bulgers.

21 Whitey Bulger, letter to Rev. Robert Drinan, June 23, 1956, part of Drinan's personal papers stored at Boston College.

Chapter 3. The University of Alcatraz

1   Classification study, August 23, 1956. Inmate Case File AZ-1428, BULGER, James Joseph Jr., "Comprehensive Inmate Case Files, 19100–1988" (ARC identifier 622809). US Penitentiary, Alcatraz. Record Group 129, the National Archives at San Bruno.

2   Present Situation report, Inmate Case File, the National Archives at San Bruno, 1956.

3   Report in Inmate Case File says he was treated on the neuropsychiatric ward from October 24 to October 26, 1956, after complaining that other men in his cell got on his nerves.

4   Whitey Bulger, letter to Rev. Robert Drinan, Inmate Case File, the National Archives at San Bruno, October 26, 1956.

5   Federal Bureau of Prisons good conduct time regulations, 1956.

6   Special Progress Report, Inmate Case File, the National Archives at San Bruno, October 19, 1961.

7   Reports in Whitey Bulger's prison file, the National Archives at San Bruno.

8   Bulger, *While the Music Lasts*, 77.

9   William Bulger, letter to US Penitentiary, Atlanta, Inmate Case File, the National Archives at San Bruno, July 30, 1958.

10 "Contract between Department of Pharmacology, Emory University School of Medicine and Human Volunteers at U.S. Penitentiary, Atlanta, Georgia," Inmate Case File, the National Archives at San Bruno, August 6, 1957.

11 John Marks, *The Search for the "Manchurian Candidate": The CIA and Mind Control—The Secret History of the Behavioral Sciences* (New York: W. W. Norton, 1979), and "Project MKUltra, the CIA's program of research in behavioral modification," Joint Hearing before the Select Committee on Intelligence and the Subcommittee on Health and Scientific Research of the Committee on Human Resources, United States Senate, 95th Congress, August, 3, 1977, 3 and 4.

12 "Contract between Department of Pharmacology, Emory University School of Medicine and Human Volunteers at U.S. Penitentiary, Atlanta, Georgia," August 6, 1957.

13 Whitey Bulger, letter to Jerry Lewis Champion Jr. from the Plymouth County Correctional Facility, postmarked August 26, 2011. Champion, a Florida-based author and Alcatraz prison historian, shared the previously undisclosed letter with the authors.

14 Ibid.

15 Richard Sunday, interview with the authors, January 2012.

16 Ibid.

17 Ibid.

18 Ibid.

19 "Out-patient Sick Call" card, Inmate Case File, the National Archives at San Bruno, entries dated January 8 and January 15, 1958.

20 Notation on Progress Report dated January 12, 1958, Inmate Case File, the National Archives at San Bruno, November 10, 1958.

21 "Contract between Communicable Disease Center-Public Health Service and Human Volunteers at U.S. Penitentiary, Atlanta, Georgia," Inmate Case File, the National Archives at San Bruno, November 29, 1958.

22 Annual Review, Inmate Case File, the National Archives at San Bruno, January 24, 1958.

23 W. H. York, associate warden, letter to Warden F. T. Wilkinson, Atlanta, Inmate Case File, the National Archives at San Bruno, January 6, 1959.

24 Letters from Bureau of Prisons director James Bennett to Congressman John McCormack and from Bennett to the Atlanta warden, National Archives at San Bruno.

25 Frank Loveland, Bureau of Prisons assistant director, memo to warden, Atlanta, Inmate Case File, the National Archives at San Bruno, March 16, 1959.

26 F. T. Wilkinson, letter to Director James V. Bennett, Inmate Case File, the National Archives at San Bruno, October 16, 1959.

27 William Bulger letter to Warden F. T. Wilkinson, Atlanta, Inmate Case File, the National Archives at San Bruno, September 1, 1959.

28 F. T. Wilkinson, letter to William Bulger, Inmate Case File, the National Archives at San Bruno, September 9, 1959.

29 F. T. Wilkinson, letter to William Bulger, Inmate Case File, the National Archives at San Bruno, September 22, 1959.

30 William Bulger, letter to F. T. Wilkinson, Inmate Case File, the National Archives at San Bruno, September 26, 1959.

31 Ibid.

32 F. T. Wilkinson, letter to Bureau of Prisons Director James V. Bennett, "Recommendation for Transfer to Alcatraz," Inmate Case File, the National Archives at San Bruno, October 16, 1959.

33 James V. Bennett, letter to Daniel O. Holland, counselor at law, Inmate Case File, the National Archives at San Bruno, November 13, 1959. Visit is referenced.

34 Jim Albright (former Alcatraz correctional officer), interview with the authors, February 2012.

35 Peter Fimrite, "Back on The Rock: Former Inmates Catch Up with Their Guards During Joyful Reunion on Alcatraz," *San Francisco Chronicle*, August 14, 2000.

36 Whitey Bulger, letter to Richard Sunday, March 23, 2012.

37 Staff notes, Inmate Case File, the National Archives at Bruno; Richard Sunday, interview with the authors, January 2012.

38 Richard Sunday, interview with the authors, January 2012.

39 Ibid.

40 Exhibit, National Park Service , which maintains Alcatraz Island, now part of the Golden Gate National Recreation Area.

41 Michael Esslinger, *Alcatraz: A Definitive History of the Penitentiary Years* (Carmel: Ocean View Publishing Company, 2003).

42 Richard Sunday and Kevin Weeks, interviews with the authors, January 2012.

43 A. G. Bloomquist, laundry foreman, letter to the Classification Committee, United States Penitentiary, Alcatraz, Inmate Case File, the National Archives at San Bruno, February 20, 1962.

44 Richard Sunday, interview with the authors, January 2012.

45 Robert Schibline, March 2012, and Richard Sunday, January 2012, interviews with the authors.

46 Whitey Bulger, letter to Rev. John O'Shea, Inmate Case File, the National Archives at San Bruno, January 6, 1960.

47 Misconduct report against Whitey Bulger, Inmate Case File, the National Archives at San Bruno, September 14, 1960.

48 T. A. Renneberg, "Informative Report" memo, Inmate Case File, the National Archives at San Bruno, September 26, 1960.

49 "Report of Good Time Forfeiture Hearing in the Case of Bulger, James J. Jr.," Inmate Case File, the National Archives at San Bruno, September 28, 1960.

50 Maurice Ordway, note to Associate Warden Olin Blackwell, Inmate Case File, the National Archives at San Bruno, October 9, 1960.

51 "Good Time Forfeited" report, Inmate Case File, the National Archives at San Bruno, October 18, 1960.

52 Inmate Case File, the National Archives at San Bruno.

53 "Out-patient Record" card, Inmate Case File, the National Archives at San Bruno, entry dated March 31, 1960.

54 Whitey Bulger, "Inmate Request to Staff Member" form, Inmate Case File, the National Archives at San Bruno, March 27, 1960.

55 Richard Barchard, letter, Inmate Case File, the National Archives at San Bruno, November 3, 1960.

56 Richard Sunday, interview with the authors, March 2012.

57 Annual Review, Inmate Case File, the National Archives at San Bruno, March 22, 1961.

58 A. G. Bloomquist, letter to the Classification Committee, March 22, 1961.

59 Whitey Bulger, "Inmate Request to Staff Member," August 17, 1961.

60 Special Review, Inmate Case File, the National Archives at San Bruno, October 19, 1961.

61 A. G. Bloomquist, letter to the Classification Committee, February 20, 1962.

62 John Herring, celhouse-officer-in charge, Special Report memo, Inmate Case File, the National Archives at San Bruno, February 20, 1962.

63 Annual Review, Inmate Case File, the National Archives at San Bruno, March 8, 1962.

64 Whitey Bulger, "Inmate Request to Staff Member," September 18, 1963.

65 "Visitors Voucher," Inmate Case File, the National Archives at San Bruno, January 16, 1964.

66 Judy Meredith, interview with the *Boston Globe* Spotlight Team, 1988.

67 Andrew P. Marinak (Catholic chaplain), letter, US Penitentiary, Lewisburg, Pennsylvania, March 12, 1964.

68 "Report of Interview or Telephone Call" memo, Inmate Case File, the National Archives at San Bruno, March 13, 1964.

69 Progress Report, Inmate Case File, the National Archives at San Bruno, April 1964.

70 Memo, US Penitentiary, Lewisburg, Pennsylvania, Inmate Case File, the National Archives at San Bruno, May 27, 1964.

Chapter 4. Becoming Untouchable

1 Stephen J. Flemmi debriefing by the DEA and Massachusetts State Police, October 29, 2003. Flemmi told investigators that Buddy McLean told him about the origins of the gang war and why he shot Bernie McLaughlin in broad daylight.

2 Shelley Murphy, "Sidekick's Double-Dealing Career Worthy of Master Spy," *Boston Globe*, July 20, 1998.

3 Stephen J. Flemmi debriefing by the DEA and Massachusetts State Police, October 29, 2003.

4 While there is a record of Flemmi's army serial number and his discharge at the rank of corporal, his full military records are believed to have been destroyed in a 1973 fire at the National Personnel Records Center (NPRC) in St. Louis, according to NPRC officials. Flemmi gave an account of his military service to law enforcement officials in October 2003, and it has been referred to in various court proceedings. In addition, the authors have interviewed some of Flemmi's war buddies, one of whom, James Lang, served with Flemmi in the 187th Airborne from 1951 to 1954.

5 Stephen J. Flemmi debriefing by the DEA and Massachusetts State Police, October 29, 2003.

6　Frank Salemme, testimony before the US House Committee on Government Reform, 2003.

7　Stephen J. Flemmi debriefing by the DEA and Massachusetts State Police, October 29, 2003.

8　Gerard O'Neill, Dick Lehr, Shelley Murphy, and Mitchell Zuckoff, the *Boston Globe* Spotlight Team report, 1998. The John Connolly interviews were conducted by Murphy.

9　William Bulger, *While the Music Lasts*, 276. Will McDonough, the *Boston Globe* sportswriter and longtime Bulger family friend, claimed in a 2002 letter to US District Court Judge Joseph Tauro that he arranged the courthouse job for Whitey.

10　Ann McCarthy, interview with the *Boston Globe* Spotlight Team, 1988.

11　Patrick Nee, interview with the authors, February 2012.

12　US Probation Department report, 1969.

13　Kevin Weeks, interview with the authors, January 2012.

14　Patrick Nee, interview with the authors, February 2012.

15　Ibid.

16　Kevin Weeks, interview with the authors, January 2012. Weeks said Whitey gave him a detailed account of shooting Donald McGonagle by mistake. Flemmi gave a similar account to law enforcement officials during his October 2003 debriefing.

17　Kevin Weeks, interview with the authors, January 2012.

18　Patrick Nee, interview with the authors, February 2012.

19　Whitey Bulger, letter to Richard Sunday, March 23, 2012.

20　Ray Richard, "Killeen Was on Gangland 'Hit List' for Two Years, Hub Police Aide Says," *Boston Globe*, May 16, 1972.

21　Patrick Nee, interview with the authors, February 2012.

22　Howie Winter, interview with the authors, August 2012.

23　Ibid.

24　Stephen J. Flemmi debriefing by the DEA and Massachusetts State Police, October 29, 2003.

25　Patrick Nee, interview with the authors, February 2012.

26　Lindsey Cyr, interview with former *Boston Globe* staffer Stephen Kurkjian and Shelley Murphy, September 2009.

27　Ibid.

28　Stephen Kurkjian and Shelley Murphy, "Whitey Bulger Was His Dad," *Boston Globe*, January 24, 2010.

29　Ibid.

30　Howie Carr, *Hitman: The Untold Story of Johnny Martorano, Whitey Bulger's Enforcer and the Most Feared Gangster in the Underworld* (New York: Tom Doherty Associates, 2011), 201.

31 Kurkjian and Murphy, "Whitey Bulger Was His Dad," *Boston Globe*, January 24, 2010.

32 Teresa Stanley, interview with the authors, April 1998, September 2009, and January 2012. Stanley died August 16, 2012, at the age of seventy-one.

Chapter 5. Just Don't Clip Anyone

1 Francis Dooher (a cousin of John Connolly's), in a letter in support of leniency to Judge Joseph Tauro, June 2002.

2 FBI memo, September 19, 1968.

3 Whitey Bulger's FBI informant file.

4 In his 661-page ruling in 1999, Judge Mark Wolf found that Flemmi had let Paul Rico and Dennis Condon know that he and Salemme were in New York while on the lam. Wolf found that Condon contacted John Connolly in New York and sent him "general information and sent him several photographs" of Salemme before Connolly spotted Salemme on the street and arrested him. "Both Flemmi and Condon deny that Flemmi provided the FBI with information that led to Salemme's arrest," Wolf wrote. "In the context of all the credible evidence in this case, it appears that this claim is not correct."

5 Stephen J. Flemmi debriefing by the DEA and Massachusetts State Police, October 29, 2003.

6 John Connolly, interview with the authors, September 1997.

7 Howie Winter, interview with the authors, August 2012.

8 Ibid.

9 Gerard O'Neill, Dick Lehr, Shelley Murphy, and Mitchell Zuckoff, *Boston Globe* Spotlight report, 1998. The John Connolly interviews were conducted by Murphy.

10 Ibid.

11 John Connolly, interview with the authors, February 1998.

12 Ibid.

13 John Martorano, testimony in US District Court, Boston, at Connolly's racketeering trial, May 12, 2002. Bill Bulger testified before the US House Committee on Government Reform in June 2003 that he never asked Connolly to protect Whitey.

14 John Connolly, interviews with the authors, February 1998.

15 Stephen Flemmi, testifying before Judge Mark L. Wolf in US District Court, Boston, August 20, 1998.

16 The account of Whitey Bulger and John Connolly's encounter on Wollaston Beach was detailed in the *Boston Globe* Spotlight report in July 1998 by Gerard O'Neill, Dick Lehr, Shelley Murphy, and Mitchell Zuckoff. The series of interviews with Connolly were done by Murphy.

17 Kevin Weeks, January 2012, and Patrick Nee, February 2012, interviews with the authors.

18 Patrick Nee, interview with the authors, February 2012.

19 Kevin Weeks, interview with the authors, January 2012.

20 Patrick Nee, February 2012, and Howie Winter, August 2012, interviews with the authors.

21 Stephen J. Flemmi debriefing by the DEA and Massachusetts State Police, October 29, 2003.

22 Patrick Nee, interview with the authors, February 2012.

23 Stephen J. Flemmi debriefing by the DEA and Massachusetts State Police, October 29, 2003.

24 Patrick Nee, February 2012, and Kevin Weeks, January 2012, interviews with the authors.

25 The account of the murder of Tommy King is based on the authors' interviews with Kevin Weeks, January 2012, and Patrick Nee, February 2012, and the testimony at various trials by Steve Flemmi and John Martorano.

26 Whitey Bulger's FBI informant file.

Chapter 6. Southie Is His Hometown

 1 The account of Whitey Bulger's torching of the John F. Kennedy birthplace is based on author interviews in 2012 with Patrick Nee, who declined Whitey's invitation to join him that night, and Kevin Weeks, who listened to Whitey's story about what happened that night. It is also based on two separate law enforcement reports about the arson attack: a Brookline Police report, September 8, 1975, which includes interviews with neighbors who reported seeing Whitey's car, and a September 9, 1975, report by state fire marshal Joseph Sneider.

 2 Brookline Police report, September 8, 1975.

 3 Patrick Nee, February 2012, and Kevin Weeks, January 2012, interviews with the authors.

 4 Brookline Police report, September 8, 1975.

 5 Ibid.

 6 Kevin Weeks, interview with the authors, January 2012.

 7 US Census, 1970.

 8 Louis P. Masur, *The Soiling of Old Glory* (New York: Bloomsbury, 2008), 32–40.

 9 Ibid., 33.

10 Bulger, *While the Music Lasts*, 120.

11 Kevin Weeks, interview with the authors, January 2012.

12 Whitey Bulger, letter to Richard Sunday, March 2012.

13 In interviews with the authors both Kevin Weeks, January 2012, and Patrick

Nee, February 2012, said that they believed Whitey was racist, based on their interactions with him over the years and the language he used. In a July 6, 2011, interview with the FBI, Joshua Bond, the property manager at the building in Santa Monica where Whitey lived, said that Whitey "was definitely racist."

14 Patrick Nee, February 2012, and Kevin Weeks, January 2012, interviews with the authors.

15 Joseph Keough, interview with the authors, April 2001.

16 Ibid.

17 Ione Malloy, *Southie Won't Go* (Chicago: University of Illinois Press, 1986), 5.

18 Jim Miara, interview with the authors, May 2012.

19 Robert diGrazia, interview with the *Boston Globe* Spotlight Team, 1988.

20 Ibid.

21 Bulger, *While the Music Lasts*, 165.

22 Christopher Lydon, "Kevin White and the Boston He Imagined," Radio Open Source, February 1, 2012.

23 Ibid.

24 William M. Bulger, interview with the *Boston Globe* Spotlight Team, 1988.

25 Kevin Weeks, Whitey's longtime associate, was among those who held that view. He was working as security aide at South Boston High School when Michael Faith was stabbed and helped detain his attacker.

26 Bulger, *While the Music Lasts*, 147.

27 Whitey Bulger, letter to Richard Sunday, April 2012.

28 *Boston Globe*, "Shots Fired at Globe Plant," October 8, 1974.

29 Whitey Bulger, letter to Richard Sunday, March 2012.

30 Kevin Weeks, interview with the authors, January 2012.

31 Whitey Bulger, letter to Richard Sunday, April 2012.

32 Kevin Weeks, interview with the authors, January 2012.

33 Ibid.

34 Ibid.

35 Kevin Weeks, January 2012, and Patrick Nee, February 2012, interviews with the authors.

36 Kevin Weeks, interview with the authors, January 2012.

37 David S. Nelson, interview with the *Boston Globe*, 1988.

38 Joe Oteri, interview with the authors, January 2012.

39 The account of Brian Wallace's long car ride and conversation with Whitey Bulger is based on an interview with Wallace by the authors, March 2012.

40 Helen Drinan, interview with the authors, March 2012.

Chapter 7. A Beautiful Friendship

1   Stephen J. Flemmi debriefing by the DEA and Massachusetts State Police, October 29, 2003.

2   Ibid.

3   Ibid.

4   Ibid., 53–54.

5   Ibid., 2.

6   Ibid., 13.

7   Stephen Flemmi, testimony at John Connolly murder trial in Miami-Dade Circuit Court, September 22, 2008.

8   Stephen J. Flemmi debriefing by the DEA and Massachusetts State Police, October 29, 2003, 54.

9   Stephen Flemmi, testimony at John Connolly murder trial in Miami-Dade Circuit Court, September 24, 2004.

10 Stephen J. Flemmi debriefing by the DEA and Massachusetts State Police, October 29, 2003, 5.

11 Ibid., 54.

12 Ibid., 54–55.

13 John Connolly, interview with the authors, March 1998.

14 Stephen Flemmi, testimony at John Connolly murder trial in Miami-Dade Circuit Court, 2008.

15 The FBI informant files of Whitey Bulger and Stephen Flemmi.

16 John Connolly, interview with the authors, June 1997.

17 John Connolly, interview with the authors, September 1997.

18 Carr, *Hitman*, 74.

19 John Martorano, testimony at Whitey Bulger racketeering trial in US District Court in Boston on June 17, 2013. The jury found on August 12, 2013, that prosecutors had failed to prove that Whitey was legally responsible for O'Toole's murder.

20 Stephen J. Flemmi debriefing by the DEA and Massachusetts State Police, October 29, 2003, 57.

21 Jerome Sullivan, "Police Lured from Scene of Boxer's Slaying," *Boston Globe*, June 13, 1975.

22 James Ayres, "Ex-Boxer Shot to Death in Dorchester," *Boston Globe*, June 13, 1975 (graphic photo by Bob Dean).

23 Stephen J. Flemmi debriefing by the DEA and Massachusetts State Police, October 29, 2003, 58.

24 John Martorano, testimony at John Connolly murder trial in Miami-Dade Circuit Court, September 17, 2008.

25 Ibid.

26 Ibid.

27 Howie Winter, interview with the authors, August 2012.

28 John Connolly, interview with the authors, September 1997.

29 John Martorano, testimony at John Connolly murder trial in Miami-Dade Circuit Court, September 17, 2008.

30 Sandra Castucci, testimony in US District Court in Boston on June 10, 2009, during a civil trial over her wrongful death suit against the government.

31 Tom Daly, testimony at John Connolly murder trial in Miami-Dade Circuit Court, October 2008.

32 Joe Oteri, interview with the authors, January 2012.

33 Stephen J. Flemmi debriefing by the DEA and Massachusetts State Police, October 29, 2003, 68.

34 This scene is based on testimony that John Morris gave in April 1998 in hearings before Judge Mark Wolf in US District Court, Boston, and on Morris's testimony in 2002 in the John Connolly racketeering trial in US District Court, Boston. It is supplemented by testimony before Judge Wolf in 1998 by Stephen Flemmi and FBI agents Nick Gianturco, John Newton, and James Ring during pretrial hearings in the racketeering case against Flemmi, Whitey, John Martorano, Frank Salemme and Robert DeLuca.

35 Teresa Stanley, interviews with the authors, September 2009.

36 Margaret McCusker, letter to US District Judge Douglas P. Woodlock, June 4, 2012, before the sentencing of her twin sister, Catherine Greig.

37 Sally Jacobs, "The Long, Unlikely Journey of Cathy Greig," *Boston Globe*, November 20, 2011.

38 Charles "Chip" Fleming, interview with the authors, January 2012.

39 Margaret McCusker, letter to US District Judge Douglas P. Woodlock, June 4, 2012.

40 Jacobs, "The Long, Unlikely Journey of Cathy Greig."

41 Ibid.

42 William St. Croix (Steve Flemmi's son), interview with the authors, November 2011; Shelley Murphy, "Breaking Silence, Flemmi Son Says Gangster's Kin Also Victims," *Boston Globe*, January 2, 2012.

43 Stephen J. Flemmi debriefing by the DEA and Massachusetts State Police, October 29, 2003, 90.

44 Steve Davis (brother of Debra Davis), interview with the authors, June 2011.

45 Stephen J. Flemmi debriefing by the DEA and Massachusetts State Police, October 29, 2003, 90.

46 Stephen Flemmi, testimony in US District Court, Boston, July 9, 2009.

47 Ibid.

48 Stephen J. Flemmi debriefing by the DEA and Massachusetts State Police, October 2003, 90–91.

49 Ibid. Teresa Stanley told the authors in an interview in April 1998 that she did not know Whitey was an FBI informant until the fact was disclosed in court in 1997.

50 Stephen Flemmi, testimony in US District Court, Boston, July 9–10, 2009.

51 Victor Davis (brother of Debra Davis) interview with the authors, March 1998.

52 Patrick Nee, interview with the authors, February 2012.

53 Stephen Flemmi, testimony in US District Court, Boston, July 10, 2009.

54 Ibid.

55 Patrick Nee, interview with the authors, February 2012.

56 Stephen J. Flemmi debriefing by the DEA and Massachusetts State Police, October 29, 2003, 92. Patrick Nee, in an interview with the authors in 2012, denied being present for Davis's burial.

57 Steve Davis, interview with the authors, June 2011.

58 Stephen J. Flemmi debriefing by the DEA and Massachusetts State Police, October 29, 2003.

59 Steve Davis, interview with the authors, June 2011. The Davis family blames Flemmi's exploitation of Michelle Davis for her later drug addiction. She died of a heroin overdose in 2006 at the age of thirty-seven.

60 Drug Enforcement Administration, interviews with witnesses who were involved in the disappearance and missing persons investigation of Debra Davis, filed in US District Court, Boston, September 15, 2003.

61 Stephen Flemmi, testimony at John Connolly murder trial in Miami-Dade Circuit Court, September 22, 2008.

62 Stephen J. Flemmi debriefing by the DEA and Massachusetts State Police, October 29, 2003, 75–76.

63 Ibid, 87–88.

64 Ibid.

Chapter 8. Lancaster Street

1 Bob Fitzpatrick, interview with the authors, June 2011.

2 The account of the state police bugging operation at Lancaster Street is based on interviews with the principal investigators, Rick Fraelick, Bob Long, and Jack O'Malley, and with Tim Burke, the prosecutor who obtained court authorization for the bugs, 1988.

3 Bob Long (former state police detective), interview with the authors, 1988.

4 John O'Donovan, interview with the authors, January 1996.

5 John Connolly, interview with the authors, February 1998.

6 Ibid.

7 John Connolly, FBI memo, October 30, 1980.

8 Lawrence Sarhatt, FBI memo, November 25, 1980, debriefing of Whitey Bulger.

9 Ibid.

10 John Connolly, FBI memo, December 2, 1980.

11 Kevin Cullen, "Mobster's Charges Put the FBI on the Defensive," *Boston Globe*, July 5, 1997.

Chapter 9. Circles Within Circles

1   The dialogue for the Dining Room scene at the Ritz is as recalled by Kevin Weeks, in an interview with the authors, January 2012.

2   Kevin Weeks, interview with the authors, 2012.

3   Kevin Weeks, interview with the authors, January 2012.

4   Kevin Weeks and Phyllis Karas, *Brutal: The Untold Story of My Life Inside Whitey Bulger's Irish Mob* (New York: HarperCollins, 2006), 37.

5   Ibid., 44.

6   Kevin Weeks, interview with the authors, January 2012.

7   Mike Swidwinski (retired DEA agent), interview with the authors, January 2007. Swidinski took Whitey's keys to make sure he didn't take off when they were questioning him.

8   Teresa Stanley, interview with the authors, January 2012.

9   Shelley Murphy, "Tales from the Whitey Watch—Former DEA Agent Recounts 2 Years of Stealth, Frustrations," *Boston Globe*, January 18, 2007.

10 Frank Dewan (retired Boston Police detective), interview with the authors, January 2007.

11 Kevin Weeks, interview with the authors, January 2012.

12 Ibid.

13 Patrick Nee, interview with the authors, February 2012.

14 Kevin Weeks, interview with the authors, January 2012.

15 Stephen J. Flemmi debriefing by the DEA and Massachusetts State Police, October 29, 2003, 117.

16 Paul Brown, interview with the authors, 1990.

17 Kevin Weeks, interview with the authors, January 2012.

18 Brian Mooney, "Eerie Graffiti Pops Up in City," *Boston Globe*, September 13, 1990.

19 Kevin Weeks, interview with the authors, January 2012.

20 Frank Bellotti, interview with the authors, August 2012.

21 Bulger, *While the Music Lasts*, 202.

22 Kevin Weeks, interview with the authors, January 2012.

23 Kevin Weeks, testimony at John Connolly racketeering trial in US District Court, Boston, May 15, 2002. All of the agents except Morris denied receiving money from Whitey and Flemmi. Jim Ring testified that he did not receive any gifts from the pair.

24 Kevin Weeks, testimony at John Connolly racketeering trial in US District Court, Boston, May 15, 2002.

25 Nicholas Gianturco, testimony during hearings before Judge Mark L. Wolf in US District Court, Boston, January 15, 1998.

26 John Morris, testimony at John Connolly racketeering trial in US District Court, Boston, May 9, 2002.

27 Jim Ring, testimony during hearings before Judge Mark L. Wolf in US District Court, Boston, June 10, 1998.

28 Kevin Weeks, testimony at John Connolly racketeering trial in US District Court, Boston, May 15, 2002.

29 Kevin Weeks, interview with the authors, January 2012.

30 Stephen J. Flemmi debriefing by the DEA and Massachusetts State Police, October 29, 2003.

31 Stephen Flemmi, testimony at John Connolly murder trial in Miami-Dade District Court, September 22, 2008.

32 Kevin Weeks, interview with the authors, January 2012.

33 John Connolly, interview with the authors, September 1997; Kevin Weeks, interview with the authors, December 2012.

34 John Connolly, interview with the authors, September 1997.

35 John Connolly, interview with the authors, July 1998.

36 IRS special agent Sandra Lemanski, testimony at John Connolly murder trial in Miami-Dade District Court, September 25, 2008.

37 FBI assistant Denise Taiste, testimony at John Connolly murder trial in Miami-Dade District Court, September 25, 2008.

38 Stephen Flemmi, testimony at John Connolly murder trial in Miami-Dade District Court, September 22, 2008.

39 National Park Service Public Affairs Office, Golden Gate Park, February 2012.

40 Richard Sunday, interviews with the authors, December 2002 and January 2012.

41 Teresa Stanley, interview with the authors, January 2012.

42 Whitey Bulger, letter to Richard Sunday, April 20, 2012.

43 Teresa Stanley and Richard Sunday, interviews with the authors, January 2012.

44 Peter Dracopoulos (operator of Alcatraz book and souvenir shack on Pier 41 in San Francisco), interview with the authors, February 2012.

45 Robert Embry (former director of the Atoke Funeral Home), interview with the authors, December 2004.

46 Ibid.

47 Whitey Bulger, letter to Jerry Champion (author and Alcatraz historian), July 2011.

48 Kevin Weeks and Peter Dracopoulos, interviews with the authors, January and February 2012.

49 Leon Thompson's book, *Last Train to Alcatraz*, self-published, inscribed

to Whitey, and letter tucked inside seized by FBI's Bulger Task Force and viewed by the authors.

50 Whitey Bulger, letter to Jerry Champion, July 2011.

51 Ibid.

52 Peter Dracopoulos, interview with the authors, February 2012.

53 Teresa Stanley, interview with the authors, September 2007.

54 Kevin Weeks, interview with the authors, January 2012.

55 FBI ad placed in *Plastic Surgery News* seeking tips on Whitey and Greig's whereabouts, April-May 2010.

56 Margaret McCusker's testimony before a federal grand jury, February 9, 2012.

Chapter 10. Overreach

1 Robert Lenzner and Donald Lowery, "Boston's Links to Jai Alai World," *Boston Globe*, June 7, 1981.

2 David Wessel, "The Life and Death of John B. Callahan," *Boston Globe*, August 8, 1982.

3 Robert Boyle and Nancy Williamson, "The Spreading Scandal in Jai Alai," *Sports Illustrated*, June 11, 1979.

4 David Kindred, "The Hit at Southern Hills," *Golf Digest*, June 2001.

5 George Getschow, Neil Maxwell, Steve Frazier, and Chester Goolrick, "Friends of Slain Telex Chairman Believe He Wanted to End Interests in Gambling," *Wall Street Journal*, June 1, 1981.

6 Robert Lenzner and Donald Lowery, "Boston's Links to Jai Alai World," *Boston Globe*, June 7, 1981.

7 John Martorano, testimony at John Connolly murder trial in Miami-Dade Circuit Court, September 17, 2008.

8 Ibid.

9 Stephen J. Flemmi debriefing by the DEA and Massachusetts State Police, October 29, 2003.

10 Stephen Flemmi, testimony at John Connolly murder trial in Miami-Dade Circuit Court, September 22, 2008.

11 Kevin Weeks, testimony at John Connolly racketeering trial in US District Court, Boston, May 15, 2002, and interview with the authors, January 2012.

12 Ibid.

13 Stephen J. Flemmi debriefing by the DEA and Massachusetts State Police, October 29, 2003.

14 Kevin Weeks, interview with the authors, January 2012.

15 Kevin Weeks, recalling conversations with Whitey while testifying at John Connolly racketeering trial in US District Court, Boston, May 2002, and in interview with the authors, January 2012.

16 John Martorano, testimony at John Connolly murder trial in Miami-Dade Circuit Court, September 17, 2008.

17 Ibid.

18 Ibid.

19 Kindred, "The Hit at Southern Hills."

20 Tulsa Police Department, report on the murder of Roger Wheeler, May 1981.

21 Stephen Flemmi, testimony at John Connolly murder trial in Miami-Dade Circuit Court, September 22, 2008.

22 Sergeant Michael Huff (homicide squad, Tulsa Police Department), letter to US District Court Judge Joseph Tauro, September 4, 2002.

23 John Morris, testimony at John Connolly's racketeering trial in US District Court, Boston, May 9, 2002.

24 Ibid.

25 Daniel Golden, "The Last King of Chinatown," *Boston Globe Sunday Magazine*, November 3, 1991.

26 Commonwealth v. Salemme, Supreme Judicial Court of Massachusetts, April 1, 1985.

27 William Murphy, interview with the authors, February 2012.

28 Brian Halloran, summary of debriefings with FBI agents Leo Brunnick and Gerald Montanari, February 23, 1982.

29 John Morris, testimony at John Connolly racketeering trial in US District Court, Boston, May 9, 2002.

30 Ibid.

31 Ibid.

32 John Morris, testimony at John Connolly racketeering trial in US District Court, Boston, May 9, 2002.

33 Stephen Flemmi, testimony at John Connolly murder trial in Miami-Dade Circuit Court, September 24, 2008. In an interview with the authors in 1998, Connolly said he learned Halloran was shopping a story to the FBI but didn't know he was cooperating until after he was killed and never told Whitey and Flemmi that he was.

34 The dialogue and action described in the Pier restaurant is taken from a report, "Activities of Edward Brian Halloran," May 11, 1982, by FBI special agents Leo E. Brunnick and Gerald J. Montanari, June 23, 1982.

35 Patricia Donahue, interview with the authors, June 2012.

36 Kevin Weeks, testimony at John Connolly racketeering trial, US District Court, Boston, May 14, 2002.

37 Kevin Weeks, interview with the authors, January 2012.

38 Kevin Weeks debriefing by the DEA and Massachusetts State Police, January 24, 2001.

39   Kevin Weeks, testimony at John Connolly racketeering trial in US District Court, Boston, May 13, 2002, and interview with the authors, January 2012.

40   Ibid.

41   Ibid.

42   Judge William G. Young, US District Court, Boston, May 1, 2009.

43   Brief of the Estate of Edward (Brian) Halloran, January 20, 2010.

44   Federal Bureau of Investigation report, May 11, 1982.

45   Kevin Weeks, testimony at John Connolly racketeering trial in US District Court, Boston, May 14, 2002, and interview with the authors, January 2012.

46   Stephen J. Flemmi debriefing by the DEA and Massachusetts State Police, October 29, 2003..

47   Kevin Weeks, interview with the authors, January 2012.

48   Ibid.

49   Ibid.

50   Patricia Donahue, interview with the authors, June 2012.

51   Kevin Weeks, interview with the authors, January 2012.

52   Kevin Weeks, testimony at John Connolly racketeering trial, US District Court, Boston, May 16, 2002.

53   John Morris, testimony at John Connolly racketeering trial, US District Court, Boston, May 9, 2002.

54   Ibid.

55   Brief of the Estate of Edward (Brian) Halloran, January 20, 2010, 14.

56   Stephen J. Flemmi debriefing by the DEA and Massachusetts State Police, October 29, 2003.

57   Ibid.

58   Stephen Flemmi, testimony at John Connolly murder trial in Miami-Dade Circuit Court, September 23, 2008.

59   John Martorano, testimony at John Connolly murder trial in Miami-Dade Circuit Court, September 17, 2008.

60   Ibid.

61   Ibid.

62   Stephen Flemmi, testimony at John Connolly murder trial in Miami-Dade Circuit Court, September 23, 2008.

63   Whitey Bulger's FBI informant file.

64   John Martorano, testimony at John Connolly murder trial in Miami-Dade Circuit Court, September 17, 2008.

65   Ibid.

66   Ibid.

67   The dialogue and action described in the extortion of Michael Solimando is based on testimony by Solimando and Stephen Flemmi at John Connolly murder trial in Miami-Dade Circuit Court in the fall of 2008, and Kevin Weeks, interview with the authors, January 2012.

68 John Morris, testimony at John Connolly racketeering trial in US District Court, Boston, May 9, 2002.

69 Stephen J. Flemmi debriefing by the DEA and Massachusetts State Police, October 29, 2003.

70 Brief of the Estate of Edward (Brian) Halloran, January 20, 2010.

71 Kevin Weeks, interview with the authors, January 2012.

Chapter 11. The Wrong Man

1 In 1986, while one of the authors was riding in Connolly's FBI vehicle, Connolly made statements expressing sympathy for the IRA. When asked how he, a law enforcement agent, could support a group that was engaged in killing police officers, Connolly replied that the Royal Ulster Constabulary, Northern Ireland's police force, was corrupt and that its mostly Protestant members blatantly discriminated against Catholics.

2 O'Connor, *South Boston: My Home Town*, 121.

3 Kevin Weeks, interview with the authors, January 2012.

4 Bulger, *While the Music Lasts*, 4.

5 Kevin Cullen, "Joe Cahill, IRA Leader in Both War and Peace," *Boston Globe*, July 25, 2004. Much of the biographical information on Joe Cahill is contained in Brendan Anderson, *Joe Cahill: A Life in the IRA* (Dublin: O'Brien Press, 2002). It is supplemented by several interviews Cahill gave the authors before his death in 2004.

6 Joe Cahill, interview with the authors, June 1998.

7 John Hurley, interview with the authors, January 1996.

8 Records on file with the Irish government's Department of Foreign Affairs, Iveagh House, Dublin.

9 Kevin Weeks, interview with the authors, January 2012.

10 Patrick Nee, interview with the authors, February 2012.

11 Joe Cahill, interview with the authors, June 1998.

12 Ibid.

13 Stephen J. Flemmi debriefing by the DEA and Massachusetts State Police, October 29, 2003, 116.

14 Kevin Weeks, interview with the authors, January 2012.

15 Stephen J. Flemmi debriefing by the DEA and Massachusetts State Police on corruption, October 2003.

16 Ibid. Flemmi said he believed John Connolly was present when Newton turned the C-4 over to him and Whitey.

17 Kevin Weeks, interview with the authors, January 2012.

18 Patrick Nee, interview with the authors, February 2012.

19 Much of the information about the *Valhalla* voyage is based on interviews with Kevin Weeks, Patrick Nee, and Gary Crossen, the federal prosecutor who investigated the conspiracy. Before he died, Bob Andersen gave Nee an

extensive debriefing on what happened during the time at sea. John McIntyre also gave an extensive accounting of the voyage to Quincy Police detective Dick Bergeron and DEA agent Steve Boeri in October 1994, a report obtained for the *Boston Globe* by reporter Dick Lehr. Weeks and Nee provided most of the information about Whitey's involvement in the *Valhalla* plot. Stephen Flemmi's 2003 debriefing with law enforcement, and his and Weeks's testimony at various trials, also provide details about the organization of the gunrunning mission, what happened on the voyage, and the demise of John McIntyre.

20 Patrick Nee, interview with the authors, February 2012.

21 Ibid.

22 John McIntyre, Quincy Police/DEA interrogation, October 14, 1984.

23 Emily McIntyre, testifying in US District Court, Boston, in *McIntyre v. the United States*, June 16, 2006.

24 Patrick Nee, interview with the authors, February 2012.

25 Kevin Weeks, interview with the authors, January 2012.

26 Sean O'Callaghan told his life story and how he compromised the gunrunning mission on the *Valhalla* in a lengthy jailhouse interview with the authors in December 1994. O'Callaghan's book *The Informer* (London: Bantam Press, 1998) was used to corroborate his interviews with the authors.

27 Sean O'Callaghan, interview with the authors, December 1994.

28 John McIntyre, Quincy Police/DEA interrogation, October 14, 1984.

29 Joe Cahill, interview with the authors, June 1998.

30 Gary Crossen (former federal prosecutor who prosecuted the *Valhalla* conspiracy case), interview with the authors, December 1992.

31 Quincy Police/DEA interrogation of John McIntyre, recorded by Dick Bergeron, October 14, 1984.

32 Report by FBI special agent Roderick Kennedy, October 16, 1984.

33 Stephen Flemmi, testifying in US District Court, Boston, in *McIntyre v. the United States*, June 2006.

34 Kevin Weeks, interview with the authors, January 2012.

35 Stephen J. Flemmi debriefing by the DEA and Massachusetts State Police, October 29, 2003.

36 Kevin Weeks, interview with the authors, January 2012.

37 The dialogue and actions described in the interrogation and death of John McIntyre are derived from the testimony in US District Court, Boston, of Kevin Weeks and Steve Flemmi, June 2006, and from interviews by the authors with Kevin Weeks, January 2012, and Patrick Nee, February 2012.

Chapter 12. Deep in The Haunty

1 Kevin Weeks, interview with the authors, January 2012.

2 Ibid.

3 Whitey Bulger's FBI informant file.

4 John Morris, testimony before Judge Mark Wolf, US District Court, Boston, April 29, 1998.

5 Gerald Clemente, interview with the authors, March 1998.

6 Weeks and Karas, *Brutal*, 109.

7 Kevin Weeks, interview with the authors, January 2012.

8 Steve Flemmi, testimony in US District Court, Boston, July 2009.

9 Weeks and Karas, *Brutal*, 111; Kevin Weeks, interview with the authors, January 2012.

10 Kevin Weeks, interview with the authors, January 2012.

11 Tom Hussey, interview with the authors, June 2009.

12 Stephen J. Flemmi debriefing by the DEA and Massachusetts State Police, October 29, 2003, 111. Flemmi's son William St. Croix said Flemmi maligned his sister to justify killing her.

13 Marion Hussey, testimony in US District Court, Boston, July 20, 2009.

14 Ibid.

15 Kevin Weeks, interview with the authors, January 2012.

16 Whitey Bulger has consistently said to friends that he did not kill Debbie Hussey or Debra Davis. While Flemmi was the only witness to the Davis killing, Kevin Weeks and Flemmi gave similar accounts of the murder of Hussey.

17 Kevin Weeks, interview with the authors, January 2012.

18 Kevin Weeks, debriefing with law enforcement, January 2001, and interview with the authors, January 2012.

19 Kevin Weeks, interview with the authors, January 2012.

20 Kevin Weeks, debriefing with law enforcement, January 2001, and Stephen J. Flemmi debriefing by the DEA and Massachusetts State Police, October 29, 2003.

21 Kevin Weeks, interview with the authors, January 2012.

22 Ibid.

23 Ibid.

24 Stephen Rakes, interview with the authors, May 2001.

25 Joe Lundbohm and John Connolly, interviews with the authors, May 1998.

26 Kevin Weeks, interview with the authors, January 2012.

27 Ibid.

28 William St. Croix (Steve Flemmi's son), interview with the authors, December 2011.

29 Teresa Stanley, interviews with the authors, April 1998, September 2009, and January 2012.

30 Kevin Weeks, interview with the authors, January 2012.

31 Raymond Slinger, testimony in US District Court, Boston, September 23, 1998.

32 Ibid. Kevin Weeks claimed, in an interview with the authors, January 2012, that Whitey asked him to get Slinger a beer.

33 John Newton, testimony in US District Court, Boston, during the Wolf hearings, May 1998.

34 Roderick Kennedy, testimony in US District Court, Boston, during the Wolf hearings, April 1998.

35 Interview, by the authors, with a South Boston woman who attended the wedding and spoke on the condition of anonymity, December 1986.

36 Dan and Nancy Yotts, interview with the authors, December 1987.

37 Ibid.

38 Whitey Bulger's FBI informant file.

39 Paul Corsetti, interviews with the authors, 1988 and October 1997.

40 Ibid.

41 Whitey Bulger's FBI informant file. A judge hearing a civil suit brought by Louis Litif's family ruled that Whitey had shot Litif, but Whitey was never charged with his murder in a criminal complaint.

42 Bob Long and Jack O'Malley (retired Massachusetts State Police detectives), interviews with the authors, October 1988.

43 John Connolly, interview with the authors, February 1998.

44 John Morris, testimony in US District Court, Boston, May 9, 2002.

45 Anthony Cardinale, interview with the authors, June 2011.

46 Dick Lehr and Kevin Cullen, "Liquor Purchase Fuels Friction over FBI-Whitey Tie," *Boston Globe*, November 11, 1990.

47 Thomas Cahill, speaking to DEA undercover agent, as cited in affidavit of Boston Police detective James Carr, February 1989.

48 Mitchell Zuckoff, "FBI in Denial as Bulger Breaks Drug Pact in Southie," *Boston Globe*, July 23, 1998, part of *Boston Globe* Spotlight Team series.

49 John Martorano, testimony in US District Court, Boston, May 2002. Connolly denied receiving the ring and was not found guilty of that charge by a federal jury.

50 John Connolly, interview with the authors, February 1998.

51 William Sessions, letter to John Connolly, October 5, 1990.

52 Shelley Murphy, "Judge Denies Ex-Agent's Effort to Bar Key Prosectuion Evidence," *Boston Globe*, April 10, 2002.

53 Howie Carr, *The Brothers Bulger: How They Terrorized and Corrupted Boston for a Quarter Century* (New York: Warner Books, 2006), 254.

54 Dick Lehr and Gary S. Chafetz, "Crime Figure Invests $1M in Back Bay," *Boston Globe*, December 6, 1993.

55 Memorandum filed by US Attorney in US District Court in Boston in forfeiture case on the seizure of Whitey Bulger's lottery winnings, February 9, 2001.

56 Tom Lyons, former deputy commissioner for veterans services for the city of Boston, interview with the authors, August 2012.

57 William Murphy (former paratrooper who met Whitey at the reunion), interview with the authors, July 1990.

58 Thomas J. Foley and John Sedgwick, *Most Wanted: Pursuing Whitey Bulger, the Murderous Mob Chief the FBI Secretly Protected* (New York: Simon & Schuster, 2012), 37.

59 Tom Foley, interview with the authors, January 2010.

60 Ibid.

61 Ibid.

62 Matthew Brelis, "Chelsea Tavern Owner Guilty of Racketeering," *Boston Globe*, February 20, 1993.

63 Paul Langner, "Café Owner Is Charged with Running Mob 'Bank,'" *Boston Globe*, May 11, 1990.

64 Michael London, from intercepted conversations quoted in indictment, December 9, 1986.

65 Tom Foley, interview with the authors, January 2010.

66 Ibid.

67 Ibid.

68 Ibid.

69 Pat Greaney, interview with the authors, January 2010.

70 Ibid.

Chapter 13. A Head Start

1 John Morris, testimony, US District Court, Boston, May 9, 2002.

2 Teresa Stanley, interviews with the authors, October 2011 and January 2012.

3 Ibid.

4 Kevin Weeks, interviews with the authors, January and May 2012; Teresa Stanley, interviews with the authors, October 2011 and January 2012.

5 Kevin Weeks, interview with the authors, May 2012.

6 Teresa Stanley, interview with the authors, October 2011.

7 Kevin Weeks, interview with the authors, May 2012.

8 Donald K. Stern, testimony at John Connolly racketeering trial in US District Court, Boston, May 8, 2002.

9 Boston weather report, *Boston Globe*, December 23, 1994.

10 The dialogue in this scene comes from multiple interviews with Kevin Weeks and is corroborated by testimony Weeks gave at John Connolly's racketeering trial in US District Court, Boston, May 2002.

11 Dennis O'Callaghan, now deceased, denied being the leak during a May 15, 2002, interview with the authors and while testifying at John Connolly's racketeering trial in US District Court, Boston, May 20, 2002. He was never charged.

12 Teresa Stanley, testimony in US District Court, Boston, during the Wolf hearings, September 18, 1998, and on May 16, 2002, at the John Connolly racketeering trial in US District Court, Boston.

13 Kevin Weeks, interview with the authors, January 2012, and testimony at John Connolly racketeering trial, US District Court, Boston, May 2002. Stephen Flemmi corroborated the dialogue while testifying in several trials, including the John Connolly murder trial in Miami-Dade Circuit Court in September 2008. Former state police lieutenant Richard Schneiderhan was convicted in 2003 of leaking information to Weeks and Flemmi and was sentenced to eighteen months in prison.

14 Kevin Weeks, testimony at John Connolly racketeering trial in US District Court, Boston, May 15, 2002.

15 Mike Brassfield, "Elusive Neighbor Keeps the FBI at Bay," *St. Petersburg Times*, April 27, 1998.

16 Tom Foley, interview with the authors, January 2010.

17 Tom Duffy, interview with the authors, October 2012.

18 Tom Foley, interview with the authors, January 2010.

19 Tom Foley and Pat Greaney, interviews with the authors, January 2010.

20 Kevin Weeks, interview with the authors, January 2012.

21 Tom Foley, interview with the authors, January 2010.

22 Ibid. Retired FBI agent Mike Buckley did not respond to multiple messages seeking comment.

23 Shelley Murphy, "Retired FBI Agent Contradicts Bulger," *Boston Globe*, June 28, 2003.

24 William Bulger, testimony before federal grand jury in Boston, April 5, 2001, and before US House Committee on Government Reform, June 19, 2003.

25 William Bulger, testimony before federal grand jury in Boston, April 5, 2001.

26 Kevin Weeks, interview with the authors, May 2012.

27 John Connolly, interview with the authors, December 2008.

28 Ibid.

29 John Morris, testimony in US District Court, Boston, April 28, 1998.

30 Whitey Bulger, letter to Richard Sunday, May 17, 2012.

31 Ibid.

32 John Morris, testimony in US District Court, Boston, April 28, 1998.

33 Ibid.

34 Whitey Bulger, letter to Richard Sunday, May 17, 2012.

35 Ibid.

36 Kevin Weeks, interview with the authors, January 2012.

37 Teresa Stanley, interview with the authors, April 1998.

38 Government's sentencing memorandum filed in *United States v. Catherine E. Greig*, US District Court, Boston, June 8, 2012; NBC News, *Today*, "Sister of Mobster's Girlfriend: 'He Was a Gentleman,'" June 22, 2012.

39 Kevin Weeks, interview with the authors, January 2012.

40 Whitey Bulger, letter to Richard Sunday, March 23, 2012.

41 Shelley Murphy spent several days in Grand Isle in December 1997, interviewing the Gautreaux family and their in-laws and other locals, and the dialogue and stories recounted here are based on that reporting: Shelley Murphy, "Whitey Bulger's Life on the Run: Fugitive's Trail Crisscrosses US," *Boston Globe*, January 4, 1998.

42 Penny Gautreaux, interview with the authors, December 1997.

43 Ibid.

44 FBI agent Michael Carazza, testimony at Catherine Greig's detention hearing in US District Court, Boston, July 13, 2011.

45 Thomas Rudolph, interview with the authors, December 1997.

46 Penny Gautreaux, interview with the author, December 1997.

47 Whitey Bulger, letter to Richard Sunday, March 23, 2012.

48 Roscoe Besson Jr., interview with the authors, December 1997.

49 Kevin Weeks, interview with the authors, January 2012.

50 Alan Thistle, interview with the authors, February 2004; Shelley Murphy, "Informant in Bulger Case Embraced Work for FBI," *Boston Globe*, March 21, 2004.

51 Ibid.

52 This dialogue is based on interviews by the authors with Kevin Weeks, January 2012, and Teresa Stanley, April 1998 and March 2004.

53 Ibid.

54 Kevin Weeks, interview with the authors, January 2012.

55 Government's sentencing memorandum in *United States v. John P. Bulger*, US District Court, Boston, August 20, 2003.

56 Teresa Stanley, interview with the authors, April 1998.

57 Kevin Weeks, interview with the authors, January 2012.

58 Ibid.

59 Several law enforcement sources in interviews with the authors, 2004 and 2012.

60 Foley and Sedgwick, *Most Wanted*, 163.

61 Kevin Weeks, interview with the authors, January 2012.

62 FBI agent Michael Carazza, testimony at Catherine Greig's detention hearing in US District Court, Boston, July 11, 2011.

63 Retired Boston Police detective Charles "Chip" Fleming (former member of Bulger Task Force), interview with the authors, January 2012.

64 Ibid.

65 Weeks and Karas, *Brutal*, 235.

66 Kevin Weeks, interview with the authors, January 2012.

Chapter 14. Where's Whitey?

1 Shelley Murphy and Maria Cramer, "Whitey in Exile: The Inside Story

of His Fugitive Years and His Unlikely Capture," *Boston Globe*, October 9, 2011.

2 FBI Boston press release, April 5, 2000.

3 FBI agent Walter J. Steffens Jr., testimony in US District Court, Boston, August 11, 1998.

4 Kenneth J. Fishman (Massachusetts judge and former attorney who represented Flemmi), testimony in Miami-Dade Circuit Court, September 25, 2008.

5 Kevin Weeks, testimony at John Connolly racketeering trial in US District Court, Boston, May 2002.

6 Ibid.

7 Stephen Flemmi, testimony at John Connolly murder trial in Miami-Dade Circuit Court, September 23, 2008.

8 Judge Mark Wolf, decision in *United States v. Salemme et al.*, September 19, 1999.

9 Judge Mark Wolf, statements at Stephen Flemmi's sentencing in US District Court, Boston, August 21, 2001.

10 Donald K. Stern, press conference covered by the authors, September 9, 1999.

11 David Wheeler, interview with the authors, March 2007.

12 Kevin Weeks, interview with the authors, January 2012.

13 Ibid.

14 Ibid.

15 Ibid.

16 Massachusetts State Police Report of Investigation, January 13, 2000.

17 Frank Salemme, testimony at John Connolly racketeering trial in US District Court, Boston, May 17, 2002.

18 Attorney Robert Popeo, quoted in Shelley Murphy, "Ex-FBI Agent Joins Heads with Gangster," *Boston Globe*, January 4, 2000.

19 William Bulger, testimony before federal grand jury in Boston, April 5, 2001.

20 John Connolly, interview with the authors, May 2002.

21 Thanassis Cambanis, "Letters from Hollywood Support Connolly," *Boston Globe*, August 10, 2002.

22 Joan Costin, letter sent to Judge Joseph Tauro and contained in John Connolly's sentencing memorandum, September 11, 2002.

23 John Connolly sentencing memorandum, September 11, 2002.

24 John Connolly, interview with the authors, May 2002.

25 David Boeri, news report on WCVB Channel 5, October 4, 2000.

26 Shelley Murphy, "FBI Gets Helps in Bulger Search," *Boston Globe*, November 14, 2000.

27 Thomas Larned, FBI supervisory agent overseeing the Bulger Task Force,

interview with the authors, September 2002; Shelley Murphy, "Hunt for 'Whitey' Bulger Still Alive," *Boston Globe*, September 5, 2002.

28 Shelley Murphy, "Whitey Bulger Reported Seen on London Street," *Boston Globe*, January 3, 2003.

29 British businessman who spoke on condition of anonymity, interview with the authors, December 2002.

30 FBI report, June 28, 2000.

31 Shelley Murphy, "Gangster Listed Brother's Name on Deposit Box," *Boston Globe*, January 3, 2003.

32 Shelley Murphy, "Terror War Slows Hunt for Bulger," *Boston Globe*, December 19, 2004.

33 Judgments in *United States v. Margaret McCusker* and *United States v. Kathleen McDonough*, US District Court, Boston, May 1999.

34 William Chase (retired FBI assistant special agent in charge of the Boston office), interview with the authors, May 2012.

35 Charles "Chip" Fleming, interview with the authors, January 2012; information released by Bulger Task Force at press conference on the tenth anniversary of his disappearance.

36 Kevin Weeks, testimony in US District Court, Boston, during trial of Richard Schneiderhan, March 12, 2003.

37 Whitey Bulger, letter to Richard Sunday, postmarked April 20, 2012.

38 Ibid.

39 Bill Bulger, remarks to the media, June 2, 2003.

40 The tavern owner spoke with the authors in 1996 on the condition of anonymity.

41 Interviews with various law enforcement officials, including retired state police colonel Tom Foley, January 2010.

42 "Condominium Trends," Department of Neighborhood Development, City of Boston, July 2000.

43 Cindy Rodriguez, "Minorities Are Hub Majority, Census Finds," *Boston Globe*, March 22, 2001.

44 US Census figures cited in South Boston Planning District, Boston Redevelopment Authority, March 2011.

45 Keith Messina, interview with the authors, September 2011.

46 Gary Steiner, interview with the authors, January 2012.

47 David Boeri, "We Found Whitey . . . and He's Still Missing," *The Phoenix*, January 4, 2007.

48 FBI press release, "The 'Whitey' Bulger Case: New Campaign Focuses on Mobster's Companion," June 20, 2011.

49 The authors covered John Connolly's murder trial in Miami and were in the courtroom when he was convicted, November 6, 2008.

50 The authors spoke with the prosecution team at its subdued celebration on South Beach after John Connolly's conviction, November 6, 2008.

Chapter 15. St. Monica's West

1 Government's sentencing memorandum in *United States v. Catherine E. Greig*, US District Court, Boston, June 8, 2012.

2 Birgitta Farinelli, interviews with the authors, July and August 2011.

3 Government's sentencing memorandum in *United States v. Catherine E. Greig*, US District Court, Boston, June 8, 2012.

4 Santa Monica rent control records for the Princess Eugenia complex on file at City Hall.

5 Birgitta Farinelli, grand jury testimony US District Court, Boston, August 4, 2011, and interviews with the authors, July and August 2011.

6 Government's sentencing memorandum in *United States v. Catherine E. Greig*, US District Court, Boston, June 8, 2012, p. 8; Teresa Stanley, interview with the authors, July 2011.

7 Whitey Bulger, letter to Richard Sunday, May 20, 2012.

8 Murphy and Cramer, "Whitey in Exile."

9 FBI interview with Joshua Bond, a property manager at the Princess Eugenia, July 28, 2011.

10 Birgitta Farinelli, interviews with the authors, July and August 2011.

11 Confidential source, interview with the authors, 2012.

12 Whitey Bulger, letter to Richard Sunday, May 17, 2012.

13 Ibid.

14 Joshua Bond, interview with the authors, June 2011.

15 FBI interview with Joshua Bond, July 6, 2011.

16 Murphy and Cramer, "Whitey in Exile."

17 Among the books were those written by Kevin Weeks, his longtime right-hand man; Patrick Nee, a rival turned associate turned bitter enemy; and John "Red" Shea, who was convicted of being a member of a drug ring that was paying tribute to Whitey.

18 Whitey Bulger, letter to Richard Sunday, July 9, 2012.

19 Murphy and Cramer, "Whitey in Exile."

20 Birgitta Farinelli, interviews with the authors, July and August 2011.

21 Murphy and Cramer, "Whitey in Exile."

22 Ibid.

23 Affidavit by FBI Special Agent Philip J. Torsney filed in *United States v. Catherine E. Greig*, US District Court, Boston, June 7, 2012.

24 Murphy and Cramer, "Whitey in Exile."

25 Ibid.

26 Whitey Bulger, letter to Richard Sunday, June 30, 2012.

27 Janus Goodwin, interview with the authors, July 2011.

28   Documents filed by prosecutors in *United States v. Catherine E. Greig*, 2012; Murphy and Cramer, "Whitey in Exile."

29   Maria Cramer, "Down-on-His-Luck Vet Befriended by Bulger," *Boston Globe*, October 9, 2011.

30   Documents filed by prosecutors in *United States v. Catherine E. Greig*, 2012.

31   Murphy and Cramer, "Whitey in Exile."

32   Ibid.; California Department of Motor Vehicles records.

33   Affidavit of FBI agent Philip J. Torsney filed in *United States v. Catherine E. Greig*, US District Court, Boston, June 7, 2012; interviews and reporting by *Boston Globe* reporters Maria Cramer and Shelley Murphy.

34   Law enforcement sources told the authors that after his capture Whitey was emotional when discussing Lawlor and upset when recounting his death, June 2011.

35   Documents filed by federal prosecutors in *United States v. Catherine E. Greig*, 2012; documents obtained from the Los Angeles County coroner's office for Sidney Joe Terry, who died in July 2011.

36   Documents filed by federal prosecutors in *United States v. Catherine E. Greig*, 2012.

37   Interviews by the authors and *Boston Globe* reporter Maria Cramer with law enforcement officials and Whitey's neighbors in Santa Monica, June–October 2011.

38   South Boston attorney Richard Lane on WBZ radio show *Nightside with Dan Rea*, July 2012. Lane later told the authors he was unclear whether it was Pistone or another retired law enforcement officer whom Whitey and Greig spotted.

39   Documents filed by prosecutors in *United States v. Catherine E. Greig*, 2012; Kevin Reddington (Greig's attorney), interview with the authors, June 2012.

40   Maria Cramer and Shelley Murphy, "For Neighbors in Calif., Memories Now Seem Surreal," *Boston Globe*, June 25, 2011.

41   Janus Goodwin, interview with the authors and Maria Cramer, July 2011.

42   Birgitta Farinelli, interview with the authors, July 2011.

43   Murphy and Cramer, "Whitey in Exile."

44   Neighbor who spoke on the condition of anonymity, interview with the authors, July 2011.

45   Enrique Sanchez, interview with *Boston Globe* reporter Maria Cramer, July 2011.

46   Joshua Bond, interviews with the authors and Maria Cramer, June and July 2011.

47   Joshua Bond, grand jury testimony, US District Court, Boston, July 28, 2011.

48   Joshua Bond, FBI interview, July 28, 2011.

49   Joshua Bond, interview with the authors and *Boston Globe* reporter Maria Cramer, June and July 2011.

50 Documents filed by prosecutors in *United States v. Catherine E. Greig*, 2012; Kevin Reddington (Greig's attorney), interview with the authors, June 2012.

51 Neighbor who spoke on the condition of anonymity, interview with the authors, July 2011.

52 Interviews by the authors with John Connolly, February 1998, and Kevin Weeks, September 2012. They described how, in the winter of 1990, Whitey discovered that a feral stray had given birth to a litter of kittens in a shed behind Teresa Stanley's house in Southie. He gave them food and put a heater in the shed to keep them comfortable.

53 Murphy and Cramer, "Whitey in Exile."

54 Interview by authors with a law enforcement official who spoke on the condition of anonymity, March 2013.

55 Enrique Sanchez, interview in Spanish with *Boston Globe* reporter Maria Cramer, July 2011.

56 Interviews by the authors and Maria Cramer with neighbors, June–October 2011; documents filed by prosecutors in *United States v. Catherine E. Greig*, 2012.

57 FBI interview with Rosita D. Tan, DMD, January 26, 2012.

58 Government's sentencing memorandum in *United States v. Catherine E. Greig*, US District Court, Boston, June 8, 2012.

59 Documents filed by prosecutors in *United States v. Catherine E. Greig*, 2012.

60 FBI interview with Dr. Reza Ray Ehsan, July 19, 2011.

61 Wendy Farnetti, grand jury testimony in US District Court, Boston, July 21, 2011.

62 Ibid.

63 Patrick Nee wrote, in *A Criminal & an Irishman*, that Whitey had sexual encounters with men. In his widely panned *Street Soldier*, Ed MacKenzie contended that Whitey was a deviant who had sex with underage girls. While there have been many rumors about Whitey's sexual preferences, some of those closest to Whitey, including his longtime paramour Teresa Stanley, insisted he was straight. Weeks said that the youngest of Whitey's sexual partners he knew of was a sixteen-year-old girl whom Whitey was with when he was in his forties.

64 Affidavit of FBI agent Philip J. Torsney filed in *United States v. Catherine E. Greig*, June 7, 2012.

65 Whitey Bulger, letter to Richard Sunday, May 17, 2012.

66 Ibid.

Chapter 16. Uncontrolled Wickedness

1 This account of the impact of Michael Donahue's murder on his family and community is based on June 2012 interviews by the authors with the Donahue family: Patricia, Tommy, Michael Jr., and Shawn.

2 William St. Croix (Steve Flemmi's son), interview with the authors,

December 2011; Murphy, "Breaking Silence, Flemmi Son Says Gangster's Kin Also Victims."

3 The total of compensation sought in lawsuits filed in US District Court, Boston, between 2001 and 2003 by families of those killed by Whitey Bulger and Steve Flemmi.

4 Lawrence Wheeler, interview with the authors, February 2004.

5 Jeffrey S. Bucholtz, argument before First Circuit Court of Appeals, Boston, March 2, 2004.

6 Thomas M. Bondy, argument before First Circuit Court of Appeals, Boston, March 4, 2008.

7 Donald K. Stern, interview with the authors, August 2012.

8 Justice Department lawyer Bridget Bailey Lipscomb, opening statement in US District Court Boston, June 5, 2006.

9 Whitey Bulger claimed, in a 1983 interview with FBI agents, that Michael Donahue had driven the getaway car after Brian Halloran shot and killed a convicted drug dealer inside a Chinatown restaurant in 1981. The claim was repeated by other criminals and even by FBI agents, but it was unfounded.

10 Shelley Murphy, "Mob Victim's Mother Takes Stand," *Boston Globe*, June 17, 2006.

11 Memorandum of law in support of Plaintiff's motion for costs, filed in *The Estate of John L. McIntyre v. the United States of America*, US District Court, Boston, February 14, 2007.

12 US District Court Judge William G. Young, speaking from the bench on December 21, 2011. Bridget Bailey Lipscomb, the Justice Department lawyer, did not respond to repeated calls and emails seeking comment. A Justice Department spokesman said Lipscomb would not comment.

13 Murphy, "Mob Victim's Mother Takes Stand."

14 Tom Donahue, interview with the authors, May 2009.

15 Bruce Selya and Jeffrey Howard, majority opinion in *Donahue v. United States*, February 11, 2011.

16 Juan Torruella, dissenting opinion in *Donahue v. United States*, February 11, 2011.

17 William St. Croix (Steve Flemmi's son), interview with the authors, December 2011.

18 Lawrence Eiser, US District Court, Boston, November 5, 2009, quoted in Shelley Murphy, "Kin of Flemmi's Victims Argue for Damages," *Boston Globe*, November 6, 2009.

19 Tom Donahue, interview with the authors, June 2012.

Chapter 17. Captured: The Man Without a Country

1 Jason Islas, "Santa Monica Reacts to bin Laden's Death," *Santa Monica Lookout*, May 3, 2011.

2 Barbara Gluck, interview with *Boston Globe* reporter Maria Cramer, July 2011; Murphy and Cramer, "Whitey in Exile."

3 Murphy and Cramer, "Whitey in Exile."

4 Wendy Farnetti, grand jury testimony in US District Court, Boston, July 21, 2011.

5 David Taylor, interview with the authors, April 2012.

6 Jonathan Mitchell, interview with the authors, June 2012. Mitchell was assigned to the task force for seven years and left the US Attorney's office just a week before Whitey was captured.

7 CBS, *48 Hours Mystery*, October 2010.

8 Shelley Murphy and Maria Cramer, "TV Ads Are Latest Tactic in Hunt for Bulger," *Boston Globe*, June 21, 2011.

9 Whitey Bulger, letter to Richard Sunday, postmarked April 20, 2012.

10 Affidavit of FBI special agent Philip J. Torsney, filed in *United States v. Catherine E. Greig*, June 7, 2012.

11 Joshua Bond, grand jury testimony, US District Court, Boston, July 28, 2011. The dialogue in this section derives from Bond's July 28, 2011, grand jury testimony and from FBI reports based on interviews with Bond on July 6, 8, and 28, 2011.

12 The description of and dialogue for the arrest of Whitey Bulger are based on the authors' interviews with Janus Goodwin, a neighbor who witnessed the arrest, and with law enforcement officials, and on a letter that Whitey Bulger sent to Richard Sunday in June 2012.

13 Janus Goodwin, interview with the authors, July 2011.

14 Joshua Bond, grand jury testimony, US District Court, Boston, July 28, 2011.

15 Affidavit of FBI special agent Philip J. Torsney filed in *United States v. Catherine E. Greig*, June 7, 2012.

16 Tom Donahue, interview with the authors, June 2011.

17 Affidavit of FBI special agent Philip Torsney, filed in *United States v. Catherine E. Greig*, June 7, 2012.

18 Sources briefed on Whitey Bulger's statements, interviews with the authors, 2011 and 2012.

19 Tom Donahue, interview with the authors, June 2011.

20 The section on conditions at Plymouth County Correctional Facility and Whitey's attitude about them is based on the authors' interviews with Richard Sunday, January 2012, Jerry Champion, February 2012, and officials with Plymouth County Sheriff's Department; letters Whitey sent to Champion in August and September 2011 and to Sunday between March

and May 2012; and a video of the Plymouth County Correctional Facility, posted on the website of *The Enterprise* of Brockton, Massachusetts, May 7, 2009.

21   Whitey's views of his place in Alcatraz history and the prospect of people making money off his infamy are based on interviews by the authors with Richard Sunday, January 2012, and Jerry Champion, February 2012, and on letters Whitey sent to Sunday and Champion in 2011 and 2012.

22   The accounts of Whitey's feelings for Cathy Greig and his final reckoning with Teresa Stanley are based on interviews by the authors with Stanley and Richard Sunday; on letters he sent to Sunday between April and July 2012; and on an interview with Enrique Sanchez by *Boston Globe* reporter Maria Cramer, July 2011.

23   Jerry Champion, interview with the authors, February 2012; letter from Whitey Bulger to Champion, September 2011.

24   Information about Whitey's relationship with Richard Sunday is based on interviews by the authors with Sunday and on letters Whitey sent Sunday between March and July 2012.

25   The section on the Catherine Greig plea and sentencing, and Whitey's reaction to it, is based on interviews with Greig's lawyer, Kevin Reddington, Paul McGonagle, and Richard Sunday, June 2012; and on letters Whitey sent to Sunday between April and July 2012. The authors attended all of Greig's hearings, including the plea and sentencing hearings.

26   The section on Whitey turning more bitter after Greig's sentencing is based on interviews by the authors with Richard Sunday and Jerry Champion, and on letters Whitey sent to Champion in September 2011 and to Sunday between April and July 2012.

Acknowledgments

Having invested so much of our professional, and sometimes personal, lives in the pursuit of Whitey Bulger's story, we had long harbored a desire to write a book about him. We are deeply grateful to the people who made this possible.

This book wouldn't have happened without the enthusiastic support of Marty Baron, the former editor of the *Boston Globe*, now at the *Washington Post*, who was gracious in letting us pursue this endeavor, and Christopher M. Mayer, the *Globe*'s publisher, who backed us all the way. Mark S. Morrow, the newspaper's deputy managing editor for Sunday & Projects, did a masterful job editing the book. He is a talented wordsmith and made his mark throughout the manuscript. He stuck with the project even after seriously injuring his arm in an accident, finishing the editing process with one of his hands in a cast. We will be forever grateful for his Herculean efforts. Jennifer Peter, deputy managing editor for local news, graciously freed us from our daily duties so that we could take on this challenge. Janice Page, the *Globe*'s editor of film and book development, was with us from the get-go. Our agents, Lane Zachary and Todd Shuster, were tremendous advocates for the project. And our lawyer, David McCraw, vice president and assistant general counsel at the New York Times Company, was a patient and thoughtful influence.

From the moment we made our pitch to them at their offices in Manhattan, the team at Norton—Jeannie Luciano, John Glusman, Drake McFeely, Louise Brockett, Bill Rusin, and Nomi Victor—have been enthusiastic, encouraging collaborators. Tom Mayer edited this book with a keen eye and a deft pencil. He was a delight to work with. We are also indebted to others at Norton—Ryan Harrington, Denise Scarfi, Nancy K. Palmquist, Janet Byrne, Julia Druskin, Don Rifkin, Eleen Cheung, Ingsu Liu, and Rachel Salzman—who worked on the book.

Many colleagues at the *Globe*, some of them now retired, helped us over the years. We both did stints on the *Globe*'s Spotlight Team, first exposing Whitey as an FBI informant and then detailing the extent of the FBI's corrupt relationship with him. Gerry O'Neill led both of those teams with enormous skill and tenacity, and we benefited from the reporting of Dick Lehr, Christine Chinlund, and Mitch Zuckoff. We are grateful to two of Marty Baron's predecessors, Jack Driscoll and Matt Storin, and his successor, Brian McGrory. When Kevin Cullen told Jack Driscoll in 1988 that he believed Whitey was an FBI informant, Jack didn't hesitate in commissioning a full-blown Spotlight investigation. That got the ball rolling. Matt Storin and Brian McGrory spared no expense in following the story wherever it went, Matt when Whitey was on the run, Brian when Whitey was in custody. Stan Grossfeld, one of journalism's finest photographers, was his usual selfless self, spending an afternoon with us on Castle Island, where Whitey used to walk, to take the authors' cover shot. He's the best. Maria Cramer's stellar reporting and writing while teaming up with Shelley Murphy on a three-month project that took them from Santa Monica to Mexico to Iceland uncovered new details about Whitey's life on the run and his capture. Their special report, "Whitey in Exile," was expertly steered by editor Scott Allen. Other *Globe* editors and reporters who helped us through the Whitey years are Sally Jacobs, who did a terrific, detailed story about Cathy Greig's life, and Milton J. Valencia, Jonathan Saltzman, Thanassis Cambanis, Patricia Nealon, Ralph Ranalli, John Ellement, Steve Kurkjian, Teresa Hanafin, and Mike Bello. Scott Helman helped us negotiate the confusing boulevard of file sharing while writing collaboratively.

Over the years, we worked with *Globe* photographers who were also chasing Whitey, none more zealous and resourceful than John Tlumacki, who snapped the first shots of Whitey and Cathy Greig in 1988 from the passenger seat of Kevin Cullen's car. John has a knack for finding wiseguys, especially on Castle Island. His exclusive photos of Whitey and Greig were used by the FBI during its manhunt. *Globe* photographer Bill Greene helped chronicle the Whitey story during our trip to Iceland. Other *Globe* photographers who helped us over the years include Bill Brett, Barry Chin, Yoon S. Byun, Jim Wilson, and Jessey Dearing.

Lisa Tuite's terrific staff in the *Globe*'s library—Wanda Joseph-Rollins, Marleen Lee, Jeremiah Manion, Rosemarie McDonald, and Colneth Smiley—were troupers as we sent them scurrying for information about ancient and recent Boston history. Rosemarie McDonald also worked as one of the book's fact-checkers, along with Matt Mahoney, Ben Jacobs, and Stephanie Vallejo. Maureen Long and Frank Bright were a big help, and David Butler did a great job on the maps.

There were other journalists outside the *Globe* who helped us with both information and collegiality: Peter Gelzinis, Janelle Lawrence, and Howie Carr at the *Boston Herald*; David Boeri, first at WCVB-TV and then at WBUR radio, who has done yeoman's work on the Whitey front; Ed Mahony of the *Hartford Courant*; Dan Rea of WBZ-TV and radio; and Tim White, of WPRI-TV in Providence.

The families of Whitey's victims have been kind and generous to us, even during some difficult moments for them. Patricia Donahue and her sons, Michael Jr., Shawn, and Tom, are very good people who deserve better than the way their government treated them. The sons of Roger Wheeler, Larry and David, who were great champions of their slain father, pushed for the truth. So, too, were the other families, who fought to keep the focus on their loved ones: the Davis family—Steve, Victor, and their late mother, Olga; Tim Connors; Paul McGonagle; Mary Callahan; Bill St. Croix; Tom Hussey and Emily and Chris McIntyre; Denise Castucci; Elaine Barrett; and Patricia Macarelli.

If not for the work of Chief US District Judge Mark L. Wolf, defense attorney Anthony Cardinale, and federal prosecutors Fred Wyshak and Brian Kelly, the extent of Whitey's corrupt relationship with the FBI may never have been revealed.

The corruption of public officials that allowed Whitey to kill and menace with impunity sometimes clouds the reality that it was good, honest people in law enforcement who brought him down; and we could not have written this book without them. While many are now retired or doing other things, we'll recognize them in the capacities in which they chased Whitey and helped us.

The Boston Police Department: Frank Dewan, Ken Beers, Jim Carr, Chip Fleming, Brendan Bradley.

The Massachusetts State Police: Buddy Saccardo, Arthur Bourque, Bob Long, Rick Fraelick, Jack O'Malley, Charlie Henderson, John Tutungian, Tom Duffy, Mike Scanlan, Steve Johnson, and Tom Foley, who led the team that finally brought charges against Whitey. We regret that Foley's mentor, Pat Greaney, who did so much to help convince Chico Krantz to testify against Whitey, didn't live to see Whitey's capture, but wherever Pat is now he's smiling. The same goes for Jack O'Donovan, the state police commander who first called the FBI out over its protection of Whitey and Steve Flemmi. O'D was in the grip of Alzheimer's when Whitey was caught, and we hope that he understood when Bob Long told him that they finally got Whitey.

Suffolk County District Attorney's office: Tim Burke and John Kiernan; Norfolk District Attorney's office: Bill Delahunt, Matt Connolly, John Kivlan; Miami-Dade State Attorney's office: Michael Von Zamft.

The US Drug Enforcement Administration: Al Reilly, Steve

Boeri, Mike Swidwinski, John Coleman, and Paul Brown, who led the charge in the 1980s to destroy the myth that Whitey had nothing to do with drugs; and Dan Doherty, who teamed up with Steve Johnson and other state police investigators to finally land Whitey and Flemmi in the dock.

Others in law enforcement who helped us over the years include Dick Bergeron and the late Dave Rowell, two Quincy cops who went after Whitey in the 1980s with great zeal and courage; Mike Huff of the Tulsa Police Department; Bill Murphy and Terry McArdle of the US Bureau of Alcohol, Tobacco and Firearms; David Taylor of the US Marshals Service; and Bob Fitzpatrick of the FBI. US Attorneys Bill Weld, Donald K. Stern, Michael Sullivan, and Carmen Ortiz. Also James Herbert and Christina DiIorio Sterling of the US Attorney's office.

During the hunt for Whitey, FBI agents Ken Kaiser, Warren Bamford, Bill Chase, Tom Larned, Tom Cassano, Gail Marcinkiewicz, John Gamel, and Rich Teahan gave us access and insight into the Bulger Task Force's efforts to track him.

There were many attorneys who helped us over the years. William Christie, Steven Gordon, and Ed Hinchey were among the lawyers who represented Whitey's victims and were tireless advocates not for just the families but the truth. We can't name all the lawyers who helped us, but others who stand out were Kenneth Fishman, Martin Weinberg, Randy Gioia, Frank Libby, Paul Kelly, Edward Berkin, Albert Cullen, Victor Garo, James P. Duggan, Manuel Casabielle, Tracy Miner, George Gormley, and Bob George.

Some of those closest to Whitey over the years were very generous with their time and reflections, especially Kevin Weeks and Pat Nee. Teresa Stanley, Whitey's longtime girlfriend, was kind to us right to the end, when she died in August 2012. Some of Whitey's former associates on Winter Hill, especially the former Winter Hill Gang leader Howie Winter, were very helpful. Richard Sunday, Whitey's closest friend in prison in Atlanta and Alcatraz, was extremely generous with his time and in allowing us to read the letters Whitey sent him from jail after his capture. Sunday remains sympathetic to Whitey, and hoped he could provide another side to him. Alcatraz historian and author Jerry Champion kindly shared letters with us that Whitey sent him from jail. We are grateful to the National Park Service for arranging a tour of Alcatraz by ranger John Cantwell, a knowledgeable and entertaining guide who let us stand in Whitey's old cell and regaled us with tales of what prison life was like. The staff at the National Archives in San Bruno, California, and the staff at Waltham, Massachusetts, provided us with Whitey's decades-old prison and court files. We greatly appreciate the help that Icelander Arthur Bogason provided during our trip to Reykjavík.

We're also thankful to others who knew Whitey and shared their memories of him: Attorney Joe Oteri, Brian Wallace, the late Bobby Moakley, the late Will McDonough, and Lindsey Cyr, the mother of Whitey's only known child, who kindly shared the difficult memories of losing their son, Douglas.

We thank the family of the late Rev. Robert Drinan, his sister-in-law Helen, and his niece Betsy; and Boston Housing Authority director Bill McGonagle, whose brother was Whitey's paperboy.

We'd also like to thank John Connolly, who gave us a series of interviews before he was convicted of racketeering in 2002 and spoke to us during his trial and after his conviction in Miami for the murder of John Callahan.

From Kevin Cullen: Many thanks to my family, my wife, Martha, and my sons, Patrick and Brendan, for their love and support.

From Shelley Murphy: My deep appreciation for the love and support of my husband, Regis; my children, Liam, Ryan, Jessica, and Kerry; my son-in-law, Tom; my grandchildren, Chloe and Shane; and my mother, Barbara, and my late father, Bill.

INDEX

Adams, John, 9

Ahearn, James, 289, 293

Albright, Jim, 59–60

Andersen, Arthur, 211

Andersen, Bob, 251, 252–53, 254, 258–60, 261, 263–64

Angiulo, Danny, 172

Angiulo, Gennaro "Jerry," 104, 106–7, 147, 172, 176, 179, 220, 224, 233, 288, 292, 294, 299

Anglin, Clarence, 69

Anglin, John, 69

Ashe, George, 144

Auerbach, Red, 338

Baione, Larry, 102, 106, 147, 172, 179, 291

Baker, Dick, 200–201, 293

Banno, John, 429

Barboza, Joe, 106

Barchard, Dorothy, 43

Barchard, Richard, 42–44, 45, 65–66

Barrett, Arthur "Bucky," 5–6, 271–74, 277–78, 282, 344, 448

Baxter, Helen (Greig's alias), 323–24, 325, 326

Baxter, Thomas F., 315

Baxter, Tom (Whitey's alias), 315, 323–24, 325, 326–27, 371

Bellotti, Frank, 195–96

Bennett, Billy, 142

Bennett, Edward "Wimpy," 76–77, 79

Bennett, James, 57, 59, 67, 68–69

Bergeron, Dick, 262, 264, 266

Besson, Roscoe, Jr., 327

bin Laden, Osama, 400–401, 402, 408

Bjornsdottir, Anna, 379–80, 406–8, 411, 416

Blake, Stanford, 359

Boeri, Steve, 262–63, 266

Bond, Joshua, 377–78, 401, 408–9, 410

Bondy, Thomas M., 389

Bradley, Ed, 149

Brasco, Donnie (Pistone's alias), 375

Brennan, Hank, 428–29, 442, 444, 446

Briick, Herbert, 45–46

Brown, Paul, 195
Browne, Michael, 257–58, 261
Brunnick, Leo, 222–25
Bucholtz, Jeffrey S., 389
Buckley, Mike, 316–17
Buffett, Jimmy, 315
Bulger, Bill, 4, 5, 7, 9, 20, 21, 23–24,
    26, 27, 28, 30, 31, 33–34, 36, 39, 47,
    48, 51, 52–53, 58–59, 66, 67, 70,
    71, 80–82, 94, 99, 107, 108, 118,
    119, 120, 122, 125–26, 127, 130–31,
    132, 134, 135, 136–37, 156, 164, 177,
    183–84, 185, 194, 195, 196, 198,
    200, 230, 241, 242, 243, 270, 271,
    287, 288, 289, 290–91, 293, 296,
    297, 298, 317–18, 320, 345–46, 351,
    352, 353–55, 359, 362, 363, 364, 413,
    422, 442, 448
Bulger, Carol, 21, 67
Bulger, James Joseph, 18–19, 25, 26–27,
    28, 29, 30, 46, 69, 421
Bulger, Jean, 19, 21, 31, 38
Bulger, Jean McCarthy, 18–19, 21, 26,
    31, 33–34, 57, 63, 70, 185, 362, 421
Bulger, John "Jack," 21, 69, 70, 183,
    330–31, 352–53, 354, 448
Bulger, Mary (Bill's daughter), 363
Bulger, Mary (Bill's wife), 353, 354
Bulger, Sheila, 31
Bush, George W., 346

Cahill, Joe, 244–48, 249, 261
Callahan, John, 210–13, 214–15, 217,
    218–19, 220, 222–23, 226, 235–37,
    238, 239, 240, 274, 282, 346, 347–
    48, 417, 428
Capone, Al, 9, 59, 415
Cardinale, Anthony, 292–93, 338–39
Carnes, Clarence "The Choctaw
    Kid," 61–62, 204–5
Carney, J. W., Jr., 423, 426, 435, 437,
    439, 444, 445

Carr, Jimmy, 327
Caruana, Michael, 155
Casper, Denise, 426, 431, 439, 445
Castucci, Richie, 151–53, 167, 448
Castucci, Sandra, 153
Champion, Jerry, 417–18
Charles, Prince of Wales, 256
Chase, William, 357
Chin, Soon Yen, 220
Ciulla, Tony, 166–67, 289–90
Cleary, Brendan, 238
Clifford, Billy, 25
Clifford, Marilyn, 25–26
Coady, John, 195–96
Comeaux, David, 203–4
Condon, Dennis, 77–78, 100–101,
    142, 144–46, 147
Condon, Jimmy, 22
Connolly, James, 16–17
Connolly, John, 4, 7–8, 34–36, 37, 80,
    98–101, 104–8, 113, 114, 117, 127,
    136, 146, 147, 148–49, 151, 152, 155–
    57, 161, 163, 167, 168, 173, 174–75,
    176–77, 178–79, 180, 182, 197–98,
    199–202, 212, 218, 219–20, 223–24,
    227, 232–34, 235, 237–38, 239–40,
    241, 243–44, 249, 263–64, 266,
    269, 271–72, 280–81, 285, 288–89,
    291–93, 294–96, 297, 298, 307,
    310–11, 316, 318–19, 320–21, 332,
    336–37, 339–41, 342–43, 344–45,
    346–48, 358–60, 375, 385, 387–88,
    389, 391, 394–95, 399, 402, 403,
    413, 425, 432, 441
Connolly, Liz, 346
Connolly, Tim, 293
Connors, Eddie, 150–51, 420, 448
Connors, Tim, 420
Cooper, Jack, 213
Corsetti, Paul, 290–91
Costello, Frank (char.), 7
Coughlin, Charles, 22

Crawley, John, 250–51, 253, 254, 258, 259, 260, 261
Crosby, Bing, 36
Cullen, Kevin, 9, 289–90, 292
Cunniff, John, 80
Curley, James Michael, 27–28, 47, 122
Curran, Jack, 87
Cushing, Richard, 17
Cyr, Douglas, 94–95, 160
Cyr, Lindsey, 92–95

Dailey, Kevin, 155
Daly, Tom, 153, 167, 289–90
Dame, Sally, 32, 33
Davis, Debra, 5, 6, 161–66, 191, 276, 282, 345, 346, 391, 397, 398, 415, 439, 441–42, 448
Davis, Ed, 162
Davis, Michelle, 166, 439
Davis, Mickey, 162
Davis, Olga, 162, 165–66, 398, 439
Davis, Steve, 439, 440, 448
Davis, Victor, 164
Deegan, Teddy, 145n
Delahunt, William, 155, 391
DeLuca, Bobby, 338, 340
Depp, Johnny, 295
Dermody, Ronnie, 41–42, 78
Dershowitz, Alan, 155
DesLauriers, Richard, 414
Devaney, Tom, 58, 86–87
Dewan, Frank, 327, 341
Diana, Princess of Wales, 256
diGrazia, Robert, 125, 126, 129
Dillinger, John, 43–44
Doherty, Dan, 313, 349, 359, 386, 393, 413
Donahue, Michael, 4, 5, 226, 227–28, 229, 230–32, 233, 234, 239, 240, 274, 282, 383–85, 391, 392, 396–97, 432, 448, 449
Donahue, Michael, Jr., 5, 226, 231, 384, 411, 433

Donahue, Patricia, 5, 225–26, 227, 230–31, 384, 385, 392, 393, 396, 397, 399, 411, 413, 432, 433, 438–39, 440, 444
Donahue, Shawn, 5, 226, 384, 411
Donahue, Tommy, 5, 226, 232, 383, 384, 392, 393, 396, 399, 411, 413, 433, 438
Donovan, Richard, 213
Dracopoulos, Peter, 206
Drinan, Helen, 137
Drinan, Robert, 47, 48, 49, 52, 56, 67, 71, 120–21, 136–37
Duffy, Tom, 313–14, 349
Dukakis, Michael, 184
Durham, John, 344, 348
Dwyer, Leo, 36, 47, 362
Dwyer, Mickey, 85

Eiser, Lawrence, 398
Embry, Robert, 205

Farinelli, Birgitta, 363, 364, 365, 368
Farnetti, Wendy, 381, 402
Fawcett, Farrah, 161
Feil, Marvin, 117
Femia, Nicky, 173
Ferrara, Vinnie, 294, 300
Ferris, Martin, 257–58, 259, 261, 268, 269
Fidler, Alan "Suitcase," 111
Fitzgerald, John "Honey Fitz," 19, 27, 142
Fitzgerald, Rose, 19
Fitzpatrick, Bob, 171, 224–25, 233, 444
Flanagan, Peter, 255
Fleming, Charles "Chip," 159, 364
Flemmi, Giovanni, 144
Flemmi, Jimmy "The Bear," 144, 150
Flemmi, Mary, 161, 198, 230, 282
Flemmi, Michael, 144, 254, 276, 315, 386, 387

Flemmi, Steve, 8, 10, 39, 75–77, 79, 100–102, 106, 111–12, 131, 141–51, 152–53, 154–55, 156–57, 160–69, 170–76, 179, 182, 184, 189, 190–91, 192, 193, 194, 197, 199–200, 201, 202, 210, 215–17, 219, 222–24, 226–27, 230, 232–33, 234, 235, 236–39, 243–44, 246, 249, 254, 263, 265, 266–68, 270–78, 280, 282, 285, 286, 288, 289, 292–93, 294, 295, 296–97, 298–300, 301, 302, 310–12, 313–15, 318–19, 321, 333–34, 338, 339, 340, 341–43, 344, 346, 347–48, 352, 353, 359, 385, 386–87, 388–89, 390, 393, 394–95, 397–98, 435, 440, 441–42, 448

Floramo, Richie, 105

Flynn, Jimmy, 229, 232, 234, 385

Flynn, Ray, 132, 134, 135, 136

Foley, Dan, 298

Foley, Tom, 298–302, 313, 314, 315–16, 332, 333, 349

Ford, Gerald, 338

Foster, James, 15

Fraelick, Rick, 171–72

Friedkin, William, 347

Gaddafi, Muammar, 245

Galway John, 98–99

Gamel, John E., 317–18, 327, 328, 329

Garriola, Scott, 408–9, 410–11, 443

Garrity, W. Arthur, Jr., 116, 118, 119, 121, 122, 123, 125, 127, 129, 137–38

Gaska, Charlie, 362, 412

Gasko, Carol (Greig's alias), 362–65, 367, 371–72, 377–79, 381, 402, 407, 408–9, 416

Gasko, Charles (Whitey's alias), 362–65, 369, 371–72, 377–79, 401–2, 407, 408–9, 410, 416

Gautreaux, Glenn, 323–24, 325, 326

Gautreaux, Glenn, Jr., 325

Gautreaux, Penny, 323–24, 325, 326

Gianturco, Charlie, 314, 337

Gianturco, Nicholas, 197–98, 337

Gibbons, John, 403, 404

Gleason, Noreen, 402–3

Gluck, Barbara, 371, 401

Glynn, Ted, 46

Goodwin, Janus, 371, 376, 410

Gore, Al, 346

Gotti, John, 292

Greaney, Pat, 301–3, 314

Greco, Louis, 145n

Greig, Catherine, 4, 11, 158–60, 183, 184, 192, 207–8, 282, 284, 307–9, 313, 314, 321–26, 329, 330, 331, 332–33, 335–36, 337, 345, 348–49, 350, 352, 353, 358, 361–71, 373–82, 400, 401–2, 405–10, 412–13, 416–17, 419–21, 442

Greig, David, 208, 419

Gudmundsson, Halldor, 380

Gustav (Davis's lover), 162, 164

Hafer, Zachary, 439

Hagler, Marvin, 300

Hale, Edward Everett, 415

Halloran, Brian, 4, 212, 220–25, 226, 228–29, 230, 232, 233, 234–35, 238, 239, 240, 246, 274, 282, 340, 385, 391, 396, 432, 448, 449

Hanlon, Linda, 160

Hayes, Kevin, 448

Hearst, Patty, 104

Hegel, Georg Wilhelm Friedrich, 62

Hitchcock, Alfred, 320

Hitler, Adolf, 394

Hoover, Herbert, 20

Hoover, J. Edgar, 78, 99

Howard, Jeffrey, 396–97

Huff, Mike, 219, 238

Hurley, John, 226, 246, 247

Hussey, Billy, 160–61